Front cover
Norias *on the River Orontes
and Mosque of Nur al-Din
(558/1164), Hama*

Museum With No Frontiers *Exhibition Trails*

ISLAMIC ART IN THE MEDITERRANEAN | SYRIA

The Ayyubid Era
Art and Architecture in Medieval Syria

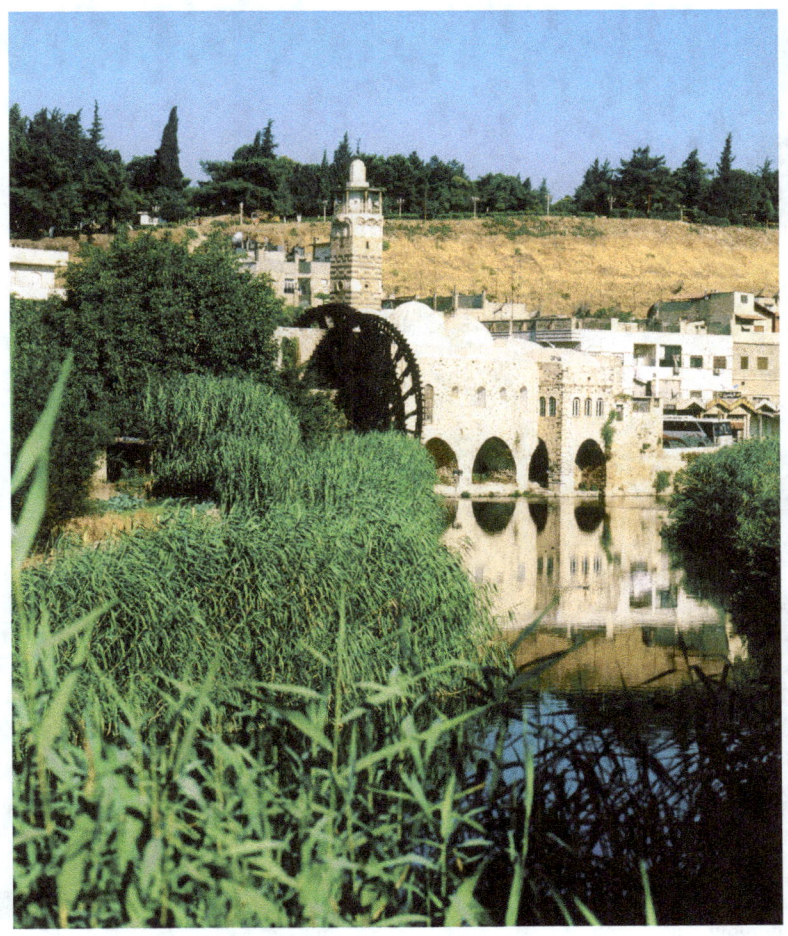

Museum With No Frontiers (MWNF)

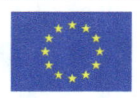 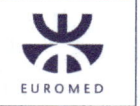

EUROPEAN UNION
Euromed Heritage

The realisation of the MWNF Exhibition Trail and related Travel Book *THE AYYUBID ERA: Art and Architecture in Medieval Syria* has been co-financed by the **European Union** within the framework of the **Euromed Heritage** programme and received the support of the following Syrian and international institutions:

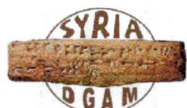

General Directorate of Antiquities and Museums
Ministry of Culture
Syrian Arab Republic

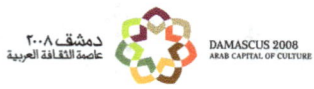

Damascus – Cultural Capital of the Arab World 2008

Official sponsor

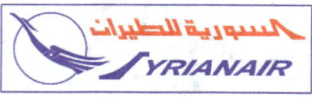

Syrian Arab Airlines

© 2015 Museum Ohne Grenzen | Museum With No Frontiers (MWNF), Vienna, Austria.

ISBN: 978-3-902782-16-8 (paperback)
ISBN: 978-3-902782-17-5 (eBook)

All Rights Reserved. No part of this publication may be reproduced, stored in a retrieval system or transmitted, in any form or by any means, electronic, mechanical or otherwise, without the prior written permission of the publisher.

For further information
www.museumwnf.org
www.mwnfbooks.net

Museum With No Frontiers
Idea and overall concept
Eva Schubert

Head of Project
Abd al-Razzaq Moaz

Project Coordinators
Samer Abdel-Ghafour
Zena Takieddine
Luna Rajab

Curatorial Committee
Mona al-Moadin
Dina Bakkour
Verena Daiber
Abd al-Razzaq Moaz
Zena Takieddine

With contributions from
Wa'al Hafian
Haytham Hasan
Balázs Major
Benjamin Michaudel
Yasser Tabbaa

Authors

Introductions
Abd al-Razzaq Moaz
Zena Takieddine

Presentation of Itineraries
Curatorial Committee
See also Index, page 11

Photography
Muhammad al-Roumi
See also photo credits page 282

Technical texts
Khaled Malas

General Map
Simon Kabboush

Schematic sketches of Itineraries
Ayham Shabans
Sergio Viguera

Monument plans (design)
Sergio Viguera

Monument plans (technical advisor)
Sakina Missoum

General Introduction
"Islamic Art in the Mediterranean"

Text
Jamila Binous
Mahmoud Hawari
Manuel Marin
Gonol Oney

Maps
Şakir Çakmak
Ertan Daş
Yekta Demiralp

Editorial Team

Editorial frame
Inci Turkoglu

Overall editorial coordination
Zena Takieddine

Editorial coordination and proofreading during pre-press production
Maria Francesca Carvelli

Copy-editing and linguistic harmonisation
Mandi Gomez

Layout and design
Christian Eckart
based on a project of
Augustina Fernández

Note

This book was prepared between 2005 and 2007, but publication was delayed because of the considerable costs involved to produce the book as an international co-edition as had occurred with the other titles of our *Islamic Art in the Mediterranean* series. However, thanks to the new publishing formats and fundraising tools that are available today, it has now been possible to complete the project and publish the English version of this book.

The Ayyubid Era: Art and Architecture in Medieval Syria is published as it was conceived by the authors before the war started. All texts, including useful information for the visit, refer to the pre-war situation and are our expression of hope that Syria, which has witnessed the evolution of civilisation since the beginnings of human history, may soon become a place of peace and the driving force behind a new and peaceful beginning for the entire region.

Acknowledgements

We thank our private donors who, in autumn 2015, made the completion of this book possible.

Sincere thanks go to: Professor Yasser Tabbaa for his generous help, in particular also during the last phase of completion of the book; Luna Rajab for her efforts to promote the book through Damascus Cultural Capital of the Arab World 2008; and Peter Heinrich Jahn for his editorial advice.

We also would like to thank all those who, while too numerous to name individually, gave their unfailing support and sound advice during the preparation of this project. However, we would like to emphasise our special thanks to the staff of the institutions listed below, who provided generous help and support whenever needed:

Ministry of Culture, Syrian Arab Republic
Directorate General of Antiquities and Museums, Damascus
National Museum Damascus
Damascus Cultural Capital of the Arab World 2008

The opinions expressed in this work do not necessarily reflect the opinions either of the European Union or of its Member States.

Photographic References

All photos in this book were taken by Muhammad al-Roumi (in 2006) except where specified differently in the legend of the image. For the complete list of photo credits for images provided by third parties, please see page 282.

Plan References
Most of the plans in this book were produced by Sergio Viguera (design) and Sakina Missoum (technical advisor). For plans taken from other sources, please refer to the plan credits on page 282.

MWNF thanks all copyright owners for their kind permission to reproduce their material. Should, despite our intensive research, any person entitled to rights have been overlooked, legitimate claims will be compensated within the usual provisions. Please contact www.museumwnf.net.

Preface

This book is dedicated to all those who believe that the key to mutual understanding and peaceful coexistence is knowledge of the other's perspective of history and cultural values, according to the other's specific historical experience.

Today we watch on with horror at developments in Syria and the surrounding region and the impact the war is having on Europe and the international community as a whole. Hundreds of thousands of Syrians have to flee their country and innocent people have to die. Nothing justifies the atrocities happening today. But, if we believe in the future and if we hope for peace in the region and for safety in the world, we have to start looking at history and cultural heritage not only as fields of academic research but, primarily, as the roots of identity and the key to human dignity. If we continue ignoring the other's perspective, the other, at a certain point of exasperation, will end up ignoring our perspective. This is where we stand today.

I am writing this preface at a time when some of the places that are described in this book – including Aleppo and Raqqa – have been severely damaged and continue to be exposed to great threat. And I remember how, between 2005 and 2007, when this book was conceived, we came together regularly in the office of Dr. Abd al-Razzaq Moaz, at that time Deputy Minister of Culture, to discuss each single detail of the described eight Itineraries. Each member of the Curatorial Committee had a different approach, ideas were discussed, and the atmosphere was excellent. Since the office was based in a residential area with no bars or restaurants in the surroundings and since each meeting lasted at least eight hours, Dr. Moaz always arrived in the morning with a large plastic bag full of tasty sandwiches and delicious damascene sweets. Wonderful smelling coffee was then prepared by the guardians of the building. At around the half way stage, a young Syrian scholar, Zena Takieddine, joined the team to take care of the overall editorial coordination of the book. Zena's enthusiasm and great empathy combined with her brilliant work, made her appear as a shining vision of Syria's bright future. After the experience of the preparation for this book, the hope that Syria, which has witnessed the evolution of civilisation since the beginnings of human history, could become a driving force for peace in the region, for all of us, became a tangible reality.

The Ayyubid Era: Art and Architecture in Medieval Syria is published as it was conceived by the authors before the war started. All texts refer to the pre-war situation and are our expression of hope that the violence in Syria may be brought to an immediate end.

Eva Schubert
Chairperson and CEO
Museum With No Frontiers

P.S. The use of the Western term "medieval" is intentional. The Curatorial Committee decided to use the term in order to include the Western dimension of the period under survey.

Advice

Transliteration of the Arabic

We have retained the common spelling for Arabic words in common use and included those in the English dictionary, such as "suq". We have maintained the phonetic spelling of the words in Arabic as determined by the authors and in accordance with Syrian standards. For all other words, we have simplified the transcription. We do not transcribe the initial *hamza* but have kept the initial *'Ayn* in personal nouns, as in 'Ali, 'Abd al-Malik, etc. We did not differentiate between short and long vowels, which are written as *a, i, ou*. Some of the proper nouns are transliterated in the text according to the *Oxford Dictionary*. The transcription for the 28 Arabic consonants are provided below as well as "a" or "at" for the ta' *marbuta*.

ء	'	ح	h	ز	z	ط	t	ق	q	ه	h
ب	b	خ	kh	س	s	ظ	z	ك	k	و	u/w
ت	t	د	d	ش	sh	ع	'	ل	l	ي	y/i
ث	th	ذ	dh	ص	s	غ	gh	م	m		
ج	j	ر	r	ض	d	ف	f	ن	n		

Words in italic in the text without an accompanying translation or explanation can be found in the glossary.

The Muslim era

The Muslim era began with the exodus of the Prophet Muhammad from Mecca to Yathrib. Then the name was changed to *Madina*, "The City" or "town of the Prophet". With his small community of followers (70 people along with family members) recently converted to Islam, the Prophet undertook the *al-hijra* (literally "the emigration") and the new era began.

The date of the emigration is the first of the month of *Muharram* in year 1 of the *Hijra*, which corresponds to 16 July of the year 622 of the Christian era. The Muslim year is made up of twelve lunar months, each month having 29 or 30 days.

Thirty years form a cycle in which the 2nd, 5th, 7th, 10th, 13th, 16th, 18th, 21st, 24th, 26th and 29th are leap years having 355 days; the others are normal years with 354 days. The Muslim lunar year is 10 or 11 days shorter than the Christian solar year.

Each day begins immediately after sunset, i.e. at dusk rather than after midnight. Most Muslim countries use both the *Hijra* Calendar (which indicates all religious events) and the Christian Calendar.

Dates

Dates given are according to the *Hijra* calendar, followed by their equivalent date on the Christian calendar after an oblique stroke. The *Hijra* date is not indicated in references derived from Christian sources, European historical events, those that occurred in Europe, Christian Dynasties, those prior to the Muslim era or those after 1918, the end of Ottoman domination in Syria.

Exact correspondence between years in one calendar and another is only possible when the day and month are given. To facilitate reading, we chose to avoid intermediate years and, in the case of *Hijra* dates falling between the beginning and the end of a century, the two centuries are mentioned. Dates prior to the beginning of the Christian era are indicated with BC. To avoid confusion, the use of the abbreviation AD is used for periods beginning before the birth of Christ and finishing after his birth.

Abbreviations:
AD = in the year of our Lord; BC = before Christ; d = death; f.h. = first half; r. = reign

Editorial Advice

Practical advice

Preliminary Remark

We would like to remind readers that The Ayyubid Era: Art and Architecture in Medieval Syria *was conceived not long before the war started. All texts reflect the pre-war situation and express our hope that the violence in Syria may be brought to an immediate end.*

This exhibition is divided into eight itineraries based on thematic concepts and including all the main cities and geographical landscapes Syria offers. Each itinerary is distinguished by a Roman numeral and represented by a schematic sketch with icons symbolizing the type of monument. The itineraries themselves are sub-divided using Arabic numerals indicating cities, villages or archaeological locations, in addition to several "optional" suggestions marked in grey. All destinations, whether optional or part of the itinerary proper, are introduced by a short italicized text that provides the visitor with information of a technical nature on how to reach each location.

Spring and autumn are the best times to visit Syria, as the weather tends to be very pleasant. The hottest (July and August) and coldest (December and January) months are probably best avoided. Visiting during the holy month of Ramadan should not pose any problems per se, but visitors may be inconvenienced by variations in opening times. As the month of Ramadan is based on a lunar calendar and therefore changes every year, it is best to check its duration with tourist information centres and travel agents.

The Directorate General of Antiquities and Museums (DGAM) operates several tourist information offices in all Syrian cities, and these offices can be consulted for information regarding accessibility to monuments and appropriate modes of travel. Visitors are advised to take advantage of typical Syrian friendliness, as everyone would be very willing to answer questions and provide assistance when approached with a smile.

Local coach-bus services are present in all cities and provide an appropriate mode of transportation between locations. More remote sites can be very easily visited using the cheap and efficient "microbus" network that also serves as public transport within busy city centres. As some of the sites described in this catalogue are off the traditionally trodden track they may require some ingenuity from travellers who are not predisposed to renting a car, but the more adventurous are likely to enjoy the charm of these excursions in particular. Alternatively, when visiting a site a few kilometres outside the city proper, hiring a taxi may be an intelligent option.

The official day off for museums and main touristic sites is Tuesday. The sites operated by the DGAM generally adhere to their opening schedules: 9:00–18:00 in the summer and 9:00–16:00 in the winter, bearing in mind that Friday noon prayers is usually observed. It is also relatively common to find many locations closed, for restoration purposes or other reasons, whereby we hope the photos and texts provided in this catalogue may offer insight to what turns out be inaccessible on the spot. However, visitors are advised to practice patience, friendliness and resourcefulness, as it is very likely that the custodian can be easily located within the immediate vicinity.

When visiting places of worship, visitors are kindly asked to adhere to established dress codes and respect the sanctity of places of worship and not interrupt the prayers.

While the catalogue's main purpose is to highlight the architectural and artistic heritage of the 11th to 13th centuries in Syria, visitors are advised to take full advantage of the depth and richness of Syria's heritage. The medieval monuments described in this catalogue often exist in total immersion with ancient structures and modern ones. They are best understood as nodes of interest within a broader cultural, historical and natural landscape.

For information on cultural or artistic events, please check the website of the Ministry of Culture, www.moc.gov.sy and for the latest in tourist information please visit www.syriatourism.org.

While we wish you a most enjoyable voyage in Syria, Museum With No Frontiers is not responsible for variations in opening times nor for any inconveniences or injuries occurring during your trip.

Khaled Malas	Zena Takieddine
Technical Texts	*Editorial Coordinator*

INDEX

- 12 **Islamic Art in the Mediterranean**
  Jamila Binous, Mahmoud Hawari, Manuela Marín, Gönül Öney

- 35 **Historical Artistic Introduction**
  Abd al-Razzaq Moaz, Zena Takieddine

- 53 **Ayyubid Art and Architecture**
  Abd al-Razzaq Moaz, Zena Takieddine

- 76 **Itinerary I** (Damascus, 2 days)
  Religion, Science and the Transmission of Knowledge under the Atabegs and Ayyubids
  Introduction and Monuments:
  Abd al-Razzaq Moaz, Zena Takieddine
  The *Bimaristans* and Public Health
  Yasser Tabbaa
  Mechanical Sciences
  Zena Takieddine

- 122 **Itinerary II** (Bosra, 1 day)
  Antique Heritage in an Ayyubid City
  Introduction and Monuments: *Verena Daiber*
  Local Traditions and Imperial Architecture in a Provincial Capital
  Verena Daiber

- 140 **Itinerary III** (Damascus Environs and Homs, 1 day)
  Christian Art and Architecture in Medieval Syria
  Introduction and Monuments: *Dina Bakkour*
  A Survey of Christian Art: Continuity and Interaction
  Dina Bakkour

- 158 **Itinerary IV** (Hama, 1 day)
  Water and Hydraulic Works
  Introduction: *Yasser Tabbaa*
  Monuments: *Wa'al Hafian*
  Memoirs of an Arab Knight
  Yasser Tabbaa
  Noria Construction
  Wa'al Hafian

- 182 **Itinerary V** (Coastal Mountains, 2 days)
  Confrontation and Coexistence: Fortifications in western Syria
  Introduction: *Benjamin Michaudel*
  Monuments: *Benjamin Michaudel, Balázs Major, Haytham Hasan*
  The Isma'iliyya Emirate of Syria
  Haytham Hasan
  Memoirs of Salah al-Din
  Yasser Tabbaa

- 212 **Itinerary VI** (Aleppo, 1 day)
  Commerce and Daily Life
  Introduction and Monuments: *Yasser Tabbaa*
  Suq of Aleppo
  Yasser Tabbaa

- 226 **Itinerary VII** (Aleppo, 1 day)
  Patronage and Court Life under the Atabegs and Ayyubids in Syria
  Introduction and Monuments: *Yasser Tabbaa*
  Inscriptions and Public Texts
  Yasser Tabbaa
  Female Patronage in Urban Development and Education
  Abd al-Razzaq Moaz

- 246 **Itinerary VIII** (The Eastern Provinces, 1 day)
  The Euphrates Region: Window onto Mesopotamia
  Introduction and Monuments: *Verena Daiber*
  The Eastern Influence in Syria
  Verena Daiber

- 265 **Glossary**

- 271 **Selected Historical Personalities**

- 279 **Further reading**

- 282 **Photographic and Plan References**

- 283 **Authors**

ISLAMIC DYNASTIES IN THE MEDITERRANEAN
The Umayyads | The Abbasids

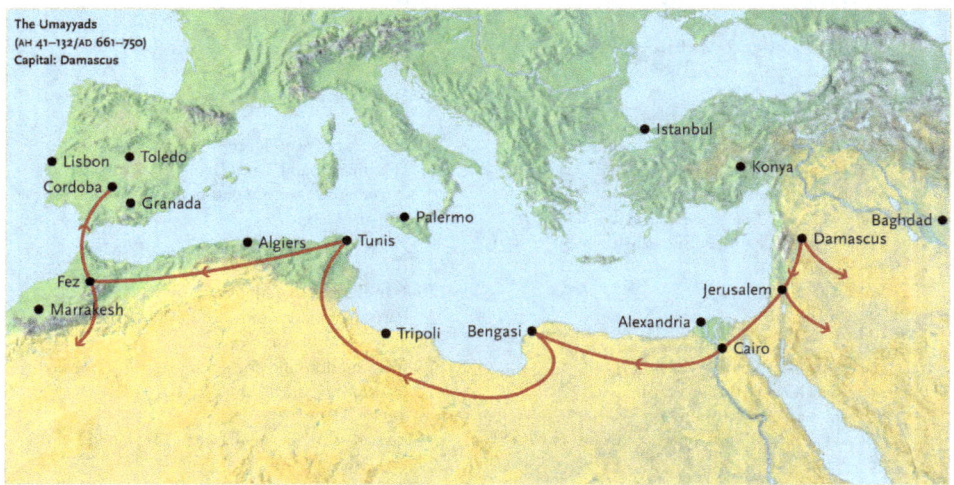

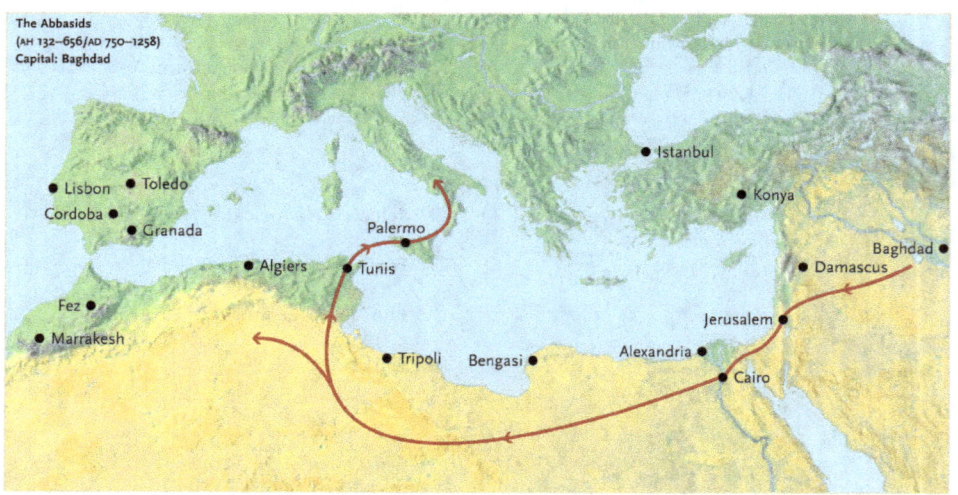

ISLAMIC DYNASTIES IN THE MEDITERRANEAN
The Fatimids | The Muslim West

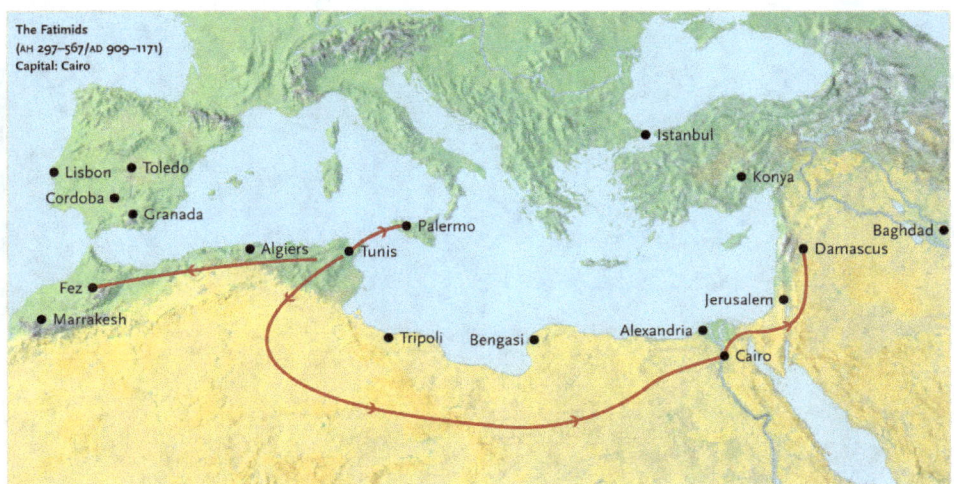

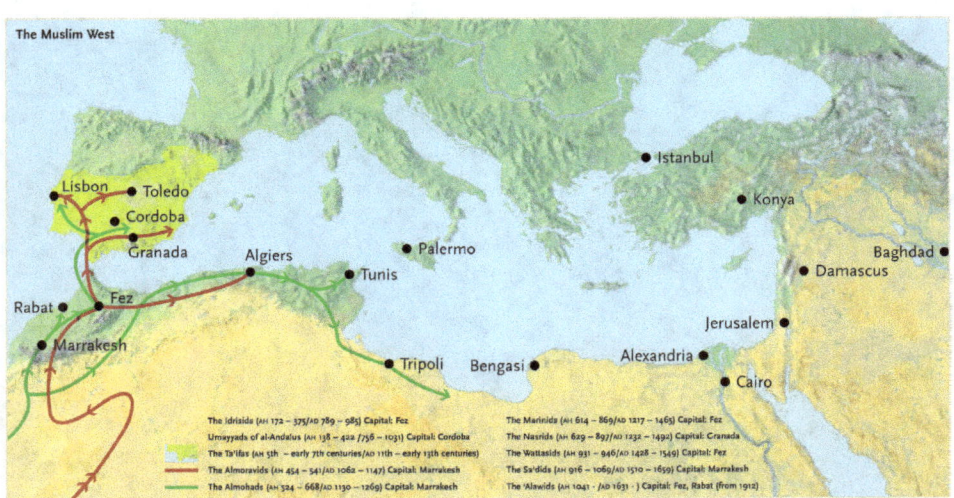

ISLAMIC DYNASTIES IN THE MEDITERRANEAN
The Central Maghreb | The Ayyubids

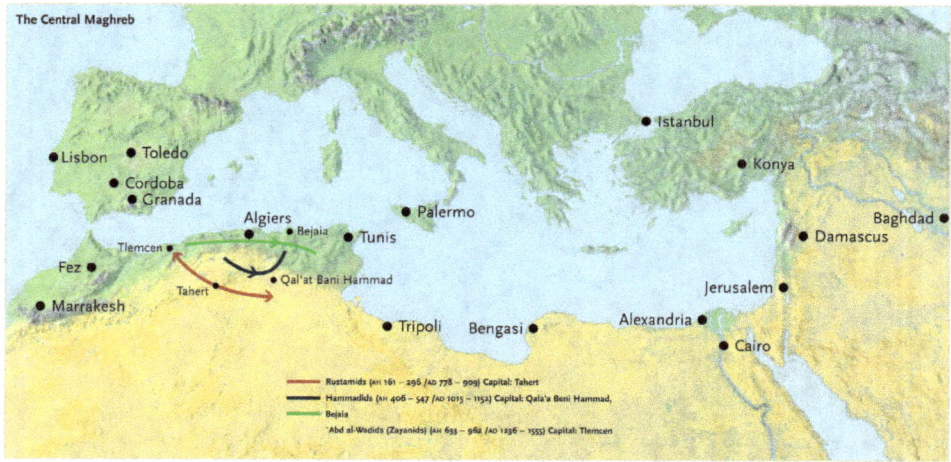

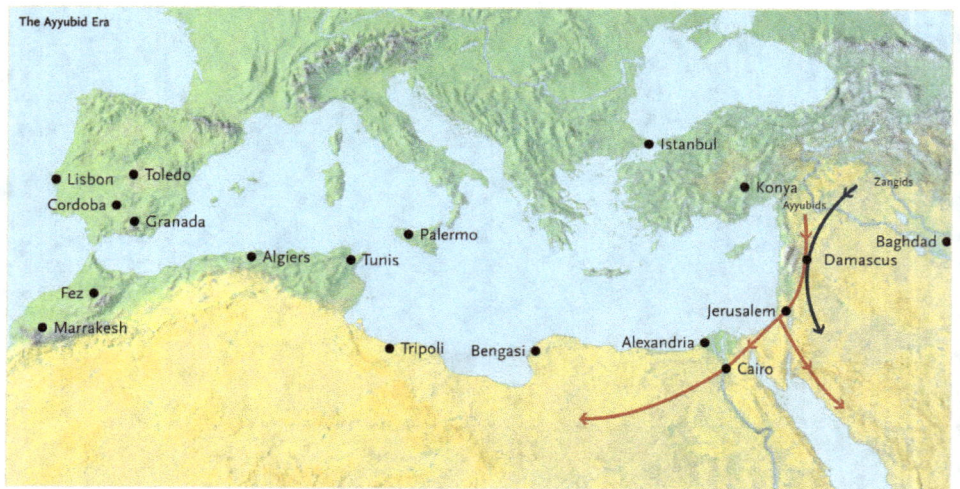

ISLAMIC DYNASTIES IN THE MEDITERRANEAN
The Mamluks | The Ottomans

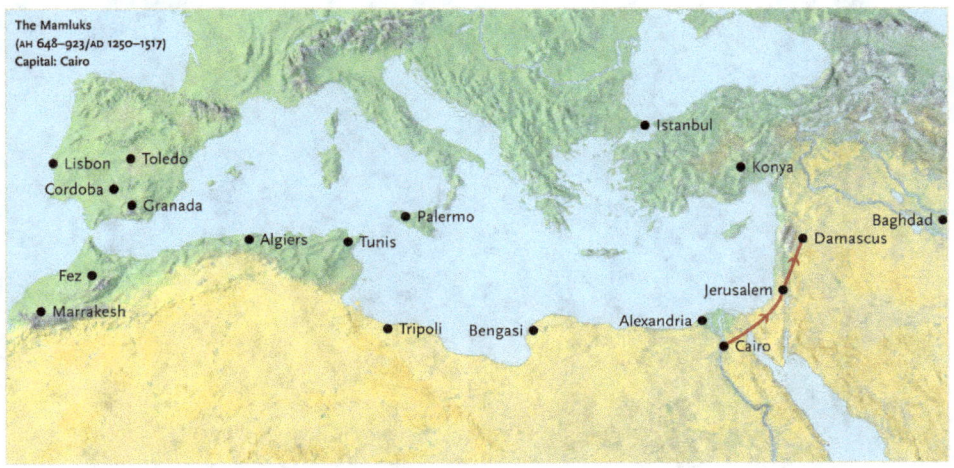

The Mamluks
(AH 648–923/AD 1250–1517)
Capital: Cairo

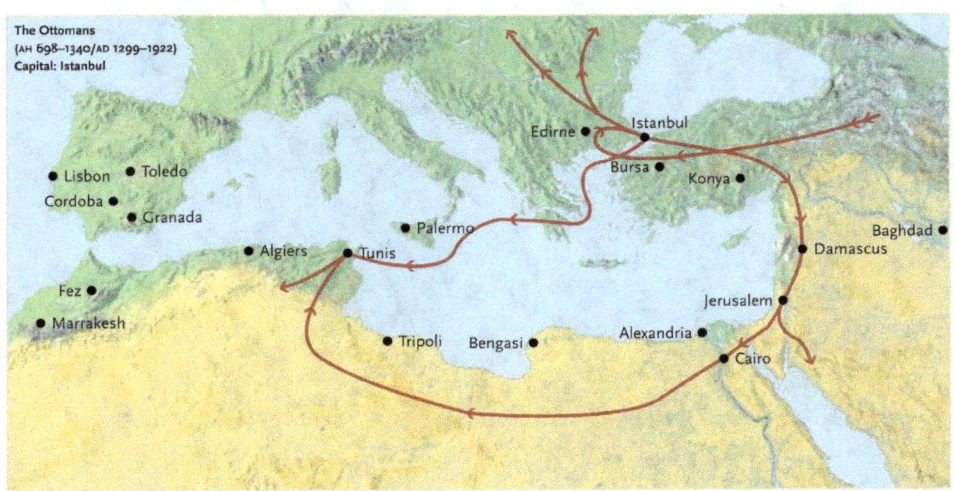

The Ottomans
(AH 698–1340/AD 1299–1922)
Capital: Istanbul

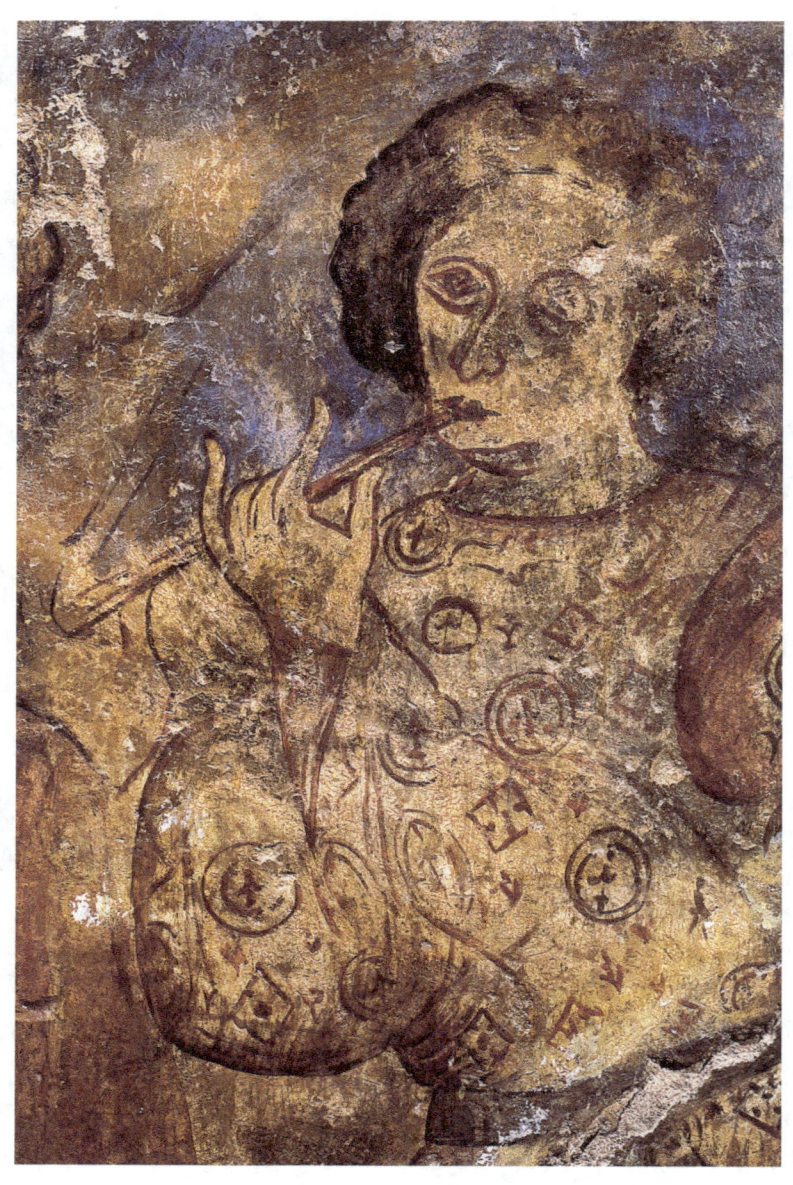

Qusayr 'Amra, mural in the Audience Hall, Badiya of Jordan.

ISLAMIC ART IN THE MEDITERRANEAN

Jamila Binous
Mahmoud Hawari
Manuela Marín
Gönül Öney

The Legacy of Islam in the Mediterranean

Since the first half of the $1^{st}/7^{th}$ century, the history of the Mediterranean Basin has belonged, in remarkably similar proportion, to two cultures, Islam and the Christian West. This extensive history of conflict and contact has created a mythology that is widely diffused in the collective imagination, a mythology based on the image of the other as the unyielding enemy, strange and alien, and as such, incomprehensible. It is of course true that battles punctuated those centuries from the time when the Muslims spilled forth from the Arabian Peninsula and took possession of the Fertile Crescent, Egypt, and later, North Africa, Sicily, and the Iberian Peninsula, penetrating into Western Europe as far as the south of France. At the beginning of the $2^{nd}/8^{th}$ century, the Mediterranean came under Islamic control.

This drive to expand, of an intensity seldom equalled in human history, was carried out in the name of a religion that considered itself then heir to its two immediate antecedents: Judaism and Christianity. It would be a gross oversimplification to explain the Islamic expansion exclusively in religious terms. One widespread image in the West presents Islam as a religion of simple dogmas adapted to the needs of the common people, spread by vulgar warriors who poured out from the desert bearing the *Qur'an* on the blades of their swords. This coarse image does away with the intellectual complexity of a religious message that transformed the world from the moment of its inception. It identifies this message with a military threat, and thus justifies a response on the same terms. Finally, it reduces an entire culture to only one of its elements, religion, and in doing so, deprives it of the potential for evolution and change.

The Mediterranean countries that were progressively incorporated into the Muslim world began their journeys from very different starting points. Forms of Islamic life that began to develop in each were quite logically different within the unity that resulted from their shared adhesion to the new religious dogma. It is precisely the capacity to assimilate elements of previous cultures (Hellenistic, Roman, etc.), which has been one of the defining characteristics of Islamic societies. If one restricts his observations to the geographical area of the Mediterranean, which was extremely diverse culturally at the time of the emergence of Islam, one will discern quickly that this initial moment does not represent a break with previous history in the least. One comes to realise that it is impossible to imagine a monolithic and immutable Islamic world, blindly following an inalterable religious message.

If anything can be singled out as the *leitmotiv* running through the area of the Mediterranean, it is diversity of expression combined with harmony of sentiment, a sentiment more cultural than religious. In the Iberian Peninsula —to begin with the western perimeter of the Mediterranean— the presence of Islam, initially brought about by military conquest, produced a society clearly differentiated from, but in permanent contact with Christian society. The importance of the cultural expression of this Islamic society was felt even after it ceased to exist as such, and gave rise to perhaps one of the most original components of Spanish culture, Mudejar art. Portugal maintained strong Mozarab traditions throughout the Islamic period and there are many imprints from this time that are still clearly visible today. In Morocco and Tunisia, the legacy of al-Andalus was assimilated into the local forms and continues to be evident to this day. The western Mediterranean produced original forms of expression that reflected its conflicting and plural historical evolution.

Lodged between East and West, the Mediterranean Sea is endowed with terrestrial enclaves, such as Sicily, that represent centuries-old key historical locations. Conquered by the Arabs established in Tunisia, Sicily has continued to perpetuate the cultural and historical memory of Islam long after the Muslims ceased to have any political presence on the island. The presence of Sicilian-Norman aesthetic forms preserved in architectural monuments clearly demonstrates that the history of these regions cannot be explained without an understanding of the diversity of social, economic and cultural experiences that flourished on their soil.

In sharp contrast, then, to the immutable and constant image alluded to at the outset, the history of Mediterranean Islam is characterised by surprising diversity. It is made up of a mixture of peoples and ethnicities, deserts and fertile lands. As the major religion has been Islam since the early Middle Ages, it is also true that religious minorities have maintained a presence historically. The Classical Arabic language of the *Qur'an,* has coexisted side-by-side with other languages, as well as with other dialects of Arabic. Within a setting of undeniable unity (Muslim religion, Arabic language and culture), each society has evolved and responded to the challenges of history in its own characteristic manner.

The Emergence and Development of Islamic Art

Throughout these countries, with ancient and diverse civilisations, a new art permeated with images from the Islamic faith emerged at the end of the $2^{nd}/8^{th}$ century and which successfully imposed itself in a period of less than a hundred years. This art, in its own particular manner, gave rise to creations and innovations based on unifying regional formulas and architectural and decorative processes, and was simultaneously inspired by the artistic traditions that proceeded it: Greco-Roman and Byzantine, Sasanian, Visigothic, Berber or even Central Asian.

The initial aim of Islamic art was to serve the needs of religion and various aspects of socio-economic life. New buildings appeared for religious purposes such as mosques and sanctuaries. For this reason, architecture played a central role in Islamic art because a whole series of other arts are dependent on it. Apart from architecture a whole range of complimentary minor arts found their artistic expressions in a variety of materials, such as wood, pottery, metal, glass, textiles and paper. In pottery, a great variety of glaze techniques were employed and among these distinguished groups are the lustre and polychrome painted wares. Glass of great beauty was manufactured, reaching excellence with the type adorned with gold and bright enamel colours. In metal work, the most sophisticated technique is inlaying bronze with silver or copper. High quality textiles and carpets, with geometric, animal and human designs, were made. Illuminated manuscripts with miniature painting represent a spectacular achievement in the arts of the book. These types of minor arts serve to attest the brilliance of Islamic art.

Figurative art, however, is excluded from the Islamic liturgical domain, which means it is ostracised from the central core of Islamic civilisation and that it is tolerated only at its periphery. Relief work is rare in the decoration of monuments and sculptures are almost flat. This deficit is compensated with a richness in ornamentation on the lavish carved plaster panelling, sculpted wooden panelling, wall tiling and glazed mosaics, as well as on the stalactite friezes, or *muqarnas*. Decorative elements taken from nature, such as leaves, flowers and branches, are generally stylised to the extreme and are so complicated that they rarely call to mind their sources of origin. The intertwining and combining of geometric motifs such as rhombus and etiolated polygons, form interlacing networks that completely cover the surface, resulting in shapes often called arabesques. One innovation within the decorative repertoire is the introduction of

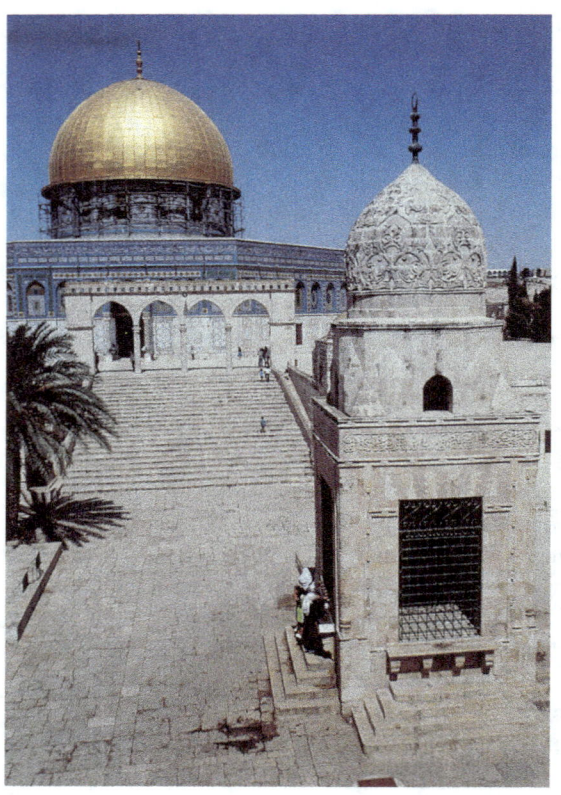

Dome of the Rock, Jerusalem.

epigraphic elements in the ornamentation of monuments, furniture and various objects. Muslim craftsmen made use of the beauty of Arabic calligraphy, the language of the sacred book, the *Qur'an,* not only for the transcription of the Qur'anic verses, but in all of its variations simply as a decorative motif for the ornamentation of stucco panelling and the edges of panels.

Art was also at the service of rulers. It was for patrons that architects built palaces, mosques, schools, hospitals, bathhouses, *caravanserais* and mausoleums, which would sometimes bear their names. Islamic art is, above all, dynastic art. Each one contributed tendencies that would bring about a partial or complete renewal of artistic forms, depending on historical conditions, the prosperity enjoyed by their states, and the traditions of each people. Islamic art, in spite of its relative unity, allowed for a diversity that gave rise to different styles, each one identified with a dynasty.

The Umayyad dynasty (41/661- 132/750), which transferred the capital of the caliphate to Damascus, represents a singular achievement in the history of Islam. It absorbed and incorporated the Hellenistic and Byzantine legacy in such a way that the classical tradition of the Mediterranean was recast in a new and innovative mould. Islamic art, thus, was formed in Syria, and the architecture, unmistakably Islamic due to the personality of the founders, would continue to bear a relation to Hellenistic and Byzantine art as well. The most important of these monuments are the Dome of the Rock in Jerusalem, the earliest existing monumental Islamic sanctuary, the Great Mosque of Damascus, which served as a model for later mosques, and the desert palaces of Syria, Jordan and Palestine.

Islamic Art in the Mediterranean

When the Abbasid caliphate (132/ 750-656/1258) succeeded the Umayyads, the political centre of Islam was moved from the Mediterranean to Baghdad in Mesopotamia. This factor would influence the development of Islamic civilisation and the entire range of culture, and art would bear the mark of that change. Abbasid art and architecture were influenced by three major traditions: Sassanian, Central Asian and Seljuq. Central Asian influence was already present in Sassanian architecture, but at Samarra this influence is represented by the stucco style with its arabesque ornamentation that would rapidly spread throughout the Islamic world. The influence of the Abbasid monuments can be observed in the buildings constructed during this period in the other regions of the empire, particularly Egypt and Ifriqiya. In Cairo, the Mosque of Ibn Tulun (262/876-265/879) is a masterpiece, remarkable for its plan and unity of conception. It was modelled after the Abbasid Great Mosque of Samarra, particularly its spiral minaret. In Kairouan, the capital of Ifriqiya, vassals of the Abbasid caliphs, the Aghlabids (184/800-296/909) expanded the Great Mosque of Kairouan, one of the most venerable congregational mosques in the Maghrib. Its *mihrab* was covered by ceramic tiles from Mesopotamia.

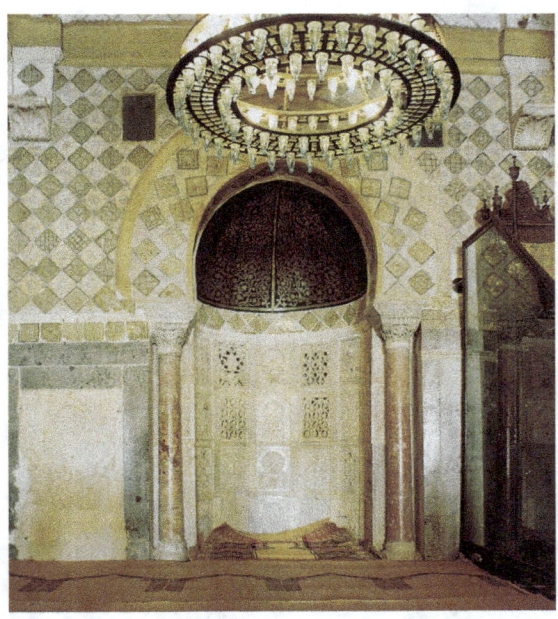

Kairouan Mosque, mihrab, Tunisia.

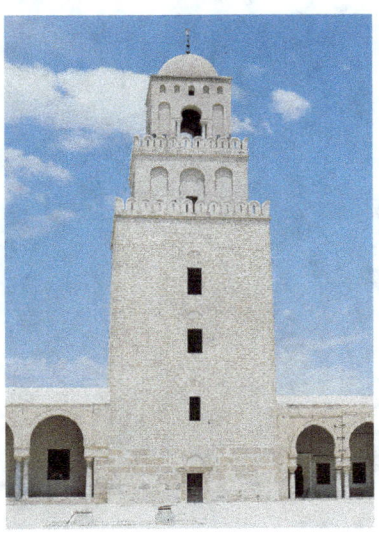

Kairouan Mosque, minaret, Tunisia.

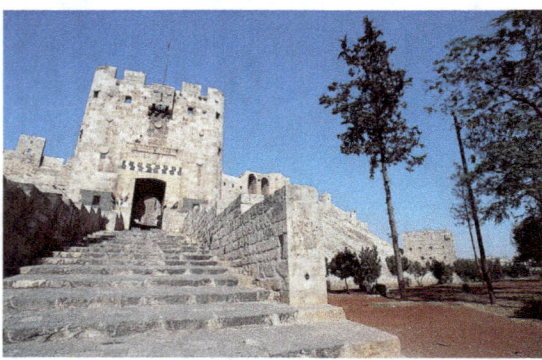

Citadel of Aleppo, view of the entrance, Syria.

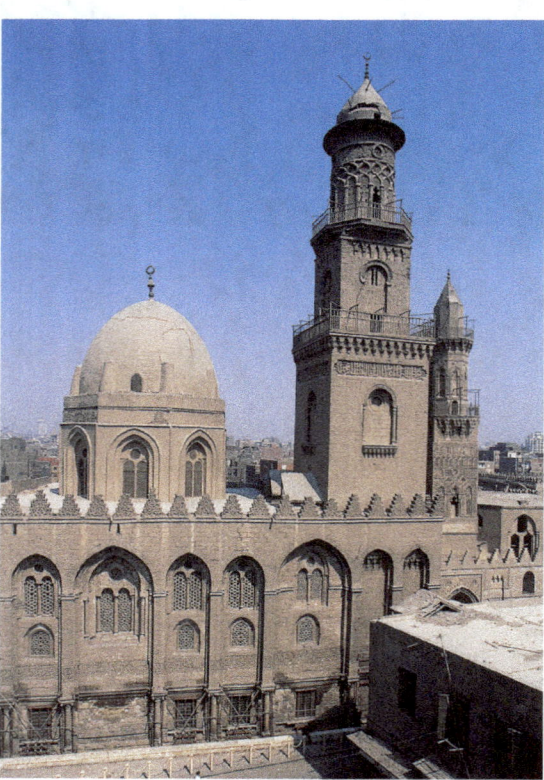

Complex of Qaluwun, Cairo, Egypt.

The reign of the Fatimids (297/909-567/1171) represents a remarkable period in the history of the Islamic countries of the Mediterranean: North Africa, Sicily, Egypt and Syria. Of their architectural constructions, a few examples remain that bear witness to their past glory. In the central Maghrib the Qal'a of the Bani Hammad and the Mosque of Mahdiya; in Sicily, the Cuba (*Qubba*) and the Zisa (*al-'Aziza*) in Palermo, constructed by Fatimid craftsmen under the Norman king William II; in Cairo, the Azhar Mosque is the most prominent example of Fatimid architecture in Egypt.

The Ayyubids (567/1171-648/1250), who overthrew the Fatimid dynasty in Cairo, were important patrons of architecture. They established religious institutions *(madrasas, khanqas)* for the propagation of *Sunni* Islam, mausoleums and welfare projects, as well as awesome fortifications pertaining to the military conflict with the Crusaders. The Citadel of Aleppo in Syria is a remarkable example of their military architecture.

The Mamluks (648/1250-923/1517) successors to the Ayyubids who had successfully resisted the Crusades and the Mongols, achieved the unity of Syria and Egypt and created a formidable empire. The wealth and luxury of the Mamluk sultan's court in Cairo motivated artists and architects to achieve an extraordinarily elegant style of architecture. For the world of Islam, the Mamluk period marked a rebirth and renaissance. The enthusiasm for establishing religious foundations and reconstructing existing ones place the Mamluks among the greatest patrons of art and architecture in the history of Islam. The Mosque of Hassan (757/ 1356), a funerary mosque built with a cruciform plan in which the four arms of the cross were formed by four *iwans* of the building around a central courtyard was typical of the era.

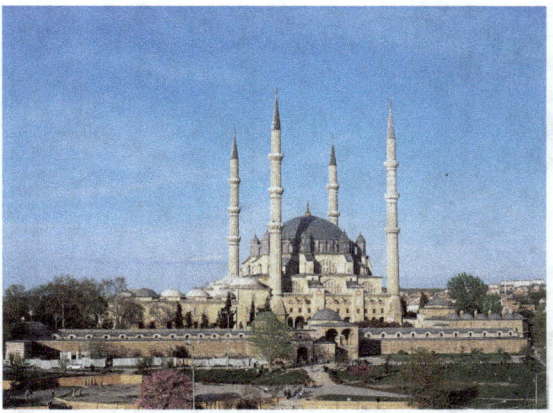

Selimiye Mosque, general view, Edirne, Turkey.

Anatolia was the birthplace of two great Islamic dynasties: the Seljuqs (571/1075-718/1318), who introduced Islam to the region; and the Ottomans (699/1299-1340/1922), who brought about the end of the Byzantine Empire upon capturing Constantinople, and asserted their hegemony throughout the region.

A distinctive style of Seljuq art and architecture flourished with influences from Central Asia, Iran, Mesopotamia and Syria, which merged with elements deriving from Anatolian Christian and antiquity heritage. Konya, the new capital in Central Anatolia, as well as other cities, were enriched with buildings in the newly developed Seljuq style. Numerous mosques, *madrasas, turbes* and *caravanserais,* which were richly decorated by stucco and tiling with diverse figural representations, have survived to our day.

Tile of Kubadabad Palace, Karatay Museum, Konya, Turkey.

As the Seljuq emirates disintegrated and Byzantium declined, the Ottomans expanded their territory swiftly changing their capital from Iznik to Bursa and then again to Edirne. The conquest of Constantinople in 858/1453 by Sultan Mehmet II provided the necessary impetus for the transition of an emerging state into a great empire. A superpower that extended its boundaries to Vienna including the Balkans in the West and to Iran in the East, as well

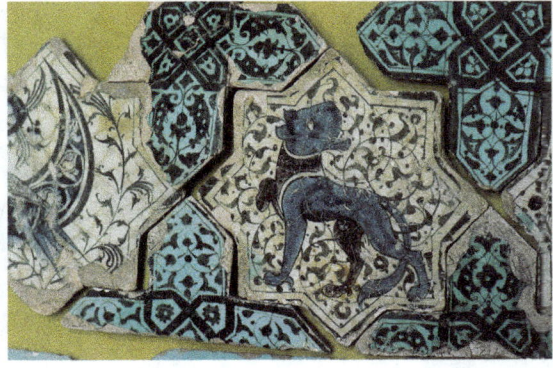

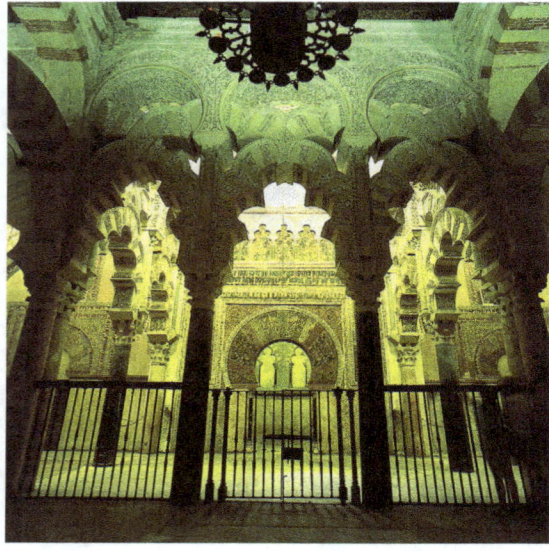

Great Mosque of Cordoba, mihrab, Spain.

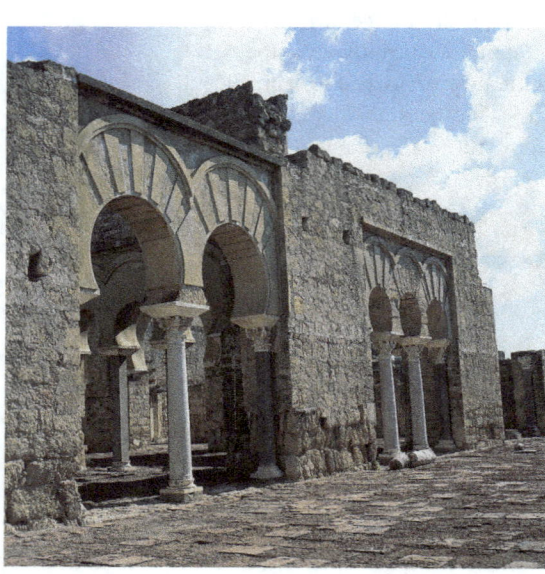

Madinat al-Zahra', Dar al-Yund, Spain.

as North Africa from Egypt to Algeria, turning the Eastern Mediterranean into an Ottoman sea. The race to surpass the grandeur of the inherited Byzantine churches, exemplified by the Hagia Sophia, culminated in the construction of great mosques in Istanbul. The most significant one is the Mosque of Süleymaniye, built in the $10^{th}/16^{th}$ century by the famous Ottoman architect Sinan, epitomises the climax in architectural harmony in domed buildings. Most major Ottoman mosques were part of a large building complex called *kulliye* that also consisted several *madrasas*, a Qur'an school, a library, a hospital (*darussifa*), a hostel (*tabhane*), a public kitchen, a *caravanserai* and mausoleums (*turbes*). From the beginning of the $12^{th}/18^{th}$ century, during the so-called Tulip Period, Ottoman architecture and decorative style reflected the influence of French Baroque and Rococo, heralding the westernisation period in arts and architecture.

Al-Andalus at the western part of the Islamic world became the cradle of a brilliant artistic and cultural expression. 'Abd al-Rahman I established an independent Umayyad caliphate (138/750-422/1031) with Cordoba as its capital. The Great Mosque of Cordoba would pioneer innovative artistic tendencies such as the double tiered arches with two alternating colours and panels with vegetal ornamentation which would become part of the repertoire of al-Andalus artistic forms.

In the 5th/11th century, the caliphate of Cordoba broke up into a score of principalities incapable of preventing the progressive advance of the reconquest initiated by the Christian states of the Northwestern Iberian Peninsula. These petty kings, or Taifa Kings, called the Almoravids in 479/1086 and the Almohads in 540/1145, repelled the Christians and reestablished partial unity in al-Andalus.

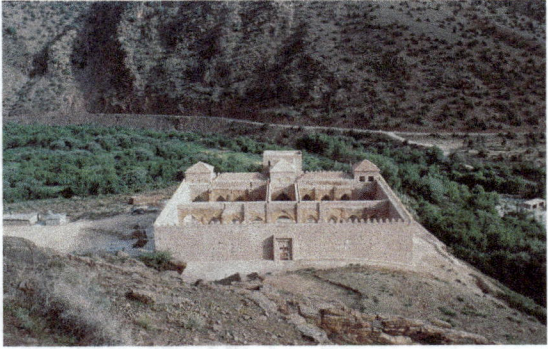

Tinmal Mosque, aerial view, Morocco.

Through their intervention in the Iberian Peninsula, the Almoravids (427/1036-541/1147) came into contact with a new civilisation and were captivated quickly by the refinement of al-Andalus art as reflected in their capital, Marrakesh, where they built a grand mosque and palaces. The influence of the architecture of Cordoba and other capitals such as Seville would be felt in all of the Almoravid monuments from Tlemcen, Algiers to Fez.

Under the rule of the Almohads (515/1121-667/1269), who expanded their hegemony as far as Tunisia, western Islamic art reached its climax. During this period, artistic creativity that originated with the Almoravid rulers was renewed and masterpieces of Islamic art were created. The Great Mosque of Seville with its minaret the Giralda, the Kutubiya in Marrakesh, the Mosque of Hassan in Rabat and the Mosque of Tinmal high in the Atlas Mountains in Morocco are notable examples.

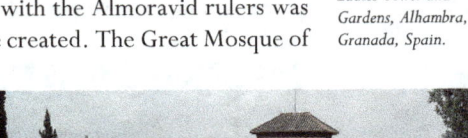

Ladies Tower and Gardens, Alhambra, Granada, Spain.

Upon the dissolution of the Almohad Empire, the Nasrid dynasty (629/1232-897/1492) installed itself in Granada and was to experience a period of splendour in the 8th/14th century. The civilisation of Granada would become a cultural model in

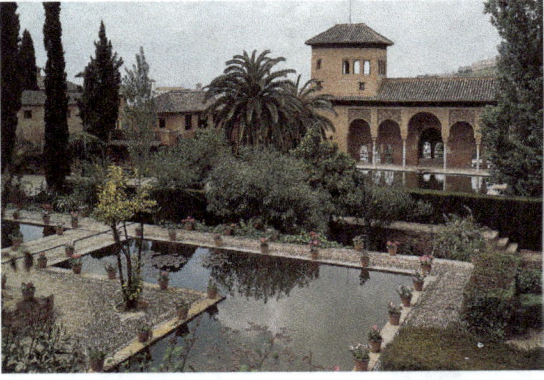

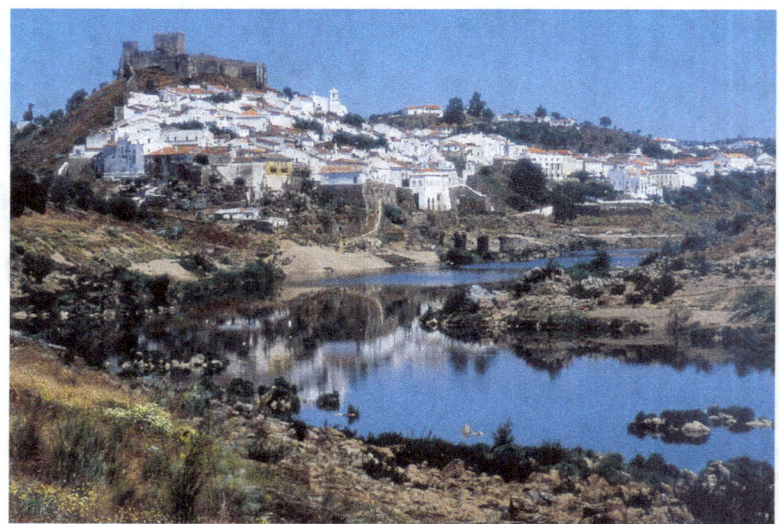

Mertola, general view, Portugal.

future centuries in Spain (Mudejar Art) and particularly in Morocco, where this artistic tradition enjoyed great popularity and would be preserved until the present day in the areas of architecture and decoration, music and cuisine. The famous palace and fort of *al-Hamra'* (the Alhambra) in Granada marks the crowning achievement of al-Andalus art, with all features of its artistic repertoire.

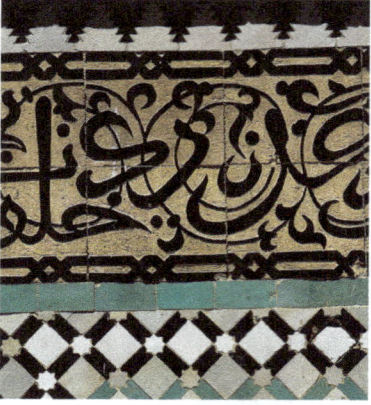

Decoration detail, Abu Inan Madrasa, Meknes, Morocco.

At the same time in Morocco, the Merinids (641/1243-876/1471) replaced the Almohads, while in Algeria the 'Abd al-Wadid's reigned (633/1235-922/1516), as did the Hafsids (625/1228-941/1534) in Tunisia. The Merinids perpetuated al-Andalus art, enriching it with new features. They embellished their capital Fez with an abundance of mosques, palaces and *madrasa*s, with their clay mosaic and *zellij* panelling in the wall decorations, considered

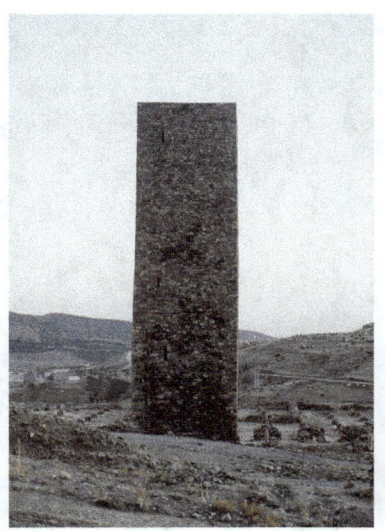
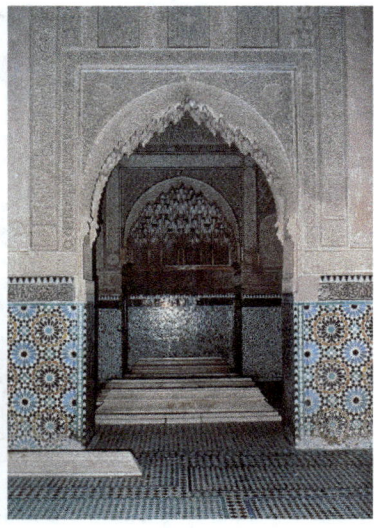

Qal'a of the Bani Hammad, minaret, Algeria.

Sa'adian Tomb Marrakesh, Morocco.

to be the most perfect works of Islamic art. The later Moroccan dynasties, the Sa'adians (933/1527-1070/1659) and the 'Alawite (1077/1659 – until the present day), carried on the artistic tradition of al-Andalus that was exiled from its native soil in 897/1492. They continued to build and decorate their monuments using the same formulas and the same decorative themes as had the preceding dynasties, adding innovative touches characteristic of their creative genius. In the early $11^{th}/17^{th}$ century, emigrants from al-Andalus (the *Moriscos*), who took up residence in the northern cities of Morocco, introduced numerous features of al-Andalus art. Today, Morocco is one of the few countries that has kept traditions of al-Andalus alive in its architecture and furniture, at the same time modernising them as they incorporated the architectural techniques and styles of the $15^{th}/20^{th}$ century.

ARCHITECTURAL SUMMARY

In general terms, Islamic architecture can be classified into two categories: religious, such as mosques, *madrasas*, mausoleums, and secular, such as palaces, *caravanserais*, fortifications, etc.

Religious Architecture

Mosques

The mosque for obvious reasons lies at the very heart of Islamic architecture. It is an apt symbol of the faith that it serves. That symbolic role was understood by Muslims at a very early stage, and played an important part in the creation of suitable visual markers for the building: minaret, dome, *mihrab*, *minbar*, etc.

The first mosque in Islam was the courtyard of the Prophet's house in Medina, with no architectural refinements. Early mosques built by the Muslims as their empire was expanding were simple. From these buildings developed the congregational or Friday mosque (*jami'*), essential features of which remain today unchanged for nearly 1400 years. The general plan consists of a large courtyard surrounded by arched porticoes, with more aisles or arcades on the side facing Mecca (*qibla*) than the other sides. The Great Umayyad Mosque in Damascus, which followed the plan of the Prophet's mosque, became the prototype for many mosques built in various parts of the Islamic world.

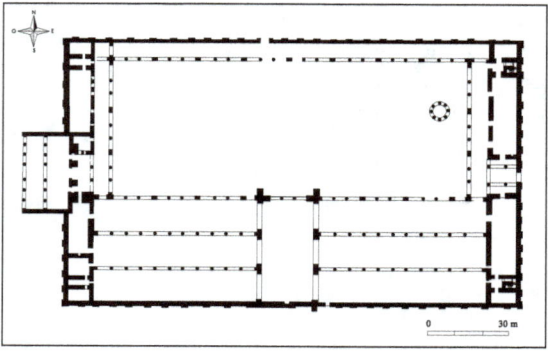

Umayyad Mosque of Damascus, Syria.

Two other types of mosques developed in Anatolia and afterwards in the Ottoman domains: the basilical and the dome types. The first type is a simple pillared hall or basilica that follows late Roman and Byzantine Syrian tradition, introduced with some modifications in the $5^{th}/11^{th}$ century. The second type, which developed during the Ottoman period, has its organisation of interior space under a single dome. The Ottoman architects in great imperial mosques created a new style of domed construction by merging the Islamic mosque tradition with that of dome building in Anatolia. The main dome rests on hexagonal support system, while lateral bays are covered by smaller domes. This emphasis on an interior space dominated by a single dome became the starting point of a style that was to be introduced in the $10^{th}/16^{th}$ century. During this period, mosques became multipurpose social complexes con-

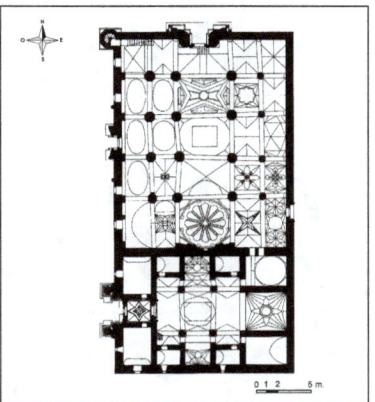

Great Mosque, Divriği, Turkey.

sisting of a *zawiya*, a *madrasa*, a public kitchen, a bath, a *caravanserai* and a mausoleum of the founder. The supreme monument of this style is the Sülaymeniye Mosque in Istanbul built in 965/1557 by the great architect Sinan.

The minaret from the top of which the *muezzin* calls Muslims to prayer, is the most prominent marker of the mosque. In Syria the traditional minaret consists of a square-plan tower built of stone. In Mamluk Egypt minarets are each divided into three distinct zones: a square section at the bottom, an octagonal middle section and a circular section with a small dome on the top. Its shaft is richly decorated and the transition between each section is covered with a band of *muqarnas* decoration. Minarets in North Africa and Spain, that share the square tower form with Syria, are decorated with panels of motifs around paired sets of windows. During the Ottoman period the octagonal or cylindrical minarets replaced the square tower. Often these are tall pointed minarets and although mosques generally have only one minaret, in major cities there are two, four or even six minarets.

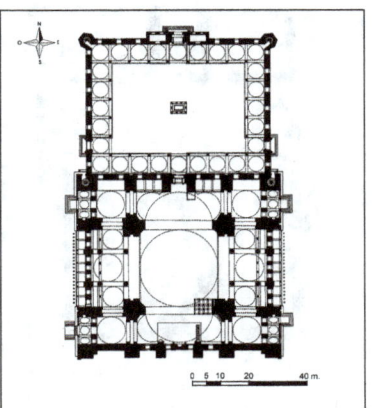

Sülaymeniye Mosque, Istanbul, Turkey.

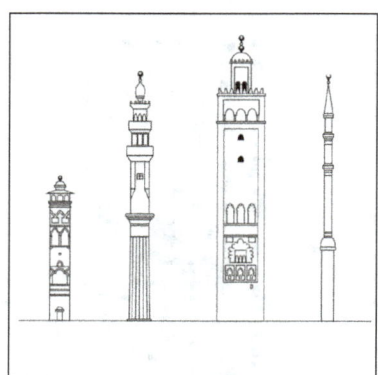

Typology of minarets.

Madrasas

It seems likely that the Seljuqs built the first *madrasas* in Persia in the early 5th/11th century when they were small structures with a domed courtyard and two lateral *iwans*. A later type developed has an open courtyard with a central *iwan* and surrounded by arcades. During the 6th/12th century in Anatolia, the *madrasa* became multifunctional and was intended to serve as a medical school, mental hospital, a hospice with a public kitchen (*imaret*) and a mausoleum. The promotion of *Sunni* (orthodox) Islam reached a new zenith in Syria and Egypt under the Zengids and the Ayyubids (6th/12th–early 7th/13th centuries). This era witnessed the introduction of the *madrasa* established by a civic or political leader for the advancement of Islamic jurisprudence. The foundation was funded by an endowment in perpetuity (*waqf*), usually the revenues of land or property in the form of an orchard, shops in a market (*suq*), or a bathhouse (*hammam*). The *madrasa* traditionally followed a cruciform plan with a central court surrounded by four *iwans*. Soon the *madrasa* became a dominant architectural form with mosques adopting a four-*iwan* plan. The *madrasa* gradually lost its sole religious and political function as a propaganda tool and tended to have a broader civic function, serving as a congregational mosque and a mausoleum for the benefactor.

The construction of m*adrasa*s in Egypt and particularly in Cairo gathered new momentum with the coming of the Mamluks. The typical Cairene *madrasa* of this era was a

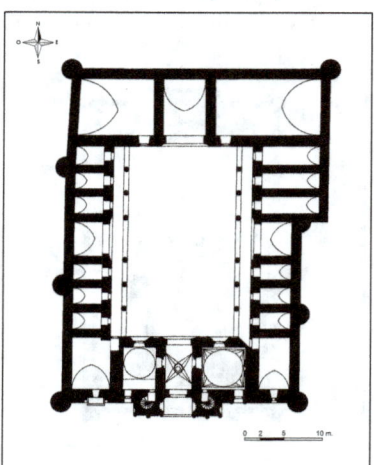

Sivas Gök Madrasa, Turkey.

multifunctional gigantic four-*iwan* structure with a stalactite (*muqarnas*) portal and splendid façades. With the advent of the Ottomans in the 10th/16th century, the joint foundation, typically a mosque-*madrasa*, became a widespread large complex that enjoyed imperial patronage. The *iwan* disappeared gradually and was replaced by a dominant dome chamber. A substantial increase in the number of domed cells used by students is a characteristic of Ottoman *madrasa*s.

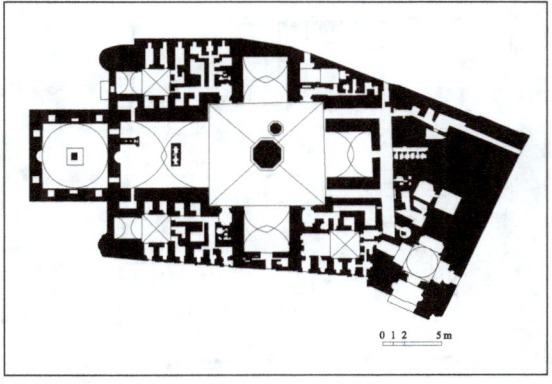

Mosque and madrasa Sultan Hassan, Cairo, Egypt.

One of the various building types that by virtue of their function and of their form can be related to the *madrasa* is the *khanqa*. The term indicates an institution, rather than a particular kind of building, that houses members of a Muslim mystical (*sufi*) order. Several other words used by Muslim historians as synonyms for *khanqa* include: in the Maghrib, *zawiya*; in Ottoman domain, *tekke*; and in general, *ribat*. Sufism permanently dominated the *khanqa*, which originated in eastern Persia during the 4th/10th century. In its simplest form the *khanqa* was a house where a group of pupils gathered around a master (*shaykh*), and it had the facilities for assembly, prayer and communal living. The establishment of *khanqa*s flourished under the Seljuqs during the 5th/11th and the 6th/12th centuries and benefited from the close association between Sufism and the *Shafi'i madhhab* (doctrine) favoured by ruling elite.

Mausoleums

The terminology of the building type of the mausoleum used in Islamic sources is varied. The standard descriptive term *turbe* refers to the function of the building as for burial. Another term is *qubba* that refers to the most identifiable, the dome, and often marks a structure commemorating Biblical prophets, companions of the Prophet Muhammad and religious or military notables. The function of mausoleums is not limited simply to a place of burial and

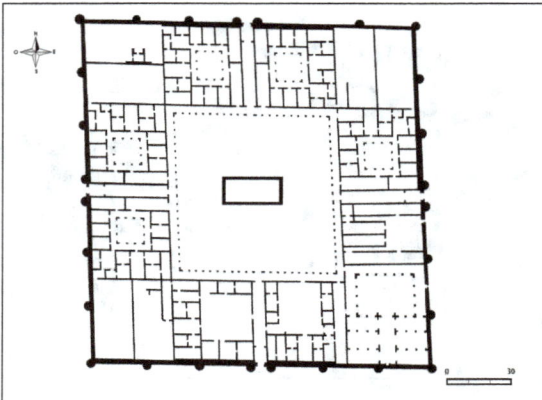

Qasr al-Khayr al-Sharqi, Syria.

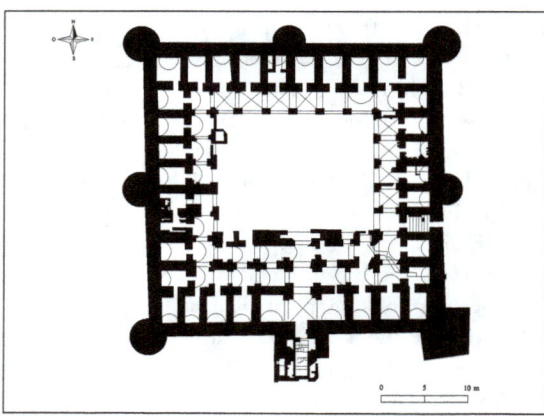

Ribat of Sousse, Tunisia.

commemoration, but also plays an important role in "popular" religion. They are venerated as tombs of local saints and became places of pilgrimage. Often the structure of a mausoleum is embellished with Qur'anic quotations and contains a *mihrab* within it to render it a place of prayer. In some cases the mausoleum became part of a joint foundation. Forms of Medieval Islamic mausoleums are varied, but the traditional one has a domed square plan.

Secular Architecture

Palaces

The Umayyad period is characterised by sumptuous palaces and bathhouses in remote desert regions. Their basic plan is largely derived from Roman military models. Although the decoration of these structures is eclectic, they constitute the best examples of the budding Islamic decorative style. Mosaics, mural paintings, stone or stucco sculpture were used for a remarkable variety of decorations and themes. Abbasid palaces in Iraq, such as those at Samarra and Ukhaidir, follow the same plan as their Umayyad forerunners, but are marked by increase in size, the use of the great *iwan*, dome and courtyard, and the extensive use of stucco decorations. Palaces in the later Islamic period developed a distinctive style that was more decorative and less monumental. The most remarkable example of royal or princely palaces is the Alhambra. The vast area of the palace is broken up into a series of separate units: gardens, pavilions and courts. The most striking feature of Alhambra, however, is the decoration that provides an extraordinary effect in the interior of the building.

Caravanserais

A *caravanserai* generally refers to a large structure that provides a lodging place for travellers and merchants. Normally, it is a square or rectangular floor plan, with a single projecting monumental entrance and towers in the exterior walls. A central courtyard is surrounded by porticoes and rooms for lodging travellers, storing merchandise and for the stabling of animals.

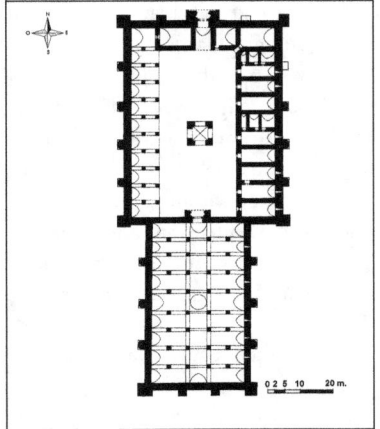

Aksaray Sultan Khan, Turkey.

The characteristic type of building has a wide range of functions since it has been described as *khan, han, funduq, ribat*. These terms may imply no more than differences in regional vocabularies rather than being distinctive functions or types. The architectural sources of the various types of *caravanserais* are difficult to identify. Some are perhaps derived from the Roman *castrum* or military camp to which the Umayyad desert palaces are related. Other types, in Mesopotamia and Persia, are associated with domestic architecture.

Urban organisation

From about the 3rd/10th century every town of any significance acquired fortified walls and towers, elaborate gates and a mighty citadel (*qal'a* or *qasba*) as seat of power. These are massive constructions built in materials characteristic of the region in which they are found; stone in Syria, Palestine and Egypt, or brick, stone and rammed earth in the Iberian Peninsula and North Africa. A unique example of military architecture is the *ribat*. Technically, this is a fortified palace designated for the temporary or permanent warriors of Islam who committed themselves to the defence of frontiers. The *ribat* of Sousse in

Tunisia bears resemblance to early Islamic palaces, but with a different interior arrangement of large halls, mosque and a minaret.

The division of the majority of Islamic cities into neighbourhoods is based on ethnic and religious affinity and it is also a system of urban organisation that facilitates the administration of the population. In the neighbourhood there is always a mosque. A bathhouse, a fountain, an oven and a group of stores are located either within or nearby. Its structure is formed by a network of streets, alleys and a collection of houses. Depending on the region and era, the home takes on diverse features governed by the historical and cultural traditions, climate and construction materials available.

The market (*suq*), which functions as the nerve-centre for local businesses, would be the most relevant characteristic of Islamic cities. Its distance from the mosque determines the spatial organisation of the markets by specialised guilds. For instance, the professions considered clean and honourable (bookmakers, perfume makers, tailors) are located in the mosque's immediate environs, and the noisy and foul-smelling crafts (blacksmith, tanning, cloth dying) are situated progressively further from it. This geographic distribution responds to imperatives that rank on strictly technical grounds.

THE ITINERARIES

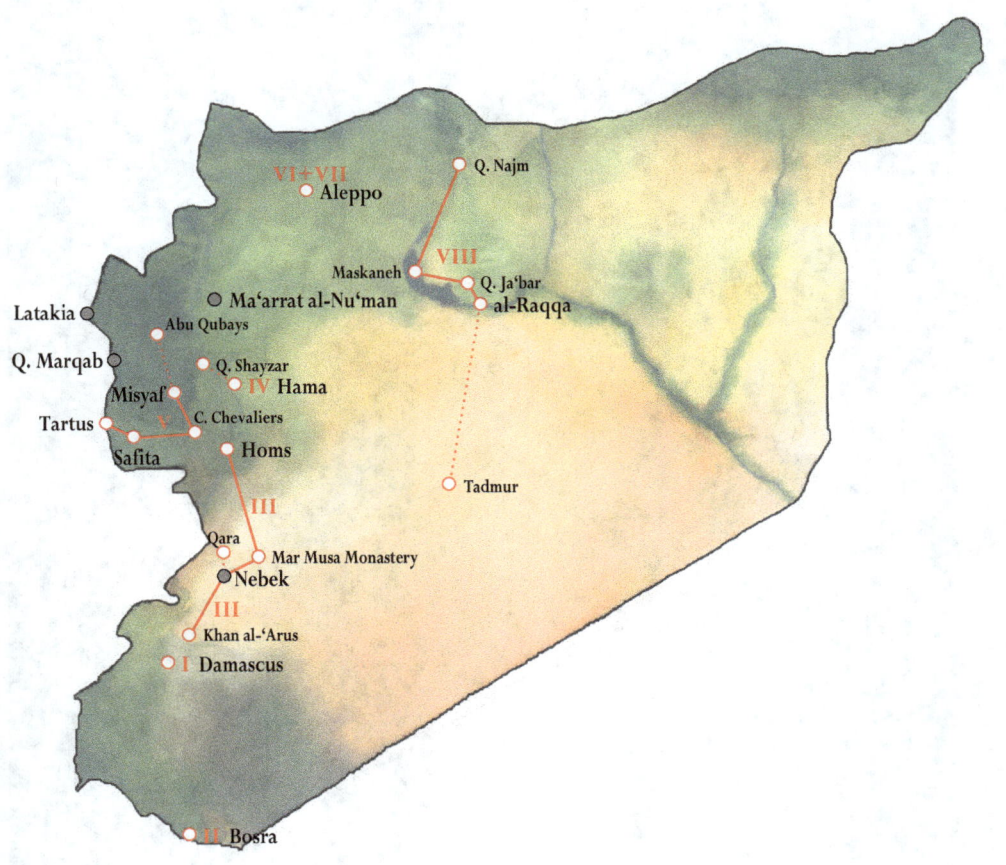

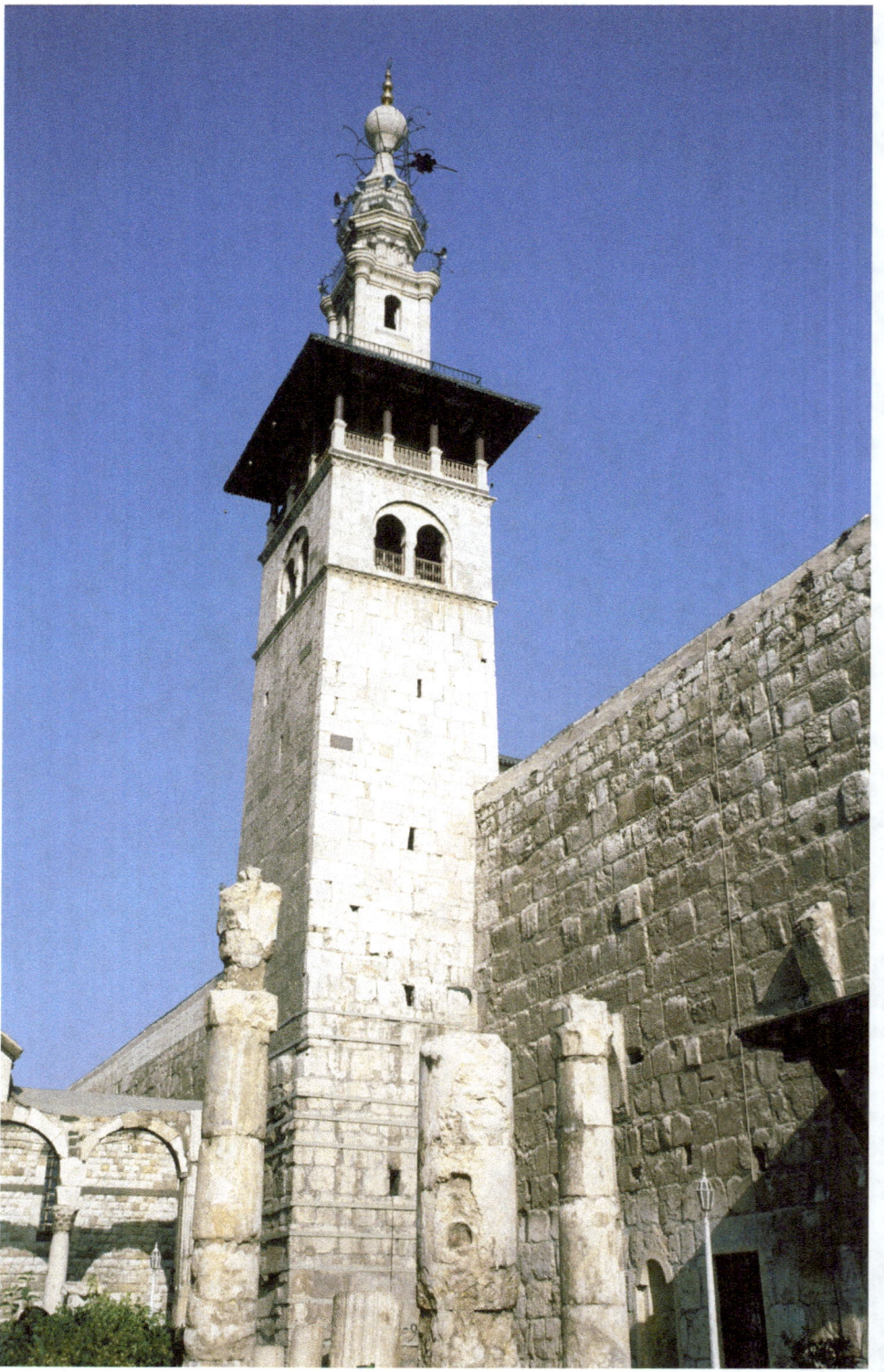

HISTORICAL INTRODUCTION

Abd al-Razzaq Moaz, Zena Takieddine

The era presented by this catalogue, from the mid-5th/-11th century until the mid-7th/-13th century, emerges from a background of turbulence in the Muslim world. This is because the period of unity and prosperity founded by the 'Abbasid Caliphate in 132/750 with its monumental capital in Baghdad, a veritable Golden Age of human civilisation under the banner of Islam, had by the 4th/10th century begun to disintegrate. Due to its wide expanse, 'Abbasid-appointed governors were growing gradually autonomous and some were even fragmenting into smaller independent states, greatly weakening Baghdad's central authority. Moreover, a Persian military dynasty from northern Iran, known as the Buyids, or Buwayhids, had even taken the capital by 333/945, rendering the 'Abbasid caliph a puppet. Most astounding of all was the proclamation of an Isma'ili counter-caliphate led by the Fatimid Dynasty in Ifriqiya (Tunisia) in 269/909. The Fatimid caliphate grew immensely powerful and extended eastward to establish a new Islamic capital in Egypt called al-Qahira "the Victorious", modern-day Cairo, in 358/969. The 'Abbasids were incapable of decisively countering the Fatimids, and Cairo flourished into a magnificent court with a strong economic and political Mediterranean presence. The Fatimids even took over the holy lands in Palestine and Arabia. These lands were formerly under 'Abbasid governance and played a crucial role in the bolstering of government legitimacy since they held the sacred shrines of Islam, Mecca, Medina and Jerusalem.

The antagonism between 'Abbasid Baghdad and Fatimid Cairo wrought havoc in the lands lying between them, known as Bilad al-Sham, and namely Syria. This included the stretch of the eastern Mediterranean coast from Alexandretta and Antioch in the north, to the River Jordan in the south, which then swept inland in the famous "Fertile Crescent" fashion, and included the central sweep of desert-like steppes, reaching the Euphrates and the Tigris rivers. The land that these two rivers surround is known as "the Island" or al-Jazira, which to this day is used in reference to north-west Syria.

An additional and ever-present pressure on the Muslim world of this region came also from the north, the Byzantine Empire, which indulged in expansionist campaigns encroaching into northern and coastal Syria. A local tribe known as the Hamdanids made great efforts to establish a strong court in Aleppo to counter the Byzantine menace, particularly under the leadership of Sayf al-Dawla (d. 356/967) the heroic deeds of whom were celebrated by the court poet al-Mutanabbi, but made little headway with the Byzantines. Meanwhile, the Fatimids in the south had taken Damascus in 358/970 causing the outbreak of warring militias and the destruction of the Great Umayyad Mosque, the spiritual focal point of the community and the major urban landmark of the city. These external pressures, marking a difficult century of Syrian history, further aggravated internal

Great Umayyad Mosque of Damascus, view of the minaret of the Bride (al-'Arus).

Chronological table of the 'Abbasid and Fatimid Caliphs.

The 'Abbasid Caliphate		The Fatimid Caliphate	
Abu 'Abbas al-Saffah	132-136/750-754		
Al-Mansur	136-158/754-775		
Al-Mahdi	158-169/775-785		
Al-Hadi	169-170/785-786		
Harun al-Rashid	170-193/786-809		
Al-Amin	193-198/809-813		
Al-Ma'mun	198-218/813-833		
Al-Mu'tasim	218-227/833-842		
Al-Wathiq	227-232/842-847		
Al-Mutawakkil	232-247/847-861		
Al-Mustansir	247-248/861-862		
Al-Musta'in	248-252/862-866		
Al-Mu'tazz	252-255/866-869		
Al-Muhtadi	255-256/869-870		
Al-Mu'tamid	256-270/870-892		
Al-Mu'tadid	270-289/892-902		
Al-Muktafi	289-295/902-908		
Al-Muqtadir	295-320/908-932		
Al-Qahir	**320-322/932-934**[1]	'Ubayd Allah al-Mahdi	297-322/909-934[2]
Al-Radi	322-329/934-940	Al-Qa'im	322-334/934-946
Al-Muttaqi	329-333/940-944		
Al-Mustakfi	333-334/944-945	Al-Mansur	334-341/946-953
Al-Muti'	**334-363/945-974**[3]	**Al-Mu'izz**	**341-365/953-975**[4]
Al-Ta'i'	363-381/974-991	Al-'Aziz	365-386/975-996
Al-Qadir	381-422/991-1031	Al-Hakim bi Amr Allah	386-411/996-1021
		Al-Zahir	411-427/1021-1036
Al-Qa'im	**422-467/1031-1075**[5]	Al-Mustansir	427-487/1036-1094[6]
Al-Muktafi	467-487/1075-1094	Al-Musta'li	487-495/1094-1101
Al-Mustazhir	487-512/1094-1118	Al-Amir	495-525/1101-1130
Al-Mustarshid	512-529/1118-1135	Al-Hafiz	525-544/1130-1149
Al-Rashid	529-530/1135-1136	Al-Zafir	544-549/1149-1154
Al-Muqtafi	530-555/1136-1160	Al-Fai'z	549-555/1154-1160
Al-Mustanjid	555-566/1160-1170	**Al-'Adid**	**555-567/1160-1171**[7]
Al-Mustadi'	566-575/1170-1180		
Al-Nasir	575-622/1180-1225		
Al-Zahir	622-623/1225-1226		
Al-Mustansir	623-640/1226-1242		
Al-Musta'sim	**640-656/1242-1258**[8]		

Source: "Abbasids", Encyclopaedia of Islam, vol 1, p. 22; "Fatimids", Encyclopaedia of Islam, vol. 2, p. 850.

[1]) The 'Abbasid Caliphate is challenged by a Fatimid counter-Caliphate.
[2]) The Fatimids found the first Shi'a caliphate in Islamic history.
[3]) Baghdad falls to the Buyids.
[4]) Fatimids found Cairo as new capital 358/969.
[5]) Baghdad taken by the Seljuqs, founding Seljuq Sultanate, and re-instating 'Abbasid Caliphate.
[6]) The Fatimids lose Syria and the Holy Lands to the Seljuqs under Toghril Beg between 447/1055 and 473/1088.
[7]) End of Fatimid Caliphate by Salah al-Din.
[8]) The Mongols destroy Baghdad.

disintegration and shifty alliances. The pervasive sense of insecurity and continuous warfare is lamented by the Syrian poet Abu al-'Ala' al-Ma'arri (d. 449/1057): "Falsehood hath so corrupted all the world, Ne'er deal as true friends they whom sects divide ... Each party defends its own creed, I wonder in vain where the Truth lies!"

The Seljuqs

Promise of a Syrian revival came from the Seljuqs. These nomadic Turkmen tribes from Central Asia (Transoxiana) were greatly skilled warriors and adept military leaders who desired to recover and reunite the fallen lands of the once great 'Abbasid caliphate. The Seljuqs took over Baghdad from the Buyids in 447/1055 and struck an alliance with the weakened 'Abbasid Caliph, al-Qa'im (d. 467/1075) thus establishing legitimacy for their rule. Many of their Turkmen armies headed towards Armenia, the Caucasus and Anatolia to fight back the Byzantines and their allies. Under the leadership of Sultan Alp Arslan (d. 1072/470), so-called for his valiant fighting skills, the Seljuqs achieved astounding victory at the Battle of Manzikert in 463/1071, even capturing the Byzantine Emperor himself, Romanos IV Diogenes. These Turkmen, known as the Seljuq-Rum, settled in Anatolia. With the Byzantine army wrecked, the main branch of the Seljuqs proceeded to occupy Syria and push the Fatimid powers out. Seljuq rule therefore redeemed the Muslim state from Syria to Central Asia and re-strengthened the prestige of the 'Abbasid caliphate.

The Seljuqs attached great importance to Syria as the westward extension of their powerful position, especially since it marked the frontier with their Fatimid rivals. The Fatimids no longer held Syrian territory and suffered internal

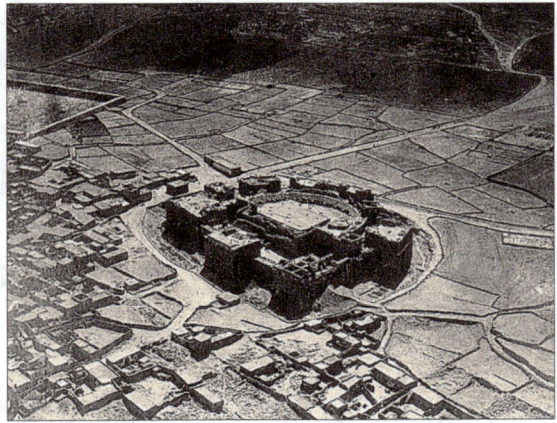

Aerial view of Bosra, 1934 (Huot and Kardous, 2001, photo 39).

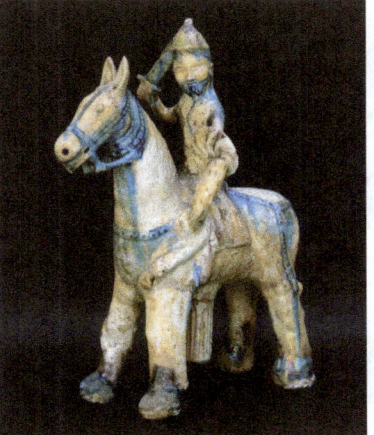

Ceramic statue depicting a Seljuq knight and known as the "Faris al-Raqqa" or the "Horseman of al-Raqqa", National Museum of Damascus (Inv. Num. 5819/ع).

Genealogy of the Seljuq Sultans.

The Seljuq Dynasty

Toghril Beg	447-455/1055-1063[1]
Alp Arslan	455-464/1063-1072
Malik Shah	465-485/1071-1092[2]
Mahmud b. Malik Shah	485-487/1092-1094
Berk Yaruq b. Malik Shah	487-498/1094-1104
Malik Shah b. Berk Yaruq b. Malik Shah	498/1104-1105
Mahmud b. Malik Shah	498-511/1105-1118
Sanjar b. Malik Shah	511-552/1118-1157[3]
Mahmud b. Muhammad b. Malik Shah	511-525/1118-1131[4]
Dawud b. Mahmud b. Muhammad b. Malik Shah	525/1131
Toghril b. Muhammad b. Malik Shah	525-529/1131-1134
Mas'ud b. Muhammad b. Malik Shah	529-547/1134-1152
Malik Shah b. Mahmud b. Muhammad b. Malik Shah	547/1152-1153
Muhammad b. Mahmud b. Muhammad b. Malik Shah	547-554/1153-1159
Sulayman b. Muhammad b. Malik Shah	555/1160
Arslan b. Toghril b. Muhammad Malik Shah	555-557/1160-1175
Toghril b. Arslan b. Toghril b. Muhammad b. Malik Shah	571-590/1175-1194

Source: Klausner, C. L., *The Seljuk Vezirate: A Study of Civil Administration (1055-1194)*, Center for Middle Eastern Studies, Harvard University, 1973, pp. 105-110.

[1] The 'Abbasid Caliphate is challenged by a Fatimid counter-Caliphate.
[2] The Fatimids found the first Shi'a caliphate in Islamic history.
[3] Baghdad falls to the Buyids.
[4] Fatimids found Cairo as new capital 358/969.

weaknesses. A major rift had occurred among them with the death of their Caliph, al-Mustansir, in 487/1094, dividing their followers between adherents to two his two sons; supporters of Nizar suppressed by those who supported al-Musta'li, the elder son. The Nizaris, therefore, fled Egypt and founded a militant Isma'ili community in the mountainous regions of Syria. Known as the Assassins, from the Arabic term *Hashashin*, they added further to the diversity and political interplay of the region.

The Seljuqs became rulers of an empire stretching right across Iran, Iraq and Syria. In their far-reaching power they did not claim to be caliphs upholding the belief in a single 'Abbasid caliphate for all of Islam, but, instead, they referred to themselves as Sultans. With their political rejuvenation, the Seljuqs had a cultural impact too, adding Eastern (Iranian and Central Asian) traditions to the Islamic governmental system and the Arab lands, as well as influencing the indigenous artistic and architectural repertoire.

In order to galvanise the fragmented society into taking heed of their leadership, the Seljuqs embarked on massive urban-development campaigns that

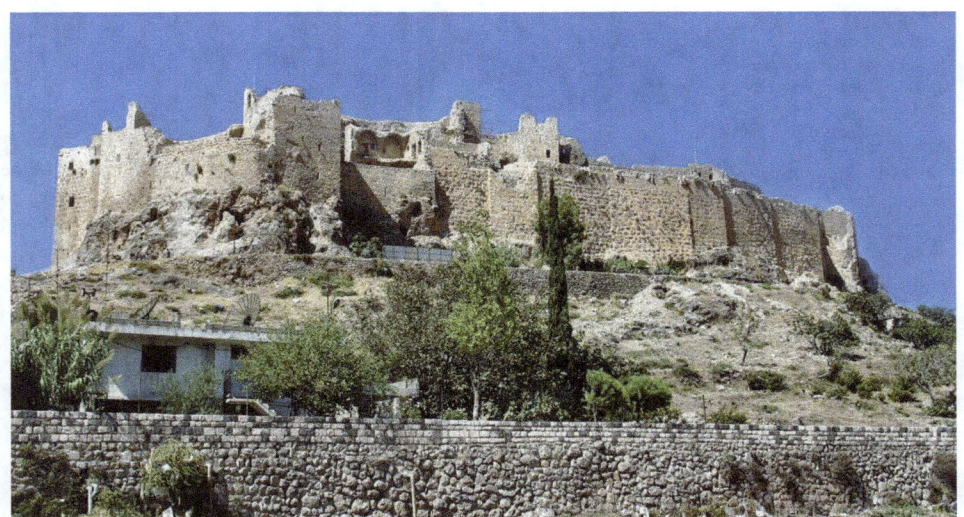

Misyaf Castle, once the headquarters of the Isma'iliyya Nizariyya in the Syrian coastal mountains.

served to protect the cities, ensure the safety of city-dwellers and rebuild the largely destroyed urban centres. Most importantly, they sought to re-educate the people so that they may serve in their new administrative system and counter the sway of Fatimid shi'ite authority. Thus, the Seljuqs built *madrasas* (colleges for legal and theological study) in abundance. These were generally dedicated to the transmission of knowledge along orthodox Sunni lines, which went hand in hand with re-establishing the dominance of the 'Abbasid caliphate.

Although the prestigious Madrasa Nizamiyya, founded in Baghdad by the powerful Seljuq vizier Nizam al-Mulk in 457/1065, is not the first *madrasa* in the Arab world, it is certainly the most famous due to its strong patronage and methodical systemisation. It was also in this period that Muhammad al-Ghazali (d. 505/1111), one of the most celebrated scholars of Islam and a distinguished professor at Madrasa Nizamiyya, produced his important work *Ihya' 'Ulum al-Din (Revival of the Religious Sciences)*. The work gave new impetus to traditional regulations of Islam and brought the mystical approach of the Muslim faith, Sufism, within the folds of traditional Islamic practice, attracting a wider and more nuanced scope of believers.

The Seljuq ruler of Syria, Taj al-Dawla Tutush I (d. 488/1095) and his wife Khatun Safwat al-Mulk (d. 512/1119) were powerful rulers who were also important patrons of religious architecture. Safwat al-Mulk was a capable regent as a widow. In Damascus, she built a funerary compound known as Qubbat al-Tawawis – the Peacock Cupola – which

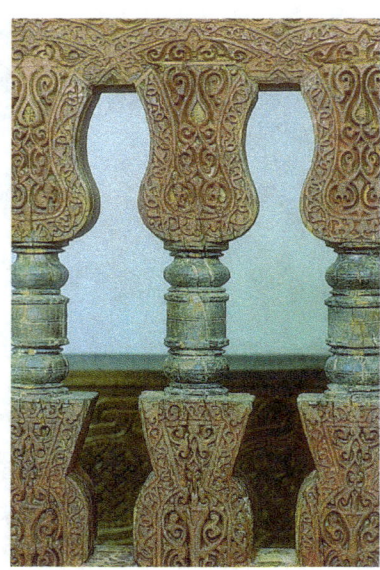

Detail of wooden screen from the Mausoleum of Sultan Duqaq in Damascus, National Museum of Damascus (Inv. Num. 97 ع).

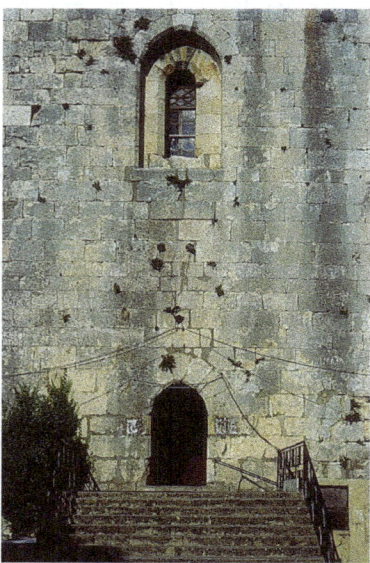

Burj Safita, near Tartus, entrance to a Crusader donjon.

included a mosque, a *khanqa* (Sufi hospice) and a mausoleum for herself and her son, Duqaq. Though this exemplary Seljuq monument has not survived to the present day it set an example for subsequent rulers, male and female, and the Seljuqs' patronage of public institutions to support their social, political and cultural revival, was a practice enthusiastically adopted by their Atabeg governors and the Ayyubid Dynasty.

The Faranj

Amidst this busy period of transition, a new and unexpected threat appeared. These were the Latin Crusaders, known by the Arabs as *al-Faranj*, or *al-Ifranj*, who invaded the Eastern Mediterranean lands in the name of Christendom in the late 5th/11th century. They first appeared on the Syrian coast in the autumn of 490/1097 where they lay siege to Antioch for nine months before it finally succumbed. They then went on to devastate the city of Ma'arrat al-Nu'man; both Arab and Latin chroniclers express shuddering despair in recording the depravity of the battle. Finally, they conquered the holy land of Jerusalem in 492/1099, causing popular outrage from all faiths of the local population. This sudden and unprecedented appearance of the Franks and their plundering of the Holy Land shocked the community. But the political rulers – Seljuq princelings, Turkish and Kurdish *atabeg*s and various other Arab tribal dynasties – were unable to unite. The main reason for this lack of unity was that they sought to preserve their local territories and were reluctant to form military alliances that might threaten their respective authorities. The Latin settlements thus remained for over two centuries; the Arwad Island off the coast of Tartus was the last Crusader position in Syria, repossessed in 701/1302. The complicated political fabric of the region influenced the internal policies of the Seljuqs in building a strong, obedient and unified society. The Zangid and Ayyubid dynasties, which exemplify Syria during this period, originated from the Seljuq sultanate. The Zangids of Syria were a two-generational dynasty, beginning with the reign of an Atabeg by the name of 'Imad al-Din Zangi in 521/1127 and ending with the death of his son Nur al-Din bin Zangi in 569/1174. The Ayyubids, founded by Salah al-Din al-Ayyubi in the same year, covers four generations of the family's leadership up until approximately 658/1260, after which some branches of the family remained as vassals to other powers.

The Atabegs

The Seljuqs had a strong policy of reconstructing the wearied cities to support their religious, economic and political revival. Given the wide expanse of territory, they often maintained local rulers, together with the employment of members of the Seljuq family as provincial governors, known as Atabegs. The term "Atabeg" is the title given to a Seljuq dignitary – "*ata*" meaning father and "*beg*" meaning leader. The first person to be given the title of Atabeg was Nizam al-Mulk (d. 485/1092), one of the most powerful figures of the Seljuq court in Baghdad and a vizier to the sultan. The title generally meant "teacher", whereby an Atabeg would be given the charge of instructing a young prince in the skills of military leadership and state governance.

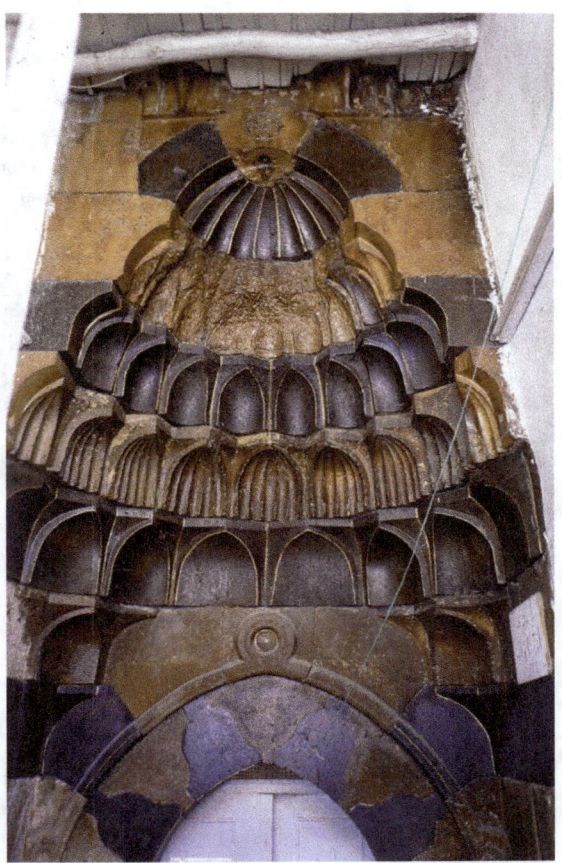

Madrasa Atabakiyya, detail of the stone muqarnas portal, Damascus.

Quite often, Atabegs actually held control of entire states, competing with each other to secure the wealth and prosperity of their lands.

In Syria, the focal point of the rivalry was between the Atabegs of Aleppo ruling under the Seljuq prince Ridwan, and the Atabegs of Damascus ruling under the Seljuq prince Duqaq, while the smaller cities that lay in between them came under alternating spheres of influence.

Though war marked the period, so did refortification and urban expansion, largely thanks to the might of the Seljuqs. If the status of Syrian cities at the end of Fatimid domination was to be compared with their situation under the Seljuq Atabegs, it would not be an exaggeration to say that they witnessed a second coming; a re-founding.

Crusader sword, Tartus Museum (photo courtesy of Balázs Major).

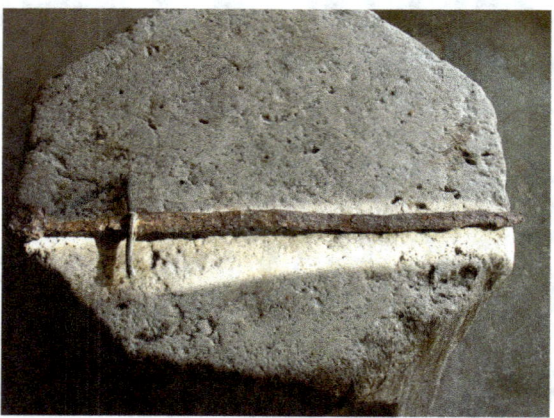

The Zangids

'Imad al-Din Zangi, the Atabeg ruler of Aleppo, was one of the most important Atabegs to consolidate his autonomy within the Seljuq Empire, thanks to his many successful expeditions. By 521/1127 he had control of Mosul and Aleppo where he used his position to further consolidate his power and limit the expansion of the Artuqids, another Turkman dynasty based in Asia Minor with influences in northern Syria. In 523/1129, the Seljuq sultan Mahmud knew Zangi as King of the West "Malik al-Gharb". When he conquered Edessa from the Crusaders in 539/1144, he became a *jihad* hero.

A Frankish slave murdered Zangi in 540/1146, leaving the city suddenly vulnerable to an encroaching Crusader invasion. His son, Nur al-Din (r. 541–69/1146–74), quickly took over his father's position and managed to rally a united Muslim offensive against their Frankish opponents. Under Nur al-Din's leadership the Crusaders, ward off Aleppo were compelled to withdraw from Edessa. This was one of the strongest victories of the Muslim warriors against the Crusaders, and Nur al-Din was everywhere extolled for his virtues as a defender of Islam.

As a far-sighted ruler Nur al-Din sent official homage to his elder brother, ruler of Mosul, Sayf al-Din bin Zangi. This secured inner unity and shared efforts of *jihad* against their common enemy. With the regions of northern Syria thus secured, Nur al-Din turned to Damascus in the spring of 541/1147, negotiating a peaceful alliance with its rival governor,

Historical Introduction

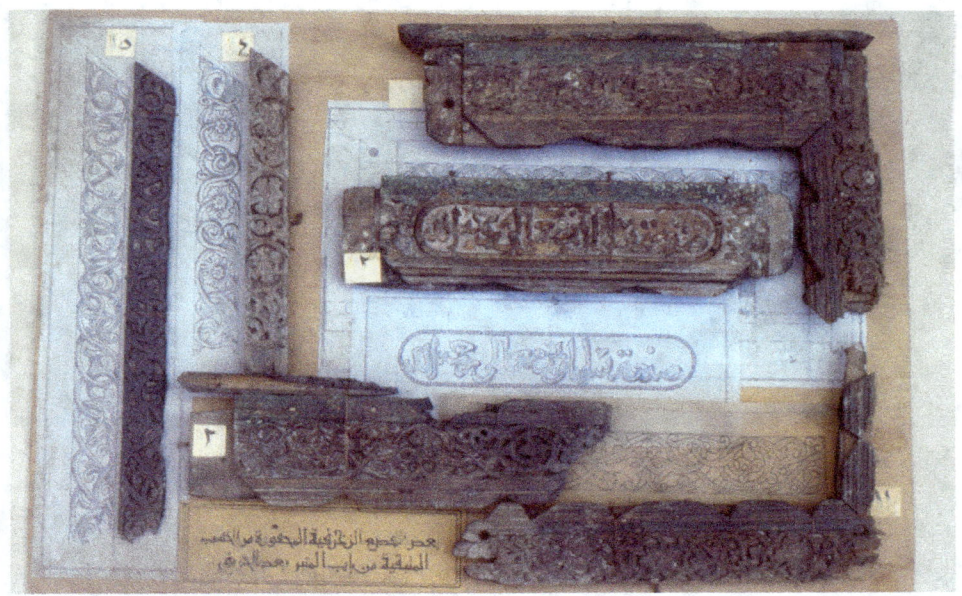

Mu'in al-Din Unur al-Atabeki (d. 543/ 1149) by marrying his daughter. Unur was powerful enough to ward off the Second Crusade's siege of Damascus in 542/1148, and when he died the following year, Nur al-Din took control of the city. United, thus, under one visionary leadership, Damascus and Aleppo created a solid front to counter the Crusader states.

Nur al-Din rebuilt all of Syria's cities. He founded new mosques, many of which are referred to colloquially as Nuri mosques in his name, as well as schools, hospitals and fortifications. Nur al-Din endowed his mosques with innovative finely carved wooden *minbar*s or pulpits, from which weekly sermons methodically propagated his vision, calling for piety, unity and *jihad* to liberate Jerusalem from the Frankish invaders. On an economic level, this unification of northern and southern Syria also gave him access to the fertile lands and granaries of Hauran and Bosra in the south which were necessary to keep his war-threatened cities well fed and prosperous. All in all the arrival of Nur al-Din to Damascus marked the beginning of a new era for Syria.

From the northern regions of Aleppo and the Byzantine frontiers, through the cities of Hama and Homs, to the new capital of Damascus and all the way south to the region of Bosra where pilgrims set off to the Holy Lands of Arabia, all of Syria became a united front. Nur al-Din

Fragments of the wooden minbar *commissioned by Nur al-Din for the Aqsa Mosque in Jerusalem, Islamic Museum, al-Aqsa Mosque (Inv. Num. 142/40), Jerusalem.*

45

Historical Introduction

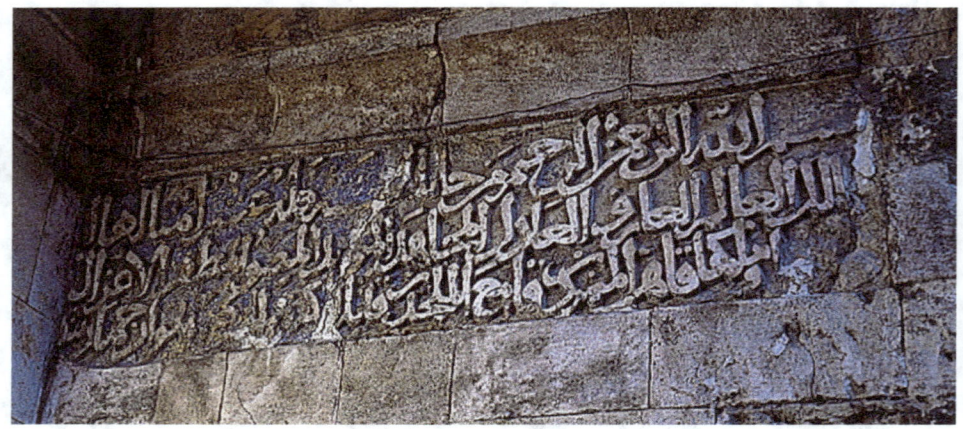

Madrasa al-Hallawiyya, detail of Nur al-Din's monumental inscription, Aleppo.

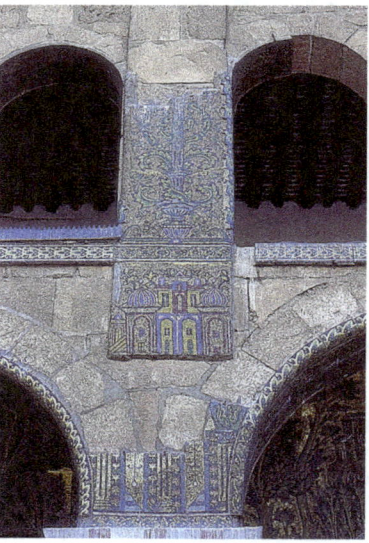

Great Umayyad mosque, detail of Nur al-Din's restoration of the mosaics, Damascus.

guaranteed food supplies for all the Muslim towns and launched a thorough fortification campaign of all the major cities. Despite two large earthquakes that ravaged the land, one in 525/1157 and the other in 565/1170, his building endeavours never ceased.

By the middle of the 6th/12th century, the seat of Islamic power had shifted to Syria, thanks to the concerted efforts of Nur al-Din. The city of Damascus witnessed a veritable political, economic and cultural renaissance becoming in every sense an imperial capital that revived a legacy, which dates back to the Umayyad Caliphate some 400 years earlier. Not surprisingly, in the inscription of the Madrasa al-Hallawiyya in Aleppo built in 543/1149, Nur al-Din no longer considered himself an Atabeg of the Seljuq sultan, but is bestowed with grander honorific titles, most notably, *al-Mujahid*, "the fighter for the faith". The style of the inscription, a thick and easily legible cursive script known as *thuluth*, also marks a decisive change in monumental epigraphy and reflects Nur al-Din's willful transformation of both form and content of Syria's leadership.

Syria's cities expanded, the population grew and the construction of various mosques, *madrasas* and centres for religious, legal and scientific study marked his reign. He restored the Great Umayyad Mosque of Damascus and he sought to liberate the Holy Land of Jerusalem, dedicating a magnificent *minbar* to the Masjid al-Aqsa. Amidst his copious city building and military activity, he also managed to perform the *hajj*, the Muslim pilgrimage, in 556/1161, where he showed great generosity to the inhabitants of the cities he passed and devoted attention to the improvement of the wells in the Arabian Desert. He died in the residence that he had constructed in the citadel of Damascus in 569/1174, but he had already introduced his most capable lieutenant Salah al-Din, known in the West as Saladin, to the region as a barrier to Frankish intervention. Interred in the funerary *madrasa* that he was in the process of constructing to the southwest of the Great Umayyad Mosque, the tomb to this day is the object of popular veneration.

The Ayyubids

The Sultan al-Nasir Salah al-Din Yusuf ibn Ayyub (d. 589/1193), known as Saladin, was one of Nur al-Din's most brilliant lieutenants. He had risen to fame during Nur al-Din's reign thanks to his final disposal of the Fatimid caliphate in Cairo in 566/1171. Upon Nur al-Din's death, this skilled warrior of Kurdish descent spent a decade consolidating his military authority and fighting with other claimants to the throne, until he was at last able to proclaim himself founder of the Ayyubid Dynasty in 579/1183. That year he was able to capture Aleppo, where allegiance to members of Nur al-Din's family was the strongest, and thus proclaim undisputed authority. His unification of Egypt and Syria resulted from the formation of a large and very well organised military force and it was at this point that he turned his attention to the Crusaders, leaving his heroic mark in Islamic history. Salah al-Din's successful campaigns saw the conquest of some 50 Crusader positions, including Chateau de Saone, which he besieged in 584/1188. Renamed as Saladin's Citadel, or Qal'at Salah al-Din, it is one of the finest surviving examples of military architecture on a spectacular mountainous ravine.

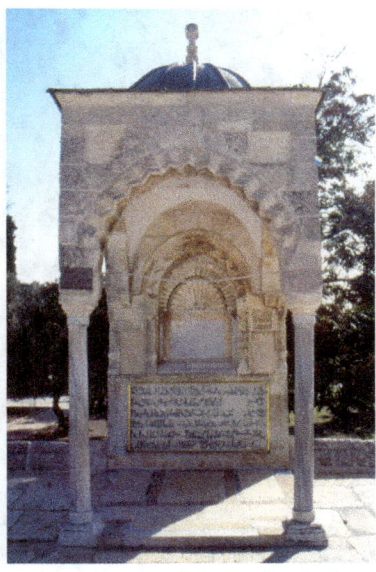

Marble inscription panel commemorating the liberation of Jerusalem by Salah al-Din and signifying his aspirations for peace, Islamic Museum, al-Aqsa Mosque, Jerusalem.

Historical Introduction

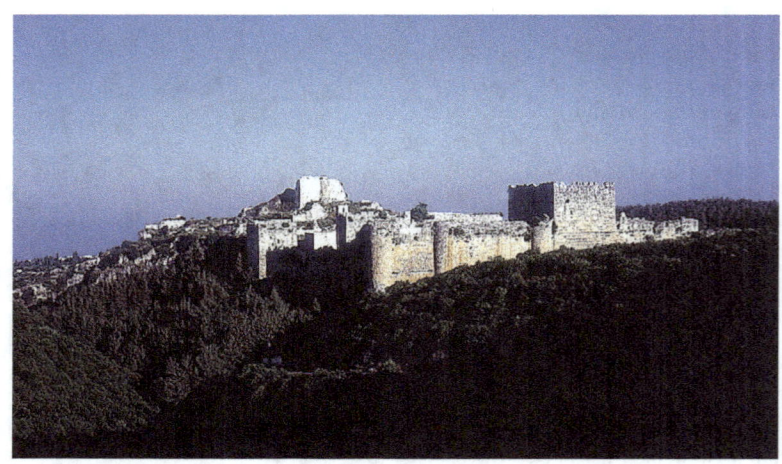

Qal'at Salah al-Din, previously Château de Saone, near Latakia.

Genealogical Tree of the Ayyubid Dynasty.

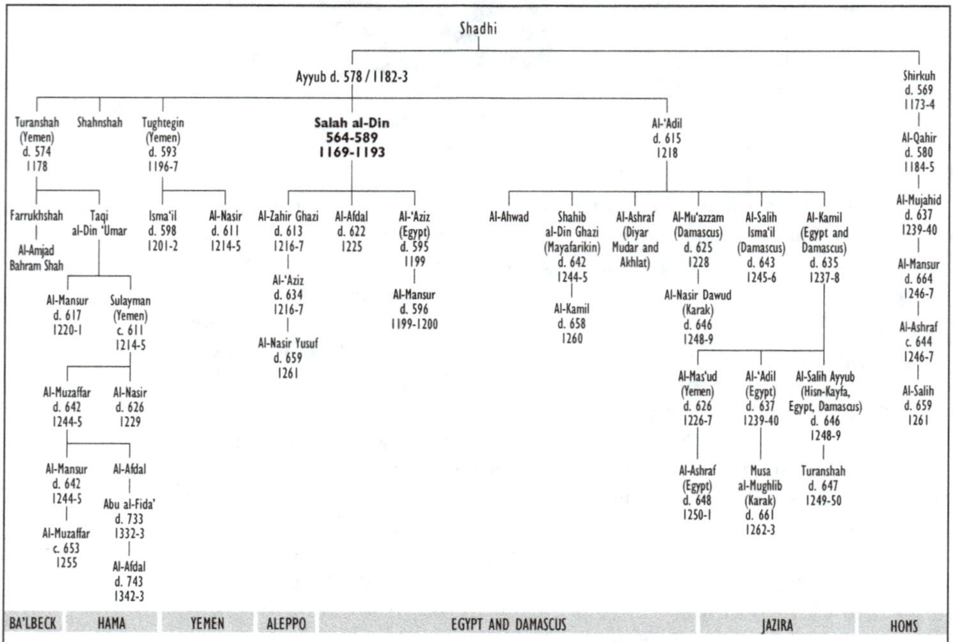

| BA'LBECK | HAMA | YEMEN | ALEPPO | EGYPT AND DAMASCUS | JAZIRA | HOMS |

Source: "Ayyubids", Encyclopaedia of Islam, vol. I, pp. 796–807.

By far the greatest triumph of Salah al-Din was the Battle of Hittin, which took place in 583/1187 and marked a major turning point in the warfare between the Muslim and the Crusader forces. Salah al-Din's resounding success at the Battle of Hittin precipitated the fall of the Crusader Kingdom of Jerusalem and the long-awaited liberation of the Holy Land of Palestine. To this day, the memory of Salah al-Din is a vibrant symbol of Islamic heroism and many political leaders and foreign conquerors have visited his tomb in acknowledgement of his esteemed legacy.

The key to the success of the Ayyubid Dynasty was that control remained within the hands of Ayyubid-family members. Although a relatively brief reign lasting some 80 years in most parts of Syria (a little longer in Hama), it was full of accomplishments. After Salah al-Din's death in 589/1193, his brother al-'Adil (d. 615/1218) took control of Damascus and spearheaded a major refortification campaign of Damascus Citadel. His brother's son al-Kamil (d. 635/1238) followed in his father's footsteps, one of capable domination in Egypt and in Damascus. Meanwhile, Salah al-Din's son al-Zahir Ghazi (d. 613/1216) had become the Ayyubid ruler of Aleppo and the region of the Jazira. He managed to bring under his sovereignty several castles and towns of central Syria, such as Harim, Manbij, Najm and Apamea. His reign brought a period of peace and prosperity. In 604/1207, al-Zahir turned to the coast and took control of the important port city of Latakia, opening for his kingdom an outlet to the Mediterranean Sea. Not coincidentally, in the same year, he signed the first trade agreement between the Ayyubids and the Venetians. Under the Ayyubids, the cities of Syria as well as those of Jordan and Palestine were all refortified. In Egypt too, the great Citadel of Salah al-Din is a lasting landmark, while the Madrasa al-Salih Ayyub and the Mausoleum of Imam al-Shafi'i are prominent examples of the urban and ideological development spearheaded by the Ayyubids. By al-Salih Isma'il's reign (d. 643/1246) in Damascus and that of al-Nasir Yusuf's

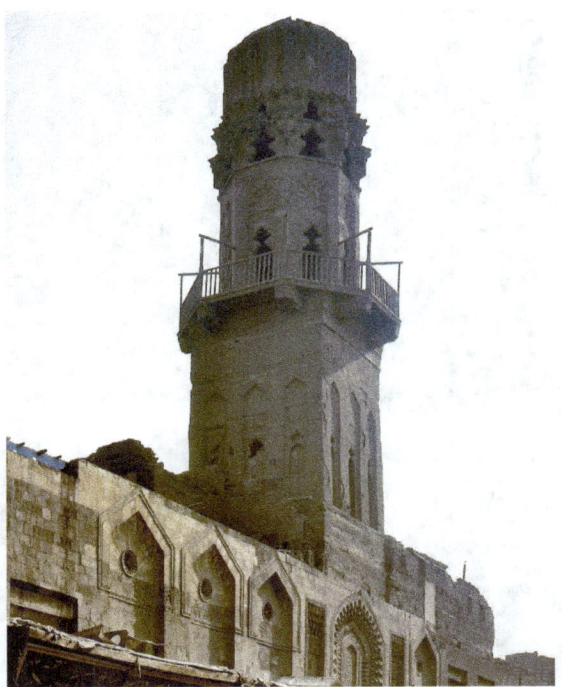

The Madrasa of al-Salih Najm al-Din Ayyub, which was built in Fatimid Cairo, Egypt, to teach the rites of Sunnism. (photo courtesy of Sheila Blair and Jonathan Bloom. © Sheila Blair & Jonathan Bloom).

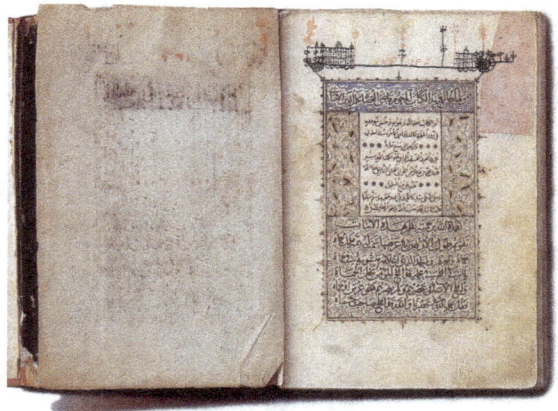

Taqwim al-Buldan, *a manuscript on geography written by Abu al-Fida', the Ayyubid ruler of Hama, National Museum of Damascus (Inv. Num. 14689/ﻉ).*

(d. 659/1261) in Aleppo, a gradual shift of authority was taking place towards Cairo, foreshadowing the rise of the Mamluk regime which would supplant the Ayyubid Dynasty.

The socio-cultural impact of the Seljuq, Zangid and especially the Ayyubid reigns is still strongly evident in Syria's medieval art and architecture. Just as it was intended, so much urban development brought a change upon the population. Education, religion, trade and military training attracted all kinds of people to Syria. These travellers had access to the many caravan routes that criss-crossed the Syrian lands. They brought with them commercial activity as well as spiritual reverence. As noted by the al-Andalus pilgrim Ibn Jubayr (d. 614/1217), the routes were well protected even during military campaigns, as the assurance of safe travel was critical to the prosperity of the dynasty. Once the caravans reached a city, they would find *suqs* (markets) selling an impressive range of goods: silk, perfume, jewellery, gold, spices, glassware, metalwork and ceramic vessels. In the heart of the suq would be the great communal mosque, several smaller mosques, as wells as charitable institutions of scientific and religious education, all patronised by members of the ruling court. *Madrasas* in particular played an important role in shaping cultural and religious life as well as in the reconfiguration of the urban landscape of Islamic cities, notably for Ayyubid Damascus and Aleppo, but also for Mamluk Cairo, Seljuq Anatolia and Marinid Fez in Tunisia.

Supported by *waqf*, non-taxable endowments, such public institutions were charitable, as charity is an important foundation of Islamic cities. Meanwhile, members of the Ayyubid military managed to earn their wages through an Islamic system of feudalism called *iqta'*. Similar to a long-term lease on a revenue-producing property; its main purpose was to provide military commanders with a steady income in return for equipping and training a specified number of horsemen. Their religious and civic institutions revived the cities of Syria, making the capital Damascus a magnet for scholars from all across the Islamic lands. Literacy levels were high and patronage of scientific as well as artistic works flourished.

Arabic culture blossomed in the Ayyubid cities and institutions; the Arabic language used not only for the dissemination of religious and scientific knowledge, but

Historical Introduction

Marvered glass vessel, probably used for perfume, National Museum of Damascus.

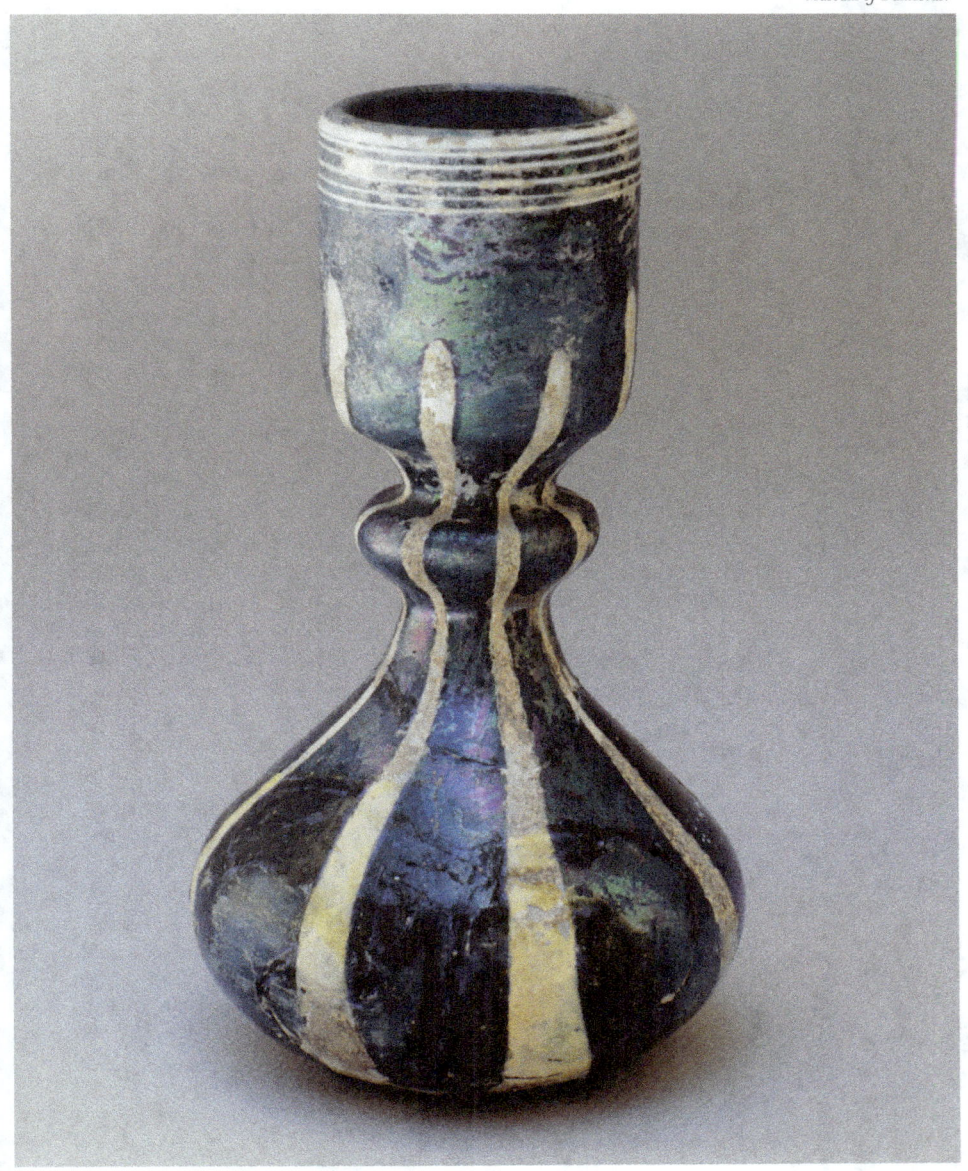

also as the main language of governance even though the rulers were not of Arab descent. This can be contrasted with the later phase of Islamic high culture, in which the Persian (farsi) and Turkish languages came to the fore. At this point, however, Arabic continued to be honoured and cultivated as the language of administration, scholarship and *belles-lettres*. Though the Ayyubids themselves were of Kurdish origin, the 25 Ayyubid rulers all had Arabic surnames, with the exception of Turan Shah the ruler of Yemen; they also spoke fluent Arabic. Many were themselves poets, historians, scientists, judges and theologians. Al-Zahir Ghazi of Aleppo and al-Mu'azzam 'Isa of Damascus are both known to have composed Arabic poetry, an art that required great linguistic expertise and cultural sensitivity. Thus the Ayyubids of Syria, unlike the later Mamluks or even their contemporary the Rum-Seljuqs, were substantially Arabised

and Arabic culture, more than Kurdish heritage, formed the main conponant of their identity.

The Mongols and the Mamluks

The decisive fall of the Ayyubid Dynasty came at the hands of the Mongols, fierce warriors from Eastern Asia. Their fearful reputation preceded them, causing the migration of whole communities westward in an attempt to escape their fury, as can be seen by the settlement of artisans from Afghanistan, in both Mosul and in Damascus. The Mongols, lead by Hulagu (d. 1265/663), soon reached the heart of the Muslim world. They devastated the capital of Baghdad in 656/1258 with exceptional cruelty and continued to invade Syria, capturing Aleppo and Damascus in 658/1260. From Egypt came the definitive resistance to the Mongol onslaught, headed by the Mamluk Sultan Baybars, a former member of the Ayyubid private guard (called *mamluk*s). Baybars defeated the Mongols in Palestine at the Battle of 'Ayn Jalut in 658/1260 and took control of Syria. Following in Salah al-Din's footsteps the Mamluks were heroic warriors against the Crusaders, breaching their most important stronghold, Crac des Chevaliers, in 669/1270–1 and conquering Acre in 690/1291. The swift victories of the Mamluks against both the Mongols and the Franks heralded a new era of Islamic revival.

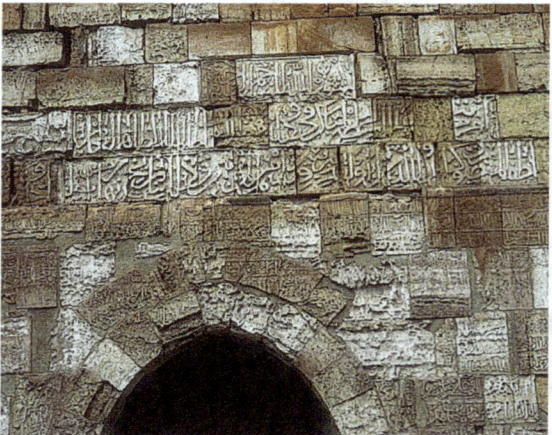

Crac des Chevaliers, detail of the Mamluk inscriptions.

AYYUBID ART AND ARCHITECTURE

Abd al-Razzaq Moaz, Zena Takieddine

If the Mamluk era is a period of great importance for the production of art and architecture in Egypt, and the same for the Ottoman era in Turkey, the Ayyubid period also has a particular place in the history of Islamic architecture in Syria. Ayyubid architecture is distinguished by its harmony, sobriety, logic and clarity. The introduction of new architectural forms and new decorative repertories into Syria saw the formation of public institutions such as the *madrasa*s and *bimaristan*s (hospitals) which bear Eastern-inspired architectural features, such as the *muqarnas* brick dome. Much of these imported elements became absorbed into the local traditions of Syria's city centres. The impact of Ayyubid patronage inaugurated a second era of Islamic art and architecture in Syria, more sober and militaristic in taste, quite unlike the formative years of Islamic art and architecture. In general, decoration was minimal and the perfection of construction based on mathematically harmonious dimensions, highly esteemed. Many important masterpieces have survived from this period, leaving their mark on the history of Islamic art.

Architecture

Usually, in the Arab world, buildings take on their patrons' names, particularly during the Atabeg and Ayyubid periods when architectural patronage was so copious. Many of the monuments mentioned in this catalogue will therefore have names made of genitive titles, which usually end with the suffix *-i*, or in the case of the feminine, *-iyya*; thus, the bathhouses, Hammam al-Nuri and the Madrasa al-Nuriyya respectively are named after Nur al-Din.

As for the building style, two prominent developments of this period are the use of the structural *iwan* and ornamental *muqarnas*.

Iwan is a Persian word for a space enclosed by three walls, usually barrel-vaulted, with the open side usually overlooking a fountain, garden, or courtyard. It had been a ubiquitous architectural form in Iran and Iraq since before the rise

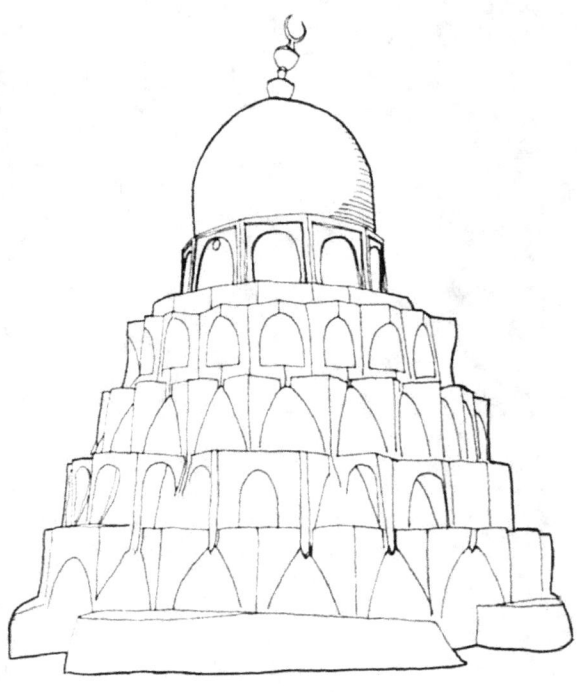

Illustration of the muqarnas dome in the mausoleum of Madrasat Nur al-Din, Damascus (Hillenbrand, 1999 fig. 3.19; Hillenbrand, 1994).

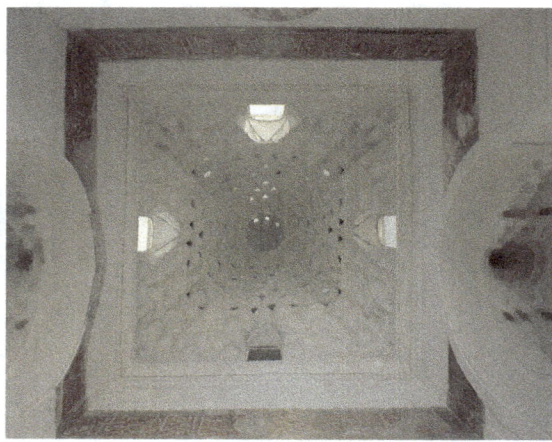

Bimaristan Nur al-Din, interior view of the muqarnas dome, Damascus.

of Islam, revived under the Seljuqs, and subsequently brought to Syria. In both Iraq and Iran, the four-*iwan*s-in-axial-symmetry plan was the standard. There were some local adaptations to this form in Syria, seen particularly in *madrasa*s (colleges) featuring one main *iwan*, a long prayer-hall and chambers on the second floor.

*Iwan*s offered a suitable meeting place for all kinds of activities, thanks to their enclosed and shaded, yet spacious and resonant, space. They served as a focal point for many kinds of monuments. Since similar layouts can serve many functions, the monument's purpose is gleaned often from epigraphic inscriptions found on their door- and window-lintels usually offer information regarding their purpose, sponsorship and date of construction.

The *muqarnas*, also called stalactite or honeycomb vaulting, is one of the most original and ubiquitous features of Islamic architecture from this period as well. Rather than a discrete architectural form, *muqarnas* is in fact an ornamental mode — consisting of spherical sections, brackets and pendants — applied to various architectural forms such as cornices, capitals, vaults and domes.

Generally accepted is the view that the development of the first *muqarnas* forms took place in Iran in the early 5th/11th century, but the earliest construction of *muqarnas* vaults took place about half a century later in Iraq. In Syria, the earliest instances of *muqarnas* vaulting can be seen in the hospital and funerary *madrasa* of Nur al-Din in Damascus, dated 549/1154 and 567/1172 respectively. Both have fully developed brick and plaster *muqarnas* domes in the Iraqi style; the hospital also has a *muqarnas* portal vault, the earliest in Islamic architecture.

The translation of the Iraqi prototype into stone-built *muqarnas* first appeared in Syria, specifically Aleppo, in the late 6th/12th century, producing a style of *muqarnas* vaults and domes that would spread to Seljuq Anatolia and Mamluk Egypt. This demanding process resulted in precise, robust and rather curvilinear vaults, usually consisting of three rows of *muqarnas* cells capped by a scalloped dome. In Syrian domes, *muqarnas* was restricted to the transition zone, often resulting in a complete halo of two or three tiers. In view of its luxurious and mysterious effect, it seems likely that *muqarnas* vaulting was a mark of distinction and an indication of spiritual values.

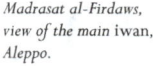

Madrasat al-Firdaws, view of the main iwan, Aleppo.

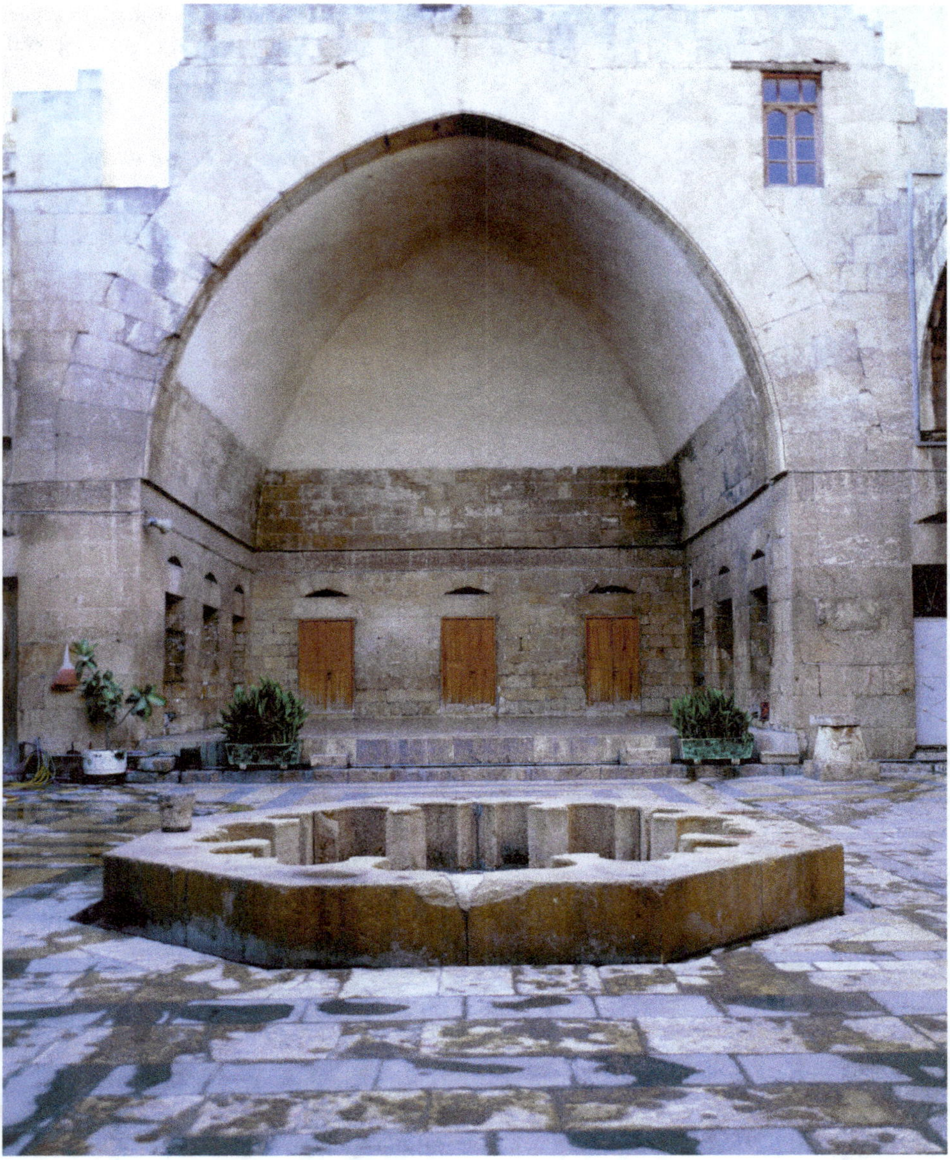

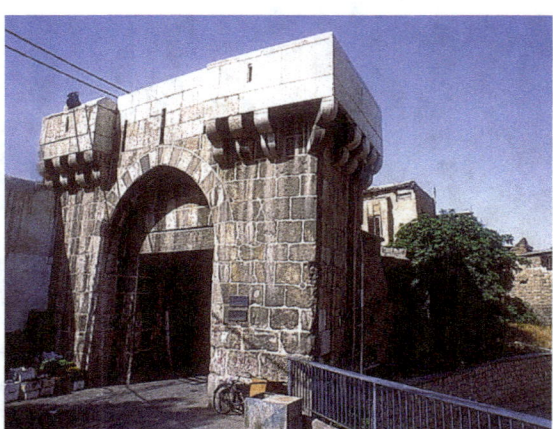

Bab al-Salama, an Ayyubid gate on the northern wall that surrounded old Damascus.

Military Gates, Towers and City Walls

The most important development to occur in Syria during the reign of the Ayyubid Dynasty was the refortification of its defence systems. The strengthening of all the city walls established Syria as a frontier region, offering the city formidable protection that allowed for successful urban development. In the main cities of Damascus and Aleppo, city gates and walls are typical defensive characteristics. Gates, known in Arabic as *bab*, could have a single or a double entrance giving a protective additional thickness, whereby a barrel-vault or cross-vault covered and connected the two gates. Arrow loops and machicolations – overhanging slits from which soldiers would pour hot oil onto enemies below – usually protected city gates. Machicolations such as these also appear in protruding-box formation. Gates often featured flanking towers with salient towers appearing at regular intervals along city walls.

Citadels, Castles and Palaces

The Arabic word for a citadel is *qal'a*. The use of this term means a fortification located either amidst cities or in distant mountainous regions. Often the distinction between a citadel and a castle is that the former is purely military while the latter is both a fortification and residence. During the Ayyubid period, however, the leadership built residential palaces inside the walls of the citadel. Therefore, a citadel or a castle can also include a palace, mosque and *hammam* for the residing military elite.

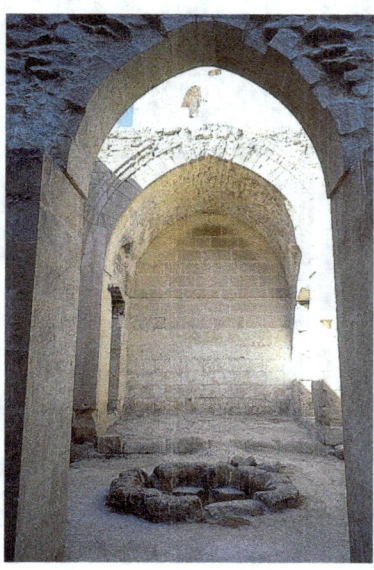

Qal'at Najm, view of the palatial courtyard and of the northern iwan.

Ayyubid art and architecture

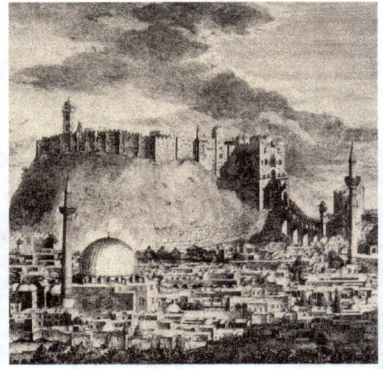

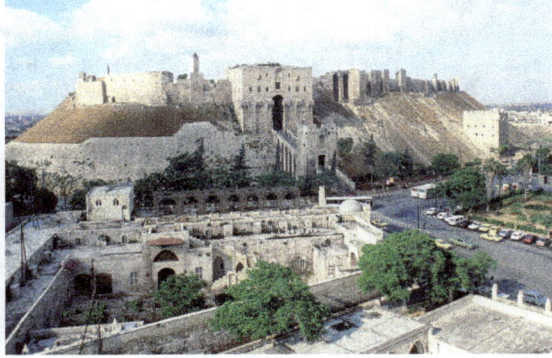

An 18th-century etching of Aleppo Citadel amidst the city (Sauvaget, 1941, plate XLVIII; Drummond, 1745).

Aleppo Citadel, modern aerial view.

Citadels became more massive, their walls thicker and higher, their entrances more cleverly protected, often surrounded by a moat and accessed through a drawbridge. The increased dimensions grew out of the development in military equipment, particularly the *manjaniq*, or mangonel, with its catapult mechanism. Merlons, machicholations and arrow loops are defensive features that usually mark the walls and towers of citadels. Architectural ornamentation appears usually focused on the entrance, while the bulk of Ayyubid architecture remains plain. In the case of the gate of Aleppo Citadel figurative talismans appear, such as serpents or lions, where they symbolised the power of the state. Another important feature of Ayyubid architecture related distinctly to 6th-/12th-century military constructs, is the usage of portcullis – defensive sliding metal gates. The traces of grooves along the sides of entrances have served to indicate the usage of such mechanisms, which helps establish the Ayyubid dating for certain monuments. Several of the citadels in Syria's coastal mountains, as well as citadels in urban settings, reveal such usage.

The most important change to the function of fortresses and citadels during this period of construction is that they now incorporated the residential palaces of the leadership as well. These Ayyubid citadel palaces and ceremonial rooms regularly feature the four-*iwans*-in-axial-symmetry layout, as in Aleppo, Bosra and Qal'at Najm in the Euphrates Region.

Aleppo Citadel, detail of entwined serpents above the main gate.

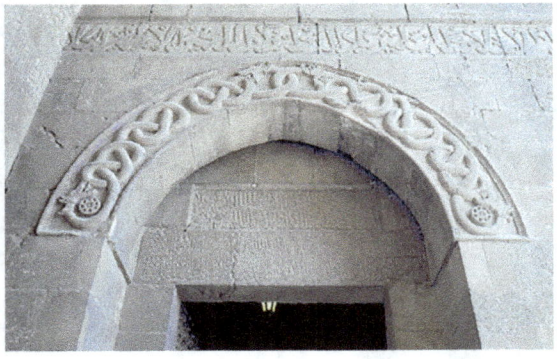

57

It is important to note that the massive construction of citadels, fortifications and castles, left its impact on civilian architecture too; what certain scholars refer to as "the militarisation of artistic taste". Even non-military buildings begin to exhibit strong military features. This is probably because the same workforce that built the expert military constructs were employed for civil buildings as well. Even a contemporary traveller to Syria, the pilgrim Ibn Jubayr from al-Andalus who arrived in Damascus in 580/1184, noted the militaristic style of civilian architecture in the region.

Civic Architecture

Madrasa

Often translated as "law school" or "theological college", the *madrasa* is a centre of higher education that is usually designated according to the *madhhab*, or the juridical school, it follows. The enthusiastic patronage of *madrasa*s during the Atabeg, Zangid and Ayyubid periods was crucial in the bid for political solidarity. It served to equip society with the theoretical and practical knowledge necessary for a cohesive and well functioning government oriented towards Sunnism and the 'Abbasid caliphate. In the Arab region *madrasa*s were first built in Iraq and then, as power shifted from the Seljuqs to Ayyubids, they were more prolifically constructed in Syria. The first *madrasa* introduced in Damascus came by way of the Seljuqs at the end of the 5th/11th century, a tradition that was continued by the Atebegs and the Ayyubids for the explicit purposes of propagating unity. Nur al-Din himself is recorded to have "constructed *madrasa*s for the transmission of knowledge, the combat of heresies and the restoration of the religion", namely, Sunnism.

As an institution, the *madrasa* functioned as a centre for higher education, which also offered free accommodation for scholars and visiting guests. The majority of Syrian *madrasa*s followed a local type composed mainly of a rectangular hall in the south suitable for prayer, a main *iwan* in the north suited to a library, and lodgings surrounding the courtyard often found on the upper floors. Typically, a central basin furnished the courtyard. It was quite common to see the juxtaposition of *madrasa* with the mausoleum – known in Arabic as *turba* or *darih* – of its founder or its founder's family members, in order that the deceased would receive the blessings of the students and visitors within, especially considering that education in the Islamic world is a form of worship.

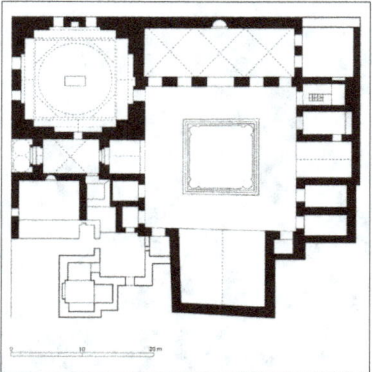

Floor-plan of Madrasa al-'Adiliyya, Damascus.

Certain *madrasas* adopted the four-*iwans*-in-axial-symmetry plan from Iran, though often adapting it to their own styles. The Syrian versions of Ayyubid *madrasas* are exemplified by the Madrasat al-Firdaws in Aleppo and the Madrasa al-'Adiliyya in Damascus, which are considered to be in a league of their own. As for building aesthetics, the entrance façade is typically very plain, sober and perfectly smooth, with the *muqarnas* portal standing out as the only decorative element.

The role of the *madrasas* in the city, as can be seen by the generosity of the *waqfs* or endowments assigned to them, was to develop a more entrenched educational and charitable institution designed to reshape the social fabric of the main Ayyubid cities.

Dar Hadith

As an educational institution, dar *hadiths* were dedicated to the study of *Hadith*, or "Sayings of the Prophet". This type of institution was first introduced by Nur al-Din in 549/1118, and it reveals the level of specialisation and diversity the Zangid ruler wished to propagate when it came to the educational development of his city's population. Thus, it functioned like a *madrasa* and followed a similar layout, equipped with courtyard, prayer-hall and lodgings. Interestingly, the Dar Hadith of Nur al-Din was the teaching ground for the famous historian of Damascus, Ibn 'Asakir in 569/1174 and also served as lodgings for the pilgrim voyager and writer Ibn Jubayr. Unfortunately, not many *dar hadiths* have survived, but they are notable as part of Nur al-Din's urban revival of Syria, particularly in the capital Damascus.

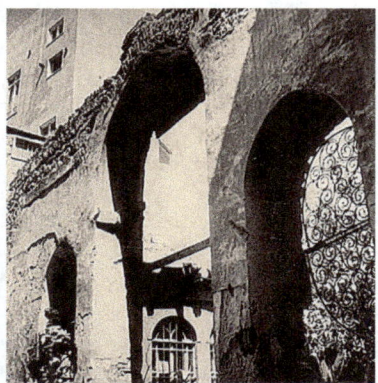

Dar al-Hadith Nuriyya, view of the triple archway leading into the southern bay, Damascus (photo courtesy of Khaled Moaz).

Khanqa

The sponsorship of *khanqas*, dwellings for Sufis, served as a mystical alternative to the academic culture of the *madrasa*. The *khanqa*, on the other hand, focused on mystical practices and offered dwellings for Sufis, practitioners of mystical Islam. Sufis were considered blessed and were typically poor, relinquishing all material pleasures for the attainment of spiritual liberation. *Khanqas* were, therefore, charitable institutions that housed these wandering, otherworldly mystics. The

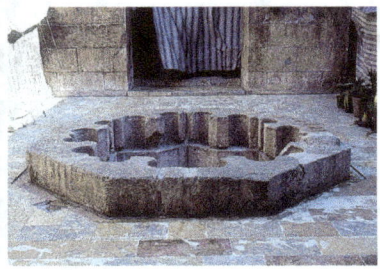

Khanqa al-Farafra, view of the courtyard basin, Aleppo.

no longer extant Khanqa Sa'd as-Su'ada was founded by Salah al-Din in 568/1173 and, considered a highly revered location where people would gather to watch the 300 dervishes who lived there when they went out for their Friday prayers. The Khanqa al-Farafra in Aleppo is one of the rare and best examples still standing.

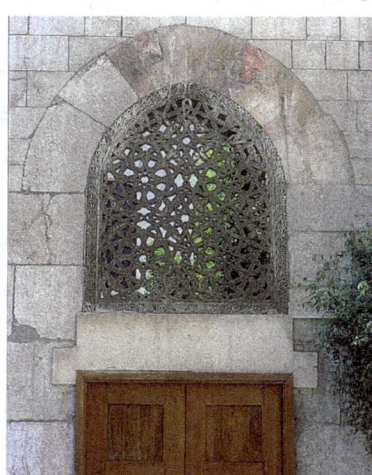

Bimaristan Nur al-Din, view of the pierced stucco window, Damascus.

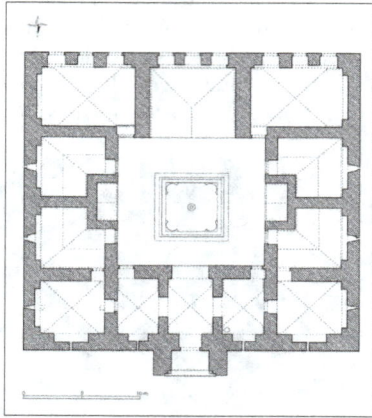

Floor-plan of Bimaristan al-Qaymari, Damascus.

Its plan is nearly identical to that of the typical *madrasa*, distinguished by the cells for solitary meditation, or *khalwa*. Such cells have, however, also been found in *madrasa*s. Evident in almost every *khanqa* is accommodation for both occasional and for long-term visitors. The sheikh himself would live, with his family, in one of the quarters of the compound and see his disciples at fixed hours to supervise their spiritual progress. A compound such as this stood at one time near the Shibliyya Mausoleum in Damascus and continues to exist in the Madrasat al-Firdaws in Aleppo.

Bimaristan

The *bimaristan* is an important urban construction introduced to Syria by Nur al-Din. The *bimaristan* treated both physical and psychological illnesses, offering treatment without charge, and medical education for aspiring physicians. Architecturally the layout again follows the four-*iwan*s-in-axial-symmetry plan, featuring a central courtyard with a pool. The abundance of water was crucial for the upkeep of hygiene in the *bimaristan* and for the administration of different forms of medication. Generally, *bimaristan*s were soothing places. They had rooms overlooking pleasant views to help patients recover, and expert musicians playing calming music. Nur al-Din built two *bimaristan*s, one in Damascus and the other in Aleppo, and a Kurdish prince of the Ayyubid elite built the Bimaristan al-Qaymari in the Salihiyya district of Damascus. They all have attractive monumental entries and grand *iwan*s.

Ayyubid art and architecture

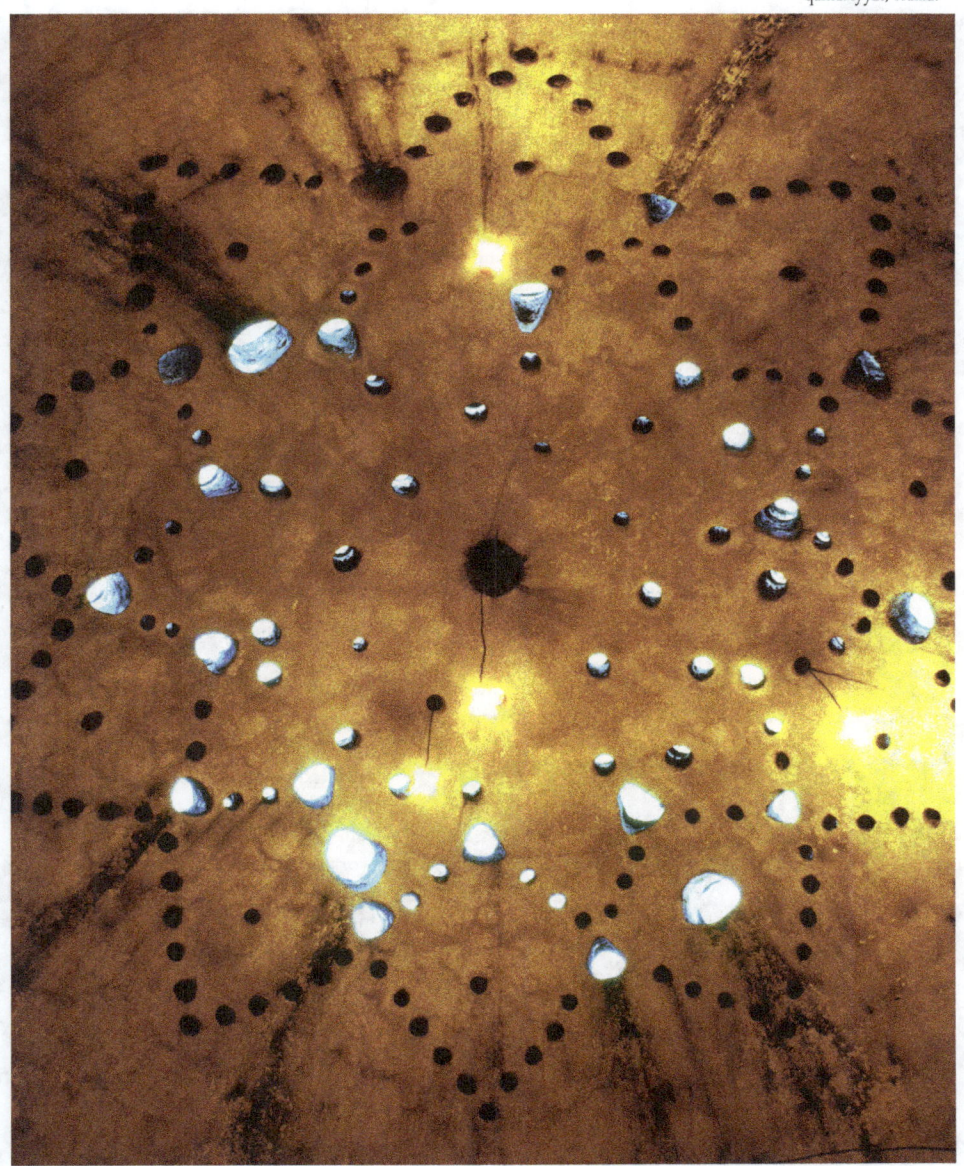

Hammam al-Nahassin, detail of the domed interior with qamariyyat, Hama.

Hammam

The *hammam* is a common feature in Islamic urban planning. Ritual cleanliness for the daily prayers and weekly bathing at the *hammam* were the norm for all members of the city. The *hammam*, designed architecturally to include a reception room and three large chambers for cold water, warm water and steam, followed the Roman example. Emphasis was on the warm-water room during the Islamic period. As a regular gathering place, the *hammam* was an important part of urban interaction. The interiors, often richly decorated with multiple domes punctuated by glass knobs known as *qamariyyat*, added to the experience. The 6th-/12th-century Damascene historian Ibn 'Asakir records the existence of 40 *hammams* inside the old city of Damascus and 17 outside.

Khan

The establishment of the *khan*, a kind of hostel and storage area for merchants and their goods, played an important part in the flourishing Ayyubid economy. Two kinds of *khan* existed: one the type embedded in the city amidst the busy commercial activity of the *suq*; the other built on trade and pilgrimage routes outside the cities. Defensive features are more characteristic of the latter type, but both offer plenty of compartmentalised space and an abundant water supply.

Religious Architecture

Mosque

There are generally two kinds of mosques. The Friday mosque, which is larger and supplied with a *minbar* (pulpit), designated for the weekly sermon and communal noontime prayers on Fridays. The smaller mosques can be found in any location and offer a clean place for everyday prayer. The larger mosques are generally known as *jami'* while the smaller mosques are known as *masjid*, but the terms are often used interchangeably. Mosques are always oriented towards the Ka'ba and the holy city of Mecca, and this orientation is called the *qibla* – the direction in which worshippers stand in prayer. In Syria, the *qibla* is south facing, the direction always indicated by a niche, or *mihrab*, in the *qibla* wall of the mosque's prayer-hall.

The great mosques of Syria's cities were restored and, in addition, many new ones were built during the Atabeg and Ayyubid periods, particularly under Nur al-Din. It was a period of religious revival. The 6th-/12th-century historian of Damascus, Ibn 'Asakir, sites the building and restora-

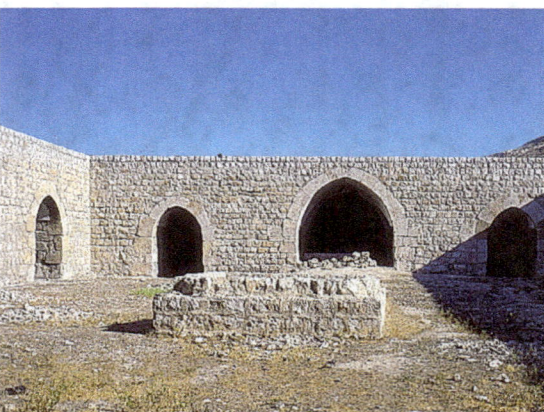

Khan al-'Arus, view of the courtyard and storage vaults, Damascus environs en route to Homs.

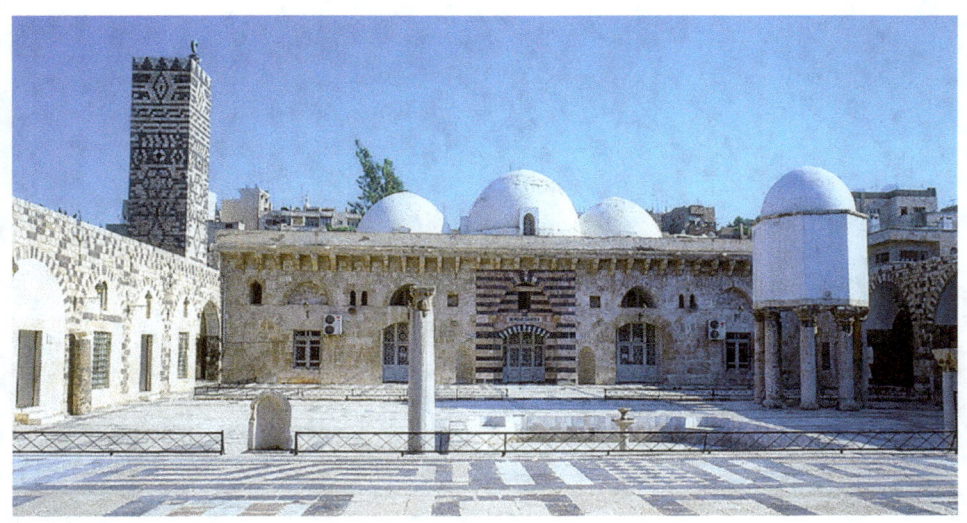

Mosque of Nur al-Din, Hama.

tion of 241 mosques inside the old city walls of Damascus and 178 outside. Most importantly, the Great Umayyad Mosque of Damascus was repaired after many years of neglect.

Minaret

The minaret has long been an architectural symbol of Islam and an urban landmark that defines the silhouette of the city. During the Atabeg and Ayyubid periods, minaret construction reveals the continuation of local styles in the various cities of Syria. Cities in the west usually featured square-based minarets made of stone, a clear continuity of Umayyad mosque minarets. Stone-carving virtuosity flourished in the north-west, particularly in Aleppo. In Hama are seen local variations in the colour of the stonework patterning, where black-and-white stone

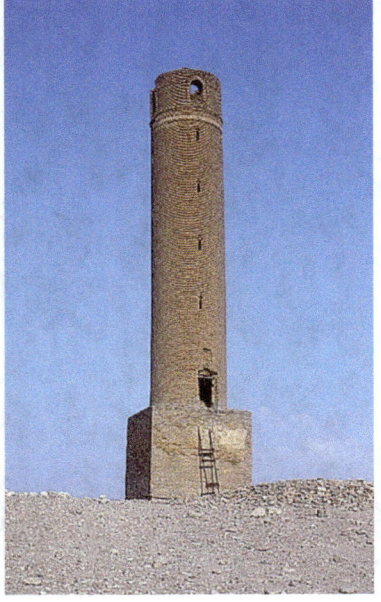

Mosque of Nur al-Din, view of the cylindrical brick minaret nearby, Qal'at Ja'bar, Raqqa.

Great Mosque, view of the square-based stone minaret, Aleppo.

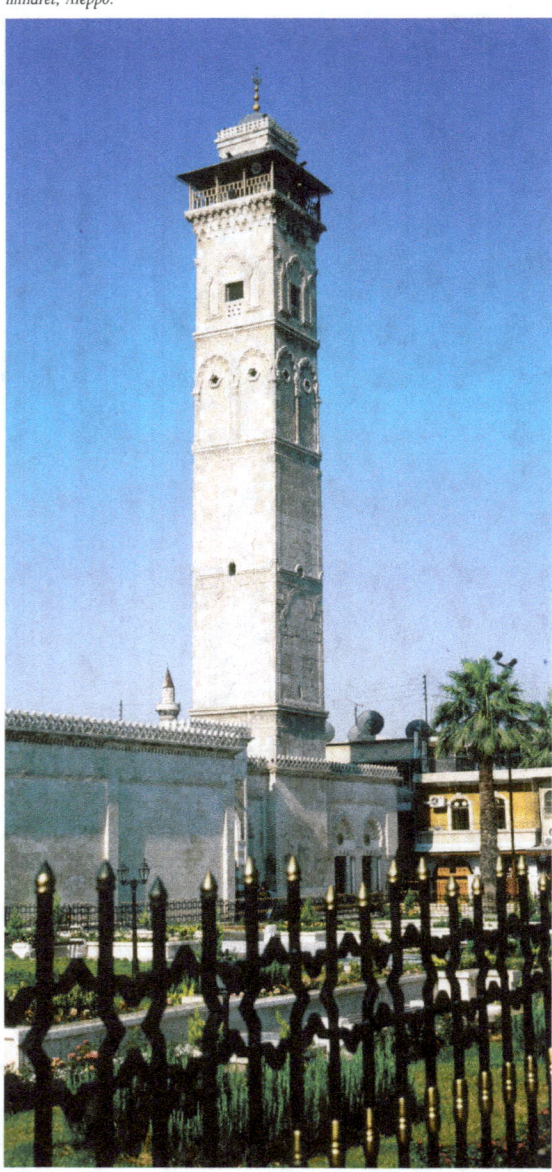

blocks followed a distinctive diamond motif (*ablaq*). As for the cities in eastern Syria, the minarets found in Qal'at Ja'bar, Raqqa and Abu Hurayra are round, following the shape found predominantly in the Eastern Muslim world, and they are brick-built. They rise in contrast to the square counterparts of western Syria.

Mausoleum

During this period, the importance of the mausoleum is felt by their sheer abundance. They are usually domed structures as the dome has long been an honorific type, commemorating the deceased and attracting the prayers of passers-by. There was also a kind of mausoleum dedicated to martyrs, known as shrine or *mashhad*.

The most distinctive feature of a mausoleum is the dome. These could have several shapes: *muqarnas*, lobed, or smooth. The transition from square room to domed ceiling also followed varying techniques. In Damascus, it was typical to have one or two polygonal drums, or tambours. There are exceptions, however, such as in the mausoleum of Madrasa al-Shamiyya that has a vault rather than a dome. In Aleppo, spherical-triangular pendentives, or squinches supported the dome. As for the *muqarnas* dome, this style was imported into Damascus from Mesopotamia by Nur al-Din, a form that is raised, basically, by corbelled bricks. Interaction between the various styles of dome building in Syria is evident in several monuments. For example, the squinches of the tomb-chamber in Madrasa al-'Adiliyya in

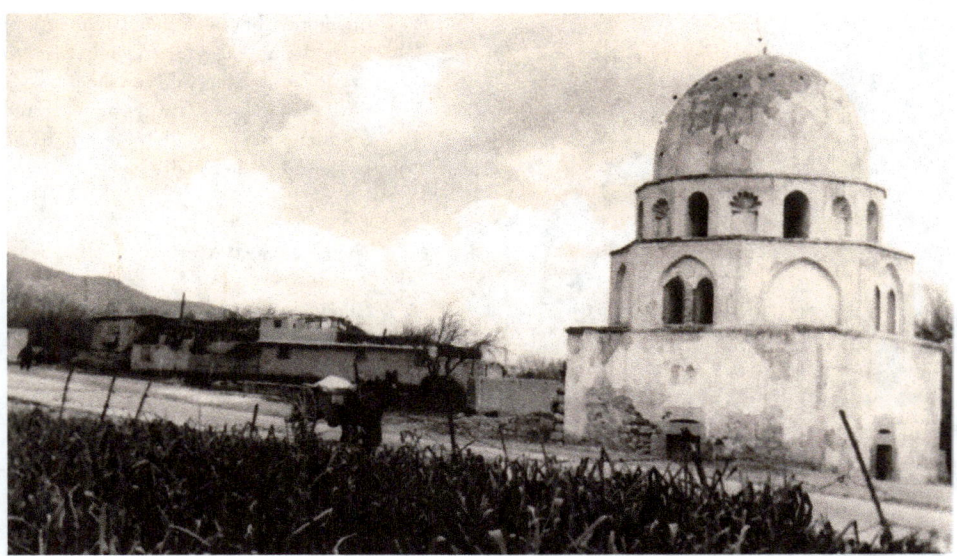

Badriyya Mausoleum, Damascus, in the 1950s (Moaz, 1954; photo courtesy of Khaled Moaz).

Damascus, reveals a strong Aleppine influence since Damascene domes usually rest on drums, not squinches.

It was generally desirable to build mausoleums in religiously prestigious locations. The vicinity of the Great Umayyad Mosque and the southern region of the Maydan from which the pilgrim's road towards Mecca began were favourite locations. Salah al-Din, for example, requested burial there in order to receive the blessings of the annual pilgrimage caravans and soldiers that would be heading for *jihad*. His sons, however, chose another location near to the Great Umayyad Mosque in Damascus. The new district of Salihiyya, north of Damascus, was also well-chosen as it had become an influential religious centre with the activism of prominent sheikhs who came from Palestinian refugee families fleeing the Crusades, as well as renowned Sufi mystics.

A mausoleum often attached to a *madrasa* as a charitable foundation, offered higher education for religious scholars and a space for reading the Qur'an, which reflected beneficially on the memory of the deceased. The link between mausoleum and *madrasa* is so prominent that some scholars have coined the term "funerary colleges". Sometimes, the size of the mausoleum dominates that of the *madrasa*, indicating that the function of the *madrasa* was secondary to the primary goal of the "*madrasa*-mausoleum"- complex: to attract blessings and prayers to the deceased patron. Nevertheless, even when mausoleums and *madrasas* are attached to one another, there is a clear

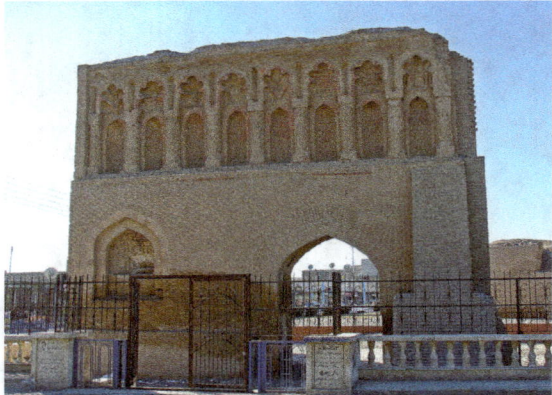

Bab Baghdad,
a ceremonial gateway,
Raqqa.

Madrasat al-Firdaws,
detail of the interlacing
marble on the mihrab,
Aleppo.

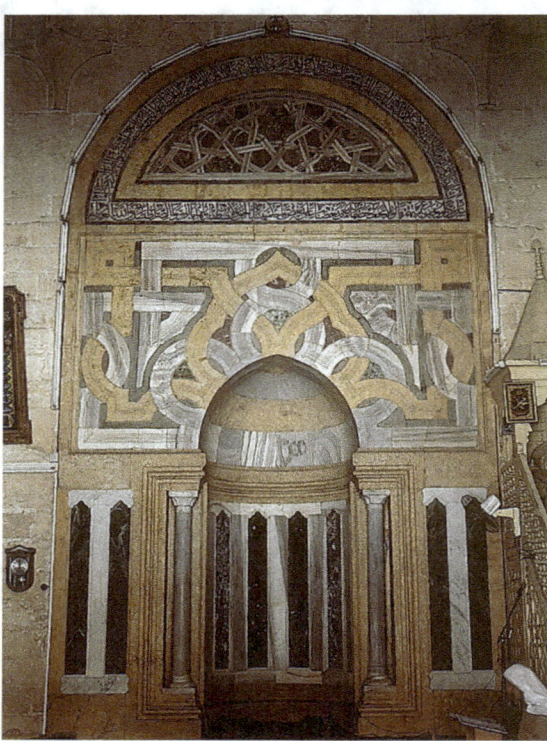

distinction between their architectural spaces because it is forbidden in Islam to pray to anyone but God and the presence of a cenotaph must always be separated from the prayer-hall so as not to be perceived as intermediary.

Architectural Media

Brick

Brick as a medium is utilised mostly on the buildings of eastern Syria as an extension to the Mesopotamian and Iranian regions. Monuments built in eastern Syria exhibit decorative architectural features in the exterior patterning of the brickwork, as found in various religious as well as secular buildings. The buildings of Raqqa are primary examples of the aestheticism of brick. The use of corbelled brick for the construction of domes, initiated in western Syria by Nur al-Din, distinguishes both his mausoleum and his *bimaristan* in Damascus. It was otherwise foreign to the region and the patterning of brick-work on building facades remained an Eastern specialty. By the end of the 6th/12th century, it was the architectural influence of northern Syria, one dominated by stone, which became a stronger influence on the building style of the capital, as can be seen in the Madrasa al-Rukniyya.

Stone

Ayyubid architecture in general and the architecture of Aleppo city in particular, is renowned for its flawless stone-carving techniques. Made under the abundant patronage of Nur al-Din, are some of the best surviving examples of stone carving in the region, found, most notably, in the remains of the Madrasa al-Shuʻaybiyya entablature. Its frieze is a masterpiece in stone carving and decoration, with vegetal scrolls and monumental Atabeg *kufic* inscriptions cut with deep incisions and expert dexterity. More examples of magnificent stone carving, offering a variety of decorative styles, decorate the entrance of Mashhad al-Hussein, a shrine in Aleppo. Additionally, the penchant for marble-capped *mihrab*s, found abundantly in the *madrasa*s of Aleppo, carries the "taste for stone" even further, since these decorative elements were fashioned from carved marble blocks rather than the more commonly used inlaid marble.

Stucco

The fashion for decorating interiors with pierced and painted panels of carved stucco is an Eastern-inspired technique, made famous in the ʻAbbasid capital of Samarra in the 2nd/8th century, and re-invigorated under Ayyubid patronage. Decorative motifs found on stucco panels include calligraphic banners in Atabeg *kufic* script, polygonal fields of vegetal motifs, and floral or geometric medallions that emphasised funerary halls or main *iwan*s in *madrasa*s and in *bimaristan*s. Stucco decorated the majority of mausoleums, but not all have survived.

Stucco application was particularly common in buildings made of brick. Once the fashion for stone from northern Syria began to dominate the building style, stucco decoration diminished. In eastern Syria, brick had always been the preferred building material, thus stucco decoration continued to flourish there. Some of the best surviving examples still *in situ* can be found in the Madrasa al-Shamiyya, Bimaristan al-Qaymari and the Badriyya Mausoleum in Damascus, the ʻUmari Mosque in Bosra, and the

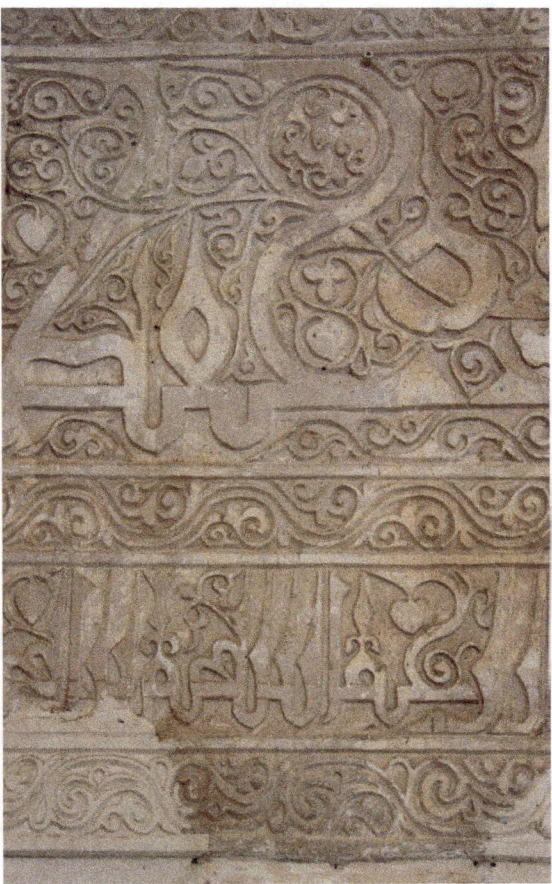

Jamiʻ al-ʻUmari ('Umari Mosque), detail of the carved stucco, Bosra.

decorated stucco niches in the western hall of Qasr al-Banat in Raqqa.

Wood

Syrian woodwork played a pivotal role in Islamic art during this period: geometric polygonal shapes, inter-crossing star designs, precisely carved vegetal motifs, and calligraphic inscriptions of various styles. Artisans in wood appreciated a variety of different woods for their grain, colour and shine when polished. Many monumental gates constructed for urban buildings as well as ritual furnishings for mosques were of wood. Wooden doors received a high level of decoration in comparison to the general architectural sobriety of Ayyubid Syria. Wood was a specialty of Syrian artisans; good examples of this artistry are the geometric patterned doors of the *bimaristan*s of Nur al-Din in Damascus and Aleppo. Another important masterpiece is the wooden screen, or *maqsura*, from the mausoleum of the Seljuq Sultan Duqaq in southern Damascus, currently held at the National Museum of Damascus. Although little survives, wood was also used in the construction of elaborate ceilings in important reception halls.

Similarly, carefully and beautifully decorated wooden *minbar*s (pulpits), which played such a crucial role in the spread of religious and political unity, were constructed. The famous carpenter from Aleppo, al-Akhtarini, was commissioned by Nur al-Din to design a *minbar* for the Aqsa Mosque in Jerusalem in anticipation of its liberation from the Franks. The *minbar*s thus constructed acted as the visual articulation of the Zangid leader. Although the Aqsa Mosque *minbar* was destroyed in a fire in 1969, that from the Mosque of Nur al-Din in Hama still survives as a comparable example of contemporary woodcarving. Other prominent examples of woodcarving from the period are the cenotaph

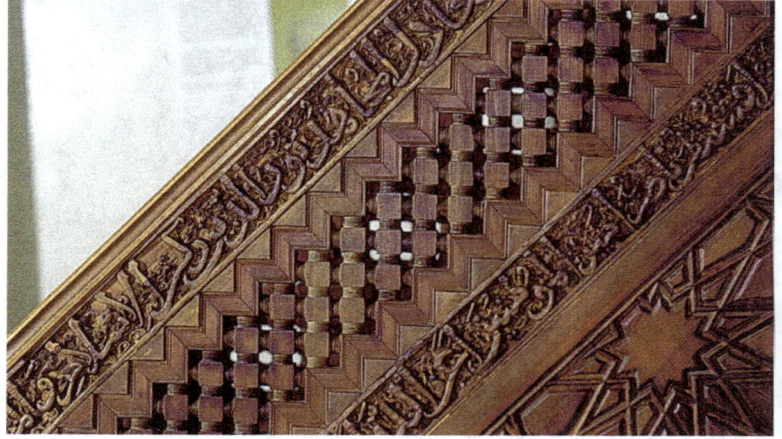

Minbar *of* Nur al-Din, detail, Hama Archaeological Museum (Inv. Num. 3266).

of Salah al-Din, ceremoniously located in his mausoleum near the Great Umayyad Mosque, and the wooden *mihrab* niche of the Madrasa al-Hallawiyya in Aleppo.

Artistic Objects

Metalwork

Syria's metalworking tradition also witnessed a revival during the Atabeg and Ayyubid periods. Military costumes and ceremonial attire would have featured important metallic artwork, offering a glimpse of aristocratic fashion. The famous Damascene swords made of highly carbonated steel and bearing the distinctive etchings of their watermarks continue to be valued, not only for their military quality, but also for their beauty. By far the most exquisite art of the period is the inlaid metalwork. The technique was brought to Mesopotamia and Syria by craftsmen migrating from Central Asia, particularly those fleeing the Mongol invasions in the region of present day Afghanistan, many of whom settled in Mosul during the reign of the Atabeg Badr al-Din Lu'lu' (607-657/1211-1259) who was well-known for his love of metal inlaid objects and lavishly commissioned such pieces. This artistic fashion had a strong influence on local metalwork production to the extent that many such items were signed "al-Mawsili", although they were produced elsewhere, such as Damascus and also Cairo.

The techniques used for inlaid metalwork were highly valued skills. Expert inlay artisans used silver, gold and copper on

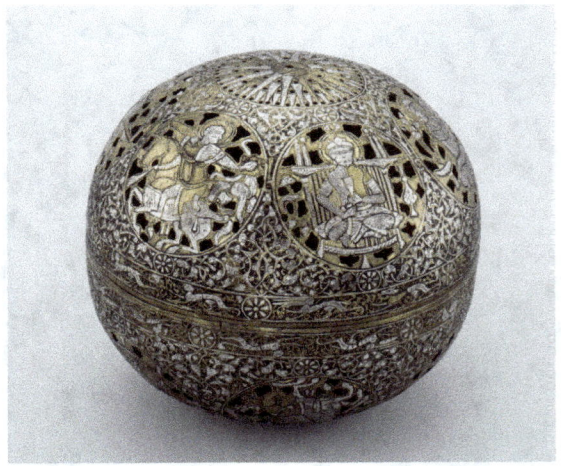

Spherical incense burner with inlaid metalwork decoration, Museum of Islamic Art at the Pergamon Museum, State Museums, Berlin (Inv. Num. MIK2774; photo by Johannes Kramer, © Museum of Islamic Art – State Museums Berlin).

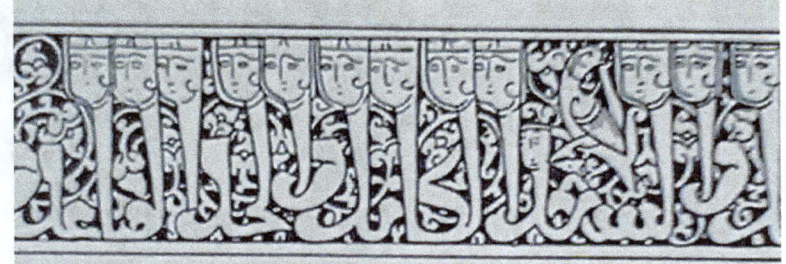

Animated inscription from an inlaid metal cup made in c.627/1230 (Hillenbrand, 1999, fig. 1.6; Rice, 1953).

Ayyubid art and architecture

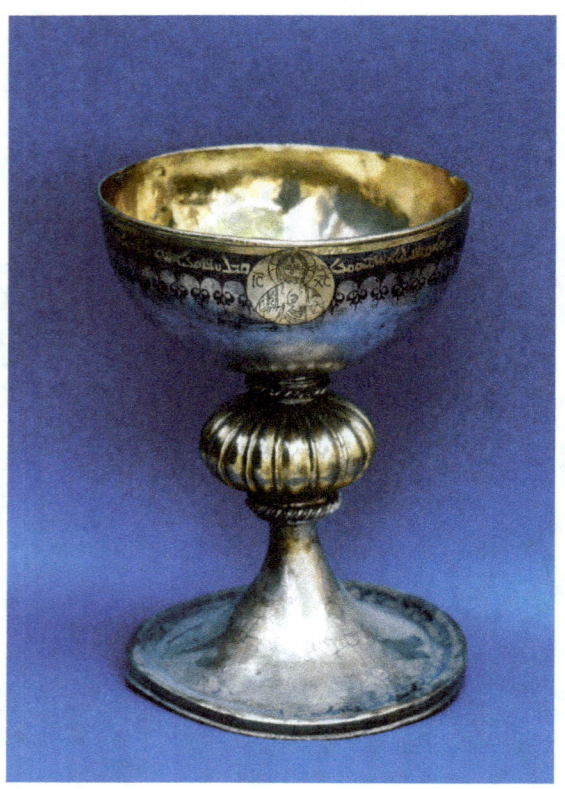

Silver chalice from the Rusafa treasure trove, National Museum of Damascus.

their artistic beauty. These metal masterpieces reveal a minuscule attention to detail and a wide repertory of images; combat scenes, hunting scenes, courtly scenes and the ever-popular astrological symbols relating to power and good fortune. Calligraphy on metal-ware usually followed in the Eastern – Central Asian – fashion, whereby the letters were sometimes animated, the vertical lines featuring human heads.

Lastly, one of the most famous Syrian examples of metalwork from the Ayyubid period is the Rusafa Treasure, an early 7th-/13th-century collection of fine silverware produced using local methods in metalworking, and dedicated to the Syrian Church of St Sergios. The treasure, hidden from the Mongols when they invaded the Raqqa region in 654/1256, survives as an example of luxurious Syrian Christian art with intermingling Christian motifs, Syriac inscriptions and Islamic arabesque decorations.

Numismatics

Typically, there were three values of coins during the Ayyubid period. The lesser denomination of *fils* was made of copper and sometimes bronze, the median denomination of *dirham* was made of silver, while the highest value coin, the *dinar*, was made of gold. With the Ayyubid Empire stretching from Syria, through the Sinai Desert to Egypt, and the strategic eastern Mediterranean ports, as well as the Red Sea down to Yemen, trade was a critical part of the empire's success. In western Syria, designs for coinage, with concentric

brass items – such as ewers, bowls and candlesticks – and, in order to highlight the contrast of the different colour metals, they delineated them with black *niello*. The depictions created by the manipulation of the inlay could be geometric, calligraphic and figurative – often a combination of all three – distributed around the vessels in concentric bands and roundels. Often the images were cleverly interrelated, adding multiple symbolism and intellectual playfulness to

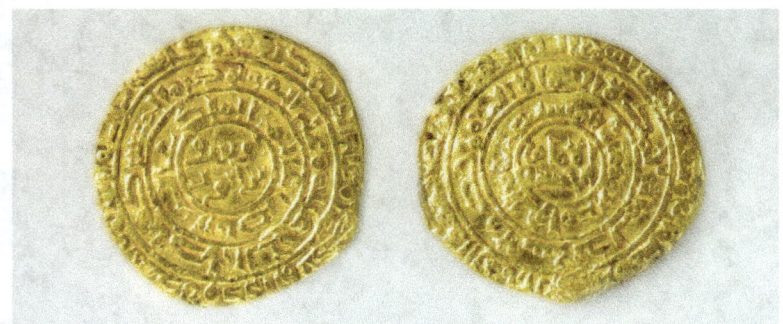

Dinar (gold coins) minted by Salah al-Din in Cairo in 574/1178, National Museum of Damascus (Inv. Num. 30178 ع د).

bands of calligraphy, follow the Fatimid precedent, a testimony to their importance on the Mediterranean trading scene. Meanwhile, the coins minted in eastern Syria and Upper Mesopotamia included figurative depictions, following the Atabeg model of the region and bearing Byzantine influence. The seated figure features mostly on bronze coins, such as that of the prince in Eastern royal attire. The first gold coin minted by Salah al-Din in Damascus in 571/1176 followed in the Fatimid tradition and played an important part in the Ayyubid Dynasty's claim to power and their emphasis on Damascus as the capital city.

An interesting outcome of Ayyubid coins is that the Crusaders of the 7th/13th century imitated them. For gold coins, they followed Salah al-Din's *dinar*, while for silver ones they imitated al-Salih Isma'il's *dirham*. The Crusaders also used the Arabic cursive, or *naskhi*, script on their coins, which sometimes featured spelling or grammatical mistakes, but they follow the Arabic *lingua franca* nonetheless.

Textiles

Despite the fact that it is rare for textiles to survive in good condition, and few examples are therefore extant, textile production in Syria and the Jazira flourished during the Atabeg and Ayyubid periods. Etymologically, seen by the continued use of the term "Muslin", an extremely fine fabric made in Mosul and the Damascene textile known in the West as "Damasco", an embroidered type. The fabrics of this period relate by the decorative repertoires to other art forms, and follow the strong influence of Eastern artistic heritage.

Manuscripts

Libraries and books were crucial as part of the cultural, scientific and religious revival in Syria. Workshops for paper production (*warraqat*) and trade in paper were important features of Damascus's suqs especially the well-known Suq al-Warraqin next to the Great Umayyad Mosque. Increased paper production supported the mass transmission of knowledge. The famous Sufi sheikh

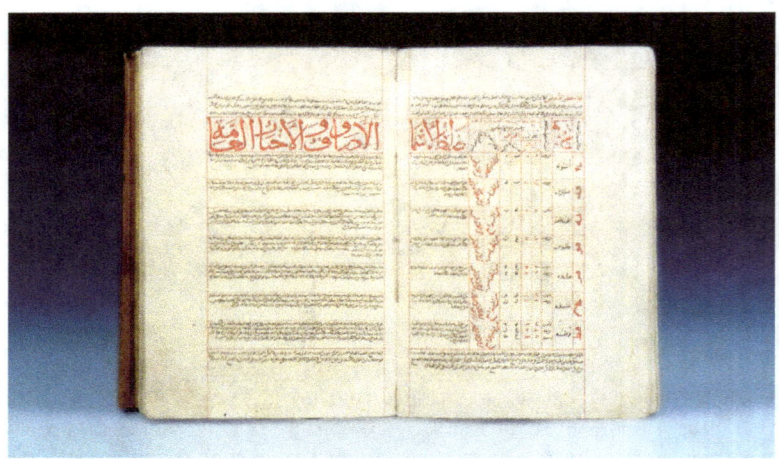

Two pages from Taqwim al-Buldan, a manuscript on geography written by Abu al-Fida', the Ayyubid ruler of Hama, National Museum of Damascus (Inv. Num. 14689/ع).

Muhyi al-Din al-'Arabi penned his voluminous Book of Poetry (*diwan*) in Damascus around 643/1237. Paper as artwork, however, finds its finest expression in manuscripts sponsored by rulers.

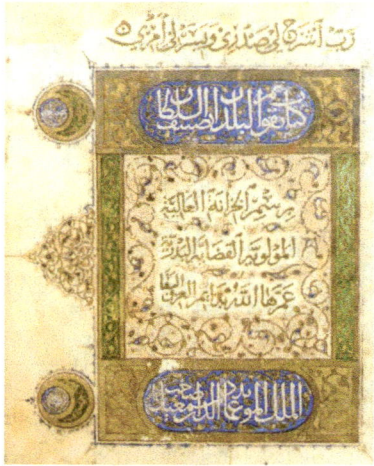

Taqwim al-Buldan, frontispiece, National Museum of Damascus (Inv. Num. 14689/ع).

Copies of the Qur'an were always the most important, most carefully copied and richly ornamented manuscripts since they carried the Word of God. An example of an illuminated Qur'an frontispiece of the Atabeg era is the Qur'an made for the library of a Zangid prince of the Jazira in around 594/1198.

The Ayyubid princes themselves were well-educated and cultured, sponsoring important manuscripts and even composing them, as can be seen by the geographical encyclopaedia written by Abu al-Fida', the Ayyubid ruler of Hama. The Arab prince of Shayzar Usama bin Munqidh even kept a diary, which has survived to offer precious insight into the first interactions of the Arabs with the Franks. It also reveals beautiful penmanship.

Also composed during this period is a rare and important manuscript on military topics, dedicated to Salah al-Din

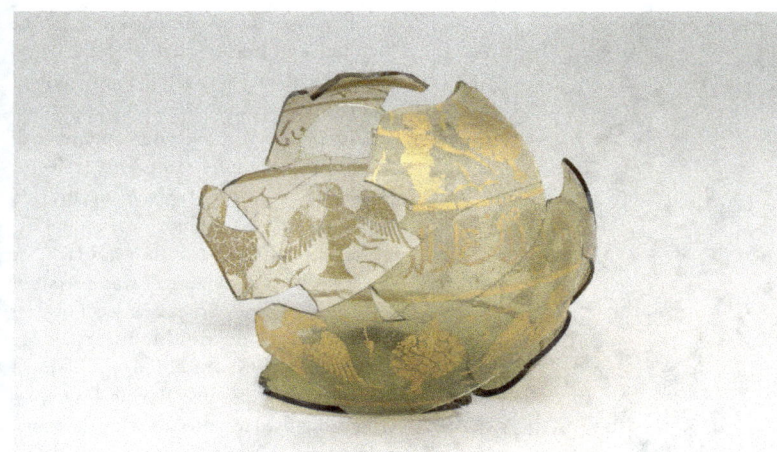

Bottle (inscribed with the name of 'Imad al-Din al-Zangi, ruler of Aleppo), 1127–46, British Museum, London (Inv. Num. 1906, 0719.1; © Trustees of the British Museum, London).

in around 583/1187. Entitled *Tabsirat Arbab al-Albab* (*The Perception of Those with Understanding*) its author, Murda al-Tarsusi, elucidates the latest mechanisms in the arts of war, it features some exceptional drawings of weapons for both man-to-man combat and siege warfare, as well as diagrammatic drawings of battle formations.

Glass

Techniques in enamelled and gilded glass were highly developed in 6th-/12th-century Syria, particularly in the Raqqa region. The decorative repertoire was wide, including gilded and enamelled cups for courtly settings, striped, marvered and moulded glass bottles and jars for perfume and kohl, and a variety of glass vessels mounted with precious or semi-precious stones such as *lapis lazuli*. Recently excavated in Hama, is an Ayyubid ewer that is embedded with *lapis lazuli* beads; it is now part of the collection at the National Museum of Damascus. The earliest datable example of luxurious glass from this period is, however, the fragmentary gilded vessel bearing the name of 'Imad al-Din Zangi, and decorated with cursive (*naskhi*) script and figurative designs along the upper and lower bands. It appears that the fashion for gilding preceded the use of coloured enamels.

Pottery

The Mesopotamian region of Syria, along the banks of the River Euphrates, was always renowned for its pottery production.

As for ceramics, i.e. glazed pottery, Raqqa was one of these production centres during the Atabeg and Ayyubid periods, producing fine glazed pottery. Excavations in the region have uncovered many kilns used to fire such wares, and

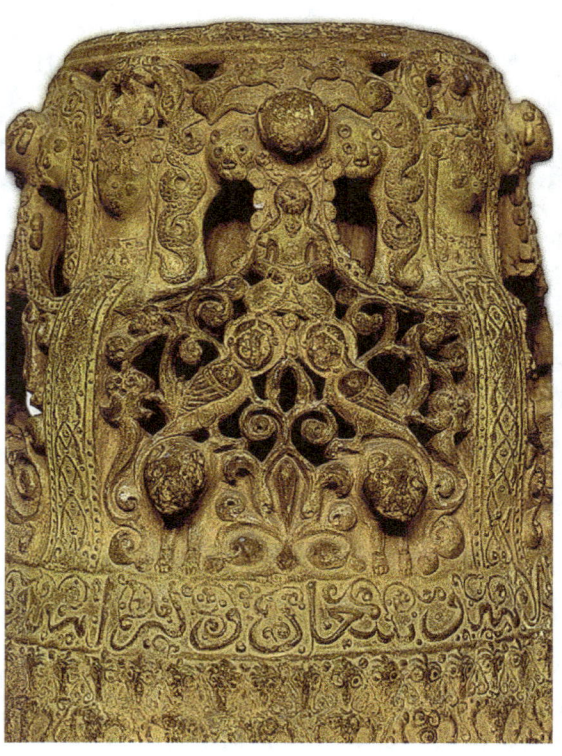

Carved and pierced khubb jar, detail, National Museum of Damascus (Inv. Num. 573 ع).

further elucidate the advanced techniques used there in the 6th/12th and first half of the 7th/13th centuries. Since Raqqa is the first and most famous place where several typical types of medieval glazed pottery was unearthed, it became known as "Raqqa ware", although it might come from other production centres, such as Rusafa or Aleppo.

This flourishing of the ceramics industry came as a result of the introduction of a new material called stone-paste, also known as fritware – a fine, white paste with a high quartz content imitating the colour and fine texture of porcelain – which had long been a preciously sought-after material known from China. Stone-paste pottery, produced in a number of centres in the Euphrates area, is distinguished by several types of decoration and glaze: most common is an under-glazed painted decoration in black, or black, blue and red, under transparent or turquoise glaze. So-called *laqabi* wares feature raised, moulded decoration painted in different colours. The most common shapes are flaring bowls on high stands, large dishes with flat rims, and vases. The inspiration for some polychromatic vessels with under-glazed paintings of figurative representations like hunters and musicians and scenes of courtly merriment, came from Iranian over-glaze painted *mina'i* wares. Most luxurious of all, however, were the lustre-painted pieces that shone in different shades of metallic gold. Their value came from the complicated firing method and time-consuming production process. Lustre, seen on all glazed colours: turquoise, blue, manganese and transparent served to imitate gold, since Islam forbade the use of gold for vessels used for eating and drinking. Their rich decorative motifs varied form abstract patterns to vegetal motifs and animals like hares, tigers and deer.

Also a type of large water jar called a *khubb* emerged, which can be as large as a metre high, a pair of which is exhibited in the National Museum of Damascus. Such unglazed pottery was well suited to water storage, since the perforated clay

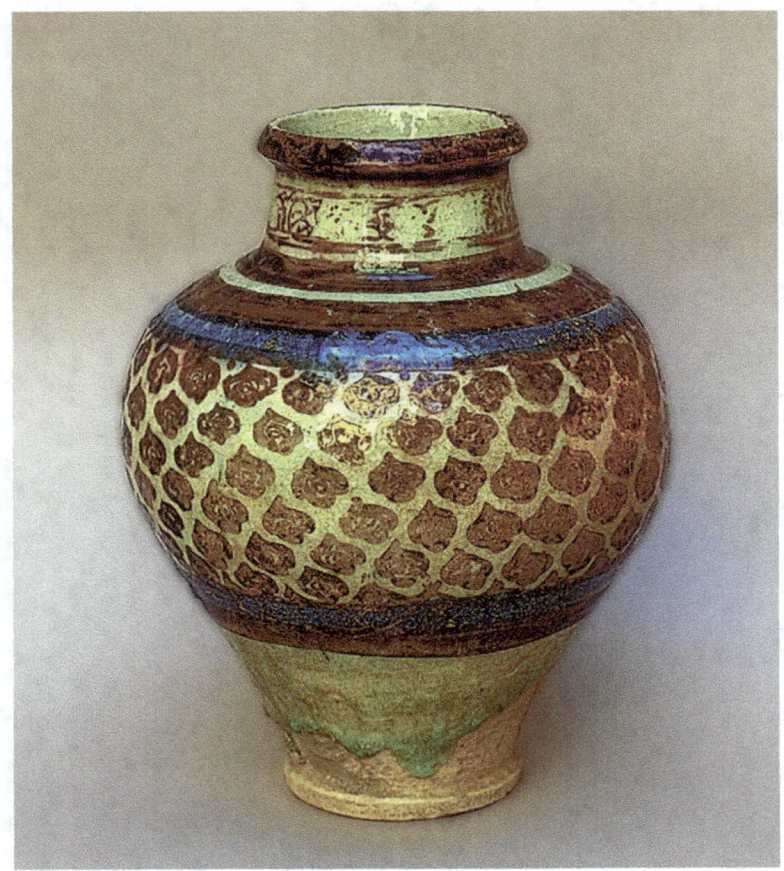

Tin-glazed vase with cobalt-blue and lustre decoration, Raqqa Museum.

body kept the water well ventilated and cool. Their surfaces, delicately decorated, except for the rounded bases (which would have been set into the ground or placed on a stand), had relief applied in various ways: moulded, incised, carved or pierced. The motifs reveal fantastical animals and esoteric symbolism juxtaposed with images of courtly life and sovereignty.

The Mongol invasion of 658/1260 not only marked a historical break but also, since nearly all the kilns in the region were destroyed, artistic production experienced an interruption. As far as we know, the centre for production then shifted to Damascus, becoming the major source of glazed wares during the subsequent Mamluk period.

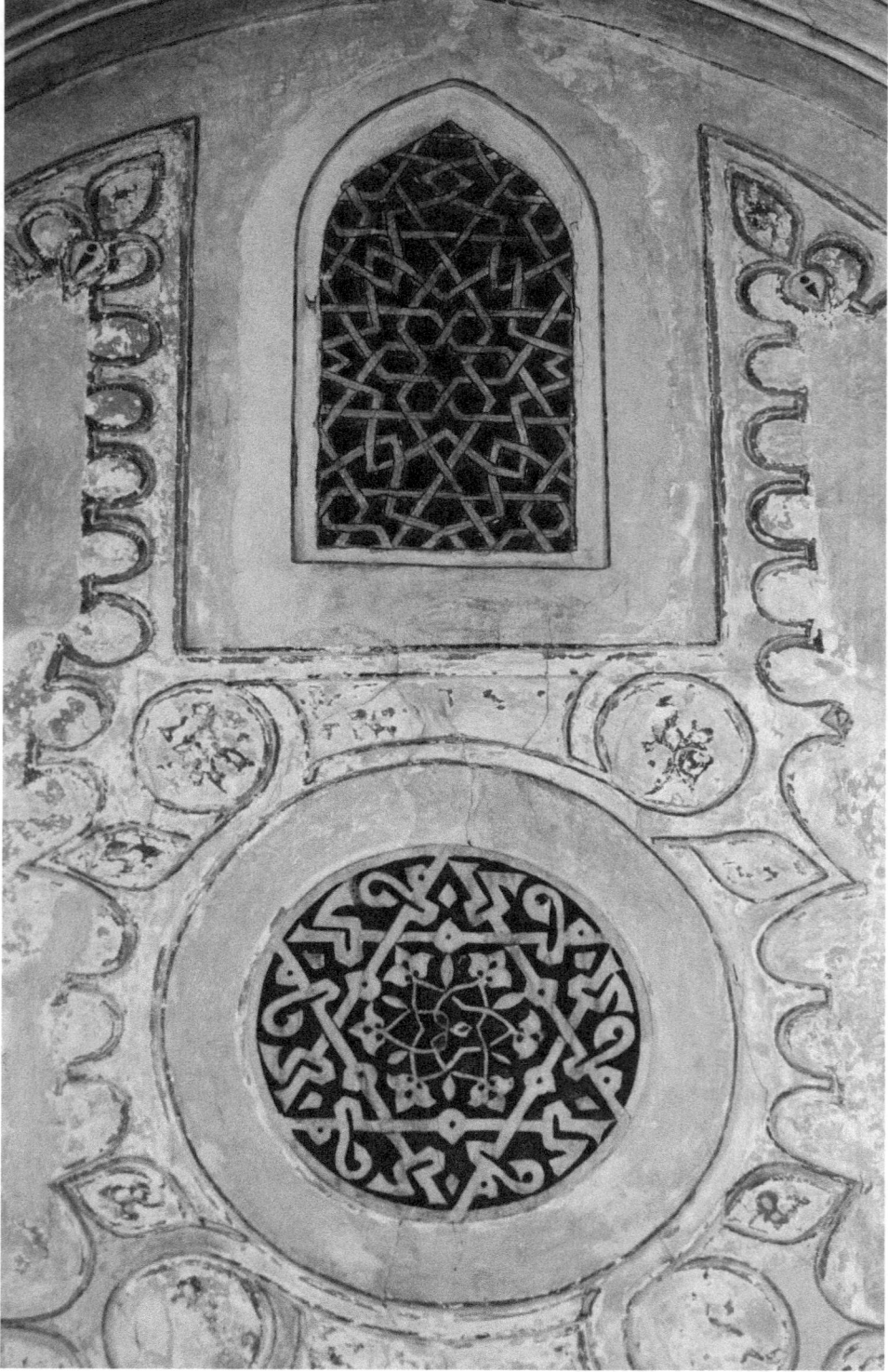

ITINERARY I
First day

Religion, Science and the Transmission of Knowledge under the Atabegs and Ayyubids

Abd al-Razzaq Moaz, Zena Takieddine

DAMASCUS

I.1 DAMASCUS: OLD CITY WALLS, TOWERS AND GATES
   I.1.a Bab Jabiya
   I.1.b Tower of Nur al-Din (Option)
   I.1.c Bab Saghir Cemetery (Option)
   I.1.d Bab Saghir
   I.1.e Bab Kisan
   I.1.f Bab Sharqi
   I.1.g Tower of al-Salih Ayyub (Option)
   I.1.h Bab Touma
   I.1.i Bab al-Salam
   I.1.j Bab al-Faradis
   I.1.k Bab al-Faraj

I.2 DAMASCUS CITADEL
I.3 BIMARISTAN NUR AL-DIN
I.4 MADRASAT OF NUR AL-DIN
I.5 HAMMAM NUR AL-DIN
I.6 GREAT UMAYYAD MOSQUE
I.7 MAUSOLEUM OF SALAH AL-DIN
I.8 MADRASA AL-'ADILIYYA
I.9 NAJMIYYA MAUSOLEUM
I.10 MADRASA AL-SHAMIYYA

The *Bimaristan*s and Public Health Yasser Tabbaa

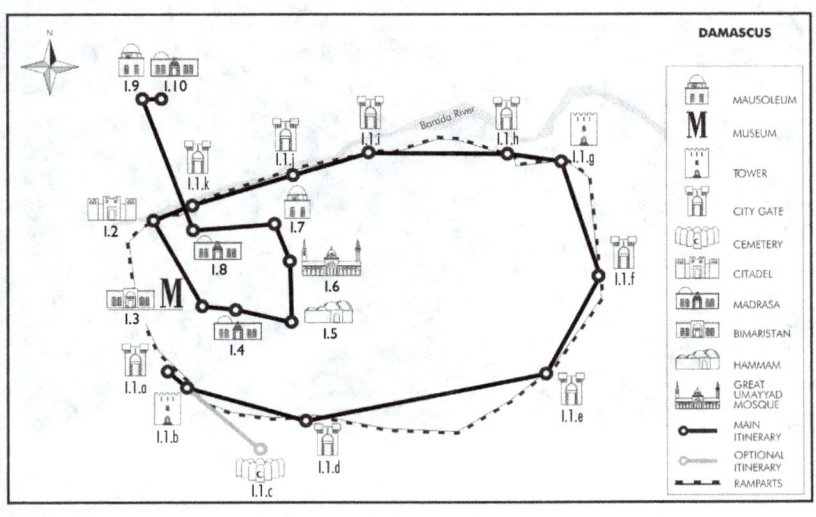

Madrasa Sitt al-Saam, Damascus, detail of stucco decoration in the mausoleum.

77

ITINERARY I *Religion, Science and the Transmission of Knowledge under the Atabegs and Ayyubids*
Introduction

The Islamic history of Damascus is important as the capital of the Umayyad Caliphate, heralding the first expansion of Islam outside the Arabian Peninsula and into the Mediterranean region in the 1st/7th century. In Damascus, the Great Umayyad Mosque was built by the caliph al-Walid bin 'Abd al-Malik in 96/715 and it was the first monumental construct of its kind, proclaiming Damascus as the vibrant capital of a new world order, and setting the standard architecturally for subsequent mosque constructions.

When the Umayyads were overcome by the 'Abbasids in 132/750 and the Islamic capital shifted to Baghdad, Damascus became a provincial city for a long time. Not until the advance of the Seljuq Turks in the 5th/11th century did it begin to experience a revival in its regional importance. When Nur al-Din succeeded in taking control of Damascus in 549/1154, the different parts of Syria were strategically united and the status of Damascus as the capital city was established once again. Nur al-Din was zealously devoted to the triumph of Islam and in Damascus he established a robust environment of theological and legal education. The construction of 100 new *madrasa*s in Damascus alone reflects his desire to change and re-educate society and revamp its urban structures. These civic developments are recorded by the historian of Damascus Ibn 'Asakir (d. 571/1176), a contemporary of Nur al-Din and a witness to the vivid architectural and religious mark he left on the city. Damascus became a magnet attracting scholars and *'ulama* (teachers) from all across the lands of the Islamic faith. They came from Iraq, Iran, Central Asia,

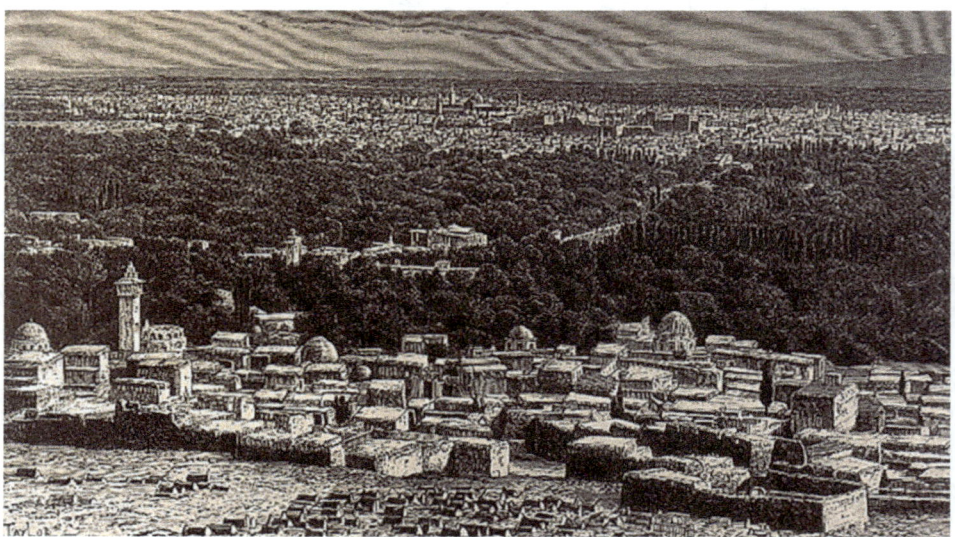

A 19th-century engraving of the Salihiyya district overlooking Damascus (Lortet, 1884).

ITINERARY I   *Religion, Science and the Transmission of Knowledge under the Atabegs and Ayyubids*
Introduction

al-Andalus (Muslim Spain), the Maghreb (North Africa) and Egypt as they fled the Crusaders, the *Reconquista*, and the Mongols. They found refuge in Damascus together with a fertile teaching ground. Damascus expanded to Mount Qasyun, some 2 km north of the old city, in what is known as the Salihiyya Quarter, and south along the pilgrimage route in what is known as al-Maydan. Both areas became important religious centres and Salihiyya in particular was famous for its *madrasa*s. Salihiyya was founded when Nur al-Din invited a handful of refugee families from Jerusalem to settle along the banks of the River Yazid. These families were of high religious standing and well educated; most famous among them are the Banu 'Asakir and the Banu Qudama, who settled there in 556/1161 and played crucial roles in Nur al-Din as well Salah al-Din's campaigns. Salihiyya expanded rapidly as a highly respected neighbourhood and a centre for anti-Crusader propaganda. It was a self-sufficient and independently functioning district, a separate city almost. The ruling elite as patrons, members of the Ayyubid family and their brothers and sisters, wives and husbands, courtiers and freed-slaves, all participated in its growth. The Ayyubids practiced an exceptionally generous patronage of writers and scholars. By the end of the Ayyubid reign in 658/1260, the Salihiyya district had become an area of thriving urbanism nestled between the Qasyun slopes of the River Yazid, attracting the best of noble patronage and charitable institution.

Under Nur al-Din and then the Ayyubids, the city walls, *burj*s and gates of Damascus were refortified and the Damascus Citadel completely redressed. The Ayyubids ensured the security for the city to thrive. *Madrasa*s, *Dar Hadith*s and mausoleums (*turba*s or *darih*s) were never too far away from *suq*s, *bimaristan*s and *hammam*s. Prior to all these institutions, it was the mosque that served – and continues to serve to this day – as a basic centre for education, with larger mosques

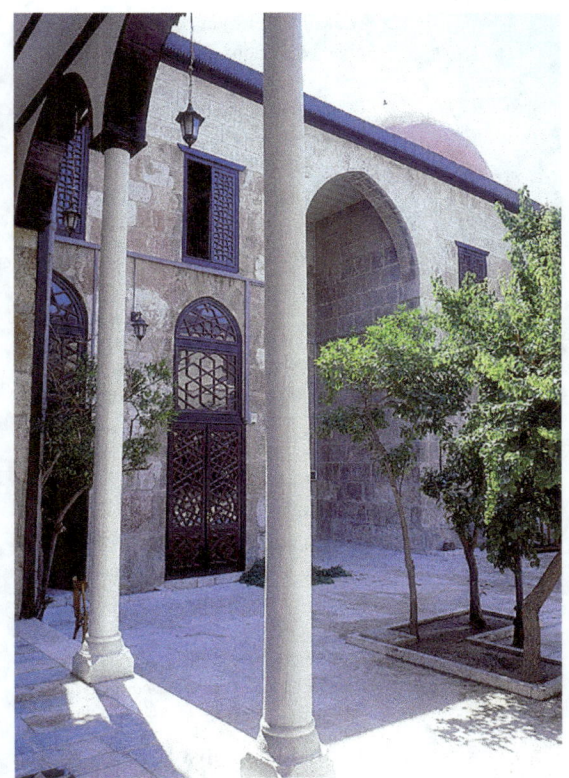

Madrasa al-'Adiliyya, view of arcade and courtyard, Damascus.

generally including libraries too. Thus public education is not new to the Muslim world, and the development of *madrasas* can be seen as a continuation of what was already offered in mosques and public libraries. It in is their quantity and specialisation that attention is drawn to the systematic approach applied to the re-education of society.

1.1 DAMASCUS: OLD CITY WALLS, TOWERS AND GATES

Start early at 08.00 am when it is cool and traffic is low. On Thawra Street, face the modern equestrian statue of Salah al-Din, and turn right. With the citadel to your left, walk around the circumference of the city in an anti-clockwise direction, visiting all eight gates, and arriving back, full circle, to the citadel. This will take between two and three hours.

1.1.a Bab al-Jabiya

Starting with Bab al-Jabiya, located at the south-western edge of the city, this gate is located inside the second-hand clothes market behind the Ottoman period Sinaniye mosque. First right behind the mosque's north entrance, the gate will appear on your left.

Bab al-Jabiya was built by the Atabeg ruler, Nur al-Din Mahmud bin Zangi in 560/1164, re-using Roman stone blocks, and it was completed by the Ayyubid ruler, al-Malik al-Mu'azzam, in 624/1227. The brackets of the defensive machicolations are visible from the exterior while on the interior is an Arabic inscription set in a *tabula ansata* (a rectangular frame with triangular edges) recording the patronage of Nur al-Din. The market, which extended out from Bab al-Jabiya, is closely related to the needs and trading activities of pilgrims and travelling merchants as it is considered to be the nearest extension of the pilgrimage route that heads southward to Mecca. Such economic activity oriented towards people passing through, as opposed to the inhabitants of the town, created order and security.

1.1.b Tower of Nur al-Din *(Option)*

Continuing 40 m south of the Sinaniye Mosque is the Tower of Nur al-Din.

This tower is located inside the courtyard of a small workshop/hotel called Funduq al-Islah and it features one of the best-preserved inscription bands in Arabic, recording Nur al-Din's refortification efforts of 568/1173.

1.1.c Bab al-Saghir Cemetery *(Option)*

Continuing down the Sinaniyya suq that parallels the old walls, Bab al-Saghir Cemetery lies to the right. It is the oldest cemetery in Damascus and, as is usual, cemeteries are located just outside old city walls. An entrance is accessible through a cobble-stoned street called al-Jarrah.

This cemetery is venerated by all Muslims and it holds many important tombs, including those of the Prophet's family, his

ITINERARY I *Religion, Science and the Transmission of Knowledge under the Atabegs and Ayyubids*
Damascus: Old City Walls, Towers and Gates

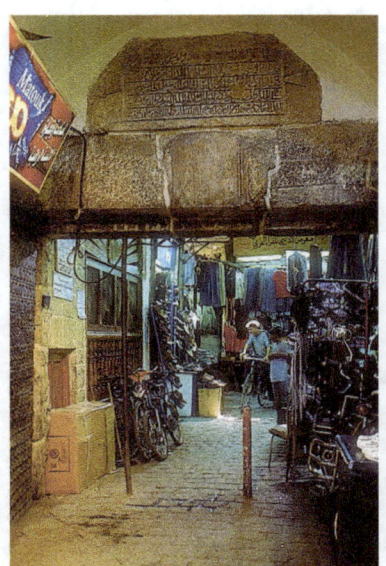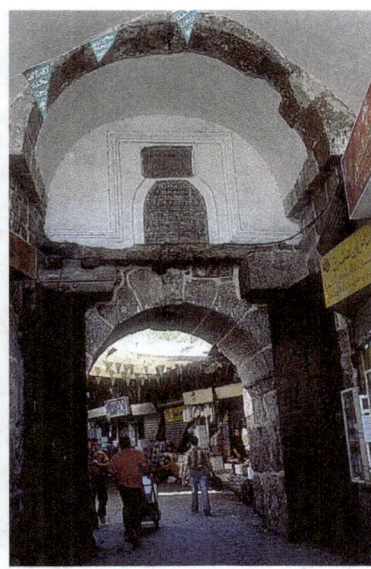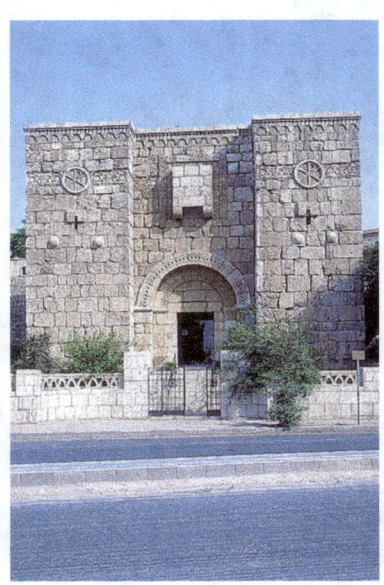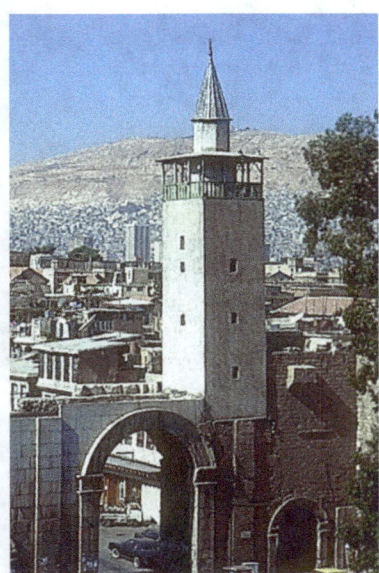

*City Gates, Damascus.
Clockwise:
Bab al-Jabiya,
Bab al-Saghir,
Bab Kisan,
Bab Sharqi.*

81

ITINERARY I   *Religion, Science and the Transmission of Knowledge under the Atabegs and Ayyubids*
Damascus: Old City Walls, Towers and Gates

companions and many of the city's elite throughout the centuries. Some of the oldest existing tombstones date to the 5th/10th and 6th/11th century with distinctive floriated *kufic* epigraphy, testimony to the attention and restorations given to the cemetery during the Atabeg and Ayyubid period.

I.1.d **Bab al-Saghir**

Turning away from the cemetery bearing right until you reach a small garden, take a left then a right, thus returning to the city walls embedded in the urban fabric where, 60 m to your left is the Bab al-Saghir (Little Gate).

It was rebuilt by Nur al-Din in 551/1156 on the foundations of the Roman Gate of Mars. It is the southernmost gate of the city. As the name indicates, its scale is small, more easily defensible, and it is equipped with machicolations.

I.1.e **Bab Kisan**

Walking eastwards through the busy Shaghour Market to Amin Street Square and continuing past the school buildings, vegetable stalls and the fire station until you reach a large roundabout, the city walls will reappear on your left. Immediately thereafter is a 20th-century church, which now incorporates the next gate en route, Bab Kisan.

Bab Kisan is also based on an original Roman gate, dedicated to Saturn, its lower courses of large stone blocks still in place. It was rebuilt during the initial Arab conquests in the 1st/7th century, with remains evident inside the chapel, and again entirely refortified by Nur al-Din in 549/1154. As a city gate, Bab Kisan was again renovated by the Mamluks before it finally became incorporated into the church building.

I.1.f **Bab Sharqi**

Return to the busy street, and continue to walk eastwards, facing the traffic. Walk past the tower and the walls as they curve northwards reaching the triple-arched gate known as Bab Sharqi (Eastern Gate).

Bab Sharqi is the oldest extant standing monument in Damascus. It still preserves its original Roman form, attributed to the reign of Augustus (d. AD 14), during which it was called the Gate of the Sun, and mentioned in the Bible as the "Street Called Straight". Bab Sharqi comprises a triple passageway, a large central arch and two flanking smaller arches. A single gate being more defensible, the two side entrances were blocked up during the Islamic period. The minaret is evidence of Nur al-Din's reconstructions, as are the extensions of the wall, albeit with smaller stones, the arrow slits and the machicolations.

I.1.g **Tower of al-Salih Ayyub**
(Option)

Continue walking around the walls for a further 500 m, past the traffic triangle, cemetery and contemporary mosque on your left. Directly facing the mosque is the base of the square tower.

ITINERARY I *Religion, Science and the Transmission of Knowledge under the Atabegs and Ayyubids*
Damascus: Old City Walls, Towers and Gates

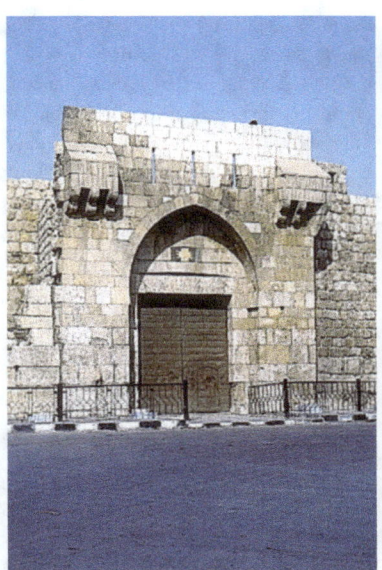
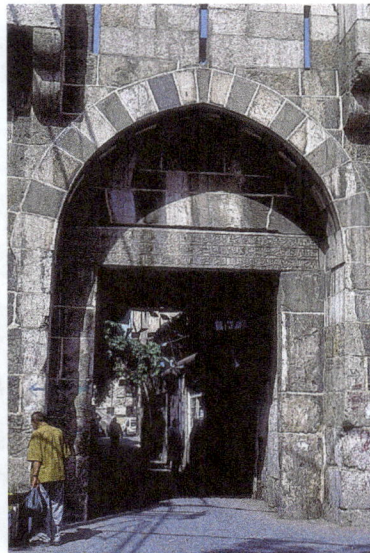
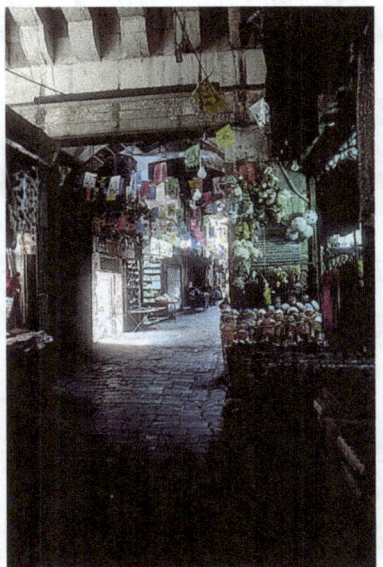
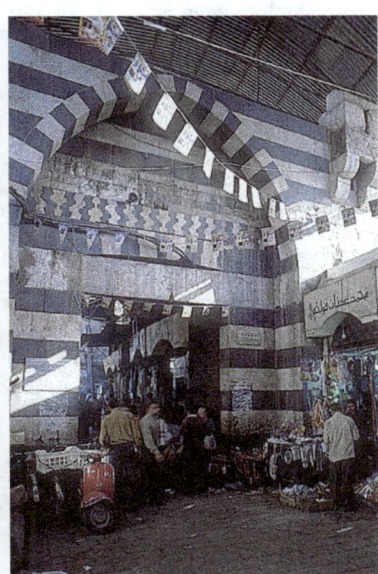

City Gates, Damascus.
Clockwise:
Bab Touma,
Bab al-Salam,
Bab al-Faradis,
Bab al-Faraj.

The Tower of al-Salih Ayyub allocates the north-eastern corner of the city walls. It is part of the final refortification programme of the Ayyubid period under al-Salih Ayyub (d. 646/1247–8). Traces of the gardens that once bloomed along the northern stretches of the city wall and the Barada river are faintly echoed by the patches of greenery around the tower.

I.1.h Bab Touma

A further 250 m to the west, is Bab Touma (St Thomas's Gate), separated from the city walls and located on an island amidst traffic.

Bab Touma, which was in Roman times the Gate of Venus, stands as a stately double gate, which underwent reconstruction during the Ayyubid period in 624/1227, and Mamluk defensive and decorative additions in 734/1333–4. The exceptionally well-preserved quality of this gate is exemplary. It features a guardroom and arrows slits above the arch, flanked by a pair of box machicolations.

I.1.i Bab al-Salam

From Bab Touma, walk westwards into the narrow street between the remains of the river and the city wall. Continue walking down this street for 450 m until you arrive at Bab al-Salam.

Known in the medieval period, Bab Salama – the Gate of Soundness, health and peace – it is one of the most beautiful gates of the city. There is a prominent monumental inscription on the gate's lintel. This is a 7th-/13th-century Ayyubid reconstruction built by al-Salih Isma'il, smoothly incorporating Roman blocks and Nur al-Din's extensions of 561/1171–2. The attractive masonry along the arch of the gate is decorated with a pronounced ablaq motif of alternating limestone and basalt. Arrow-slits and box machicolations protrude around the corner to overlook the bend in the river as well as the communications routes beyond. Its riverside location made it a popular spot for tanneries which required water for the manufacture of leather goods.

I.1.j Bab al-Faradis

Continuing westwards towards Malik Faisal Street and turning left into the Amara Suq, stands Bab al-Faradis, now acting as a threshold between the inner and outer Amara neighbourhoods.

Bab al-Faradis, meaning Gate of Paradise, alludes to the once-blossoming district along the banks of the river. The structure dates from Nur al-Din's period and it was originally constructed as a double gateway, as can be seen by the cross-vaulted ceiling in front of the gate.

I.1.k Bab al-Faraj

Lastly, Bab al-Faraj is reached by returning to Malik Faisal Street and walking further west, turning left into the busy Manakhliye Suq (Market of the Sieves) where the gate is located.

Bab al-Faraj, or the Gate of Deliverance, is the only gate that has no Roman precedent but is entirely the work of Nur al-Din, built in 549/1154. Located closest to the citadel, its name indicates the sense of optimism and triumph Nur al-Din was establishing in the city. This gate was also refortified by the Ayyubids and rebuilt again in the 7th/13th century.

I.2 DAMASCUS CITADEL

At the end of Malik Faisal Street, turn left walking against the traffic to arrive at Damascus Citadel. Entry into the recently restored citadel is by the west gate, behind the equestrian statue of Salah al-Din. Opening times are Wed–Mon 9.00–18.00 during the summer, 9.00–16.00 during the winter. Parts of the Citadel are open to the public free of charge, while other areas require an entrance fee. Closed on Tuesdays and during Friday prayers (approx 11.00–13.00). The Citadel occasionally hosts special events and festivals.

Functioning as a city within the city, Damascus Citadel was extensively refortified by al-Malik al-'Adil between 599–610/1203–14. It measures approximately 220 m x 150 m; a near rectangular layout with the north-western corner curving inward to accommodate the River Barada. Built on top of Roman remains, and Seljuq restructuring of 469/1076–7, it also has some important additions by Nur al-Din and Salah al-Din. The bulk of the Citadel, however, is al-Malik al-'Adil's construction and many inscriptions attest to his systematic fortification of the site. The most prominent one is now found on the north-eastern tower's exterior. Thought to have been located originally on the north gate, known as *Bab al-Hadid*, or the Gate of

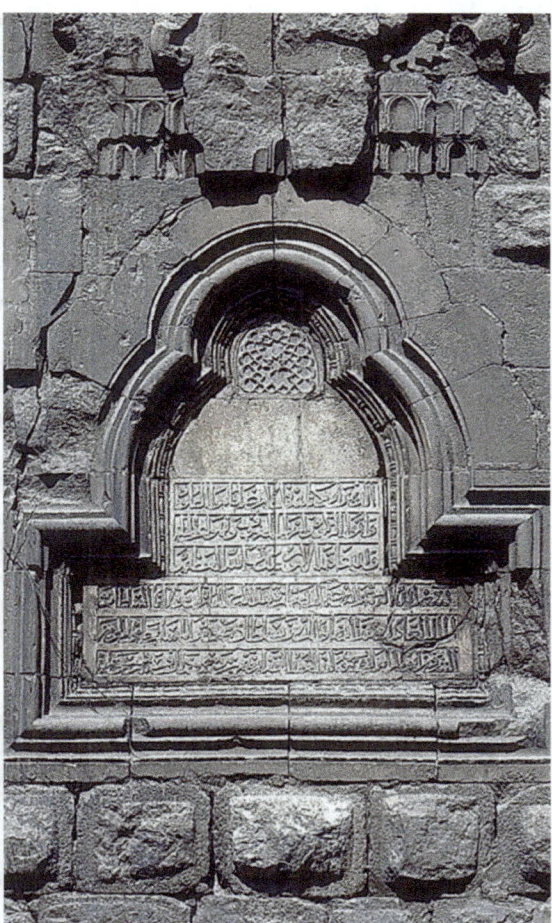

Damascus Citadel, inscription panel of al-'Adil.

ITINERARY I *Religion, Science and the Transmission of Knowledge under the Atabegs and Ayyubids*
Damascus Citadel

Damascus Citadel, detail of the eastern gate's stone muqarnas.

Damascus Citadel, view of the so-called Throne Room.

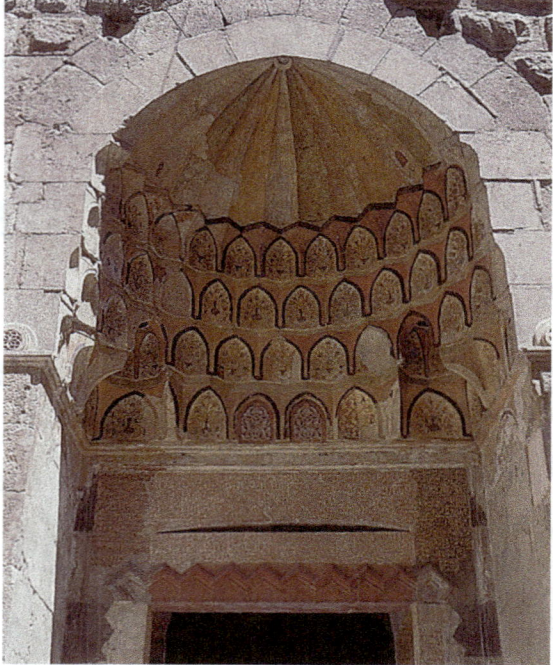

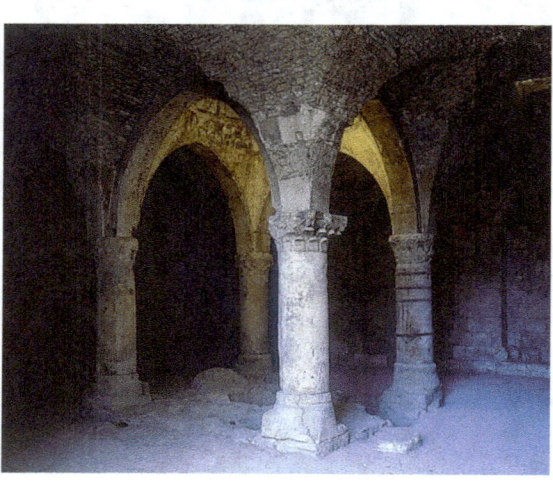

Steel, it features three surrounding *burjs* and a non-direct entry passage as well as a drawbridge across the moat. The west gate, known as the *Bab al-Sirr* or the Secret Gate, is hardly visible from the exterior, and was designed to be inconspicuous. It includes remnants of a hinge, used for a portcullis, a sliding metal gate, which is a distinctive feature of Ayyubid-period defences. This area leads to the south-west area of the citadel, thought to be the site of the Ayyubid palace. Recent excavations, however, have uncovered traces of metal-working and arrowheads, indicating that the gallery was probably used for the manufacture of military tools.

By far the most artistically magnificent, gate is the East Gate, used as the formal entry into the citadel during the Ayyubid period. It features the first stone *muqarnas* in Damascus, prior to which brick was the regular medium. This *muqarnas* is copiously inscribed and beautifully painted. The different layers of colour have been carefully removed to reveal a repertoire of decorative motifs from the Ayyubid period as well as later Mamluk and Ottoman additions. A passageway from this portal leads to a nine-vaulted hall, once thought of as a "throne room", but which has recently been re-interpreted as a reception room or meeting area. Scholars have suggested that personnel from the military North Gate and the palatial East Gate would have filed through corridors to meet up in this vaulted hall. It has a central cupola mounted on thick pillars with roman *spolia* capitals framed by a circular *muqarnas* rim.

1.3 BIMARISTAN NUR AL-DIN

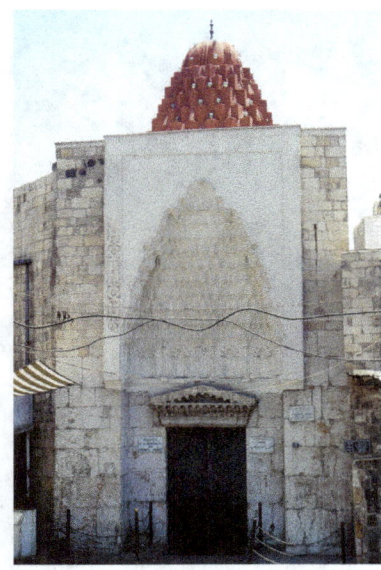

Bimaristan Nur al-Din, view of the entrance façade, Damascus.

Enter the covered market, Suq al-Hamidiyya, and walk down the thoroughfare for 250 m, counting the streets on the right that are perpendicular to the main axis. At the fifth street, turn right, the bimaristan *is on the left-hand side some 75 m further on. It is currently the Museum of Arabic Medicine and Science. Opening times are Wed–Mon 9.00–14.00. Closed on Tuesdays and during Friday prayers (approx 11.00–13.00). There is an entrance fee.*

Bimaristan Nur al-Din is immediately recognisable by its red-brick *muqarnas* dome rhythmically dotted with dark, glass bulbs. Constructed in 549/1154, this hospital features the first *muqarnas* dome in Damascus and clearly indicates the strong Eastern architectural influences, which were brought to Damascus by Nur al-Din from Mosul. It is also one of the earliest surviving *bimaristans* of the region, featuring a perfectly formed four-*iwans* in-axial-symmetry plan with a central courtyard, similarly inspired by Eastern architectural styles. It became the model for subsequent *bimaristan* constructions, such as the Bimaristan al-Qaymari in the Salihiyya district, north of Damascus.

Bimaristan Nur al-Din has an entrance block that protrudes at a right angle to the building. Its portal features an undulating and unusually tall *muqarnas* façade with a row of lobed arches at the base. These, curiously, rest on top of

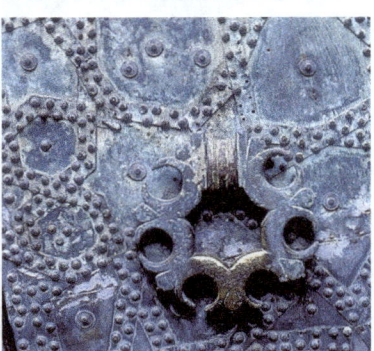

Bimaristan Nur al-Din, detail of door-knocker and geometric decoration on the gate.

a classically styled gate lintel. Another important artistic aspect of the *bimaristan*'s entrance is its wooden gate, a distinctive example of woodcarving with astral motifs. Its designer Abu al-Fadl Muhammad bin 'Abd-al-Karim al-Harithi, known as al-Muhandis, was

ITINERARY I   *Religion, Science and the Transmission of Knowledge under the Atabegs and Ayyubids*
Bimaristan Nur al-Din

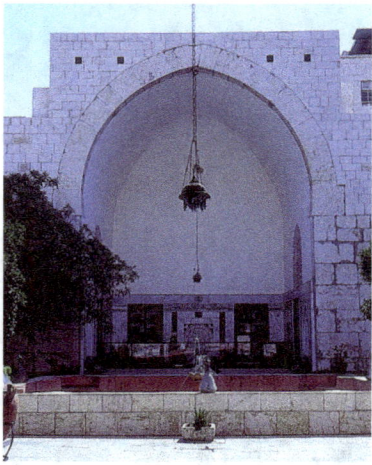

Bimaristan Nur al-Din, view of the courtyard and main iwan, Damascus.

both a medical doctor and a geometrician during the Atabeg period. The entrance leads into a spacious, square vestibule which now includes a ticketing booth to the left and a taxonomy museum to

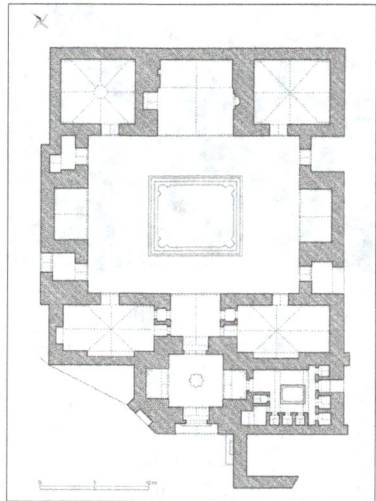

Floor-plan of Bimaristan Nur al-Din.

the right. But the overhead sight of the vestibule is a mesmerising vision of gradually receding cells pierced by beams of light, an affect created by the corbelled dome.

Inside the *bimaristan*, the symmetrical four-*iwans* plan around the rectangular courtyard measuring 20 m x 15 m, is planted with orange and almond trees that frame its central stone-carved basin, which is typically designed with bracketed inner corners. The east *iwan*, which is larger than the others and faces the entrance, would have been designated for the use of medical students to attend lectures by renowned physicians and would have given access to a medical library. A marble dado rail with a perfectly legible cursive inscription quotes passages from the Qur'an pertaining to medicine and healing, while an oval-shaped plaque indicates Nur al-Din's patronage. Overlooking the south-western corner of the courtyard, the original arched window of perforated stucco still survives. Its design is a grid of octagonal stars with interlacing floral scrolls.

The Bimaristan Nur al-Din currently functions as the Museum of Arabic Medicine and Science. Many of the objects, documents and miniature paintings on display, some originals and some reproductions, indicate the influence of Islamic medicine on the European Renaissance period and modern science, as well as the cross-Mediterranean travel of Muslim doctors to European courts. Specialised medical tools and pharmaceutical pottery containers are also on display.

ITINERARY I Religion, Science and the Transmission of Knowledge under the Atabegs and Ayyubids
Madrasat Nur al-Din

I.4 MADRASAT NUR AL-DIN

Leaving the bimaristan, turn left around the corner, walking towards the Harika Suq (Gold Market); then turn right at the covered Suq al-Khayyatin (Tailors' Market). The Madrasat Nur al-Din is situated 20 m into the suq. Now a mosque is open to visitors respecting appropriate dress codes and conduct, but it is likely to be closed apart from during prayer times (approx 11.00–13.00). A small donation is advisable. There is no public access to the mausoleum, but one can peek into it through the window grilles above the water fountain that serves the suq.

This grand *madrasa* and its annexed mausoleum belongs to Nur al-Din and, like the *bimaristan*, features a red-brick *muqarnas* dome. The writer, Ibn al-Jubayr visited this *madrasa* in 580/1184 and describes it as "one of the finest colleges in the world". The entrance to the *madrasa* is on the east side through a recessed *muqarnas* portal and a structurally impressive cross-vaulted vestibule. Historians have recorded the burial of Nur al-Din in this *madrasa* upon his death in 569/1174, and the rectangular cenotaph located to the left of the entrance is inscribed with a large and simple cursive calligraphic relief (*thuluth*) typical of Nur al-Din's constructs. A large frieze executed in a similar script circumscribes the four walls of the room under the dome and typically contains "*Ayat al-Kursi*", the most auspicious verse of the Qur'an (2:255). Typically, the tomb chamber includes windows overlooking the street, thereby receiving the blessings of passers-by, and a *mihrab* featuring two antique colonnettes in the south (*qibla*) wall to indicate the direction of Mecca.

Back in the vestibule, a staircase leads up to the residential chambers used by students and professors. Straight ahead, the *madrasa*'s courtyard pool appears, similar in design to the pool in Nur al-Din's Bimaristan, but with the addition of an above-ground water channel flowing from a fountain in the back wall of the

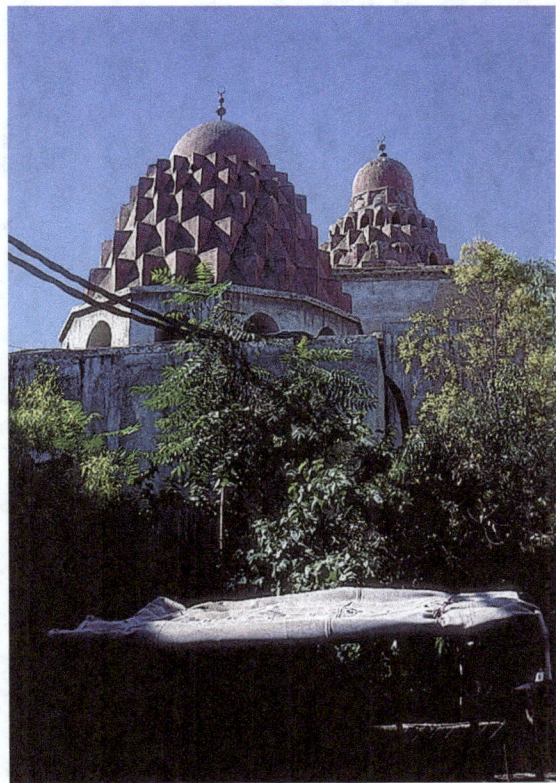

Madrasa and Mausoleum of Nur al-Din, exterior view of the muqarnas *domes, Damascus.*

ITINERARY I   *Religion, Science and the Transmission of Knowledge under the Atabegs and Ayyubids*
Hammam Nur al-Din

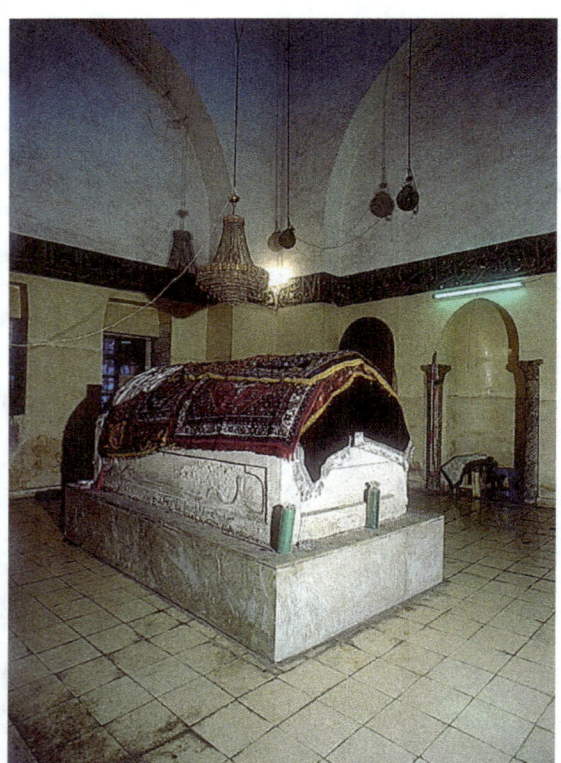

Madrasa and Mausoleum of Nur al-Din, view of the cenotaph, Damascus.

muqarnas dome does not form part of the Nur al-Din complex but is actually a Mamluk-period construct. Nevertheless, it gives visual testimony to the continuation of the architectural heritage that Nur al-Din brought with him from the East and also political testimony to the continued admiration of Nur al-Din's leadership.

I.5 HAMMAM NUR AL-DIN

Return to the entrance of Suq al-Khayyatin and turn left, walking towards Suq al-Slah (Armoury Market) and Suq al-Bzuriye (Spice Market). Upon reaching the bottom of Suq al-Bzuriye, turn right and walk up the street (south) for 30 m. Hammam Nur al-Din is on the left, just before the imposing Ottoman-era khan. As it is still in use, men may enter the hammam *to visit or to bathe at any time before midnight. Women cannot enter the* hammam *except by special appointment.*

western *iwan*, and thereby offering the glistening effect of water falling over the stone. This type of fountain is known as a *salsabil*, and Ibn Jubayr does not fail to note its beauty. To the left of the courtyard is the wide prayer-hall, including an original *mihrab* and a recently added *minbar*. Thus the visitor to this *madrasa* is greeted by the auspicious abundance of water as well as accommodation for study and prayer.

A domed-chamber to the north of the entrance with a near-identical red

Hammam Nur al-Din is one of the oldest in Damascus and still in regular use today. None of its multiple domes are apparent from the exterior, but they would have been very prominent when it was first constructed. The *hammam* has undergone many recent renovations and the large domed chamber immediately inside the entrance is from the Ottoman period. The bathing halls proper are still the original Nuri constructions. Furthest from the entrance is where the bathing experience begins, starting with the *frigidarium*, or cold-water chambers, known as *barrani* or the "exterior areas"; these are composed of three sequential square rooms with octagonal interiors and domed roofs of varying sizes. The middle room is larger than the front and back rooms, and it contains the passage-way to the *tepidarium*, or warm-water chambers, known as *wustani*, or the "middle areas". The architectural style and layout of the *hammam* underlines the centrality of the *wustani*, which is of a large octagonal shape and capped by a gored dome resting on a drum of 16 niches. The interior of the *wustani* is perfectly symmetrical. Small ledge-like annexations with pointed-arch entries, known as *maqsura*s, open up on its four diagonal sides and offer bathers some seclusion. Passageways at the front and back of the room lead to the hot and cold areas respectively, while to the right and left are two more rectangularly shaped rooms, each surmounted by two small octagonal domes. These rooms are usually used for facilities like massage and depilation.

Finally, there is the *calidarium*, the hot-water chamber, known as *juwwani* or the "interior areas", which is a wide and barrel-vaulted oblong space with curved sides. Steam enters the room through a side-vent linked to the furnace, or *bayt al-nar*, known colloquially as "*qimmim*". This is the hottest room where bathers rest on stone benches.

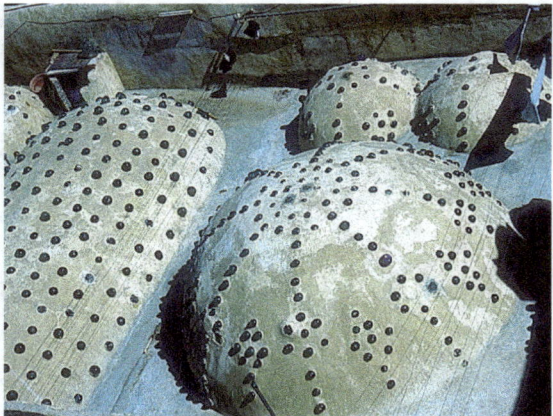

Hammam Nur al-Din, exterior view of the domes, vault and qamariyyat, Damascus.

1.6 GREAT UMAYYAD MOSQUE

Return to the bottom of the Suq al-Bzuriye (Spice Market), turn left, then right, and walk southwards into Suq Slah (Armoury Market). The Mosque, in the heart of Damascus, lies directly before you. Foreigners are advised to enter from the northern gate, announcing themselves at the cloakroom/ticket office. Respecting appropriate dress codes and conduct, the mosque can be visited any time during the day. A small donation is recommended, and tourists are expected to pay a small fee.

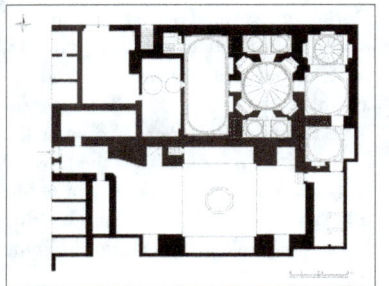

Floor-plan of Hammam Nur al-Din.

ITINERARY I *Religion, Science and the Transmission of Knowledge under the Atabegs and Ayyubids*
Great Umayyad Mosque

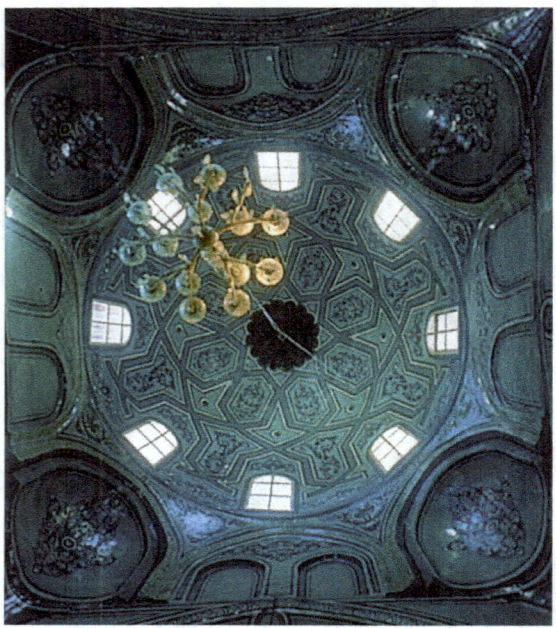

Great Umayyad Mosque, view of the Mashhad al-Hussein located inside the mosque, Damascus.

The Great Umayyad Mosque is the ultimate religious centre of **Damascus** and also one of the earliest monuments of Islam. Its open courtyard and rectilinear plan has been described as "hypostyle" in reference to the support of the prayer-hall's roof on multiple rhythmically spaced columns. The most remarkable feature of this mosque is its brilliant mosaics of green, blue and gold and its abundant use of marble.

Nevertheless, the mosque suffered many fires and required careful restoration during the Atabeg and Ayyubid reigns. During the medieval period, the Mosque's three minarets were renovated, two during Seljuq rule, distinguished by their square-based towers, and the third under Mamluk patronage. Several patches of the surviving mosaic belong to Nur al-Din's restoration period in the mid $6^{th}/12^{th}$ century, in which he clearly followed the example of the founding father of the mosque, the Umayyad caliph Al-Walid bin 'Abd al-Malik. Some of the marble re-panelling also occurred under Salah al-Din's reign. Every ruler wanted to leave his mark on the Great Umayyad Mosque in order to underline his religious piety and political legitimacy.

The most complete extant renovation from the Ayyubid period is found in the Mashhad al-Hussein, designed in typical Ayyubid-mausoleum fashion. Overly renovated and repainted in modern times, its architectural layout clearly follows the plan of the Ayyubid mausoleum: a square chamber capped by a dome, resting on an octagonal drum. The diagonals of the drum are arched niches, serving as squinches for the base of the dome, which includes eight windows.

As a centre for the dissemination of religious knowledge, mosques always played an important role as a public gathering place. The mosque courtyard was the only public square in the city. During the Ayyubid period, it supported many important circles, or *halaqas*, for teaching. The renowned theologian al-Ghazali (d. 505/1111) is known to have taught in a corner, known as the *zawiya* of the mosque. Thus the mosque was always available as a space for public education whereby scholars seeking higher or more concentrated learning would attend the *madrasas*.

ITINERARY I   *Religion, Science and the Transmission of Knowledge under the Atabegs and Ayyubids*
Great Umayyad Mosque

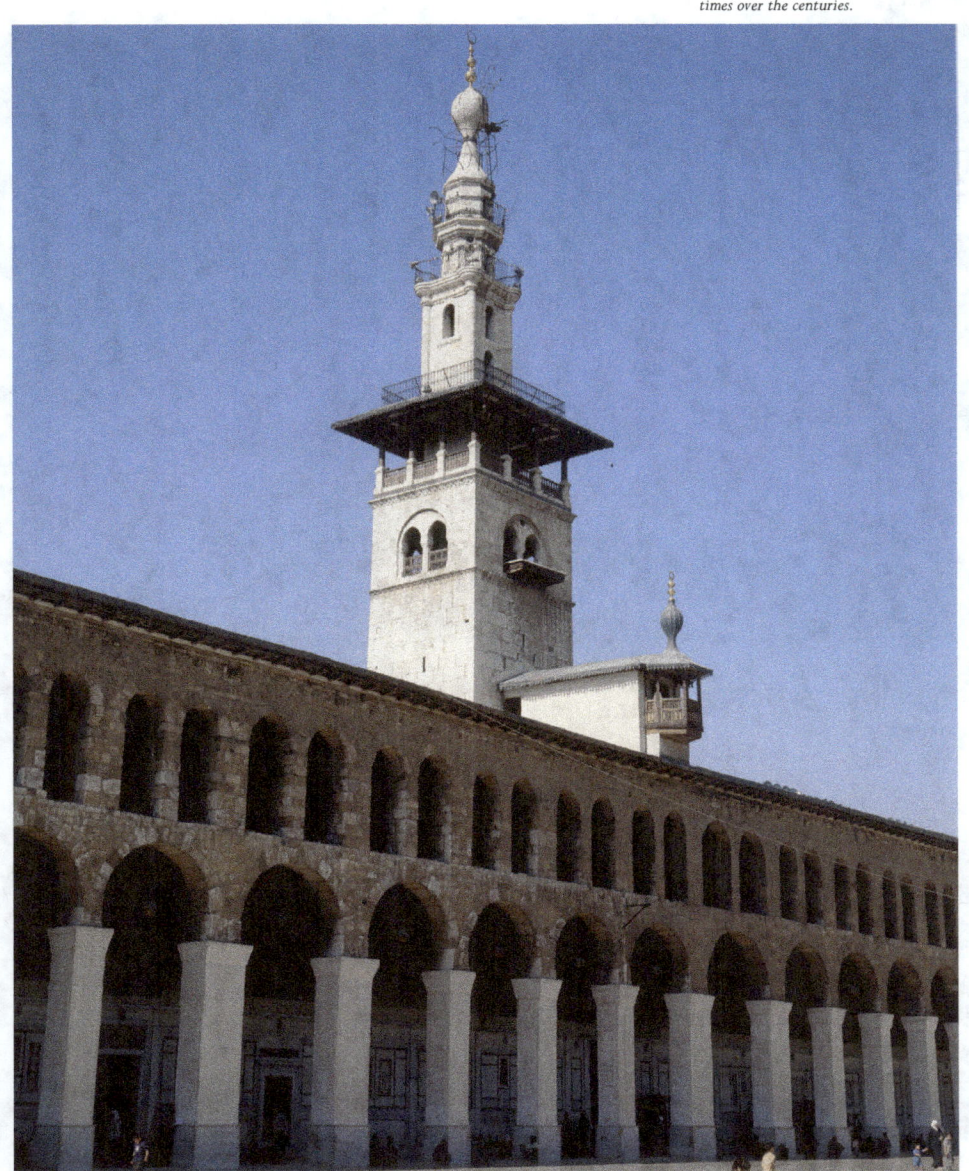

Great Umayyad Mosque, view of the courtyard and of a minaret, Damascus. The mosque has been restored at various times over the centuries.

ITINERARY I   Religion, Science and the Transmission of Knowledge under the Atabegs and Ayyubids
Mausoleum of Salah al-Din

Mausoleum of Salah al-Din, Damascus.

A 19th-century sketch of the Mausoleum of Salah al-Din, Damascus, by Harry Finn (Wilson, 1881–84).

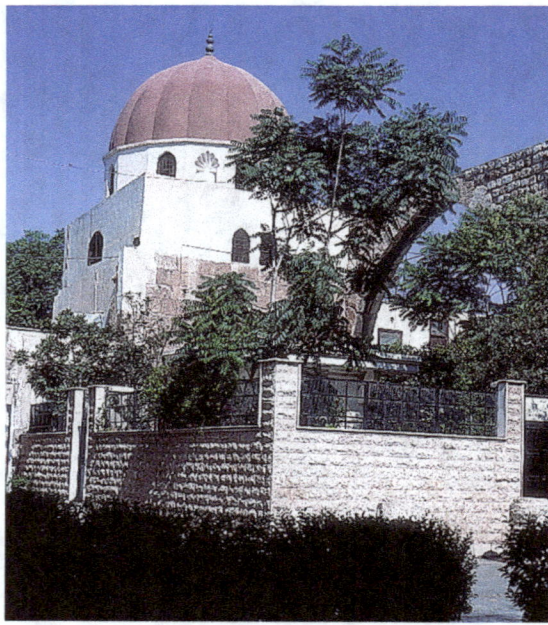

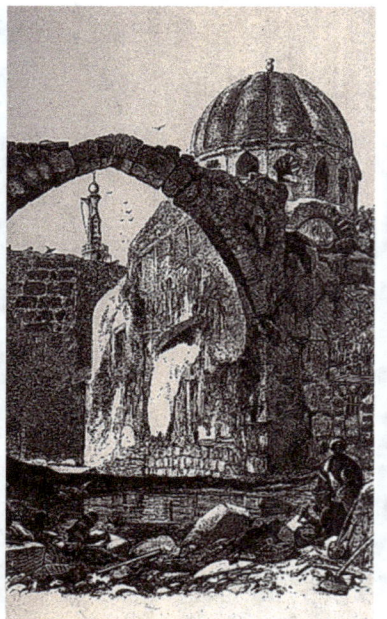

I.7 MAUSOLEUM OF SALAH AL-DIN

North of the Great Umayyad Mosque, the Mausoleum lies directly behind the chamber that serves as a cloakroom for foreigners visiting the Great Umayyad Mosque. It can be visited at any time during the day.

The construction of the tomb is typically Damascene Ayyubid: a square chamber with *ablaq* walls, and four arches capped by a cupola. The exterior of the dome is lobed. The movement from square chamber to circular dome is achieved by a transitional drum in two zones: a wide octagonal base followed by a 16-sided polygon with alternating arched windows and lobed niches. The *darih* or mausoleum was built under the auspices of one of Salah al-Din's sons, al-Afdal, while the attached *madrasa* was constructed under the orders of another of Salah al-Din's sons, al-Malik al-'Aziz, and known as Madrasa al-'Aziziyya. The wide arch that once framed the garden is the only surviving remnant of the *madrasa*.

Salah al-Din died in 589/1193 and many contemporary records of his death survive. Interred initially at the Damascus Citadel, his body was transferred to its final resting place on the holy day of

ITINERARY I *Religion, Science and the Transmission of Knowledge under the Atabegs and Ayyubids*
Mausoleum of Salah al-Din

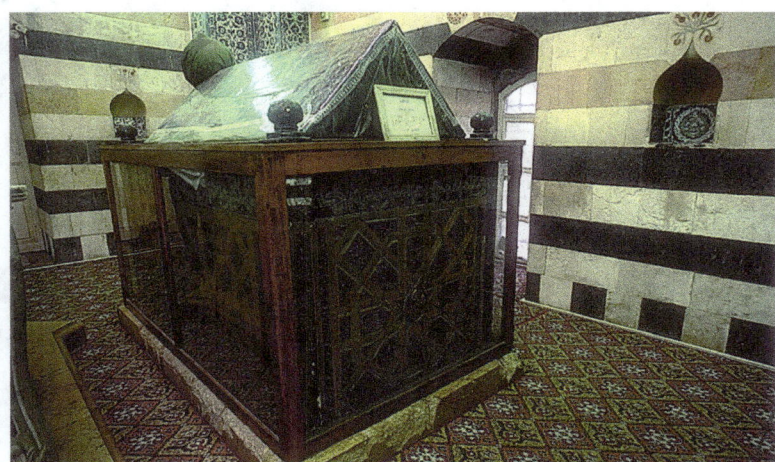

The wooden cenotaph of Salah al-Din, Damascus, partially restored.

'*Ashura* in 592/1195, once the mausoleum/*madrasa* complex was completed. There are two sarcophagi inside the mausoleum. The wooden one is the original, a masterpiece of Ayyubid aestheticism, featuring inlaid panels of octagonal designs filled-in with spiralling curves of floral motifs, with an inscription banner in *kufic* script running across the top; all the components of which are executed with faultless precision. There is some decay along the edges and two of the original side-panels are lost. As for the white marble cenotaph, it is thought to have been a gift from the German Emperor William II who visited Damascus in 1898.

The interior of the tomb-chamber is mounted with blue and green Ottoman tiles of the 11th/17th century known as *qashani*, which the Ottomans bestowed in order to leave their mark on the important monuments of Damascus and, of course, as an expression of gratitude to Salah al-Din for having liberated Jerusalem from the Crusaders.

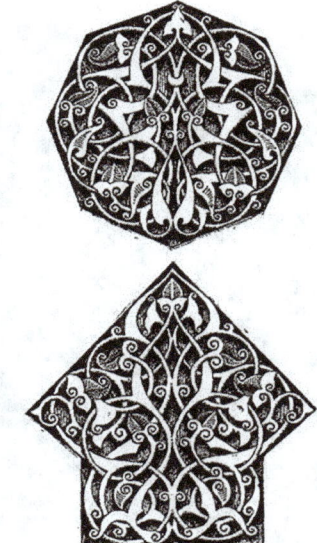

Detail of the wood-carving on the cenotaph of Salah al-Din, Damascus (Sauvaget, Revue des Arts Asiatiques, 1930).

95

ITINERARY I   *Religion, Science and the Transmission of Knowledge under the Atabegs and Ayyubids*
Madrasa al-'Adiliyya

Madrasa al-'Adiliyya, detail of the stone-carved portal, Damascus.

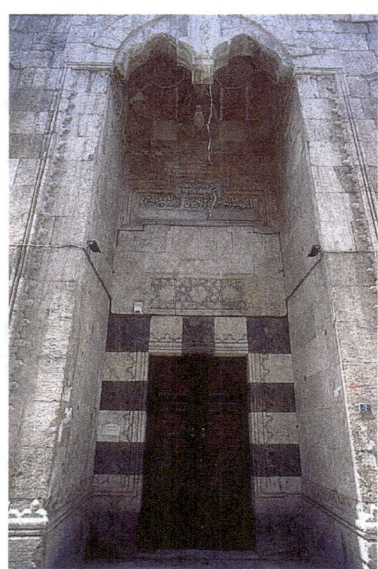

Madrasa al-'Adiliyya, view of the courtyard and basin, Damascus.

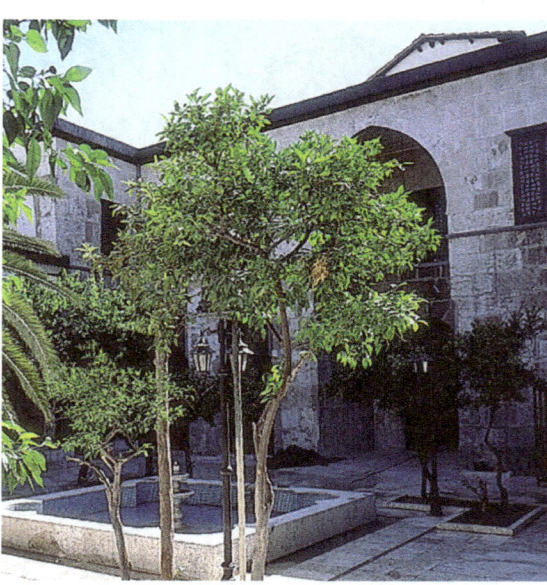

I.8 MADRASA AL-'ADILIYYA

Leave the mosque, walking past the cloakroom, turn right and then left. Arriving on Zahiriyya Street, walk 60 m and then turn right at the Zahiriyya Library, conspicuous by its large entrance and its ochre-tinted dome. The Madrasa al-'Adiliyya directly faces the Zahiriyya Library which also has a notable muqarnas *entrance. As the* madrasa *is currently undergoing restoration, access to the interior is irregular.*

One of Nur al-Din later monuments, this *madrasa* was founded in 568/1172 but its construction was interrupted by Nur al-Din's death in 569/1174. It was not until the reign of the Ayyubid al-Malik al-'Adil in 592/1196 that construction was resumed and finally completed by Al-'Adil's son, al-Malik al-Mu'azzam, who spent a further four years preparing the mausoleum for his father and instating a *waqf* or endowment for the upkeep of the *madrasa* in perpetuity. By 620/1223 it was finally complete. It is one of the best surviving examples of an Ayyubid *madrasa* in Damascus, made of large and perfectly measured blocks of stone.

The portal is unique in Ayyubid architecture, flaunting skilled stone carving that betrays a strong northern influence, probably the work of Aleppine architects. There is a frame of bracketed stone moulding around the entry, and rows of *ablaq* stone blocks. The overhanging vault is decorated with a pair of square-based *muqarnas* domes hidden behind a hanging pendant keystone and tri-lobed arches.

The entrance leads through a cross-vaulted vestibule similar to that of Madrasa Nur al-Din, into an immense central courtyard with a newly restored fountain. The northern *iwan* to the left features a barrel-vaulted ceiling. Straight ahead is a narrow *iwan* flanked by four cells used as student accommodation. A long prayer-hall with five entry bays and a central *mihrab* is accessible to the right. The northwestern corner features a small chamber made of large limestone blocks, a so-called *khalwa* used as a place for meditation or prayer in seclusion. Dominating the south-eastern corner of the *madrasa* is al-Malik al-'Adil's grand mausoleum. The mausoleum is a spacious domed chamber with a pair of windows overlooking each side of the street corner in order to invite the blessings of passers-by. Aleppine architectural techniques can be seen in the usage of squinches which carry the dome, as opposed to the local style of using load-bearing drums.

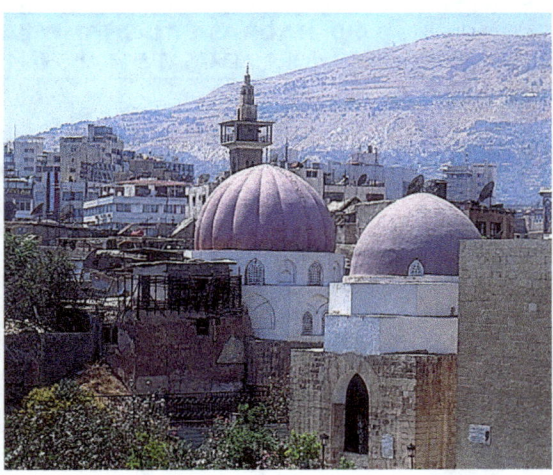

Najmiyya Mausoleum seen alongside Madrasa al-Shamiyya, Damascus.

I.9 NAJMIYYA MAUSOLEUM
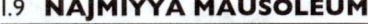

Exit the walled city north of the citadel and walk northwards towards the modern road bridge known as Jisr al-Thawra. The two monuments, Madrasa Najmiyya and Madrasa Shamiyya, are directly across from where you are standing, partially hidden behind the bridge. Use the pedestrian access to cross the street. Access to the interior is irregular.

The Najmiyya Mausoleum is a prime example of a Damascene freestanding tomb. It was built for members of the Ayyubid family and named after Salah al-Din's father, Najm al-Din Ayyub (d. 568/1172–3). The cemetery grounds in which the tomb was located originally stretched along the banks of the canalised River Barada, west of the walled city. It would have included the Madrasa Sitt al-Sham, still located on the same plot as the Najmiyya, as well as other dynastic monuments with funerary grounds. The mausoleum is typically square with a lobed dome that rises above two zones of transition, an octagon and a hexadecagon. It contains four Ayyubid tombs. On the outside, above the small entrance, are seven lines of small *thuluth* script alluding to the burial of one of Salah al-Din's son al-Malik al-Mansur Hasan in 575/1178–9. His is the southernmost tomb. Also preserved in the interior are traces of a stucco frieze with interlaced geometric ornamentation.

ITINERARY I *Religion, Science and the Transmission of Knowledge under the Atabegs and Ayyubids*
Madrasa al-Shamiyya

I.10 MADRASA AL-SHAMIYYA (OR MADRASAT SITT AL-SHAM)

The Madrasa al-Shamiyya is on the same plot of land as the Madrasa Najmiyya, next to each other.

This *madrasa* survives as one of the best-maintained examples of an Ayyubid funerary ground – or *madrasa* and *turba* complex – constructed in 585/1189. Its size and layout is unusual when compared to other types found in Damascus, and it was originally much larger than its current state. Its tomb-chamber is rectangular rather than square, with a vaulted roof rather than domed. There is a rectangular courtyard with an *ablaq* arcade creating a porch between the courtyard and the subsequent halls. There is a rectangular water-basin and a large funerary hall next to each other on the western side, and an oratory that overlooks the *turba* and a square-cut minaret to the eastern side. The complex of this *madrasa* would have included dwellings for students and teachers.

By far the most remarkable feature is the funerary hall, a rectangular arch-vaulted chamber entered from its longest side through a tripartite gate which faces the courtyard pool. It is designed in perfect axial symmetry with recessed windows on each side and a *mihrab* on the southern wall. Most exquisite of all is the survival of the painted and pierced stucco work that once covered the interior. This stucco is applied in compartmentalised fields of geometric arabesques, calligraphic banners and bracketed moulding along the frames around the different decorative

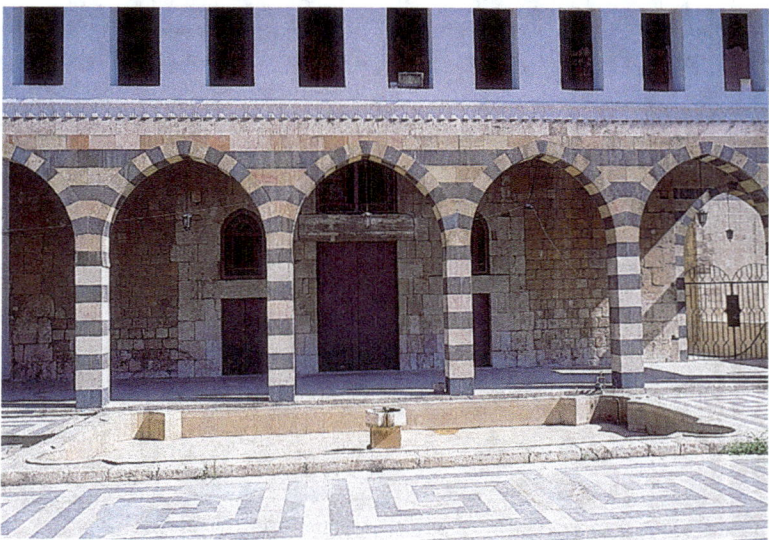

Madrasa al-Shamiyya, view of the courtyard and basin, Damascus.

ITINERARY I   *Religion, Science and the Transmission of Knowledge under the Atabegs and Ayyubids*
Madrasa al-Shamiyya

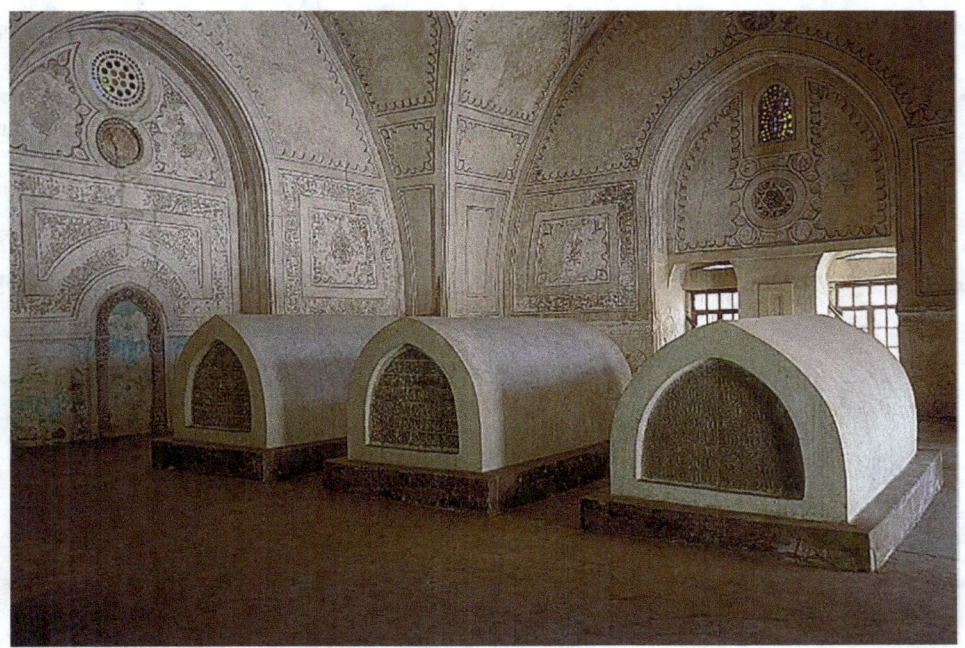

Madrasa al-Shamiyya, view of the three tombs in the stucco-decorated mausoleum, Damascus.

fields and the ribs of the vaults. A beautiful example is the interlacing medallion based on the *kufic*-style geometric rendition of the Prophet Muhammad's name, which is repeated six times to form a hexagonal pattern with a central arabesque, located in the middle of the recessed arch in the eastern wall.

Three tombs rest here and, according to the inscriptions, Sitt al-Sham began building this *turba* on the death of her brother Turan Shah, ruler of Yemen, who died in 576/1180. Turan Shah's tomb is the southernmost one, that furthest from the entrance. The middle tomb contains Nasir al-Din bin Shirkuh, ruler of Homs (d. 581/1185–6), who was Sitt al-Sham's first cousin and second husband. As for the northernmost tomb, nearest the entrance, this carries Sitt al-Sham's son, Husam al-Din Lagin (d. 587/1191). Sitt al-Sham was inhumed in her son's tomb when she died in 616/1220.

THE *BIMARISTAN*S AND PUBLIC HEALTH

Yasser Tabbaa

*Bimaristan*s were centres for both medical treatment and education, endowed with libraries, which were accessible for training physicians. Illustrated scientific manuscripts reveal scholars within affluent architectural settings, as can be seen in the Arabic *De Materia Medica* translations from Baghdad. While the first *bimaristan*s were built in Baghdad between the 2nd/8th and 4th/10th centuries, the earliest existing *bimaristan*s are those built in Syria by Nur al-Din, who was largely responsible for the revival of the hospital as an institution. His two surviving *bimaristan*s in Aleppo and in Damascus are especially important because they give us a clear idea of the architectural form of this institution, which invariably adopted the four-*iwan*s-in-axial-symmetry plan with a central pool and surrounding rooms on one level. In the Bimaristan al-Nuri in Aleppo the plan was modified in the 7th/13th century with the addition of a second hall with surrounding chambers. The Bimaristan al-Nuri in Damascus is one of the most famous hospitals in medieval Islam. It was noted for the many prominent physicians who practiced there, including Ibn al-Mutran (d. 587/1191), who was Salah al-Din's private physician. It was also influential in terms of its architectural layout, which was copied for the Bimaristan al-Qaymari in Salihiyya, and seems to have influenced several hospitals in Anatolia and in Cairo, including the famous Egyptian *bimaristan*s of Salah al-Din and Qalawun, built in 569/1174 and 656/1285 respectively.

Offering free medical care for the poor and dispensing pharmaceutical drugs for those who required them, *bimaristan*s were very expensive to operate, the reason perhaps that so few were built. Quite considerable *waqf*s were needed for them to function efficiently, often requiring the revenues from *hammam*s, shops, mills, orchards and even entire villages.

Floor-plan of Bimaristan Nur al-Din, Damascus.

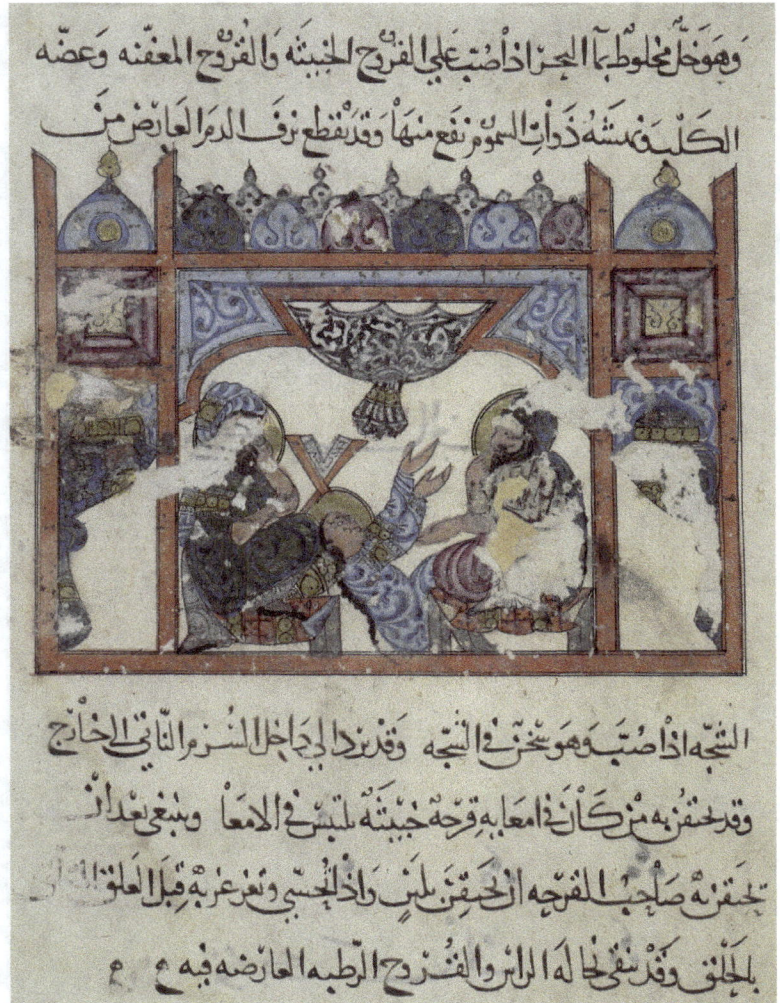

Illustration from the 6th/12th century manuscript De Materia Medica, *depicting physicians at work in fine architectural surroundings, British Museum, London (Inv. Num. 1934, 1013, 0.1; © Trustees of the British Museum, London).*

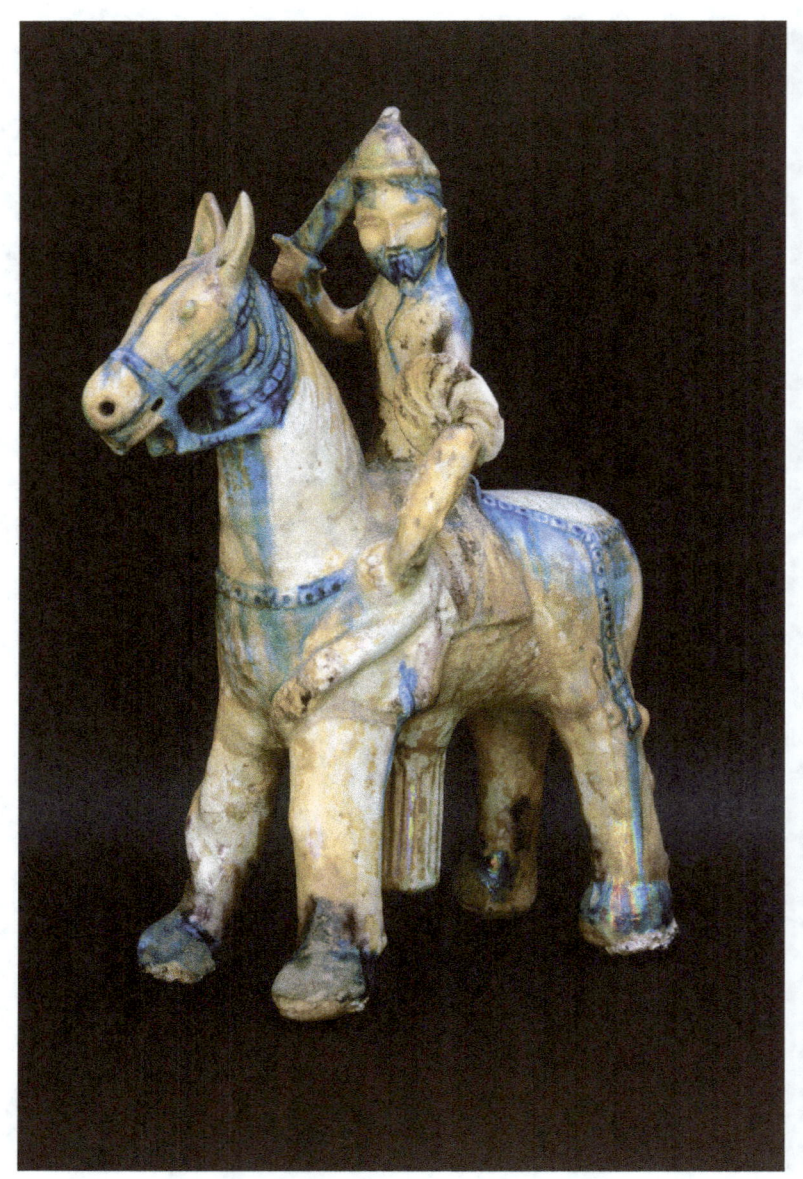

Ceramic statue of the "Faris al-Raqqa" or the "Horseman of al-Raqqa", National Museum of Damascus (Inv. Num. 5819/ج).

ITINERARY I
Second day

Religion, Science and the Transmission of Knowledge under the Atabegs and Ayyubids

Abd al-Razzaq Moaz, Zena Takieddine

NATIONAL MUSEUM OF DAMASCUS AND THE SALIHIYYA QUARTER

I.11 National Museum of Damascus
I.12 Farukhshahiyya and Amjadiyya Mausoleums (Option)
I.13 Salihiyya Quarter
I.14 Madrasa al-Jaharkasiyya
I.15 Bimaristan Qaymariyya
I.16 Hanabila Mosque
I.17 Madrasa al-Sahiba
I.18 Madrasa al-Rukniyya
I.19 Shibliyya Mausoleum
I.20 Badriyya Mausoleum
I.21 Madrasa Hafiziyya

Mechanical Sciences   Zena Takieddine

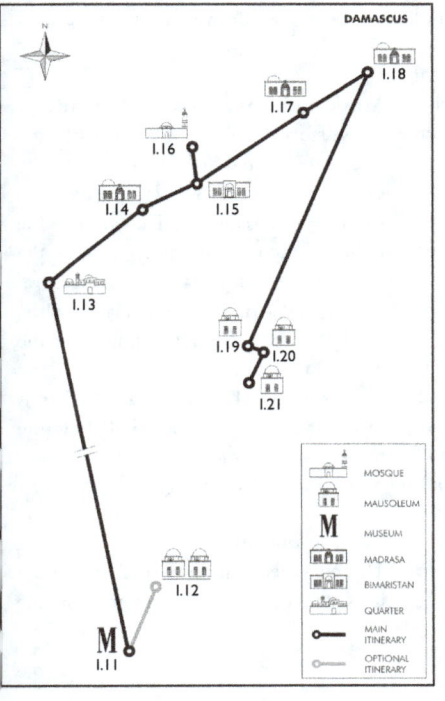

ITINERARY I *Religion, Science and the Transmission of Knowledge under the Atabegs and Ayyubids*
National Museum of Damascus

I.11 NATIONAL MUSEUM OF DAMASCUS

The museum is located on al-Quwatli Street, south of the River Barada and east of the Ottoman era Tekkiyye Suleimaniyye. Opening times are Wed–Mon 9.00–18.00 during the summer, 9.00–16.00 during the winter. Closed on Tuesdays and during Friday prayers (approx 11.00–13.00). There is an entrance fee.

The Museum building was constructed in 1936 by the French architect Michel Ecochard and includes important items from the Prehistoric era to the present. Its collection of Islamic art began in earnest when the Umayyad desert palace of Qasr al-Hayr al-Gharbi was discovered in the 1930s. The entrance to the museum incorporates the grand stucco-carved façade of the Qasr al-Hayr al-Gharbi, while the left-hand wing of the museum is dedicated to the paintings and sculptures from the palace. Ceramics, metalwork, stucco panels, woodcarving and manuscripts from the Ayyubid period are some of the most important objects on display.

"Horseman of Raqqa"

Known as the "Horseman of Raqqa" or "*Faris al-Raqqa*" this ceramic figurine exemplifies the skilled craftsmanship of the potters of Raqqa and also the strong influence the Eastern style had on the ceramics industry in Syria. The whiteness of the clay composition, known as fritware, was an invention inspired by Chinese porcelain, while the facial features, hairstyle and erect warrior pose of horse and rider are a celebration of Central Asian chivalry. The Central Asian nomadic tribes, from which the Seljuqs originated, were particularly famed for their skills as warriors and their agility on horseback. As for the method of decoration, where the surface is raised and highlighted in different colours to emphasise the ornamental features, this is known as the *laqabi* technique. Found along with this equestrian figurine, were luxury *Laqabi*-ware bowls and dishes. While production for this kind of luxurious pottery was centred in the city of Kashan in Persia, Raqqa was also an important centre for production in the region. Interaction between the two manufacturing centres was common, particularly through trade and patronage.

Maskaneh carved-stucco façade

These stucco friezes originally decorated a mosque located near the medieval city of Balis near Raqqa (VIII.2), and are dated to the $5^{th}/11^{th}$ century. They framed the façade of the tripartite prayer-hall of the mosque, with intricately carved floral and vegetal swirls that are related to the ancient stucco-carving technique of the Mesopotamian region, particularly the 'Abbasid capital of Samarra. The bands of Qur'anic phrases inscribed along the top of the niches are excellent examples of the Atabeg *kufic* calligraphic style.

Marble plaque

This engraved marble panel featured ten lines of carved inscription commemorating

ITINERARY I   Religion, Science and the Transmission of Knowledge under the Atabegs and Ayyubids
National Museum of Damascus

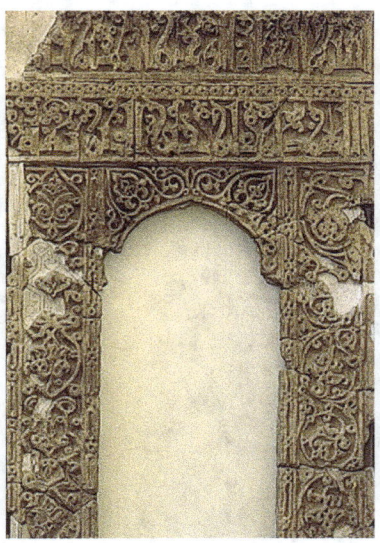

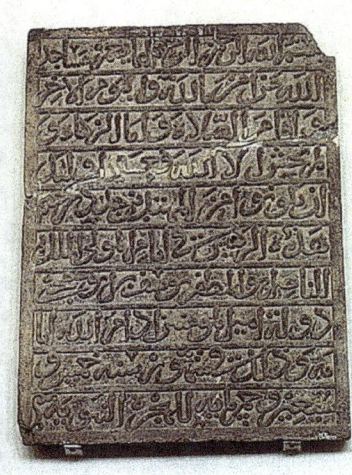

Carved stucco remains from Maskaneh and the medieval city of Balis, National Museum of Damascus.

Carved marble inscription plaque of Salah al-Din, National Museum of Damascus (Inv. Num. 13/ع).

the renovation works conducted by al-Malik al-Nasir Salah al-Din in 575/1179. One of a pair, it records the restoration of the Great Umayyad Mosque's marble panelling by this Ayyubid ruler, executed in thuluth script and arranged in the following lines:

"In the name of God,
the Merciful and Compassionate.
The people who build the mosques
of God are those who believe in God
and the Day of Judgment,
perform the prayers, give alms and
do not fear any except God, as they
are from the rightly guided. Renovation
of this two parts [of the mosque] took place
in the days of the protector, al-Malik
al-Nasir Abu al-Mudhaffar Yusuf bin
Ayyub, Reviver of the State
of the Commander of the Faithful,
may he live long
and this in the months of the year
five-hundred and seventy-five [c. AD 1179]
after the hijra of the Prophet."

Cobalt-blue glazed dish

This dark-blue ceramic dish is decorated inside with the word "*al-mulk*" (meaning power, sovereignty, or ownership). This word was carved into the bottom of the dish before the glaze was applied, which meant that the cobalt-blue gathered in the grooves, making the low points darker and the high points lighter, intensifying the effect of the decoration. The overall surface of the vessel, however, was uniform and smooth by the end of the glazing process. This method of decoration is similar to that used on wares produced in Syria and Iran, although

105

ITINERARY I   Religion, Science and the Transmission of Knowledge under the Atabegs and Ayyubids
National Museum of Damascus

Cobalt-blue glazed dish from Raqqa, National Museum of Damascus (Inv. Num. 1387/ع).

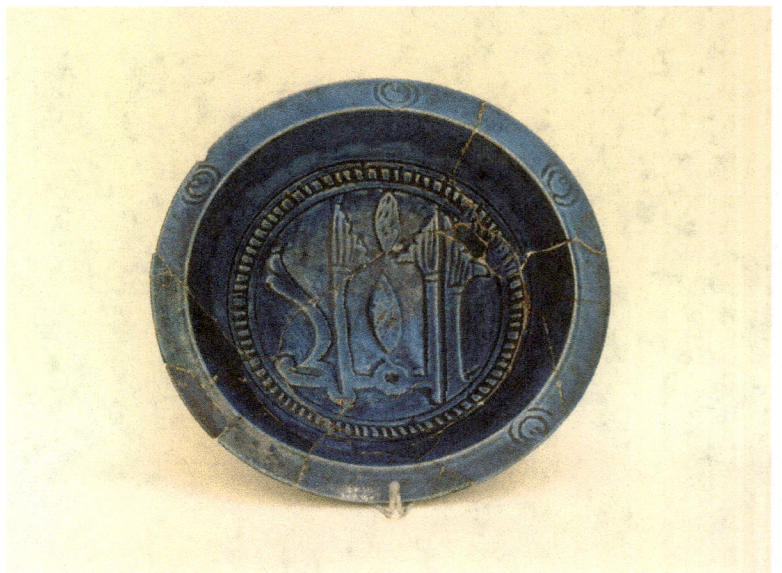

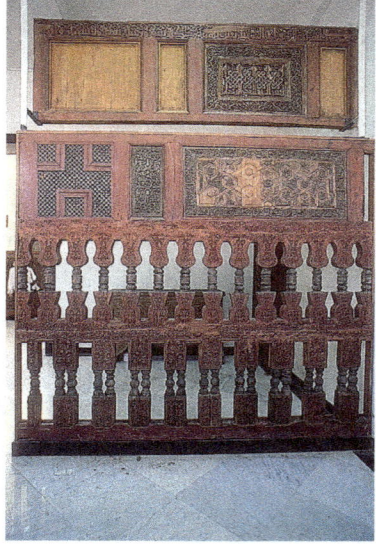

Wooden screen, or maqsura, Seljuq Damascus, National Museum of Damascus (Inv. Num. 97 ع).

pieces of this type are usually polychrome. "*Al-mulk*" is written in foliated Atabeg *kufic* script, in which each letter ends with a decorative sprout or bud.

Seljuq wooden screen

This wooden screen illustrates the importance of Syria in the field of Islamic woodwork. According to the date inscribed on it, 497/1104, it must have originally belonged to the Seljuq Sultan Duqaq, whose mausoleum was located in the Maydan district south-west of old Damascus, a favourite location along the pilgrimage route. During the Atabeg period, the screen was reworked and moved to Musalla al-'Idayn Mosque which was built by Amir Ja'far Muhammad bin al-Hasan al-'Ali nearly 100 years later.

ITINERARY I *Religion, Science and the Transmission of Knowledge under the Atabegs and Ayyubids*
National Museum of Damascus

Made up of two parts, the top section of the screen is a wooden rectangular partition with various frames that divide the surface into rectangular fields. Carved, stylised vegetal motifs and *kufic* inscriptions decorate the screen's façade. On the other side of the central top panel is the expression "… God is Islam" executed in *kufic* script and openwork carving. It indicates the final words of the Qur'anic verses (3: 18–19) that are inscribed around the frame.

Cenotaph of Bakhti Khatun

This monumental and heavily renovated wooden cenotaph is 145 cm wide, 140 cm high and 217 cm wide. According to the inscription, it belonged to a noblewoman of the Artuqid Dynasty, Bakhti Khatun (d. 648/1250). Geometric carving and astral decorations cover the cenotaph's entire surface, which is framed by two bands of Atabeg *kufic* calligraphy, ornamented with the occasional floral motifs. The topmost band features displays "*Ayat al-Kursi*" ("Throne Verse"; 2: 255), while the lower one is a glorious identification of the lineage of the deceased and his titles as follows:

"*This is the coffin of the exalted, the great, the majestic the pride of all noble ladies / the guardian of life and religion, Bakhti Khatun daughter of the sultan the king Mu'izz al-Din Qaysar Shah son of the sultan the fortunate / the martyred king of the kings of Byzantium and Armenia Qillij Arslan may Allah sanctify his soul / and brighten his coffin, and that is on the first crescent of the month of Rabi' al-Awwal in the year 648 Hijri [AD 1250].*"

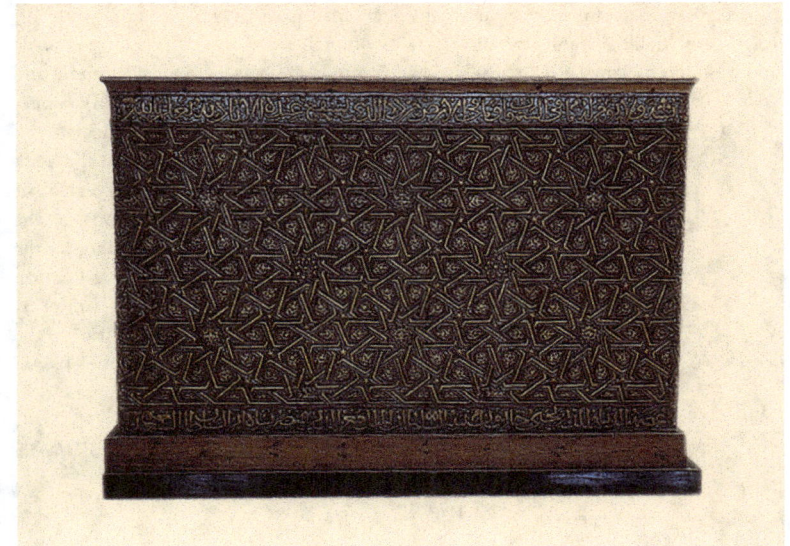

Carved wooden cenotaph, northern Syria, National Museum of Damascus.

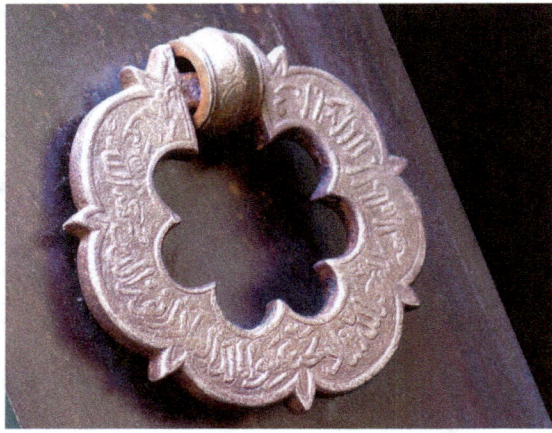

Door-knocker, National Museum of Damascus (Inv. Num. 2798/ع).

Centre spread of Taqwim al-Buldan *illustrating the author's organisation of the scientific material, National Museum of Damascus (Inv. Num. 14689/ع).*

Doorknocker

This carefully worked moulded-bronze doorknocker once belonged to the Madrasa al-Shadhbakhtiyya in Aleppo (VI.1.i). As indicated by the inscription, the *madrasa* was commissioned during the reign of al-Malik al-Zahir in 589/1193, and was built by Jamal al-Din Shadhbakht who was a freed slave, or *'atiq*, of Nur al-Din. Shadhbakht was an important patron in his own right.

Abu al-Fida' manuscript on Geography

This manuscript on geography entitled *Taqwim al-Buldan* (*The Almanac of Countries*) was written by the Ayyubid prince of Hama, Isma'il Abu al-Fida' (d. 732/1331). This copy was completed in the year 741/1340, less than a decade after the death of the author, thus highlighting its importance and continued transmission from the Ayyubid period to the Mamluk era. Its calligraphic style and colour scheme belong to the Mamluk artistic style but its author Abu al-Fida' is a legacy of the Ayyubid Dynasty, born and raised in Damascus. He completed writing this scientific work in 721/1321, and his comprehensive organisation of geographic knowledge was so very systematic and thorough that his work quickly superseded all previous geographical texts. A colophon on the last page of the book documents 741/1340 as the year of its completion, Sultan Abu al-Fida' as the author and patron, a calligrapher by the name of Muhammad bin 'Abd al-Rahman al-Qirsh as the copyist, and a painter by the name of Muhammad al-'Arari as the illuminator of its frontispiece. It was most probably produced in Hama.

Mona al-Moadin

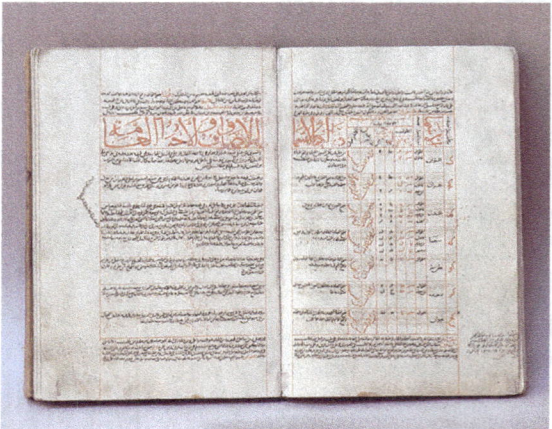

I.12 FARUKHSHAHIYYA AND AMJADIYYA MAUSOLEUMS (OPTION)

There are quite a few mausoleums en route, which are easily discernable by their generally square stone structures and smooth or lobed domes. Instead of going directly to Salihiyya district or quarter, a walk across the pedestrian bridge over the highway leads to a pair of newly renovated Ayyubid mausoleums. The *Farukhshahiyya*, commissioned by Salah al-Din's sister-in-law in 579/1182–3, and the *Amjadiyya* founded by the latter's grandson in 629/1231–2. Both were originally decorated with painted stucco which has not survived, and the complex is currently being used as a mosque. It is interesting to contrast such funerary monuments, here heavily renovated amidst a glossy new high-end commercial district, with the numerous mausoleums and *madrasa*s of the Salihiyya district, where the spiritual resonance is a life-worn and lived-in reality.

I.13 SALIHIYYA QUARTER

Take public transport to Afif Street. Walk uphill past the Afif Mosque and the small garden/traffic node to your left, arriving at a cobblestone path. Continue walking uphill towards the domed structure to your left, and enter the small street to your right. You are now at the western end of "Bayn al-Madaris" Street (The Street Between the Madrasas) which stretches all across the Salihiyya Quarter parallel to the Yazid River. During the Ayyubid period this was a place of orchards, clean water, fresh air, and lofty monuments dedicated to charity, piety and education. The first four monuments are lined up just 25 m into this street on the right-hand side, discernable by their domes, inscriptions and boarded-up windows.

The Salihiyya Quarter was founded by refugees from Jerusalem who were highly educated and played an important role in the militaries of Nur al-Din and Salah al-Din. Many patrons sought to support this district by constructing *madrasa*s and mausoleums, and all the other trappings of an independent urban centre. Currently, the Salihiyya district spreads across a long strip, and one of its main streets is known as "The Street Between the Madrasas".

From its westernmost point, the first monument on the right is the **Farnathiyya Mausoleum** (621/1224)

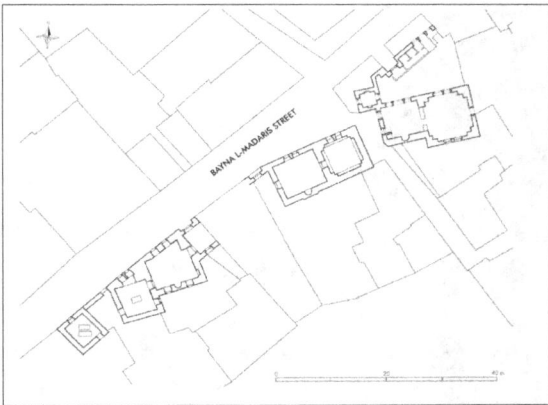

Ground-plan of the Salihiyya district of Damascus, including Turba Farnathiyya (Farnathiyya Mausoleum), Madrasa al-Murshidiyya, Dar al-Hadith al-Ashrafiyya and Madrasa al-Atabakiyya).

ITINERARY I *Religion, Science and the Transmission of Knowledge under the Atabegs and Ayyubids*
Salihiyya quarter

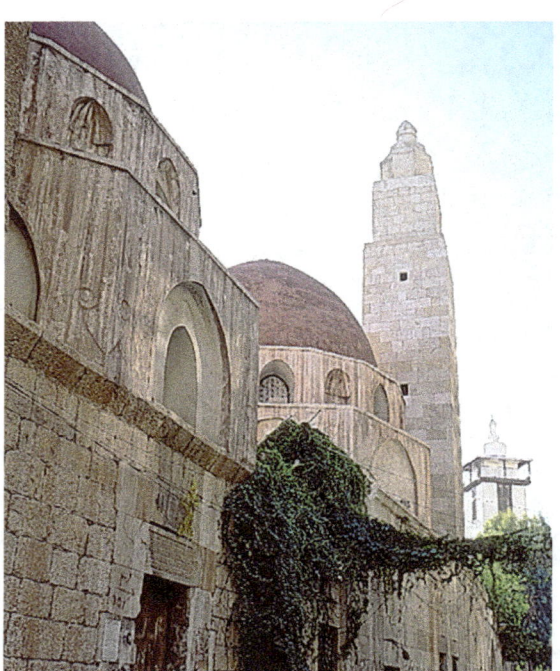

Beginning of Bayn al-Madaris Street, leading to Suq al-Jum'a in the Salihiyya district of Damascus.

which is known to have included a *zawiya* or residential area for Sufis who would have given mystical lessons to the tomb visitors. The mausoleum is a square building with a dome on top of two levels of tambours and a cursive inscription set in a *tabula ansata* above its lintel, on top of which is a single curvilinear block of inscribed basalt-stone set interlacing amidst rectilinear limestones. The gap in the stone blocks above the window is a necessary feature to relieve the pressure on the lintel. The clever discreetness of this gap, a thin horizontal line that maintains the elegance and solidity of the construction, is typical of the Ayyubid architectural style on many of the lintels above the windows and doors of the mausoleum and *madrasa*.

Next to the Farnathiyya is **Madrasa al-Murshidiyya**. Built in 654/1252, it is a funerary *madrasa* commemorating Khadija Khatun, daughter of the Ayyubid leader al-Malik al-Mu'azzam 'Isa, son of al-Malik al-'Adil. The *madrasa* has an irregular plan because it lies on a slightly hooked street. It features a beautifully well-preserved *tabula ansata* inscription in the entrance lintel with four lines of perfectly legible and diacritically marked cursive script commemorating the patron's donation. This is one of the best surviving examples of *kitaba waqfiyya*, which bears important documentations on the administrative and financial upkeep of the institution. The entrance leads into a prayer-hall and an adjacent tomb-chamber while a square minaret rises between the two rooms. This simple, square minaret is the sole Ayyubid model to have survived in the city, after-which more heavily ornamented minarets of the Mamluk and Ottoman periods dominate. Adjacent to this *madrasa* is the **Dar al-Hadith al-Ashrafiyya**, an elegant construct built by al-Malik al-Ashraf in 634/1237 as indicated by the modern plaque located next to its similarly prominent *tabula ansata* inscription with the *shahada* — declaration of faith — carved into the triangular brackets of the frame. As for the layout, it was built on two levels, probably to accommodate the slope towards the River Yazid. The entrance leads to a staircase, which descends to the courtyard, while at street-level is a prayer-hall with a *mihrab* and an adjacent tomb-chamber. The dome of the latter is set on a pair of drums, or tambours, the first one typically taller and wider than the second, and both feature alternating decorative motifs of blind arches and pierced windows.

Just a few metres past the Ashrafiyya is the **Madrasa al-Atabakiyya**, built in 640/1242 by Turkan Khatun, the wife of Malik al-Ashraf, and now used as a mosque. It is discernable by its recessed stone *muqarnas* portal with its prominent *ablaq* decoration.

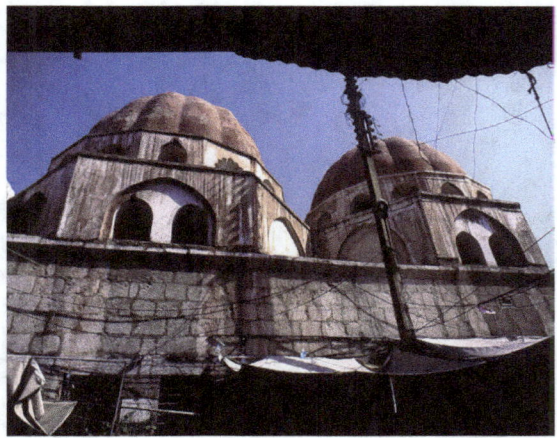

Madrasa al-Jaharkasiyya, with its two domed tomb chambers, Damascus.

I.14 MADRASA AL-JAHARKASIYYA

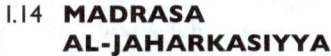

Further up the Bayn al-Madaris street, the street turns into a market place known as "Suq al-Jum'a" (Friday Market) and the madrasa appears some 100 m further on, on the left-hand side of the street, overlooking a downhill path on the right.

The **Madrasa al-Jaharkasiyya** is a rare example of a double-domed mausoleum each of which houses two coffins, a total of four. It was founded by the Ayyubid prince Fakhr al-Din (d. 607/1211), a commander of Salah al-Din's private guard. The prayer-hall of this *madrasa* is very small as prominence is given to the tomb chambers. The function of the *madrasa* was indeed overshadowed by the more important tradition of paying respects and blessings to the dead patron and his family. Withered inscriptions are discernable above the lintels of the windows.

I.15 BIMARISTAN QAYMARIYYA

Continue to walk up the Bayn al-Madaris street amidst the market. The bimaristan *will appear on your right, just before the Ottoman Mosque of Muhyidin on the corner. The entrance to the* bimaristan *may be hidden behind market stalls and access is irregular.*

This *bimaristan* was built by Sayf al-Din al-Qaymari between 646/1248 and 654/1256. The Qaymar family, or Banu Qaymar, were major patrons of urban architecture and important members of the aristocratic elite under the Ayyubids. The construction of this large *bimaristan* in the Salihiyya quarter is an indicator of the district's wealth and demonstrates its

ITINERARY I   Religion, Science and the Transmission of Knowledge under the Atabegs and Ayyubids
Bimaristan al-Qaymariyya

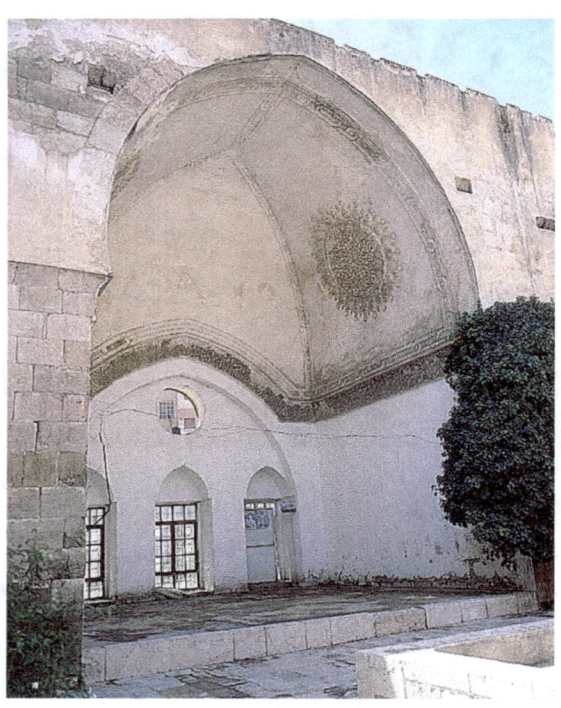

Bimaristan Qaymariyya (Bimaristan al-Qaymari), view of the courtyard and main iwan *with inscription and stucco medallion, Damascus.*

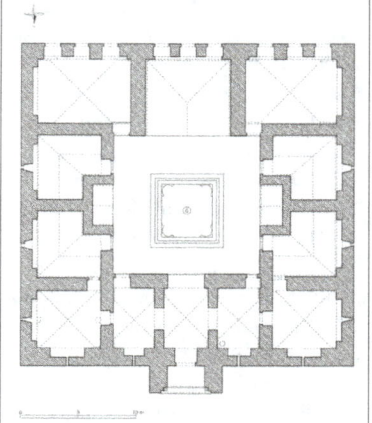

Floor-plan of Bimaristan Qaymariyya.

independence from the old City of Damascus. Yet it follows the example of Bimaristan Nur al-Din, built nearly a century earlier, with its four perfectly symmetrical *iwan*s surrounding the courtyard, albeit of larger dimensions, and with more ornate decoration. The curvilinear designs in the *ablaq* bi-colour stones that decorate not only the arch but the entirety of the recessed portal, the use of large sized and carefully punctuated *thuluth* epigraphy that stretches across all three sides of the recessed portal, and the provision of *mastaba*s, or stone ledges, for seating, shows the progression of the façade's monumentality. In the interior, a pair of intricate stucco medallions and a dado rail of calligraphic inscriptions that repeat the *shahada*, or confession of faith, decorate the *bimaristan*'s main *iwan* and exhibit a marked increase in floral ornamentation. Originally, the main rooms for patients would have overlooked the River Yazid, which unfortunately has been cemented over. The water supply for the *bimaristan* came from an ingenious waterwheel built behind it, in an alleyway known as *Hayy al-Nawa'ir*, the "Neighbourhood of Waterwheels". It is one of the few surviving *nawa'ir* on the River Yazid.

I.16 HANABILA MOSQUE

Back on Bayn al-Madaris Street, or Suq al-Jum'a (Friday Market), continue walking 20 m further. A small street, known as al-Hanabila Street, appears on your left, flanked by a bakery. Walk uphill to reach the mosque

Hanabila Mosque

on your right. It may be visited respecting appropriate dress codes and conduct, but it is likely to be closed apart from prayer times (approx 11.00–13.00). A small donation is recommended.

Previously to this mosque's construction, it was widely understood that no town could have more than one Friday Mosque for the weekly congregational prayers and sermon. The construction of Jami' al-Hanabila in the same city that holds the most monumental mosque of all, the Great Umayyad Mosque of Damascus, serves to highlight yet again the independent status of the Salihiyya quarter and its flourishing population.

The construction of this mosque was initiated by Abu 'Umar Muhammad bin Qudama al-Muqaddasi (from Jerusalem), a sheikh and grammarian of the Banu Qudama which came to Damascus fleeing the Crusader attack. To help cover the expenses, al-Malik al-Muzaffar Gokburi, lord of Irbil (near Mosul) and married to Salah al-Din's sister, sent further funds in 598/1202 and also commissioned the sinking of a well to supply the mosque with water. Inscriptions relating to Gokburi's patronage are found in a monumental *kufic* inscription above the lintel of the western gate of the mosque, above the door leading to the minaret and, most beautifully, along the top of the pierced stucco window located above the entrance to the prayer-hall, designed as a grid of symmetric leafy designs. All this highlights the close ties between religious scholars and military rulers during the Ayyubid period, and the support extended to architectural patronage from the lands east of Syria westward.

The importance of this mosque is that it is a miniature of the Great Umayyad Mosque, featuring the same open courtyard plan, hypostyle construction and triple-gabled roofing of the prayer-hall. The mosque is also known for its sundial, or *mazwala*, on the northern wall and for its Crusader capital on one of the columns. It has an important wooden *minbar*, commissioned by Prince Gokburi and crafted by a Damascene-settled carpenter named Ibrahim al-Kurdi in 604/1208. The inscription on the *minbar* also gives praise and allegiance to the 'Abbasid caliph, following the example of the Seljuqs.

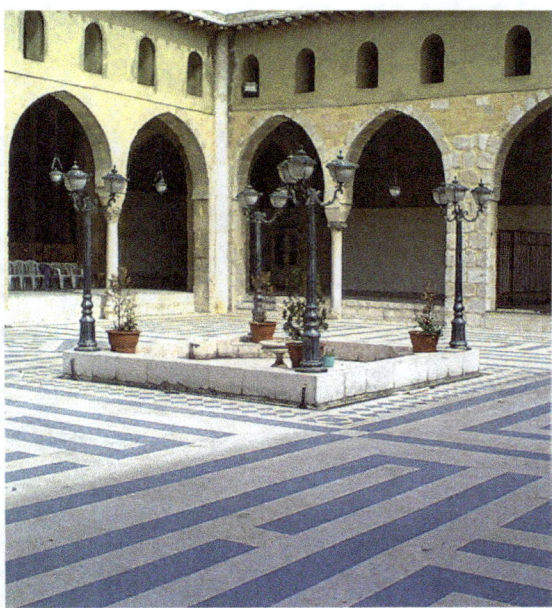

Hanabila Mosque, view of the courtyard and arcade, Damascus.

ITINERARY I *Religion, Science and the Transmission of Knowledge under the Atabegs and Ayyubids*
Madrasa al-Sahiba

Madrasa al-Sahiba, view of the muqarnas portal, Damascus.

Floor-plan of Madrasa al-Sahiba.

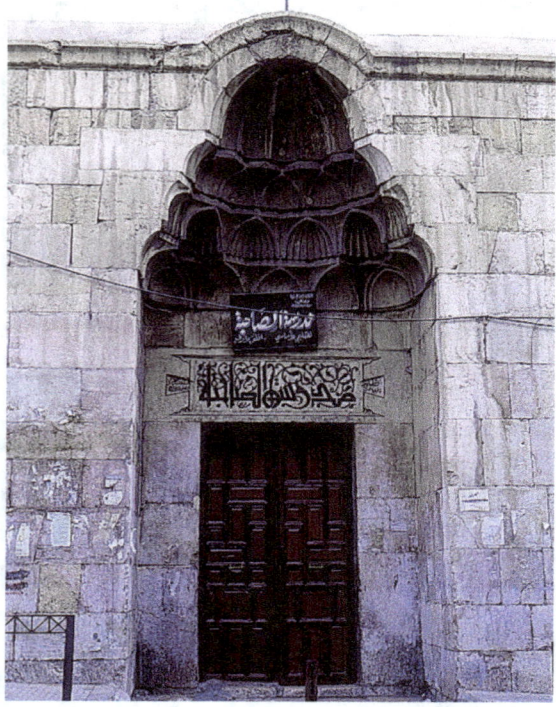

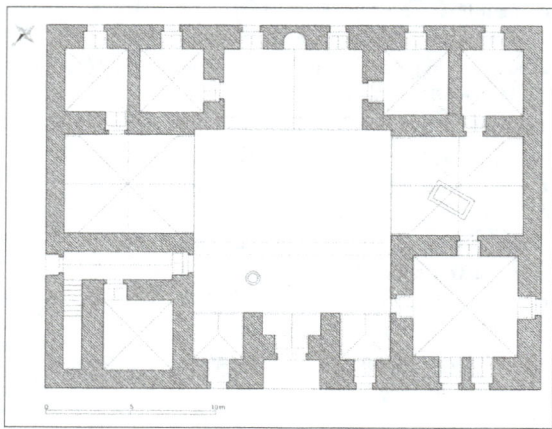

I.17 MADRASA AL-SAHIBA

Retrace your steps to return to the Bayn al-Madaris street and continue walk 300 m further towards the large mosque/theological school that appears on the skyline ahead of you. The madrasa *is the elegant stone building that appears on your left. As it is currently in use as a primary school, access to the interior may be difficult.*

This elegant *madrasa* is still in use today as an elementary school for girls. A rackety version of a founder's cenotaph sits quite casually amidst the students' desks. Generation after generation of Salihiyya schoolgirls have grown up in happy and curious awareness that their *madrasa* was built by none other than Saladin's sister, Rabi'a Khatun who was also the wife of Prince Gokburi, the patron of the district's congregational mosque Jami' al-Hanabila. Not surprisingly, the *madrasa* was dedicated to the *Hanabli* rite or *madhhab* – school of law – which was an important school in the religious revival of the 6th-/12th-century cities of Syria.

As a building, the *madrasa* is a rare example of elegance and balance. Unlike the traditional *madrasas* of Damascus, which usually feature a long prayer-hall and a main *iwan*, the layout of Madrasa al-Sahiba is perfectly symmetrical and reveals the influence of Eastern architecture, understandably so as the patron was the Princess of Irbil in Iraq. It also features the prominence of stone aesthetics, which is a northern influence from Aleppo,

ITINERARY I   Religion, Science and the Transmission of Knowledge under the Atabegs and Ayyubids
Madrasa al-Rukniyya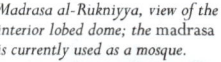

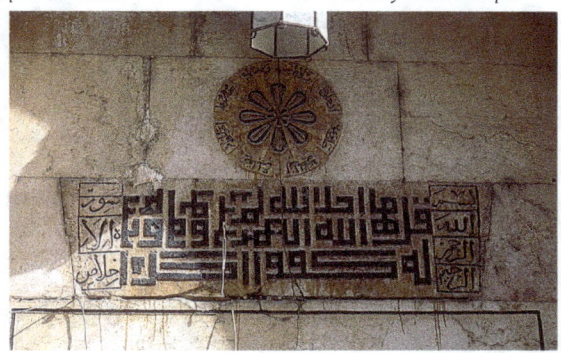

Madrasa al-Rukniyya, Qur'anic inscription and eight-petalled medallion above the entrance portal, Damascus.

Madrasa al-Rukniyya, view of the interior lobed dome; the madrasa is currently used as a mosque.

as can be seen by its elegant limestone façade with a single row of pinkish stone near the top, and a recessed central portal with a stone *muqarnas*. Subtle ornamentation is found in the geometric carving above the windows of the façade, particularly the closely spaced pair to the right. A small, square stone between the lintels of the windows, engraved with geometric strap-work and the *shahada* (declaration of monotheist faith) "*La Ilaha illa 'llah*", thus indicates the tomb-chamber.

The use of stone for the *muqarnas* is a particularly Syrian achievement of the early 7th/13th century, prior to which brick was the traditional medium. The interior is clearly laid out in the four-*iwans*-in-axial symmetry plan, a rarity in Damascene *madrasas* during this period. The façade of the courtyard comprises a row of three arches. The southern *iwan* has a central *mihrab* flanked by windows that originally overlooked the gardens laid out alongside the River Yazid. A pair of parallel open arches stretching across the courtyard is distinctive of this *madrasa*, surviving as a remnant of the second floor, which once would have served as lodgings for travelling scholars.

I.18 MADRASA AL-RUKNIYYA

Continue walking to the top of Bayn al-Madaris street and turn right, walk downhill for 30 m, the madrasa *appears on Chamdin Square. Currently used as a mosque, it may be visited respecting appropriate dress codes and*

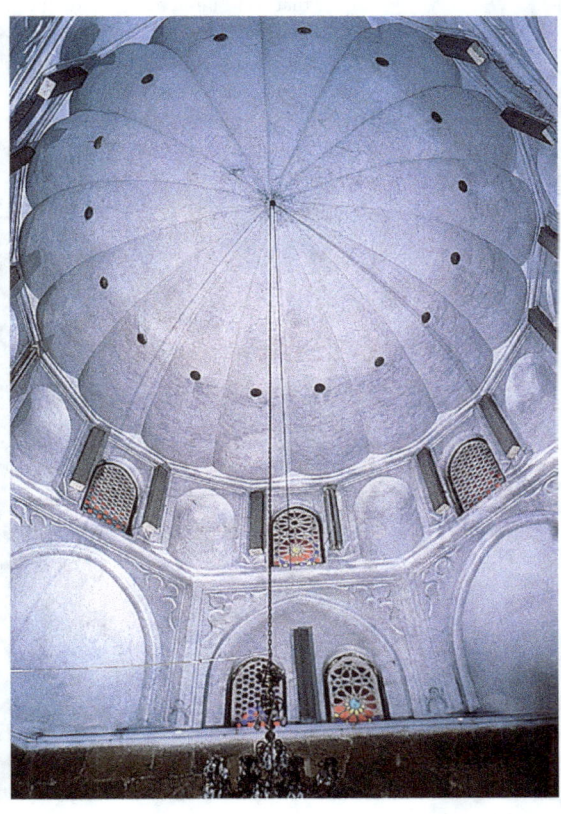

115

ITINERARY I *Religion, Science and the Transmission of Knowledge under the Atabegs and Ayyubids*
Madrasa al-Rukniyya | Shibliyya Mausoleum

conduct, but it is likely to be closed apart from prayer times (approx. 11.00–13.00). A small donation is recommended.

Built by Rukn al-Din Mengüverish al-Falaki, the building is made of two square sections, the smaller one is a mausoleum (*turba*) and the larger one a mosque. The minaret is a recent addition and did not exist in the original plan. The plan of a courtyard surrounded by three *riwaqs* shows the decorative stone-carving techniques that were influenced by Northern Syria and even Anatolia. This façade decoration is rare, with beautiful geometric *kufic* designs over the windows and over the gate. The *madrasa* also features the first Ayyubid courtyard to be covered by a dome. The mausoleum is bigger than the courtyard and the non-symmetrical portico. Meanwhile, the interior of the prayer-hall displays the simple elegance of Ayyubid architecture. The inscriptions on the mausoleum indicate that it once belonged to the *madrasa* complex; indeed mausoleums are often the only surviving evidence of a *madrasa*'s existence. This is the case of the Madrasa al-Rukniyya, which currently functions as a mosque.

Generally speaking, up until the end of the 6th/12th century, the tambours of mausoleums were made of brick, indicating the strong Eastern influence of these architectural types. By the 7th/13th century, however, the influence of northern Syria and Aleppo becomes stronger and the use of stone more dominant. This *madrasa* is a good example to illustrate this point.

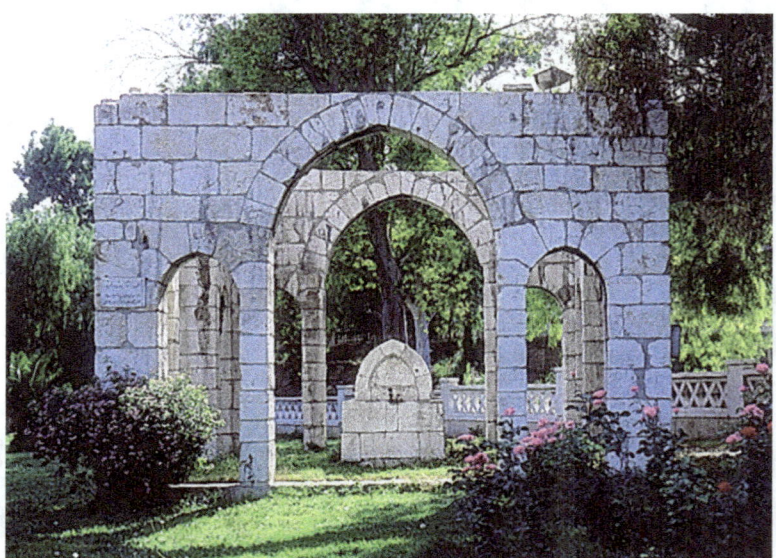

Shibliyya Mausoleum, view of the corner stones and tomb, Damascus.

ITINERARY I   Religion, Science and the Transmission of Knowledge under the Atabegs and Ayyubids
Badriyya Mausoleum

I.19 SHIBLIYYA MAUSOLEUM

Walk downhill towards Maysat Square. Two structures are discernable amidst the traffic, the domed Badriyya Mausoleum in the middle and the stone remains of the Shibliyya Mausoleum to the right. Do not cross the street into the grassed-over traffic-island from the north, but rather walk west towards the Shibliyya, visiting it first then crossing into the traffic-island at the point where the street is narrowest and safest to cross.

This mausoleum was originally part of a large architectural complex including a *madrasa* and a *khanqa*. It would have original stood in the middle of a rectangular courtyard. Only the cenotaph and the four corners of its chamber remain, now standing in the middle of a grassed-over traffic-island. The Shibliyya was built by Shibl al-Dawla, a eunuch of Husam al-Din, son of Sitt al-Sham. Shibl al-Dawla was an influential figure who sponsored the opening of a main road from the Madrasa al-Shamiyya to Mount Qasyun, increasing accessibility of the Salihiyya Quarter. He also endowed his institution with a very rich *waqf* and since his death in 623/1226 he lies buried here. His *madrasa* and *khanqa* were dedicated to the practice of mysticism and to the accommodation of Sufis. Many myths surround the character of Shibl al-Dawla and his tomb, which survives despite the demolition of the rest of the complex and the onslaught of modern urbanism.

I.20 BADRIYYA MAUSOLEUM

In the middle of Maysat Square is a grassed-over traffic-island amidst which the Badriyya Mausoleum stands. This domed chamber currently houses the offices for an environmental NGO.

This mausoleum was constructed under the auspices of Prince Badr al-Din Hasan bin al-Daya, known as *Lala* (Turkish for "educator" or "up-bringer"). Lala and his brothers were part of Nur al-Din's cultural and military aristocracy during his reign of Syria from 549/1154 to 569/1174. The construction date of this *madrasa* is uncertain, but historical sources confirm that it was before 569/1174.

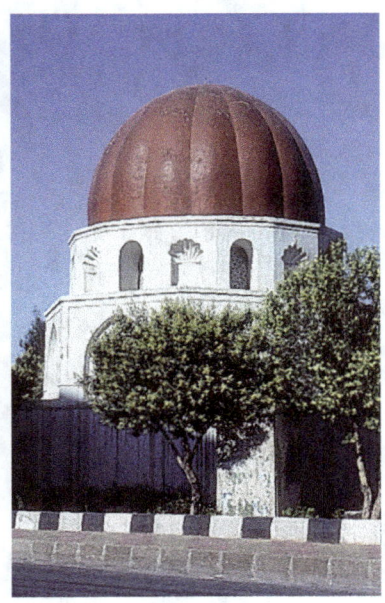

Badriyya Mausoleum, Damascus.

117

ITINERARY I   Religion, Science and the Transmission of Knowledge under the Atabegs and Ayyubids
Badriyya Mausoleum

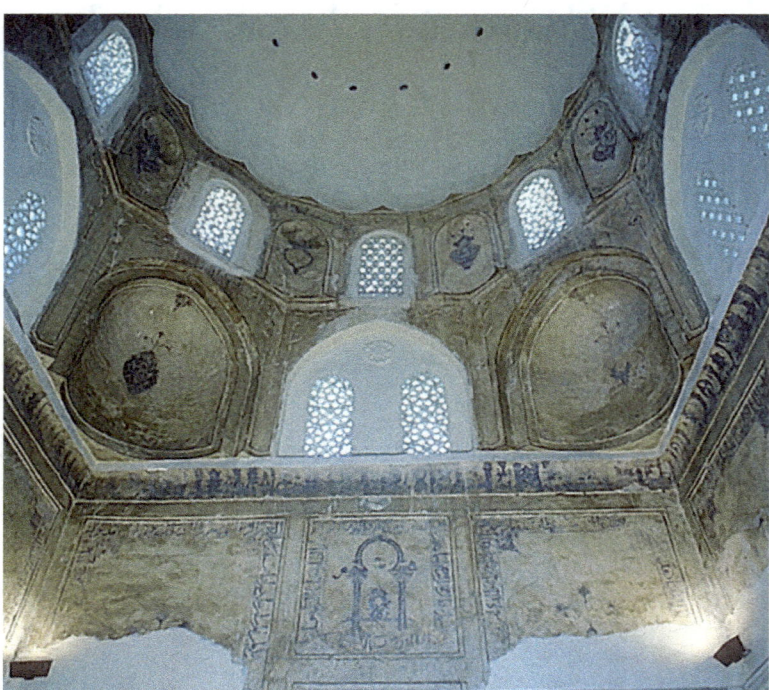

Badriyya Mausoleum, view of the stucco-decorated interior, Damascus.

Upon the death of its patron, Lala, the ruling Ayyubid king, al-Malik al-Mu'azzam, nominated the Syrian historian, Sibt bin al-Jawzi, as supervisor of the *madrasa* in 615/1218.

The mausoleum is square in form, with an arched bay on each face and a domed roof. The dome represents a type found on a large majority of Ayyubid monuments in Damascus, where an intermediary device of two polygonal drums establishes the passage from square enclosure to circular dome. The remains of blue-painted stucco decoration in the interior are a precious survival of what most other mausoleums have lost. Floral interlacing, along with depictions of flowers in vases, are framed by friezes of cursive *thuluth* script. While a prominent dado rail of angular, Atabeg *kufic* script runs around the mausoleum's four walls. In every squinched angle beneath the cupola is a small, blue medallion; the borders of the windows also feature delicate decoration. This interior decoration reveals two schools of art: the first is oriental Iranian, as seen in calligraphic banner and stucco work, while the second is local Damascene, as noted in the medallions decorating the squinches.

ITINERARY I *Religion, Science and the Transmission of Knowledge under the Atabegs and Ayyubids*
Madrasa Hafiziyya

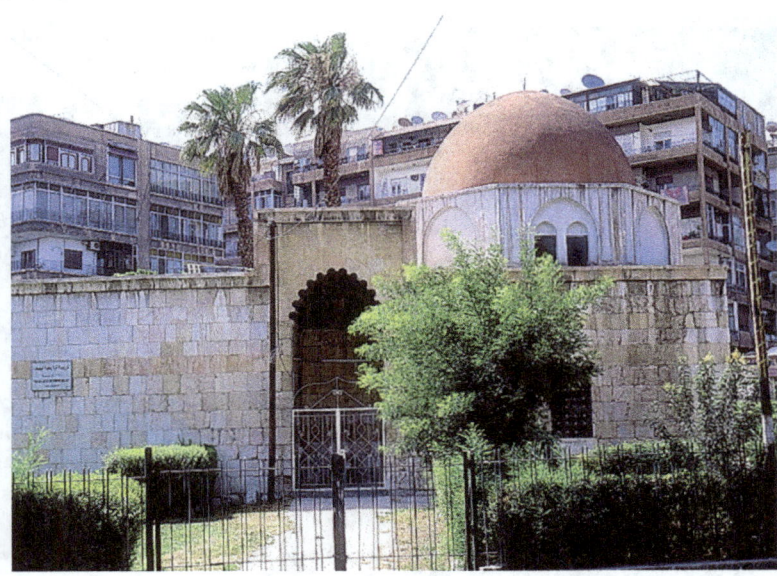

Madrasa Hafiziyya and its mausoleum, Damascus.

I.21 MADRASA HAFIZIYYA

From Maysat Square, walk south-west towards the public garden. The Hafiziyya complex, now housing the Syrian Geographical Society, is located within the garden. Access to the interior may be difficult, as the Society does not observe regular hours.

The layout of this *madrasa* is very irregular, constructed in different phases and in a transitional cusp-period straddling the late Ayyubid to early Mamluk periods. It belongs to Arghun al-Hafiziyya, a freed slave woman of al-Malik al-'Adil. She became very rich and her surname, al-Hafiz, refers to al-Malik al-Hafiz lord of Qal'at Ja'bar (VIII.3.) on the Euphrates, whom she brought up. She died in 648/1250 and was buried within the mausoleum.

The *madrasa*'s mausoleum is of a typical square plan, while the prayer hall attached to it follows a miniature cruciform plan with a vaulted courtyard, similar to that of Madrasa al-Rukniyya. The main artistic feature is the peculiar entrance: a narrow bay covered by a conch-shaped vault. The ribs of the conch stretch over the whole vault and form a lobed arch at the front. The gate opens from a side wall of the bay. This strange entrance, together with the asymmetry of the general layout reveals the extent of manoeuverability that Syrian architects exhibited in adapting the Eastern-inspired Seljuq prototype.

MECHANICAL SCIENCES

Zena Takieddine

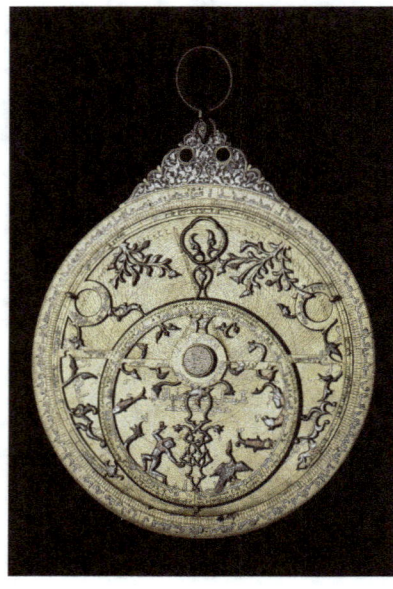

Astrolabe, Ayyubid Dynasty, British Museum, London (Inv. Num. 1855, 0709.1; © Trustees of the British Museum, London).

The construction of educational institutions was coupled with a flourishing in the applied sciences. Tools and machines devoted to time-keeping and hydraulic distribution were necessary to keep track of prayer times and to supply mosques, *madrasa*s and *bimaristan*s with water. Inventions for these purposes reveal some of the most advanced fields of study in the Muslim world. The exacting methodology and practical necessity driving their creation was also coupled with a decorative aestheticism. Ayyubid astrolabes display high scientific precision while simultaneously representing the constellations in pleasing arabesque designs. Similarly when Nur al-Din restored the Umayyad Mosque he included in its eastern gate a clock that was both technically intricate and beautiful. It featured an array of brass bird sculptures that automatically released weights into resonant cups for every hour.

Technical treatises from this period include the Damascene author Ridwan bin al-Sa'ati's, who wrote *On the Construction of Clocks and their Uses* in 600/1203; it was his father who constructed the monumental clock for the Great Umayyad Mosque, commissioned by Nur al-Din.

By far the most famous work on mechanical sciences comes from the genius inventor Badi' al-Zaman al-Jazari who, in 602/1206 not only wrote, but also illustrated his tome, *The Book of Knowledge of Ingenious Mechanical Devices*. Sponsored by the Artuqid court in northern Syria – a Turkish dynasty, which became the vassals of Salah al-Din – this work gives lucid instructions for putting together all kinds of machines, taking advantage of delayed-reaction techniques and automatic responses. In addition to clocks, these include water-dispensers, fountains with musical androids and various water-lifting machines. Al-Jazari's fanciful illustrations are entirely functional and their entertaining perks flaunt high technological expertise.

In the Salihiyya district of Damascus, there is an alleyway known as *Hayy al-Nawa'ir*, "Neighbourhood of the Waterwheels", which features a type of waterwheel following al-Jazari's instructions. An actual specimen can be found behind the Bimaristan al-Qaymari, constructed just 50 years after al-Jazari wrote his work. Unlike the *nawa'ir* of Hama, which

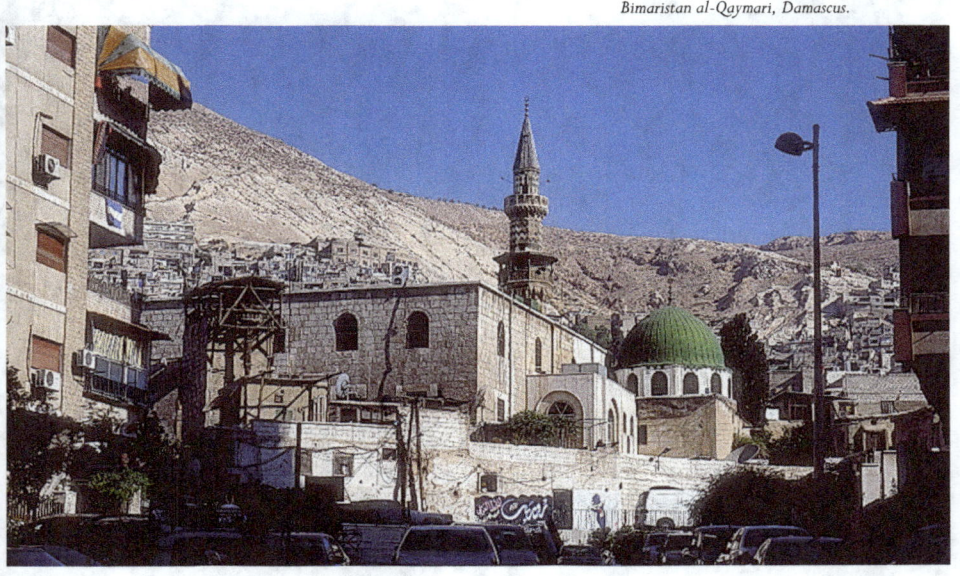

The noria in Hayy al-nawa'ir, which supplied the Bimaristan al-Qaymari, Damascus.

continue in an ancient tradition, and function in a way made possible by the Orontes' fast-flowing momentum, this *noria* on the River Yazid is a mid-7th/13th-century invention. It uses multiple vertical and horizontal wheels to raise the water in a way that takes into account geographical limitations such as the weaker momentum of smaller tributaries and the uphill area of distribution.

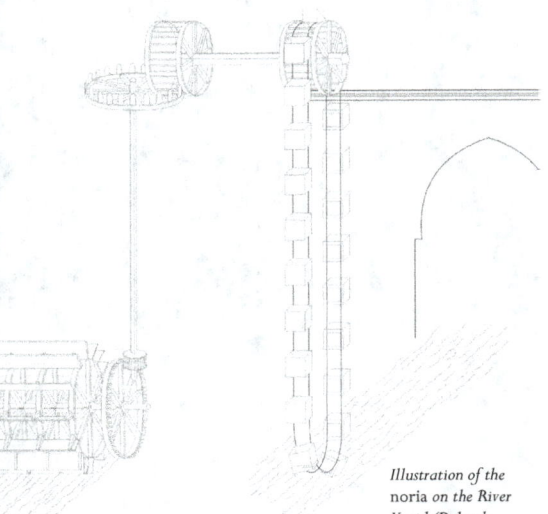

Illustration of the noria on the River Yazid (Delpech, Girard, Robin, Roumi, 1997).

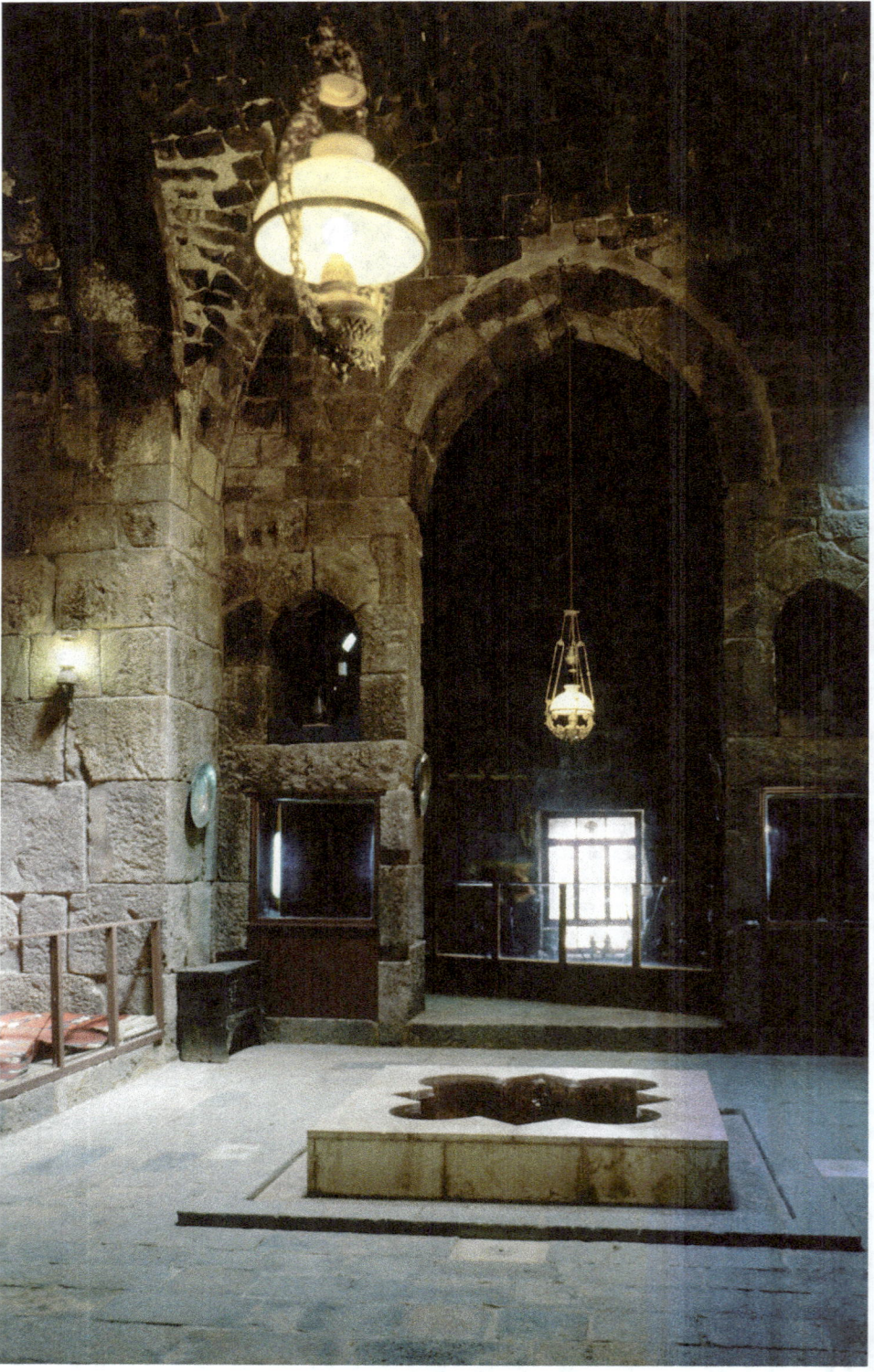

ITINERARY I

Antique Heritage in an Ayyubid City

Verena Daiber

BOSRA

II.1 BOSRA CITADEL (Museum)
II.2 MASJID KHIDR (Option)
II.3 JAMI' AL-'UMARI
II.4 MABRAK AL-NAQA MOSQUE/MADRASAT GUMUSHTAGIN
II.5 MOSQUE OF FATIMA
II.6 BIRKAT AL-HAJJ
II.7 MADRASAT ABU AL-FIDA'
II.8 MASJID YAQUT

Local Traditions and Imperial Architecture in a Provincial Capital   Verena Daiber

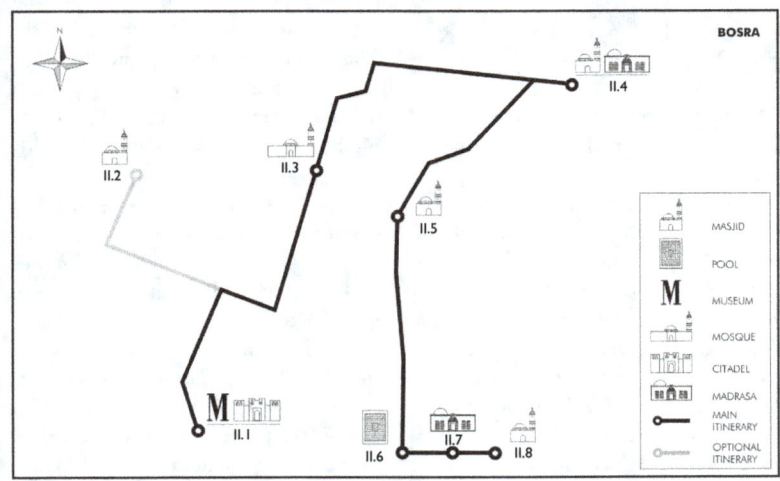

Bosra Citadel.

ITINERARY II   *Antique Heritage in an Ayyubid City*
Introduction

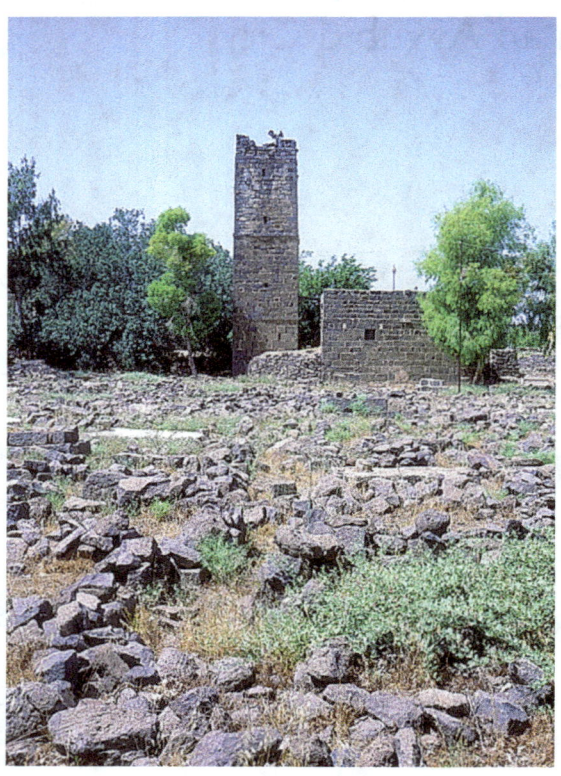

Masjid Khidr, Bosra.

Throughout the ages, Bosra remained a major city in the Hauran region that stretches to the south of Damascus between the Jabal al-Druze in the east and the Golan Heights in the west. Bosra secured its wealth by the fertile agricultural lands that had long served as the granary for the Bilad al-Sham. The Nabateans transferred their capital from Petra to Bosra in the first century AD and, after the Roman conquest in 106 AD, it became the capital of the *Provincia Arabia*. With the triumph of Islam over the region in 13/634, life continued within the Antique city; very few alterations to the infrastructure were undertaken. The only evidence of early Islamic building activity is the two reused inscriptions in the Great Mosque dating to the $2^{nd}/8^{th}$ century.

The religious and economic status of Bosra grew due to its status as an attractive market and trade centre, as well as the southernmost outpost of Damascus and the last major halt on the pilgrimage route, between Syria and the holy cities in the Hijaz. The pilgrimage caravans would halt in Bosra and arrange their provisions before entering the desert. According to the medieval traveller and historian Ibn Battuta, the city of Bosra was where the Prophet Muhammad's caravan would stop to do trade on behalf of his wife, Khadija, who was a renowned merchant in Mecca. Mabrak al-Naqa holds the imprints of the Prophet's kneeling she-camel, and the site revered as material evidence of the Prophet's visit. The biography (*Sira*) of the Prophet, sites Bosra as the place where the Christian monk Bahira who resided in the Basilica of the city, foretold Muhammad his future prophecy.

The redevelopment of medieval Bosra started with the Seljuq conquest of Damascus and the surrounding territories in 468/1076. Initial alterations were undertaken at the citadel by Shams al-Dawla Gumushtagin, who was the son of the Seljuq ruler of Damascus, Taj al-Dawla Tutush (r. 471–88/1078–95). Mostly, the redevelopments are ascribed to the Turkish general Amin al-Dawla

ITINERARY II   *Antique Heritage in an Ayyubid City*
Introduction

Gumushtagin (d. 541/1146), commissioner of Bosra under the Burid ruler of Damascus. He rebuilt the Great Mosque and founded the Khidr Mosque and the Madrasa next to the Shrine of Mabrak al-Naqa.

A major change in building politics occurred in the Ayyubid period under al-'Adil Abu Bakr (592–615/1196–1218). He undertook enormous refortification efforts throughout Syria and Egypt as a protective measure against the Crusaders. At his death the fiefdom of Bosra passed on to his son, al-Salih Isma'il (615–44/1218–46), whose rule is considered to represent Islamic Bosra's heyday. He renovated the Great Mosque and improved the infrastructure of the city by reactivating the huge pre-Islamic water reservoir, Birkat al-Hajj. His sumptuous residence, constructed within the citadel walls, included a mosque erected on top of the stage of the Roman theatre, a covered water cistern in the *orchestra* and a *hammam* in the eastern peristyle. On top of the cistern, vaulted halls served as storerooms and an arsenal. Alas, these structures were removed during several stages of restoration works between 1946 and 1970, leaving no testimony to the primetime of medieval Bosra. After the Mongol raid of 658/1260, the city never regained its previous splendour.

Leaving Damascus via the Damascus–Amman Highway, the town of Bosra lies 140 km south of Damascus. Drive 100 km south and then turn east (left) at the Dar'a/Bosra exit, and continue for a further 40 km east. Public Transport is available.

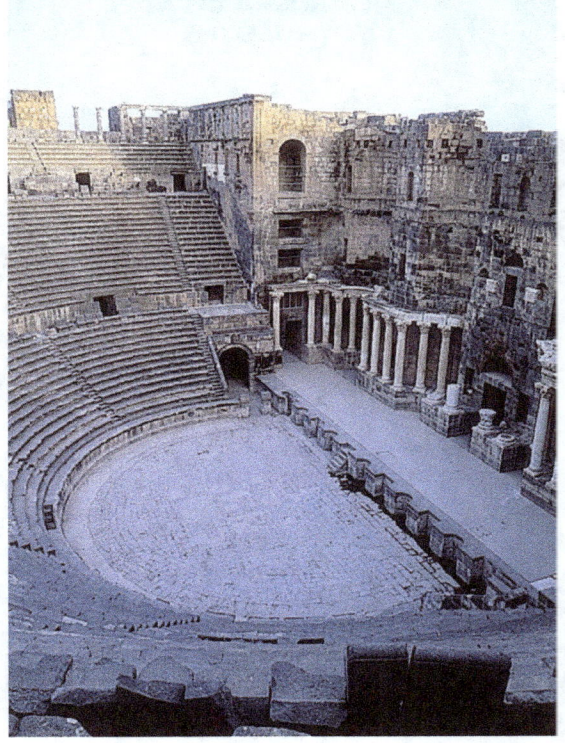

Bosra Citadel.

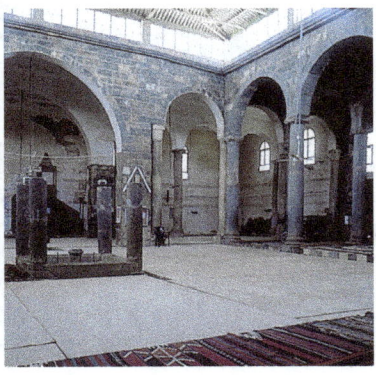

Jami' al-'Umari, Bosra.

II.1 BOSRA CITADEL (MUSEUM)

Impossible to miss, located at the centre of town, the citadel envelopes the famous Bosra Roman amphitheatre. The museum is located within the citadel ramparts to the south. Opening times are Wed–Mon 9.00–18.00 during the summer, 9.00–16.00 during the winter. Closed during Friday prayers (approx 11.00–13.00). There is an entrance fee.

As a major stronghold in the region and the palatial residence for the Ayyubid regent, the citadel became the focal point of the Islamic city. It was a Roman theatre transformed into a military structure by a series of constructions carried out during a period of more than 150 years. The initial period of alterations began under Gumushtagin in 481/1088, who built the two towers on top of the rectangular 9 m x 8 m stairwells flanking the *scaena* of the theatre (1 and 2), and consequently closed all the openings to the outside. Around 60 years later, the last Burid ruler of Damascus, Abu Sa'id Abaq (534–49/1140–54), resumed the fortification extensions. He built the tower on the south-west façade of the *cavea* (3) in 542/1147–8 in anticipation of a Crusader attack, as is evident from his epithet in the inscription: "*qatil al-kafara wal-mushrikin*", "killer of the unbelievers and the polytheists". These three towers from the first extension phase, covered in a simple and traditional way, have a flat roof of basalt-stone slabs supported by transverse arches.

The second phase of fortification began with the Ayyubid ruler of Damascus, al-'Adil Abu Bakr (r. 592–615/1196–1218). The towers, now erected at a considerable distance from the *cavea* proper, leave space for interior corridors and defence installations. Several antique structures from within the city must have been used for there is evidence of numerous *spolia* in this building phase. The additional towers, erected by al-'Adil, are distinguished from earlier extensions by their considerably larger size, the construction technique of the outer walls and the barrel-vaulted roofs. The north-western tower (4) measuring 22 m x 31 m was added in 599/1202–3, and was followed in 608–10/1211–13 by the two entrance towers (9 and 10).

Passing these, the visitor finds himself in one of the defence alleyways around the theatre proper. Climbing the stairs one reaches the northern platform serving as an exhibition space for antique statues in front of tower (11). Together with

Floor-plan of Bosra Citadel.

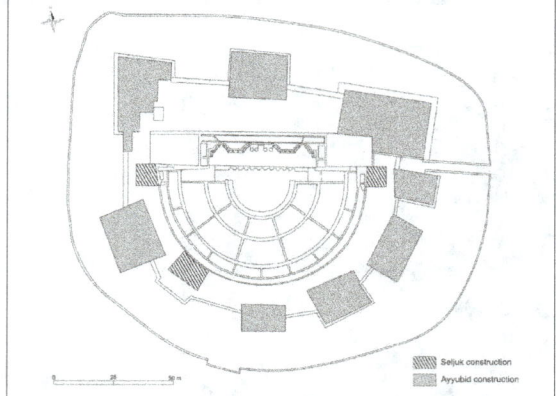

ITINERARY II *Antique Heritage in an Ayyubid City*
Bosra Citadel (Museum)

tower (5), now accommodating the ethnographic collection, and tower (7) that serves as archaeological museum, it belongs to the last, medieval, phase carried out to improve the citadel's defences. All three towers are constructed in the splendid three-*iwans* mode, arranged around a central courtyard. Tower (11), since it is easy to reach from the entrance gate, might have served as a reception hall during the reign of al-Salih Isma'il, who took up residence in the citadel.

II.2 **MASJID KHIDR** (OPTION)

Exiting the citadel from the main entrance, the ancient town of Bosra lies immediately to the north. Walking around the theatre, one arrives upon the classical ruins, organised on a clear east–west axis. Looking west, the minaret of Masjid Khidr is visible in the distance. The building's interior may be inaccessible.

About 200 m off the main north–south axis of the city, it stands as one of the oldest surviving Islamic buildings of Bosra, indicating the extension of the medieval city. The entrance inscription mentions Gumushtagin as patron in 528/1134. A modest structure, 9 m x 9.5 m, it is dedicated to the popular Muslim Saint al-Khidr. Antique building materials were recycled as décor, and the 12 m-high minaret is set 1.5 m to the west of the building, indicating a later construction date (probably inspired by the impressive minaret of the Jami' al-'Umari built in 618/1221–2). The interior follows the local architectural tradition of Hauran; two transverse arches carrying the stone slabs of a flat ceiling. An antique conch tops the prayer-niche, flanked by two antique columns.

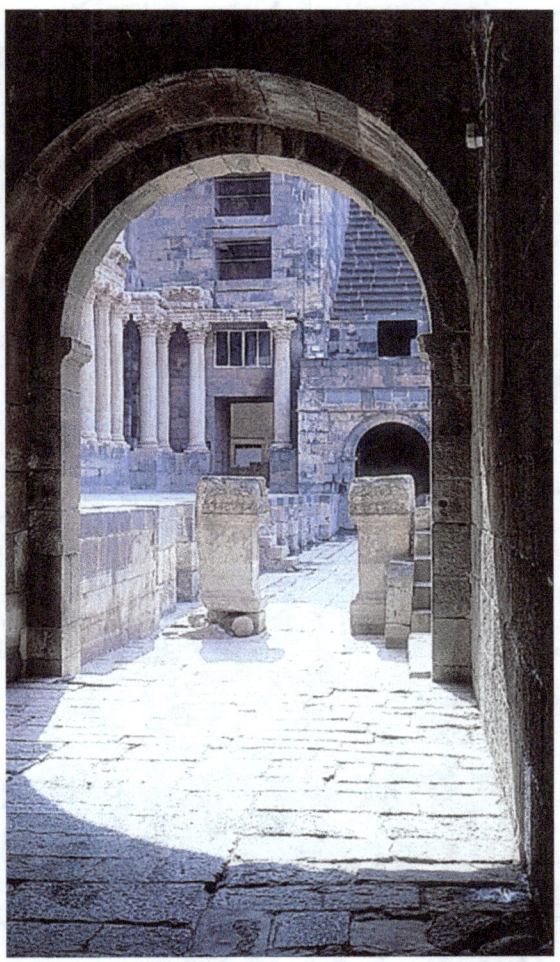

Bosra Citadel, view of the Roman scaenae frons *and orchestra.*

127

ITINERARY II   *Antique Heritage in an Ayyubid City*
Jami' al-'Umari

II.3 JAMI' AL-'UMARI

Return to the monumental east—west axis. Walk 150 m north towards the other minaret that appears on the horizon in front of you amongst the Corinthian capitals. Jami' al-'Umari is the large building that appears to the west. It can be visited respecting appropriate dress codes and conduct, but it is likely to be closed apart from prayer times (approx 11.00—13.00). A small donation is advisable.

The Friday Mosque of Bosra is the most elevated building of the city, its minaret defining the silhouette of the skyline. The main entrance is located on the east façade directed towards the main road. Three portals and five arched windows are arranged symmetrically across the façade. A row of arcades 2 m in front of the façade, accentuate the edifice. The arches rest on ten short, antique columns with Ionian capitals.
According to local tradition, the mosque is attributable to the second Rightly Guided Caliph 'Umar bin al-Khattab (r. 13–23/634–44). Although there might have been an Umayyad foundation, attributable to the caliph 'Umar II, the present structure is the result of several building phases during the 5th/11th to the 7th/13th centuries. An inscription that was once included on the eastern façade mentions the renovation efforts of Gumushtagin in 605/1112–13. The inscription supports the assumption that the redesign of Jami' al-'Umari was part of a wider programme, that saw vernacular architecture built throughout Syria in the early 6th/11th and 7th/12th centuries. Which supposition further supports the notion that the extensive restoration works carried out at the Great Umayyad Mosque in Damascus by the Seljuqs in 457/1064–5, and that by the Burids in 503/1109–10 inspired these efforts. The prestigious Umayyad Mosque is the classical example of its type and influenced the mosque architecture in the Bilad al-Sham from there on in and throughout the ages. Covering a trapezoid plot of roughly 34 m x 36 m, Jami' al-'Umari follows the *riwaq*-mosque layout: a central courtyard surrounded by single porticos on the east and west sides, and double porticos to the north and south. The carefully chosen antique columns and capitals of white limestone stand out clearly against the dark basalt arches and walls. Apart from that, the interior decoration is remarkably sober and confines itself to a simple hewn ledge above the arcades. Preserved in the prayer hall are parts of the sumptuous stucco decoration that once covered a

Jami' al-'Umari, view of the square minaret and arcades with Ionian capitals, Bosra.

ITINERARY II   Antique Heritage in an Ayyubid City
Jami' al-'Umari

strip that ran at a height of 1.80 m to 3.50 m from the ground. This strip included two rows of inscriptions, surrounded by friezes of detailed and elaborated tendrils. Amazing similarities to stucco decorations in eastern Iran and Afghanistan testify to the stylistic influence from the Seljuq homelands.

The final restoration phase was concentrated on the north portico, inscribed with a completion date of 618/1221–2. From the outside, the northern façade reveals an outstanding style. The stones used are of larger size than the rest of the building and the portal layout is composed of three doorways. Above the doorways a row of reused column-bases serve as headers, a distinguishing mark found in the entrance towers of the Bosra Citadel erected ten years earlier. Such borrowing may suggest that a local workforce employed to work on the mosque and may have copied the building style introduced to the region ten years earlier. On the east end, the square minaret protrudes from the northern wall. The 5 m-high base of the minaret, completely integrated into the stonework of the wall, indicates that it belonged to the original construction. The upper part of the 20 m-high minaret has double arched windows and a flat stone-slab roof. Remains of white paint are evidence of its once outstanding character.

From the Mamluk period, the Mosque was left to decay until several phases of restoration works carried out in the 20th century. In the last phase of 1963–5, the erection of a steel construction covered what had been originally an open court-yard. After uncovering the original street level in 1992–3, the rehabilitation of the building as the Congregational Mosque of Bosra took place.

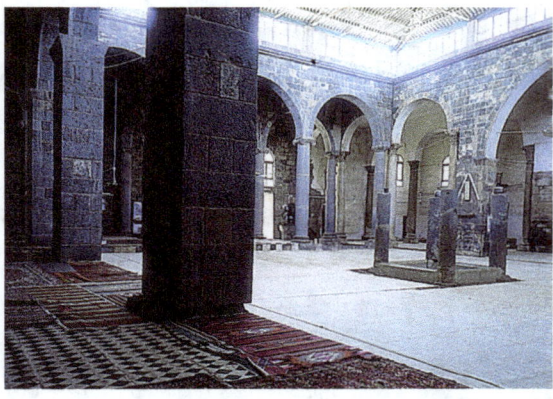

Jami' al-'Umari, interior, general view, Bosra.

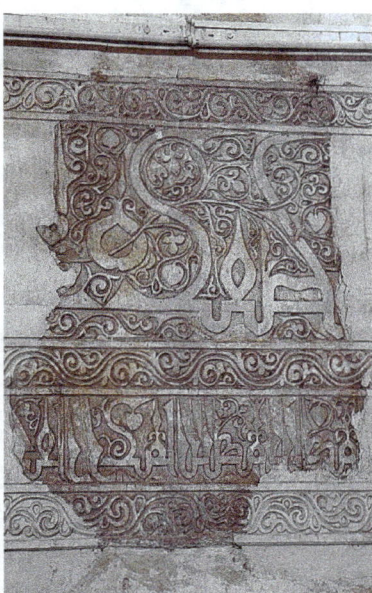

Jami' al-'Umari, fragment of stucco decoration with two-row inscription, Bosra.

II.4 MABRAK AL-NAQA MOSQUE/MADRASAT GUMUSHTAGIN

Continue walking north, and divert to the east (left) at the site of the Roman military camp. The white cupola of the Madrasat Gumushtagin is visible topping the black structure that appears in the distance, beyond the graveyard in the foreground. The shrine and the madrasa can be visited respecting appropriate dress codes and conduct, but it is likely to be closed apart from prayer times (approx 11.00–13.00). A small donation is advisable. In the event that the buildings are closed, the proprietors of the shops across the street may help you in locating the caretaker.

Situated on the north-east corner of the fortification wall, the complex covers a plot of 29 m x 15 m. The main, northern façade shows clearly the division in three parts, each provided by a proper entrance and distinguished by clear joins in the stonework. The oldest part is the so-called Mabrak al-Naqa on the western side, built of small stones of irregular size. The middle part is a prayer-hall, whilst the largest part is the *madrasa* on the eastern side.

The Mabrak al-Naqa, "the place where the she-camel kneeled" is, according to the local tradition, the place where the Prophet Muhammad let his she-camel kneel down during his visit to the city on trade. The date of the shrine itself remains unclear but it continues to be a place of prayer. Certainly, the *qibla* wall forms the oldest part of the building, whereas the square forecourt was probably added during the medieval period. The *mihrab* is decorated with *spolia* – a semicircular carved shell and two undecorated antique pillars. Below the shell there is an inscription in *kufic* script, which describes the place as "the Mosque of the Prophet". The "kneeling spot" is an antique stone slab in front of the prayer-niche with several depressions, interpreted as the imprints of the camel.

The middle part of the Mabrak complex, a small, square oratory of around 6.5 m x 6.5 m with a prayer-niche was added at a later stage, as the Mabrak itself was originally preceded by a square forecourt. The prayer-room is divided by a single transverse arch, which supports the roof-slabs in traditional local style. Here also, the prayer-niche is decorated with two antique spiral-fluted columns and topped with a carved shell.

A *madrasa* occupies the eastern half of the complex, commissioned by Gumushtagin in 530/1136, as mentioned in the inscrip-

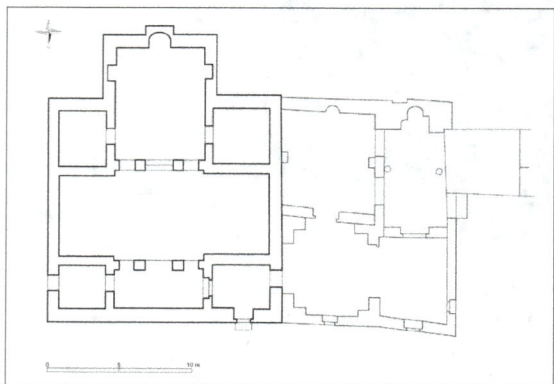

Floor-plan of Madrasat Gumushtagin, Bosra.

ITINERARY II   Antique Heritage in an Ayyubid City
Mabrak al-Naqa Mosque/Madrasat Gumushtagin

tion above the entrance. It follows the four-*iwans*-in-axial-symmetry layout whereby the four *iwans* are placed around a central courtyard. The west and east *iwans* are separated from the courtyard by a huge arch supported by antique abutments. The north *iwan* and the south *qibla iwan* have three doorways surmounted by windows with pointed arches. The *qibla iwan* is emphasised by its double depth of 8 m, requiring an extra transverse arch to support the roof. Originally, the inner walls were covered with red plaster; the yellowish plaster is a later addition.

This *madrasa* is the earliest surviving example of a religious college in Syria. Both the institution of *madrasa* and the four-*iwans*-in axial-symmetry layout are of Iranian origin, first introduced to Syria in the mid 5th/11th century and which subsequently spread all over the Muslim territories. Here, instead of barrel-vaults that were the usual covering for *iwans* in Iran, the roof is made of flat basalt slabs in the local Hauran style. Also exceptional for Iranian *madrasas*, the courtyard was covered by a dome, probably for climatic reasons but also because similar central domes have long been known in the local tradition, as can be seen in the impressive churches in Ezra en route between Damascus and Bosra.

The minaret is only accessible via the roof of the complex and was probably a later addition from the first half of the 6th/13th century.

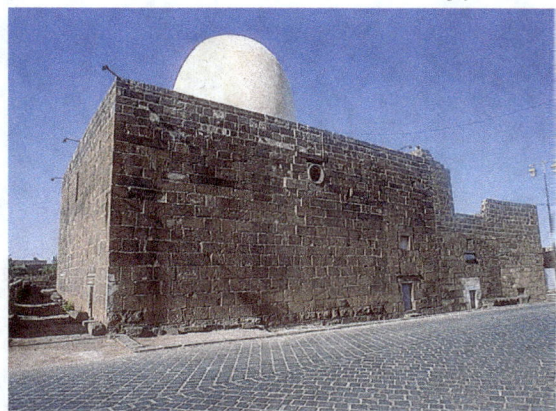

Mabrak al-Naqa Mosque/ Madrasat Gumushtagin, general view, Bosra.

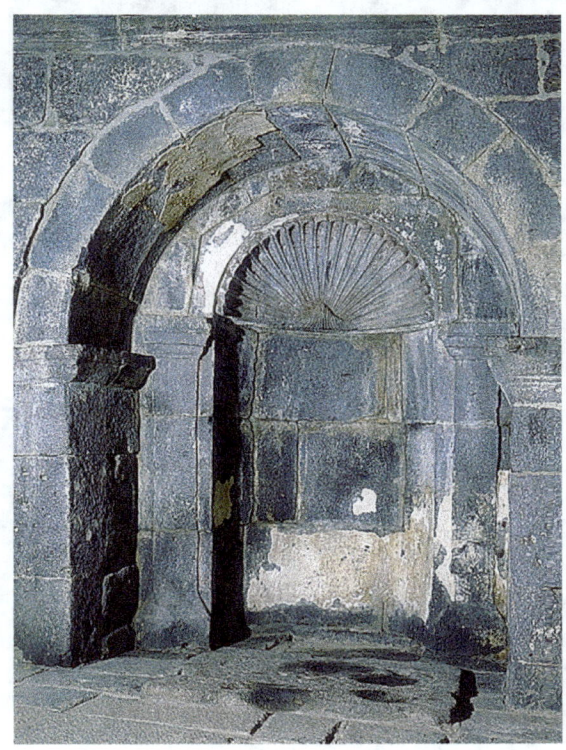

Mabrak al-Naqa Mosque/ Madrasat Gumushtagin: the mihrab decorated with spolia and the "kneeling spot", Bosra.

ITINERARY II *Antique Heritage in an Ayyubid City*
Mosque of Fatima

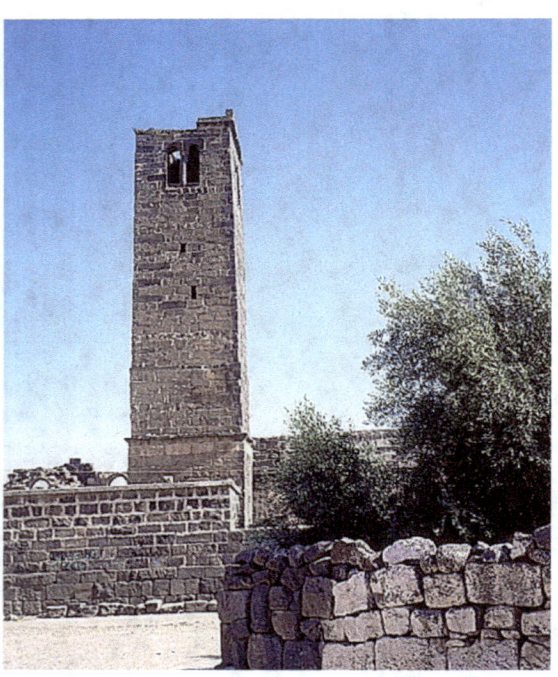

Mosque of Fatima, view of the square minaret, Bosra.

II.5 **MOSQUE OF FATIMA**

On leaving the madrasa, turn back and walk south-west for 75 m. The Mosque of Fatima is located directly behind the Basilica ruin. It can be visited respecting appropriate dress codes and conduct, but it is likely to be closed apart from prayer times (approx 11.00–13.00). A small donation is advisable

Although dedicated to the venerated daughter of the Prophet Muhammad, this mosque is a medieval structure as evident from the inscription above the west window of the entrance façade. The year and name of the patron have been extinguished, but the epigraphic style clearly points to the reign of al-Salih Isma'il (615–44/1218–46). The building of the rectangular structure, measuring 11 m x 21 m, was in two phases. The original, northern part of the structure's stonework is more irregular than that of the later, southern section, which is made of thoroughly hewn and regularly cut stones. The interior demonstrates the local building technique: six low-placed arches that support the basalt slabs forming a flat roof. The two northern arches rest on antique abutments while the third, central, arch, constructed entirely from *spolia*, marks the transition to the newer section. The extension to the south is distinguishable by larger windows and a lack of *spolia*; the arches are smaller and rest directly on the ground without abutments. Although a wider room would have been preferable for the devotional needs of the Islamic community, the mosque's extension was in its length rather than its width, because the local roofing technique made a lengthwise extension easier to manage.

Here also, the isolated minaret erected at the north-east corner of the mosque is of later date. The inscription under the horizontal ledge that protrudes from the minaret's outer wall between the ground and first level mentions the Mamluk sultan, al-Nasir Muhammad as the patron in 705/1306. It clearly copies the Ayyubid minaret of the Jami' al-'Umari which was constructed 90 years earlier.

ITINERARY II *Antique Heritage in an Ayyubid City*
Birkat al-Hajj

II.6 BIRKAT AL-HAJJ

Walk south through the alleyways of basalt houses, keeping the citadel/theatre to the east, and you will suddenly come upon a large pool of water in a basin cistern.

The Birkat al-Hajj, the "pilgrimage's reservoir", marks the most south-easterly extension of the Muslim city. The open, trapezoid-shaped reservoir measures 155 m x 122 m, edged by massive 3.5 m-thick walls of roughly hewn basalt-stone blocks. Three metre-wide projections divide the inner walls. The reservoir itself is between 6 m and 12 m deep. Stairs at the north-western, south-western and south-eastern corners provide access to the water. The Birkat al-Hajj and another, slightly smaller, reservoir to the east secured the water supply for the city, collecting rain and melted ice from the Jabal Hauran and the Wadi al-Zaydi to the west of the city.

In his description of Syria, the historian Ibn Shaddad al-Halabi mentions that the Ayyubid ruler of Damascus, al-Mu'azzam 'Isa (d. 624/1227), built a huge reservoir in the outskirts of Bosra, to serve as a drinking trough for the pilgrim's caravan that passed on its annual journey to Mecca before entering the desert region. Describing his participation in the pilgrimage from Damascus in 726/1326, the traveller Ibn Battuta gives a vivid description of Bosra as pilgrim's halt: "... we travelled on to the town of Bosra;

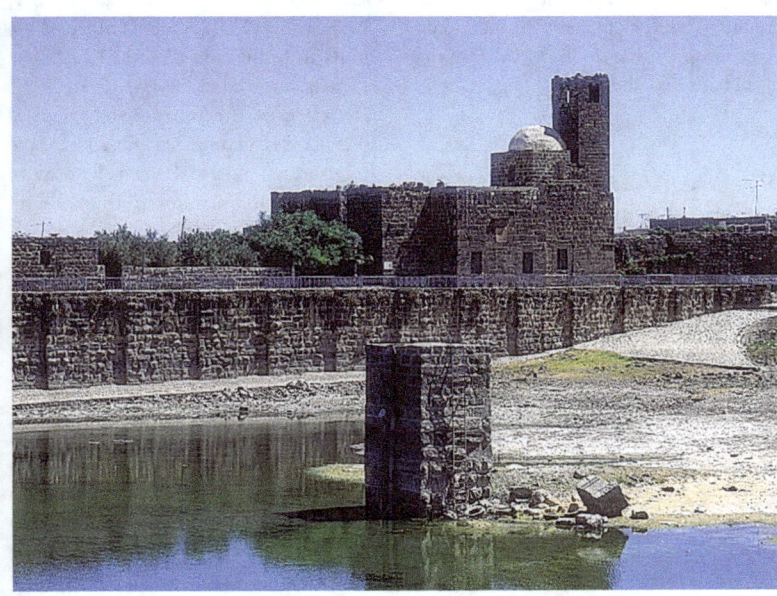

Birkat al-Hajj, general view, Bosra.

it too is a small place. It is the usual practice of the caravan to stop there for four nights. The inhabitants of the Hauran flock to this town with their produce and the pilgrims supply themselves here with provisions for the journey." The huge dimensions of the reservoir suggest that it must have provided water for a large city and not just for the pilgrims' caravans that passed through twice a year. Therefore the initial structure may date to the Roman period (5th century AD) while the historically documented efforts of al-Mu'azzam 'Isa indicate a medieval renovation. This supposition matches very well with the extension of the citadel into a palatial residence for the lord of Bosra, the brother of al-Mu'azzam, al-Salih Isma'il, since the citadel with its newly constructed mosque and *hammam* required a sufficient and well-functioning water supply that the Birkat al-Hajj may well have provided.

II.7 MADRASAT ABU AL-FIDA' also known as MADRASAT AL-DABBAGHA

It is located on the eastern side of Birkat al-Hajj, and is visible from the edge of the reservoir. The interior may be inaccessible.

This *madrasa*, built at the northern edge of the water reservoir, has well-preserved walls, up to 8 m high. Its tall minaret and the many projections and rejections of its outer walls make it an outstanding building in this part of the city. Although access to the *madrasa* is through the oblong side, the southern wall facing the reservoir has to be considered the main façade. At the base of the building, a row of rectangular openings flows into a canal running towards the west, which once provided the citadel and possibly other structures in the city with water from the reservoir. Accentuation of the protruding, middle, part of the wall is by two large windows at ground-floor level and a row of three smaller windows under the edge of the roof. In the middle of the wall surface, an inscription on a light-coloured limestone slab stands out from the dark-basalt wall. Three layers of various *spolia* – basalt, limestone, and fluted limestone – add to its peculiarity. The inscription mentions that al-Salih Isma'il commissioned the *madrasa* and that the Sultan's commander, Amir Shams al-Din Sunqur, donated the funds to build it in 622/1225–6. The *madrasa* followed in the *Hanafi* rite.

The core of the building is an axial four-*iwans* structure. Accentuation of the longitudinal axis of 19 m is by way of the oversized 9 m-long south *iwan* with a prayer-niche that served as a mosque. Two side rooms belong to the original layout although they give the impression of a later addition. Traditional transverse arches support the flat-stone roof of the prayer *iwan* proper, whereas the small room to the east of it, and the two side *iwans* in the courtyard, are roofed with pointed barrel-vaults, unrecorded in any other religious building in Bosra and evidently inspired by the interiors of the recently erected towers of the citadel.

ITINERARY II *Antique Heritage in an Ayyubid City*
Madrasat Abu al-Fida'

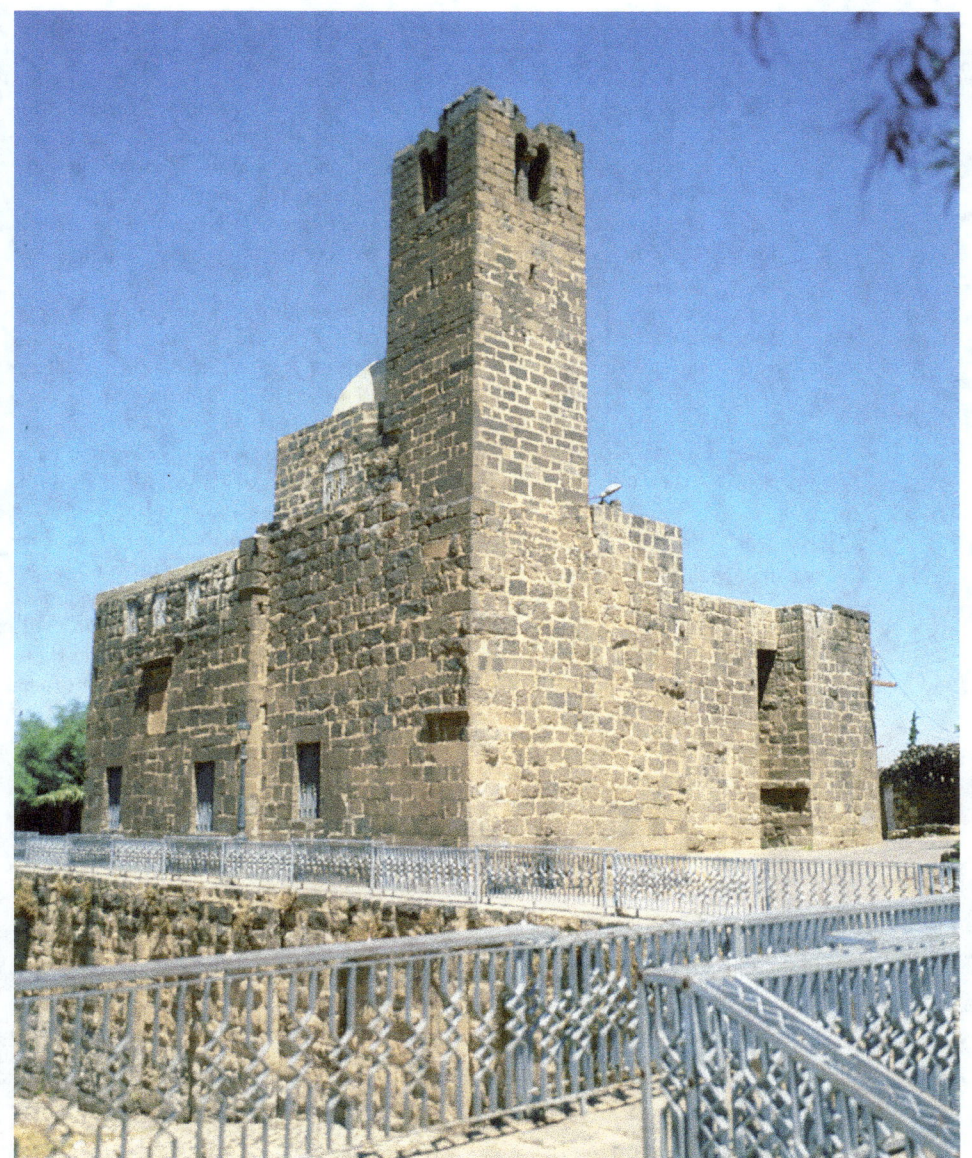

Madrasat Abu al-Fida', view of the mausoleum dome and minaret, Bosra.

ITINERARY II   *Antique Heritage in an Ayyubid City*
Masjid Yaqut

The square mausoleum at the southeastern corner of the building was added at a later stage in 630/1232–3 as a final resting place for its patron. The mausoleum's dome, which rests on an octagonal tambour, follows the example of other mausoleums, built profusely in Damascus and in other Syrian cities from the 6th/12th century, another reference to the imperial architectural tradition of the capital.

Here also, the minaret on the mausoleum roof is a later addition. The upper floor is provided with twin arcaded windows on each side of the wall, apparently it too copied the minaret of Jami' al-'Umari.

II.8 MASJID YAQUT

This small building is located to the northeast of Birkat al-Hajj, and is visible from the edge of the reservoir. The interior may be inaccessible.

The small funerary monument at the north-eastern edge of the Birkat al-Hajj is identified as the *darih* of the pilgrim Shibab al-Din Yusuf, son of Yaqut the commandant of Bosra Citadel. The inscription, on a limestone block above the entrance, mentions the founder Yaqut and the date 655/1257–8. Another carved inscription on white limestone is inserted on the western façade. As is the case with the inscription on the neighbouring Madrasa al-Dabbagha, the inscription is emphasised by a carved antique stone block. The façade layout of both this and the neighbouring structure show that Birkat al-Hajj was regarded as a representative public space, serving as the background to the arrival of the pilgrimage caravan and saturation of the animals. The cemetery located to the east of the reservoir will have inspired the erection of funerary monuments on this spot.

The building consists of two rooms, covering an area of 7 m x 14 m. Access is through a portal to the north, added at a later stage, as evidenced by the clear junction in the stonework. The door, which is 2 m wide, has a pointed niche 0.9 m deep and is accessible via a few steps; benches (*mastaba*) originally flanked the steps on each side. A courtyard once lay behind the door but it is no longer extant, while, to the right, an entrance leads to the prayer-room. The sole decoration here is the antique shell-shaped *mihrab* niche. The eastern room served as mausoleum. In contrast to the other religious monuments of the city that either employ local building techniques (Masjid Khidr and Masjid Fatima), or represent a mix of traditional with the new imperial architecture (Mabrak al-Naqa Mosque-Madrasa Complex and Madrasa al-Dabbagha), here, both rooms are covered by cross-vaults, probably influenced by the citadel towers that had been built a few years earlier. Construction of one of the towers (8) was under the supervision of Commander Yaqut, and he very likely employed the same workforce to construct his son's mausoleum.

ITINERARY II   *Antique Heritage in an Ayyubid City*
Masjid Yaqut

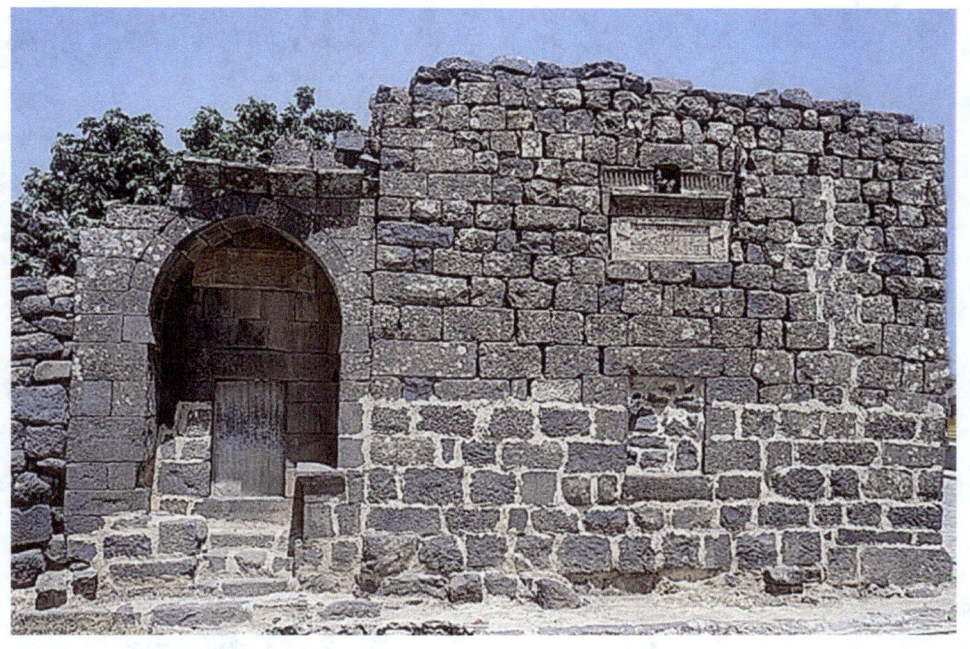

Masjid Yaqut, Bosra.

LOCAL TRADITIONS AND IMPERIAL ARCHITECTURE IN A PROVINCIAL CAPITAL

Verena Daiber

The dark stonework of the buildings in Bosra, only occasionally highlighted by pale limestone, gives the city its distinctive atmosphere. Black basalt is abundantly available in the Hauran region. Since wood is scarce, the architecture of the city thus acquired a characteristic construction technique: flat roofs of basalt-stone slabs. The heavy stone slabs required the support of transverse arches, inserted at regular intervals. The earliest Islamic structures, like the three Burid towers of the Bosra Citadel (481/1088 and 542/1147–8), Masjid Khidr (528/1134), Jami' al-'Umari (506/1112–13) and even the later Mosque of Fatima (early 7th/13th century), impressively reveal this continuity of local building traditions, which date back to the Roman structures built nearly 700 years before.

Foreign influences are introduced at the Madrasat Gumushtagin (530/1136) seen in the four-*iwan*s-in-axial-symmetry layout, first brought to Syria in the 5th/11th century by the Seljuqs from their Iranian homeland. Nevertheless, the innovation is combined with the traditional-style flat roofs. In the Ayyubid period, barrel-vaulted *iwan* structures become more widely used as the ideal plan for public constructions – *madrasa*s and palatial structures – as, for example, in the citadel palaces of Aleppo (Itinerary VII.1.h), Damascus (Itinerary I.2) and Qal'at Najm (Itinerary VIII.1.). In Bosra, the

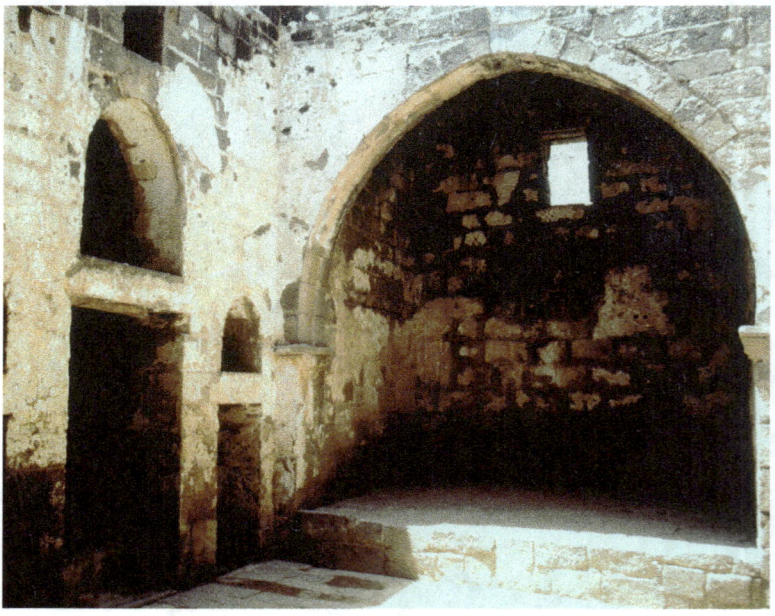

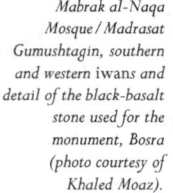

Mabrak al-Naqa Mosque / Madrasat Gumushtagin, southern and western iwans and detail of the black-basalt stone used for the monument, Bosra (photo courtesy of Khaled Moaz).

vaulted-*iwan* structure was initially introduced for use on the towers of the citadel but the style is otherwise unrecorded in the Hauran region. This suggests an intensive exchange of building expertise between the capital Damascus and the provincial city of Bosra.

This was especially the case under al-'Adil Abu Bakr (r. 592–615/1196–1218) who commissioned extensive refortifications at the citadels of both Damascus and Bosra. Thus the "International Fortification Style" was promoted in Bosra and executed by Damascene workmen who were working within the scope of a comprehensive fortification program that was sponsored by the Ayyubids throughout Egypt, Syria and the Jazira. These developments grew out of the Crusader threat, and as a response to the new techniques and weaponry used in warfare, such as the *manjaniq* (mangonel) introduced in the late 6th/12th century.

In civil architecture, the Madrasat al-Dabbagha is a good example of an architectural tripartite blending: the Iranian four-*iwans* layout, along with the innovations in imperial construction engineering – like the barrel-vault – and the continued use of the ancient, local flat-roof technique. The last building erected before the Mongol sack of 658/1260, Masjid Yaqut, is covered with cross vaults; it can, therefore, be considered the final link in the chain of 5th/11th–7th/13th century Bosran architecture that developed under the influence of the capital, Damascus.

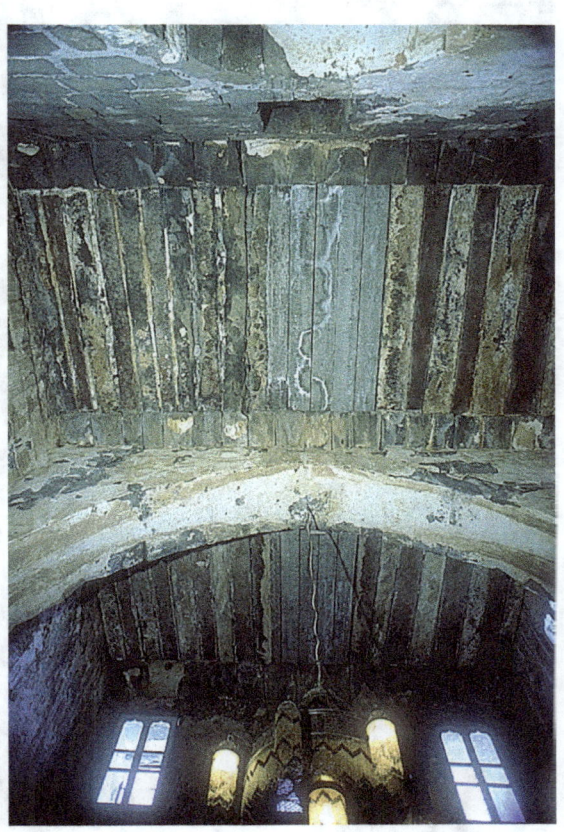

Mabrak al-Naqa Mosque/Madrasat Gumushtagin, the traditional flat roof constructed of stone slabs, Bosra.

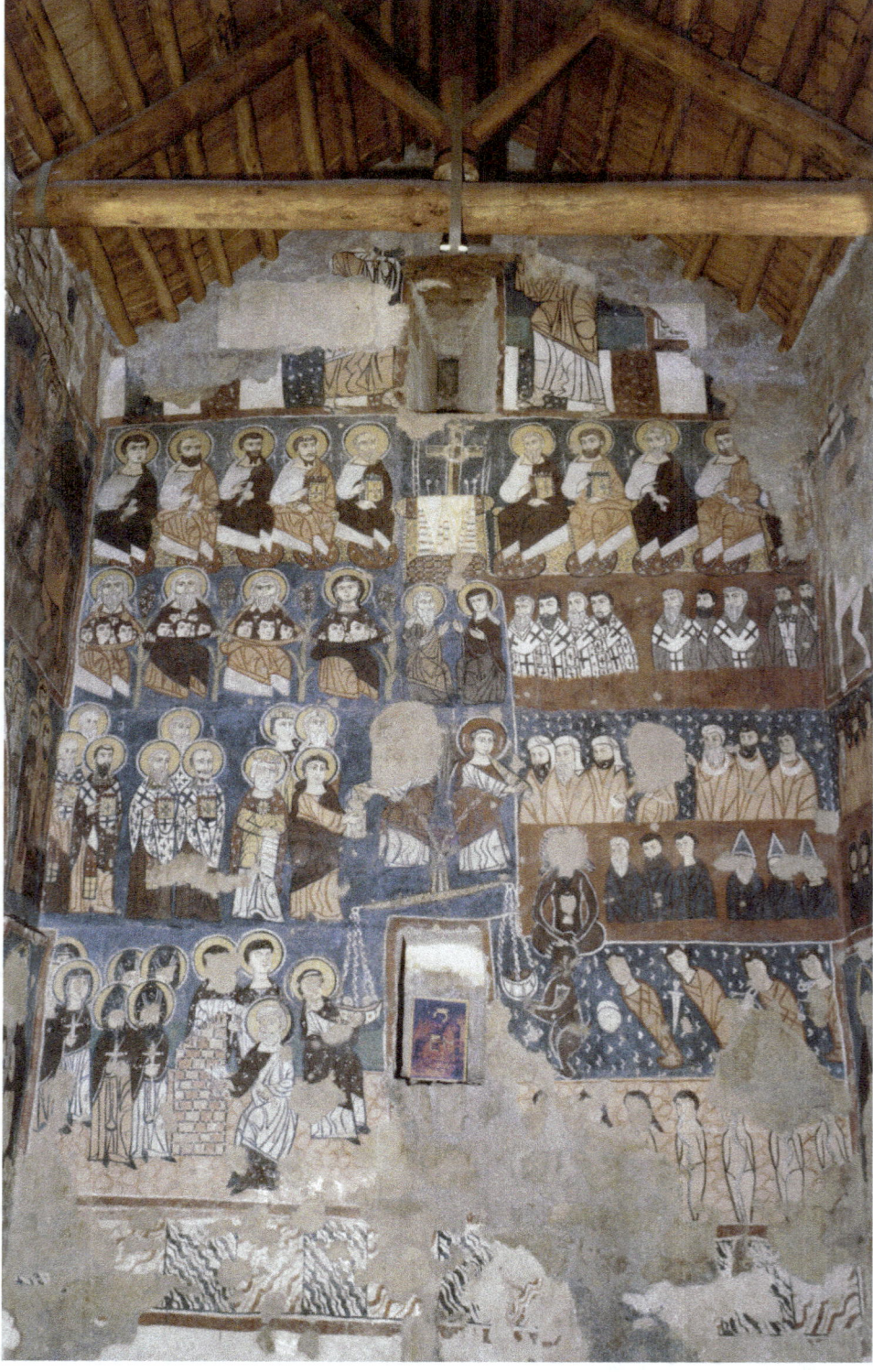

ITINERARY III

Christian Art and Architecture in Medieval Syria

Dina Bakkour

III.1 KHAN AL-'ARUS
III.2 MAR MUSA AL-HABASHI MONASTERY
III.3 TOWN OF QARA (OPTION)
III.4 HOMS
   III.4.a Homs Museum
   III.4.b Great Mosque of Nur al-Din
   III.4.c Church of St Elian

SCENIC OPTION
A Walk through Qalamun

A Survey of Christian Art: Continuity and Interaction   Dina Bakkour

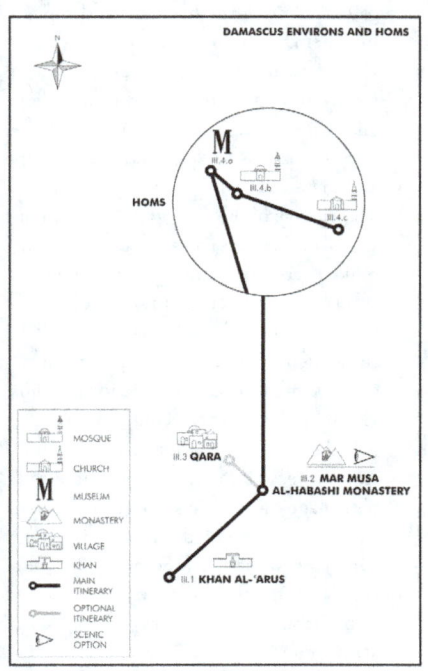

Mar Musa al-Habashī Monastery, fresco of the Last Judgement.

ITINERARY III *Christian Art and Architecture in Medieval Syria*
Introduction

Christian communities living within Syria have always been part-and-parcel of its cultural fabric. Under Islamic religious law, as stated in the Holy Qur'an their rights are fully respected as *"Ahl al-Kitab"*, "People of the Book", or *"Ahl al-Dhimma"*, "People of non-Muslim Faith", with whom there is a certain moral and legal relationship. Thus cultural interaction between Christians and Muslims of the Arab world, and particularly Syria, has always been the norm. A healthy dialogue in matters of theology, spirituality, metaphysics and morality was actually the basis for translation movements, methodical debates and cultural growth.

A wide variety of Christian communities have long existed within Syrian communities, the most prominent being the Roman Orthodox, Syriac, Armenian Orthodox and some Maronites. Their ancient and sacred traditions have continued uninterrupted by the Islamic government, and the continued development of churches and monasteries under Islamic reign attests to the continuity of their religious practices and cultural growth.

During the medieval period, covering the end of the Fatimid reign, the Atabegs, the Ayyubids, and the Mamluks, a change in the circumstances of the local Christian communities occurred: the infringement of Latin Christian Crusaders, or the Franks, into Syrian lands. This brought a new kind of political, religious and social pressure upon local Christians. The Franks criticised and sought to change the norms of cohabitation practiced by the Arab and Eastern Christians of Syria. As Western Catholics, the Franks showed total disregard for indigenous traditions. They imposed foreign rituals upon them, calling their clergy heretical and replacing them with Latin clergymen. Latin Christians also imposed taxes on Eastern Christian communities and raided their churches. Such a situation caused the local Christians to despise the Crusaders and to be wary of their intentions.

The victory of the Zangid Atabeg Nur al-Din over the Crusaders was the beginning of the Arab Christian's liberation and their return to some sense of normalcy. Salah al-Din's victory in Jerusalem and its subsequent liberation allowed for the re-establishment of safe passage for pilgrims visiting the Holy Land. Under Atabeg and Ayyubid rule, local Christian communities witnessed a revival of architectural patronage of churches and monasteries, exhibiting some of the most important surviving works of medieval Christian art. Thus, the flourishing of Christian art is inseparable from the progress of Syrian art in general.

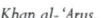
Khan al-'Arus.

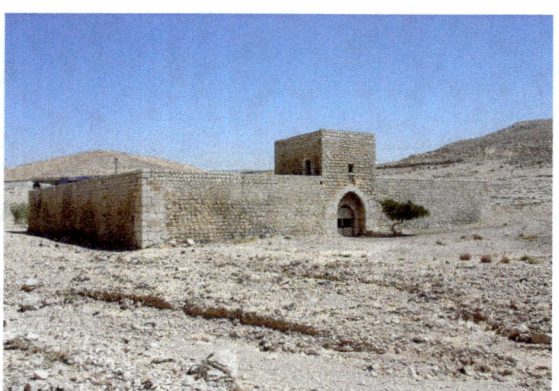

ITINERARY III *Christian Art and Architecture in Medieval Syria*
Introduction

The extensive travel-routes in Syria facilitated the existing local Christian communities, along with the free movement of Christian pilgrims visiting biblical sites. Such routes were not only frequented by pilgrims but also by merchants, and by the late 6th/12th century, a number of *khans* existed in Syrian cities, which offered not only accommodation for travellers but also storage for the goods, which were often valuable, carried by merchant caravans. Ibn Jubayr, a Muslim pilgrim from al-Andalus in Spain, travelled extensively in Syria and noted that "... The road from Homs to Damascus is little populated, except for three or four places where there are these *khanat*". One prominent example is Khan al-'Arus, built by Salah al-Din and bearing an official designation as a *funduq*, or hotel. Built in typical militaristic style as dictated by the atmosphere of the period, it offered shelter, access to clean water and storage for goods in the middle of the desert road. It thus promoted the continuation of pilgrimage and trade even in times of war.

Built for monks who sought seclusion for meditation and worship, there were many monasteries, constructed in the valleys and plains of the Syrian Desert and, more particularly, in the mountains. Mar Musa Monastery, Mar Ya'qub Monastery and Saint Sergius Church in Qara, Mar Elian in Homs, (and a church recently discovered during excavations in the Muslim city of Tell Tnaynir in al-Hasakeh north-east Syria), were all markedly restored during the Ayyubid period. Often built at scenic locations, monasteries offered distance from the hectic life of the city, and churches often exhibited beautiful works of art. They were popular destinations for travellers of all faiths.

The most striking example is Deir Mar Musa al-Habashi, or the Monastery of St. Moses the Ethiopian. It is located

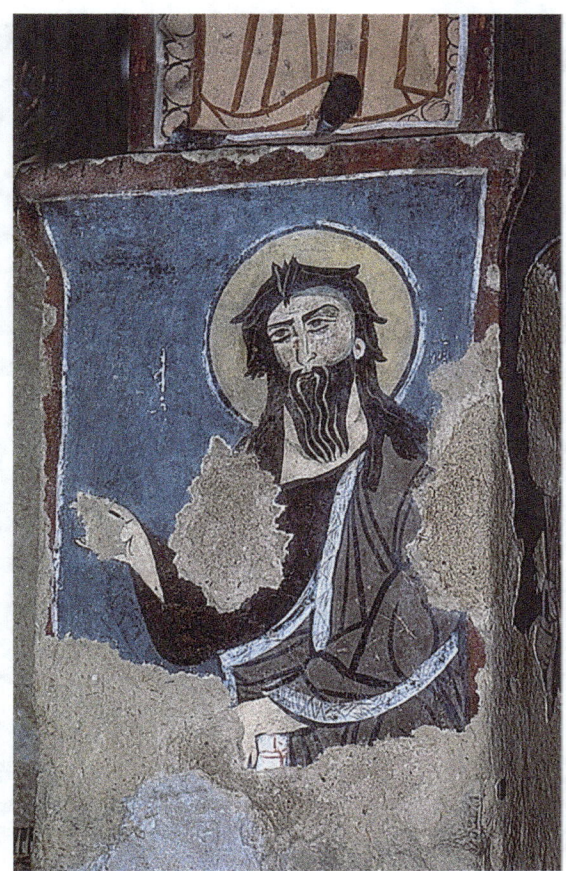

Mar Musa al-Habashi Monastery, fresco of St. John the Baptist.

143

ITINERARY III *Christian Art and Architecture in Medieval Syria*
Introduction

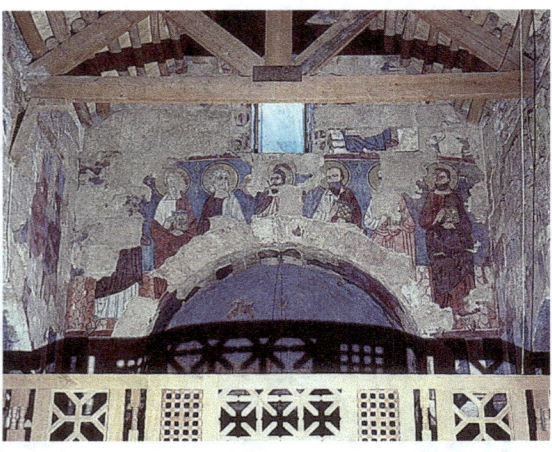

Mar Musa al-Habashi Monastery, view of the fresco in the sanctuary behind the iconostasis, depicting Jesus Christ between the Apostles St. Peter and St. Paul, and the Annunciation *of Jesus.*

on the distant cliffs of the Qalamun Mountains, immersed within a deeply spiritual atmosphere. The paintings in the monastery church survive as a rare example of a complete – though damaged – cycle of frescos still in situ. Painting of the walls was in three phases, the first of which was in the mid-5th/11th century, then the early 6th/12th century and lastly in 588/1192 – all of which are within the Seljuq, Atabeg and Ayyubid reigns. On a regional stylistic level, the paintings link to the churches of Egypt, Jerusalem and Ethiopia in addition to local Syriac expressions. The Monastery of Mar Musa was also an important centre for writing and the copying of rare manuscripts.

Iconographically, the works are clearly of Christian origin, but the style of the painting itself, such as that found in the *Last Judgement*, was utilised by both Christians and Muslims of the period. Some scholars have noted the inclusion of the image of Abraham (one of the three patriarchs holding the souls of the saved) as a deliberate expression of the common heritage shared by both Christians and Muslims, as Abraham is considered the ancestor to both faiths. This interpretation is even expressed in the journal of the 5th-/11th-century Muslim traveller from Persia, Nasir-i-Khusrow who, upon his visit to the Church of the Holy Sepulchre, describes a similar depiction of the *Last Judgement* depicted in mosaic.

The abundance of religious buildings dedicated to the Christian communities of Syria indicates a thriving Christian community living during the Islamic reign. Christians played important roles in all the crafts, in trade and in scientific practice and political diplomacy. Experts of Christian faith would have played an influential role in the caliphal court and often headed the prestigious fields of medicine and astronomy. Abu al-Faraj al-Nasrani (the Christian), was court doctor to both Salah al-Din and his son al-Malik al-Afdal, while Muwaffaq al-Din bin al-Mutran (son of the Bishop), a Damascene doctor renowned for his medical virtuosity, served in al-Malik al-Nasir's court. Many Muslim princes and governors relied on Christian subjects as viziers or ambassadors representing the Ayyubid Empire, particularly during the high period of trade with Italy. They also played an active role in banking and money-exchange.

Local Christian communities continued to prosper in the Islamic cities, and the flourishing of Christian spirituality saw no hindrance under Atabeg and

Ayyubid leadership. Not even the disruptions caused by the unexpected Crusader onslaughts could separate the local Christians from their sense of belonging.

Start early, leaving Damascus via the Damascus–Homs Highway. It is possible to schedule an overnight stay either in Homs (160 km away), or Hama (a further 50 km). Some travellers might opt to spend a night at the Monastery of Mar Musa, located in the Qalamun mountains just east of Nebek village en route to Homs thus dividing the itinerary over two days.

III.1 KHAN AL-'ARUS

This building is located 45 km north of Damascus on the Damascus–Homs Highway. It is next to a blue traffic sign indicating an exit to the village of Ma'lula, behind which is a concrete bypass bridge spanning over the highway. The khan, a few meters lower than street level, lies to your left and is very easily visible from the highway. The building is always open to the public.

It is impossible to miss this attractive building, which survives as a very important example of a medieval *caravanserai*. The 6th-/12th-century traveller Ibn Jubayr, as well as other visitors of the 13th/19th century, noted the existence of an inscription panel located above the entrance lintel which has since gone missing. A record exists of the following words:

"The construction of this blessed hotel was ordered by our leader al-Malik al-Nasir, the righteousness of the world and the religion, the Sultan of Islam and all Muslims, Abu al-Muzaffar Yusuf bin Ayyub, the reviver of the nation of the prince of the faithful, and that is in the year 577."

The date corresponds to AD 1181, the patron is Salah al-Din, and the style of this building is very much like a fortress – clear evidence of the militarisation of Islamic architecture during this period. Ibn Jubayr (d. 614/1217) passed by this building less than two years after its construction and calls it "Khan al-Sultan" in reference to its ruling patron. In his travel memoirs, he describes it as "... the zenith of strength and handsomeness, with iron doors after the fashion in the building of khanat in this part of the world ...", and he refers to many similar constructions along the travel-routes, as beautiful and well fortified.

The *khan* is nearly square; all four of its sides are about 40 m long. The entry, framed by two arches, is on the southern wall. It leads into a corridor that has

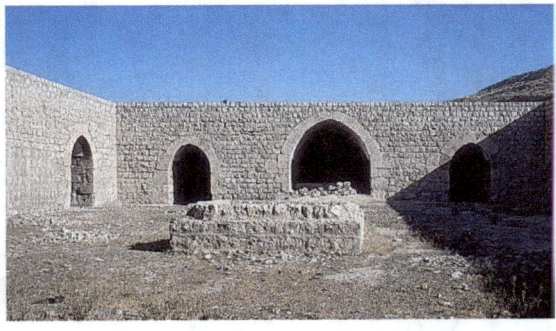

Khan al-'Arus.

ITINERARY III   *Christian Art and Architecture in Medieval Syria*
Mar Musa al-Habashi Monastery

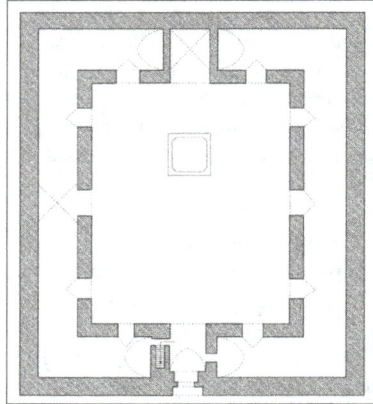

Floor-plan of Khan al-'Arus.

a staircase on the left-hand side leading to the roof. The open courtyard with its central water basin is about 29.55 m x 24.75 m, is surrounded by arched porticos, known in Arabic as *riwaq*.

The upper storey consists of a single room built on top of the entrance as a protective measure. This room is rectangular, 6.40 m x 3.85 m, with a barrel-vaulted roof. It has two windows, used for surveillance, one overlooking the courtyard and the other overlooking the entrance. Originally endowed with merlons and arrow loops on all sides the room has two doors to facilitate access to the roof.

III.2 MAR MUSA AL-HABASHI MONASTERY

Back to the Damascus-Homs highway, continue north until you reach the town of Nebek, which is half-way between Damascus and Homs, approximately 80 km from either. The monastery *lies around 15 km east of Nebek and is accessible by car. In Nebek, exit along the Nebek–Qaryatayn road and drive eastwards through the arid landscape, paying particular attention to the green signposts. Once at the foot of the hills, which cradle the monastery, park and climb the many steps up to the monastery proper. The monastery is open for visitors at all times and offers free accommodation. A small donation is advisable.*

SCENIC OPTION
A WALK THROUGH QALAMUN
An alternative route to Mar Musa al-Habashi is the ancient route following an old dirt road to the east of Nebek known as "Tariq al-Deir". The route is along an uneven path amidst the sloping Qalamun hills that should only be undertaken accompanied by a guide or someone familiar with the area. The first part is accessible by car or on a mule where, half-way along the path, there is a small barn/garage owned by the monastery, used specifically for visitors. After this point, continue on foot and cross the narrow wadi cliffs. It is an enchanting journey for those who enjoy walking and hiking in the openness of nature.

The Mar Musa Monastery is located on the surface of one of the rock formations of the Qalamun Mountains. The area, known as *"al-jebel al-mudakhin"*, or "the smoky mountain" due to its mistiness, overlooks the Palmyrene Plains. The mountain rises approximately 1,320 m above sea level. According to legend, it was named after the King of Ethiopia's son, who arrived in this region after he refused the status of royalty, choosing instead an ascetic lifestyle. He wandered through Egypt and Jerusalem, becoming a priest in one of the monasteries of Qara, and finally settling near the site of Deir Mar Musa, where he stayed in one of the caves and lived the rest of his life as a monk. Allegedly, Byzantine soldiers made martyrs of Mar Musa and some other monks because they refused the Chalcedonian rite. His family returned his body to Ethiopia and all that is left of him is his thumb, currently kept hidden as a relic within a silver glove at the Syriac Church of Nebek.

The monastery is strategically located near to the wintertime route between Damascus and Homs. It was originally a Byzantine watchtower dating back to the 5th or 6th century AD and overlooking the desert road. Remnants of this early tower are in the north-west corner of the monastery, distinguished by its large stones, and currently used as the kitchen. The monastery has a defensive quality; its entrance is very small, about 1 m high, located on the west wall, which is equipped with several arrow loops. Following the entrance is a dark corridor, a few utilitarian rooms and the church. A wide, open space overlooking the rest of the mountain follows.

The main rooms, distributed over two levels above the cliff surface, along with many additional rooms on three levels below the cliff surface, all have small windows that overlook the valley. Rainwater was also collected in the storage chambers around the monastery, after which the water distributed throughout the complex was available all year round. The monastery is currently part of the Syriac Catholic Church of Nebek. It gained a great degree of religious importance in the 10th/16th century and acquired an ecclesiastical chair due to the increased numbers of monks who reside there, and the frequency of pilgrimages to it. The monastery has also spiritual significance for the Muslims of the region who visit the site in honour of Khidr, or

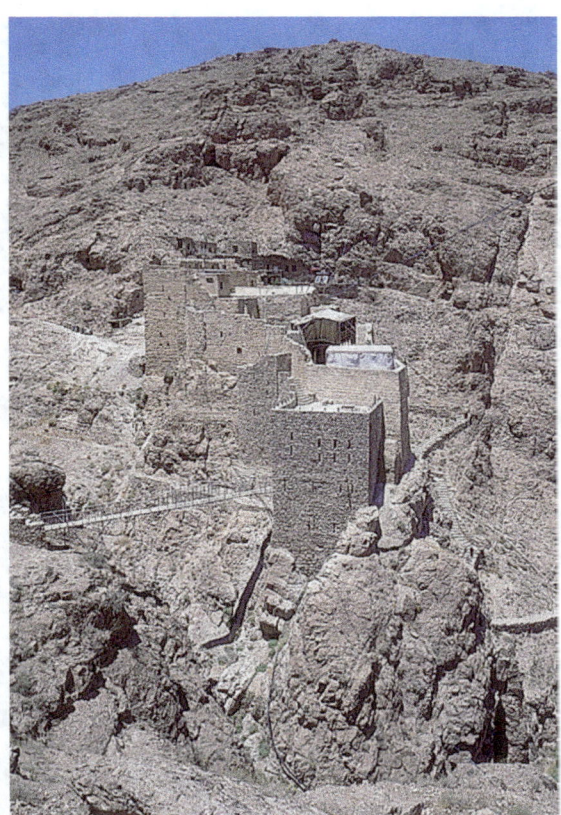

Mar Musa al-Habashi Monastery, general view.

Mar Musa al-Habashi Monastery

Saint George, offering the saint their prayers and oaths.

As for the church, founded in 450/1058, it is located to the northern side of the monastery and is square in layout, each side measuring 10 m. The entrance, through a door on its south wall, leads into the interior supported by two arcades of three bays, made up of four columns and three arches each. The eastern side of the central knave, elevated slightly, is separated by a curtain wall and topped by a semi-dome. Its lower part is made of stone while the upper section is finished in wood. A prayer-niche and sacrificial table are set in the middle of this space, designated as the Holy of Holies.

The Fresco Paintings

Paintings cover the entire surface of the church interior with scenes of Christian iconography, depicted in a mixture of styles and revealing multiple layers of work. These frescos, considered some of the richest examples of Church paintings in the region, present a fine example of local Christian art. The first layer and the oldest, includes an inscription dated to 466/1073–4. Not much of this layer is visible, the best example is the image of the Prophet Ilyas in the middle arcade, and the image of Samson painted in the arcade on the right. The inscriptions on this level of the fresco are in Greek. The second level is not much later than the first. The artist has signed and dated the work, completed on the first Sunday of Tammuz 488 (1095). The best examples found in this layer are the *Annunciation of Jesus* on the eastern wall of the church, and the *Baptism* painted on the left-hand arcade to the left of which is the image of Saint Simeon standing on his pillar, where he spent 37 years of his life. The artist in an inscription that is somewhat damaged and unclear has dated the third and most visible layer. Two readings have been offered: the first 909/1504, has often been understood as the Mamluk period, but has been re-interpreted as referring to the Seleucid calendar, which corresponds to 588/1192; while the second is of 604/1208. The most famous image from this layer of the fresco is the *Judgement Day*, making up the entire west wall of the central knave. It includes a central figure of Jesus sitting on a throne with Adam and Eve kneeling at his feet, while at either side there is a queue of people waiting for their deeds to be measured-up and weighed. The saved souls of the faithful are to the right of Jesus, while the sinners, liars and disbelievers are on the left, headed by Satan who tries in vain to tilt the scales.

Up until the 1930s Syriac monks from all over the region continued to travel to live at Mar Musa, by which time the monastery had been gradually abandoned and used by shepherds and nomads, many of whom took the wooden ceiling-planks to make fires for warmth, exposing the paintings to damage and weathering. It was not until the American University of Beirut sent an archaeological expedition in 1982 to document the damage photographically, which in turn inspired the campaign for restorative works, and revived the religious function of the site.

ITINERARY III   *Christian Art and Architecture in Medieval Syria*
Mar Musa al-Habashi Monastery

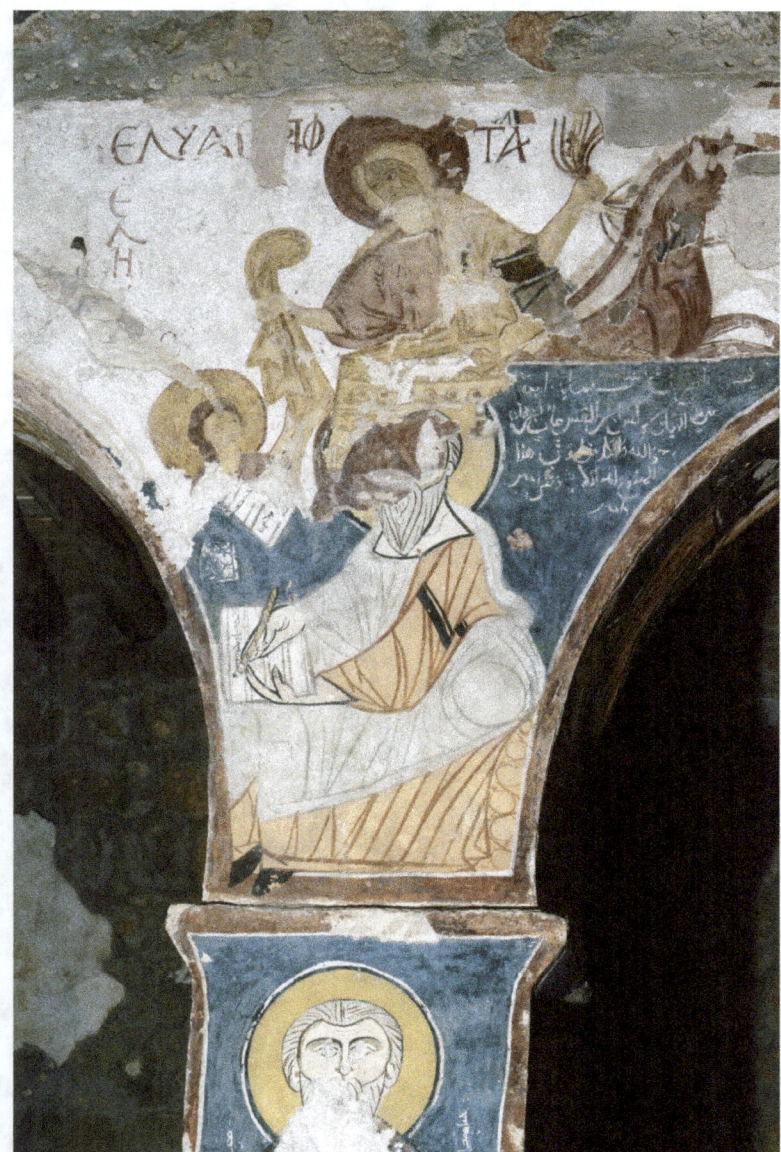

Mar Musa al-Habashi Monastery, detail of the fresco depicting Prophet Iliyas' Ascent to Heaven.

ITINERARY III   Christian Art and Architecture in Medieval Syria
Homs

III.3 **TOWN OF QARA (OPTION)**

Located 15 km north of Nebek, on the left side of the highway — requiring a detour — is the town of Qara with some striking examples of late antique and medieval Christian architecture. The Church of Saints Sergius and Bacchus, today Greek Orthodox, is located on Omar al-Mukhtar Street, one street before the main town square. It holds some beautiful fresco paintings from the 6th/11th century that are very similar to those of Mar Musa. The nearby mosque with the striking portal in the town centre is a converted Basilica. The remains of Qara Monastery, now heavily renovated, lies 2 km west of the town and includes 7th-/13th-century frescos.

III.4 **HOMS**

Return to the Damascus-Homs highway and continue heading north to reach the small and quiet city of Homs.

III.4.a Homs Museum

The museum is located on the corner of al-Quwatli Street and Ibn-Khaldun Street. The museum is open Wed–Mon 9.00–18.00 during the summer, 9.00–16.00 during the winter. Closed on Tuesdays and during Friday prayers (approx 11.00–13.00). There is an entrance fee.

Ceramic vase
This vase, approximately 31 cm high, is decorated with freely painted vegetal motifs executed in a dark-green colour upon a white tin-glazed surface with blue under-glaze. The rim is broken and missing. The style of the vase is Persian, dated approximately to the 7th/13th century, and it may have been brought west to Syria by travelling merchants along the Central Asian trade-routes.

Pilgrim's flask
Made of cream coloured pottery, it is typically disc-shaped and decorated with four protruding attachments. It is 22 cm in diameter and 32 cm high including the neck featuring the heraldic blazon of a sword in the middle of its body. The Ayyubids were the first to use blazons as symbols of military and government rank, and it was common for such blazons to appear on personal items and on architectural elements to indicate patronage. This pilgrim flask, found in a medieval well dug some 50 m from the north side of the old city walls, dates to the end of the 6th/12th century.

Dish
Dated to the 6th/12th or early 7th/13th century, this dish is an example of the famous turquoise-glazed Raqqa-ware with black under-glazed ornamentation. Such a dish would have been a popular trade commodity among luxury goods, crossing the Syrian Desert on caravans to reach the *suqs* and wealthy patrons. Its conical shape spans a diameter of 18.5 cm and it features a semi-astral sequence along the rim, and an intricate pseudo-calligraphic band along the exterior rim and interior of the dish.

ITINERARY III *Christian Art and Architecture in Medieval Syria*
Homs

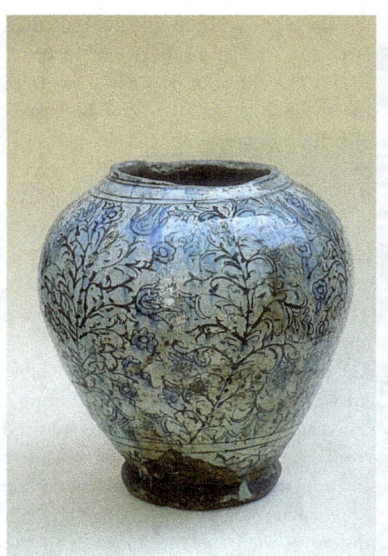

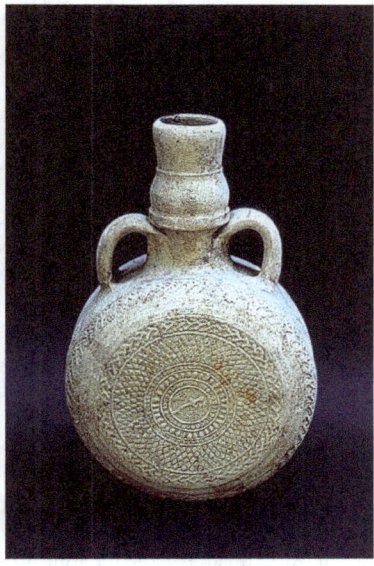

Ceramic vase,
Homs Museum.

Pilgrim flask,
Homs Museum.

Dish,
Homs Museum.

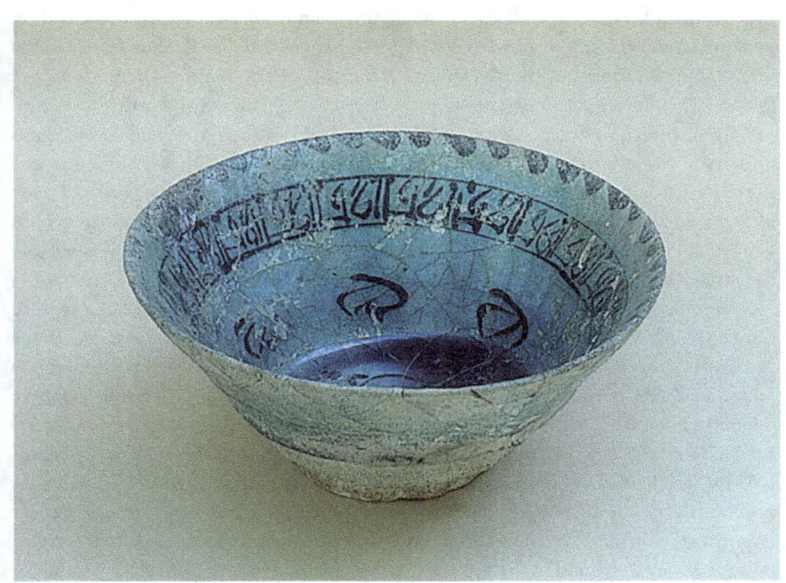

III.4.b Great Mosque of Nur al-Din

Known locally as the Jami' al-Nuri the mosque lies south of Homs's Old Clock Square. Walking ast, the mosque's entrance appears on the left amidst the shops, 20 m before the roofed suq. Respecting appropriate dress codes and conduct, it is open at any time during the day. A small donation is advisable.

Known by the residents of Homs as the Great Mosque it is one of the most important historical monuments of the city, second only to the mosque of Khalid ibn al-Walid, as well as being the largest. The site, used for spiritual purposes even before Christian times, was probably a temple to the Sun God, Apollo. Parts of the mosque, it is thought, were formerly a church dedicated to Saint John the Baptist. Corinthian column capitals in the mosque courtyard and in the decorated lintels represent most of these remains. In 359/969, during the Arab conquests, the Byzantine Emperor Nisifor Fokas destroyed the mosque that was on this site. Thus, when Nur al-Din took control of Syria during the 6th/12th century, he strengthened the Arab frontier against the Byzantines and he gave each major city a new mosque, including this one in Homs. On the south wall of the mosque is an inscription commemorating the Mamluk Sultan al-Zahir Baybars' restoration of the mosque in the 7th/13th century.

The mosque is rectangular, approximately 5.323 m-sq, divided into a prayer-hall and courtyard of nearly equal size. This layout is similar to many of the Umayyad mosque layouts as found in Syria, such as the Great Umayyad Mosque in Damascus (I.6) and the Jami' al-'Umari in Bosra (II.3). The entrance to the mosque is on the south side and may have been part of a different building that pre-dates the mosque. It leads directly to the prayer-hall. There is a western gate, which also leads directly to the prayer-hall; this latter one is modern, built in the 1950s. The final and main gate, renovated in 1197/1783, leads to the courtyard of the mosque.

The prayer-hall is an elongated rectangle measuring 17 m x 100 m. The ceiling's construction comprises a cross-vaulted stone resting on 14 stone, square pillars and a small dome. Only some parts of the prayer-hall date to the Ayyubid period: the room next to the *mihrab* and the marble dado rail and marble *minbar*, the main *mihrab* in the southern wall, as well as two smaller flanking *mihrab*s. On the top of the main *mihrab*, there are important traces of a mosaic panel. Scholars continue to debate whether it is Umayyad or Ayyubid. As for the mosque courtyard, it is also rectangular and open to the sky, surrounded by an arcade on each side. Now removed, a water basin with a well covered by a small dome furnished the courtyard. There are also the remains of an Ayyubid *madrasa*. In the middle of the northern arcade there is a circular tower, opposite to which are two circular plaques of white stone resting on pillars, these were sundials. A shorter pillar made of granite, 98 cm high, is situated between the two circular plaques and would have been used to determine the angle of the sun, especially useful for

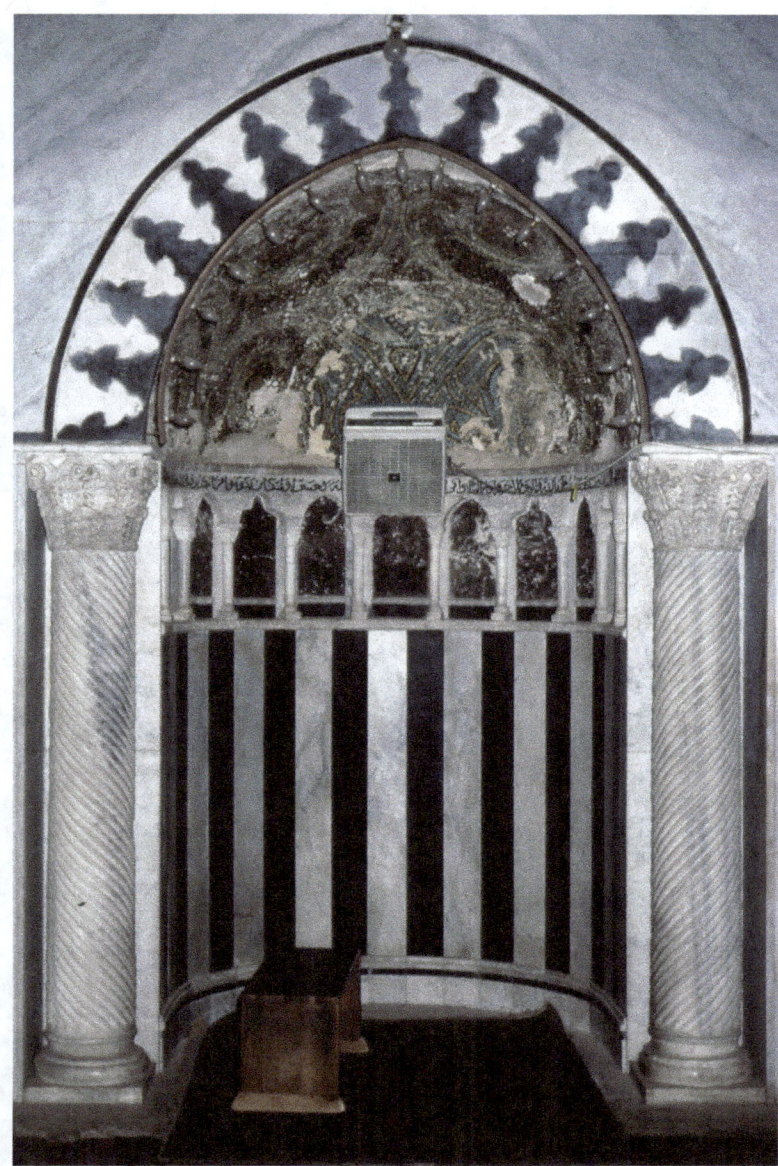

Great Mosque of Nur al-Din, the Ayyubid mihrab, Homs (photo courtesy of Yasser Tabbaa and AKDC. © Yasser Tabbaa Archive, Aga Khan Documentation Center at MIT).

determining the time of the 'Asr prayer (between noon and sunset). As for the minaret, located in the south-western part of the mosque and made of basalt stone, it follows the Umayyad style of a square-based minaret.

The Nuri Mosque is contemporaneous to the Church of Saint Elian and, in addition to its architectural and artistic importance, its patron, Nur al-Din, was a leader renowned for his religious tolerance to the different communities of Syria.

III.4.c Church of St. Elian

Known locally as Kniset Mar Elian, the church is located near the east wall of the old city. From the Great Mosque, walk east through the covered suqs and then through the narrow residential neighbourhood. Located on Bustan al-Diwan Street, the church is part of a larger monastic complex. Respecting appropriate dress codes and conduct, it is open at any time during the day. A small donation is advisable.

This Roman Orthodox Church is of unknown dating but part of the interior includes frescos from the $7^{th}/13^{th}$ century, which means that the structure must be of an earlier date. The church consists of a courtyard, a prayer-hall, a cemetery and a convent for nuns. The exterior gate is made of basalt-stone, replaced in 1914. In the south-western part of the building there is an *iwan* with two doors leading to the prayer-hall. Above the *iwan* is a separate quarter for women to pray, known as the *sha'riyya*. Above the *sha'riyya* is the bell tower. Built in the church courtyard was the convent; the church itself is a small building, 5 m x 9 m, and it contains the grave of the martyr Mar Elian, or Saint Elian. It was renewed and enlarged in 1261/1845, with the addition of two new structures along the north side. Further renovations have taken place in modern times. Currently, it is a rectangular-shaped building, 13.90 m x 14.70 m, made of two parts. The first part, located in the east side, contains the old sacrificial table and a door that leads to the cenotaph of Saint Elian, after which corridor leads to the courtyard. A wooden screen (*iconostasis*) separates one part of the church from the other. The second chamber has a ceiling supported by three arcades and four columns. In 1973, Romanian painters took charge of redecorating the whole of the interior, while the *iconostasis* was a gift from the Orthodox Church of Romania.

The cenotaph of the martyr is made of marble, a rectangular box with a pyramidal cover. The box lives in a small room with a domed roof that is altogether some

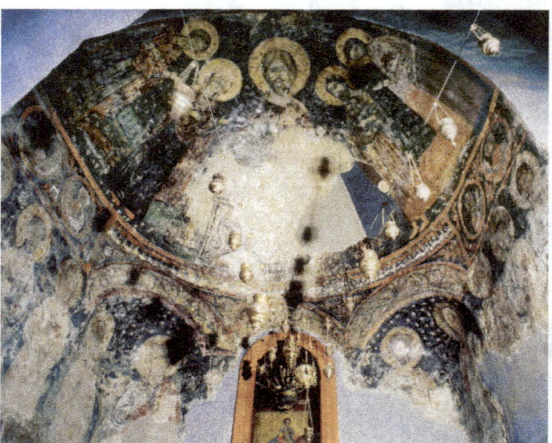

Church of St. Elian, dome fresco depicting Jesus Christ, the Virgin Mary, St. John the Baptist and saints.

ITINERARY III *Christian Art and Architecture in Medieval Syria*
Homs

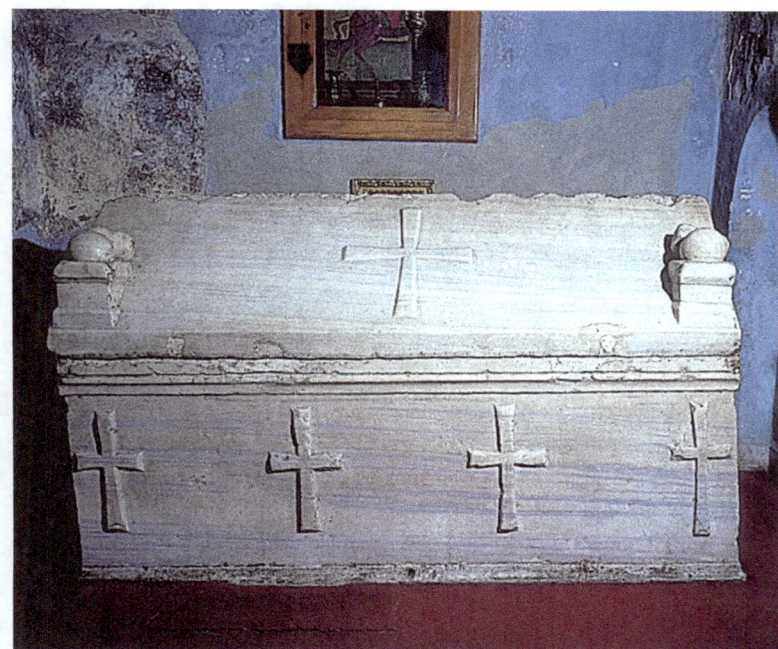

Church of St. Elian, cenotaph of Saint Elian.

2.20 m high. Decorating the walls are several layers of frescos, the cleaning and protection of which is due to the Directorate of Antiquities. The topmost layer of painting dates to the 7th/13th century, made up of two sections: above the dome Jesus is standing amidst four people; the Virgin Mary to Jesus' right dressed in a blue cloak and Saint John the Baptist to his left. Remains of the throne are also evident. In his left hand, John the Baptist holds a book that leans on his knee while his right hand, lifted in blessing, follows the Greek Orthodox style. On the second row, there are images of standing saints with halos around their heads. The inscriptions are in both Greek and Syriac. These paintings reflect the Byzantine traditions continued by the Arab Christians in Syria and maintaining the Chalcedonian rite. There are many local artistic features in these paintings, such as Jesus' head, tilted towards the right, his face human and partly obscured, as well as the vivacious movement of the characters and the soft features and non-uniformity of the beards. Scholars have suggested that such changes in artistic style are a phenomenon of the beautification of local churches during the Crusader presence in Syria, after exposure to Latin Christian art.

A SURVEY OF CHRISTIAN ART: CONTINUITY AND INTERACTION

Dina Bakkour

With the rise of the Islamic Empire and the end of Byzantine-Persian warfare, there was greater interchange, continuity and freedom of local Christian rituals and artistic expression. There was also the absorption of Christian craftsmen into the circle of Islamic patronage. To this effect, the survival of Christian archaeological, architectural and artistic remains is a good indicator of the previous civilisations that have waxed and waned in Syria. Christian art, therefore, was an essential part of the local culture, which controlled the region throughout many centuries and still to this day.

From the pre-Islamic period, the "dead cities" of the Byzantine period located in northern Syria, are not comparable to anything else in the world with their haunting beauty. These citadels, coupled with those of Sam'an and Rusafa, are also fine examples of local Byzantine art.

Of course, the churches of Damascus, Aleppo and Palmyra continued to thrive throughout the Islamic period and still do to this day. The veneration of Saint John the Baptist's shrine within the prayer-hall of the Great Umayyad Mosque in Damascus is a prime example of the spirit of respect and continuity the Islamic conquest professed towards local Christians. Under the Islamic reign, the participation of Arab Christians in the production of the fine and applied arts continued. Take for instance Ibrahim al-Nasrani (2nd/8th century), the ceramist from al-Hira, the discovery of whose many works has been in Raqqa. Further, consider the metal treasure trove discovered in the Church of Rusafa, which belong to the 6th/12th and 7th/13th centuries. The find contained three imported objects and two metal objects fabricated following local metal-working traditions, and some featuring

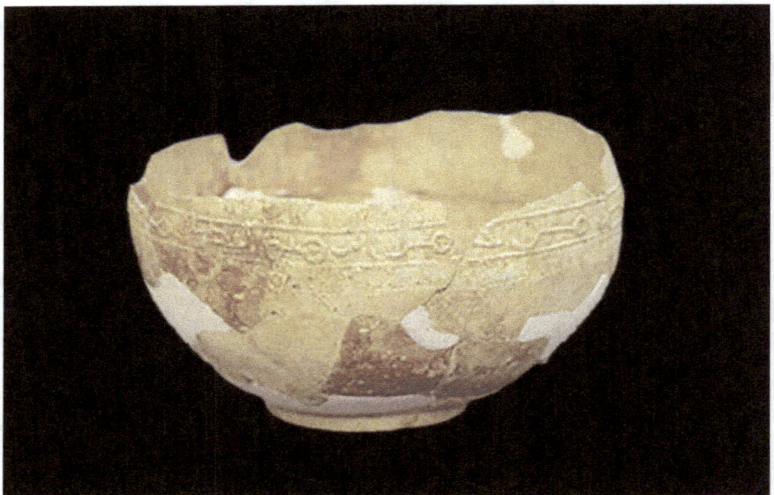

Pottery bowl made by the ceramist Ibrahim al-Nasrani (136–58/754–75), National Museum of Damascus (Inv. Num. 17261/ع).

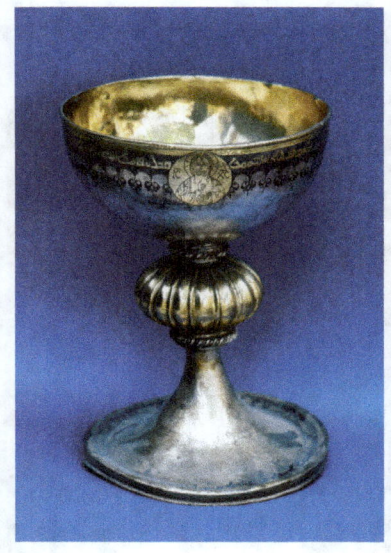

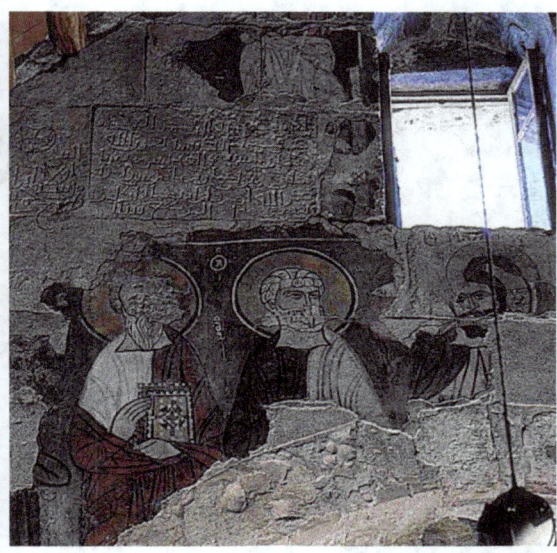

Arabic and others featuring Syriac inscriptions. The mix of Byzantine and arabesque elements in their decoration is typical of Syrian Christian art.

With the revival of artistic expression and urban development during the Ayyubid reign, the Christian mural paintings of Deir Mar Musa in Nebek, Deir Mar Ya'qub in Qara and Deir Mar Elian in Homs also underwent a complete revival. For many centuries, Christians of different religious denominations, including the Rum-Orthodox, the Syrian-Catholic, Protestant, and others, have populated the Qalamun Mountains between Damascus and Homs. Mar Musa al-Habashi in particular was also an important centre for manuscript writing and copying. Monks transported many such manuscripts to Egypt, which was an important centre for Christian monasticism in the region, thus revealing a history of continued development between the Christian communities and the Islamic Empire.

With the arrival of Islam and the development of Islamic art, which itself is an amalgamation of local Greco-Roman, Byzantine, Sassanian and indigenous Arab traditions, typical Islamic features such as the arabesque, Arabic calligraphy and spiralling foliate designs became part of the visual embellishment of local Christian art as well. Many ideological exchanges also occurred, as part of this cultural mix. Thus the inscription of the priest's son in the church of the Monastery of Mar Musa, as in many Christian texts, begins with the Islamic Basmala, the profession of the faith.

Silvery chalice from the Rusafa treasure, National Museum of Damascus.

Mar Musa al-Habashi Monastery, detail of the fresco in the sanctuary, depicting the Apostle St. Peter beside Jesus Christ.

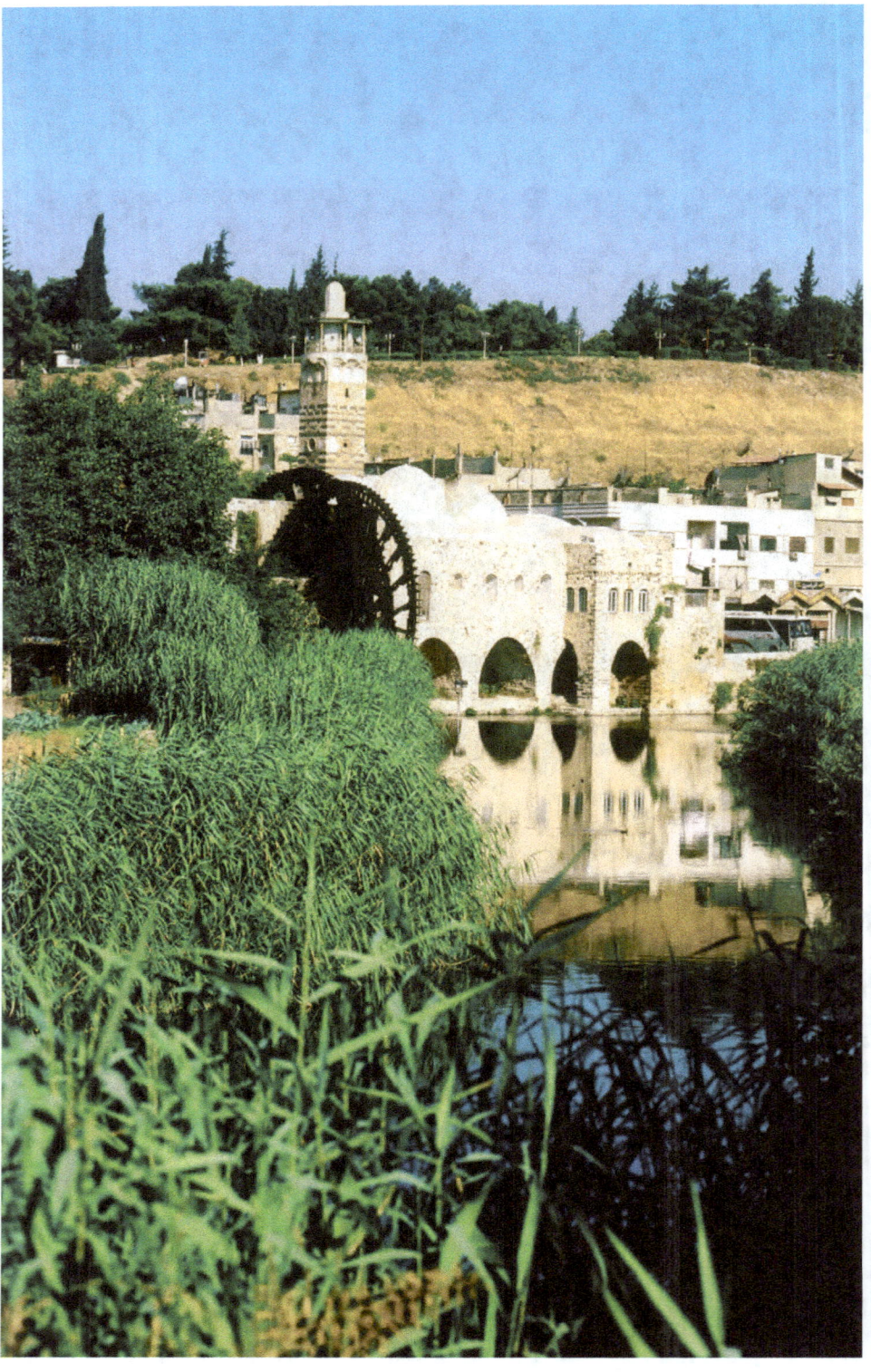

ITINERARY IV

Water and Hydraulic Works

Introduction: Yasser Tabbaa; Monuments: Wa'al Hafia

IV.1 SHMEMIS CITADEL (OPTION)

IV.2 HAMA
    IV.2.a Noria Jisriyya and Ma'muriyya
    IV.2.b Noria Ja'bariyya, Sahuniyya, and Kilaniyya
    IV.2.c Mosque of Nur al-Din
    IV.2.d Hammam al-Sultan
    IV.2.e Hama Archaeological Museum
    IV.2.f Mosque of Abu al-Fida'
    IV.2.g Noria al-Khudra, al-Dawalik and al-Dahsha
    IV.2.h Noria al-Muhammadiyya
    IV.2.i Great Mosque of Hama
    IV.2.j Mosque of al-Hasanayn

IV.3 QAL'AT SHAYZAR

Memoirs of an Arab Knight	Yasser Tabbaa
Noria Construction	Wa'al Hafian

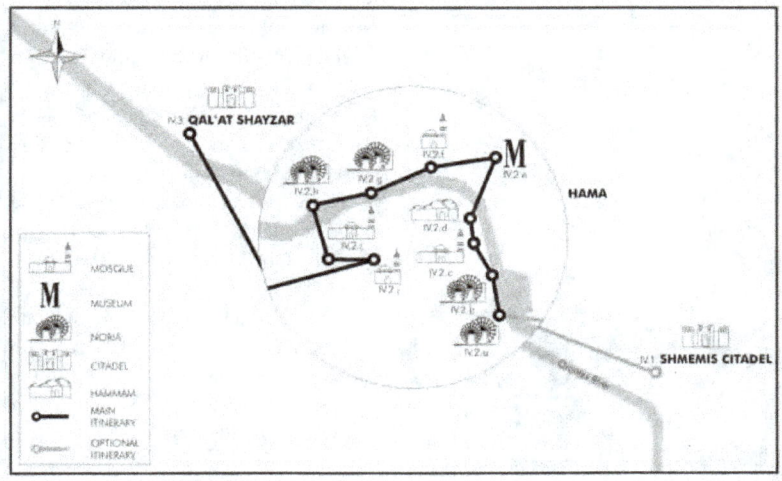

Norias, Hama.

ITINERARY IV *Water and Hydraulic Works*
Introduction

The generally arid climate of most Middle Eastern countries placed a high value on water, making it a central feature in religious and royal iconography and an important vehicle for technological innovations. The provision of water is one of the great meritorious acts of Islamic piety, so that both the Atabegs and Ayyubids spent considerable efforts on canalisation, water-elevating machines, as well as cisterns, pools and public fountains. In Ayyubid Aleppo, water, brought from a northern source through Qanat Haylan, led to an elaborate system of canalisation that fed the entire city. These waters also fed the moat around the citadel, in addition to its various wells, a *hammam* and fountains. While in Ayyubid Damascus, the seven branches of the Barada river were channelled to nourish every private home and public space.

Once inside a religious or a palatial structure, water became almost a semi-precious substance: pouring out of a lion's mouth, running through narrow channels, filling a decorative pool and spurting from a central jet. Ibn Jubayr (d. 614/1217), who visited Damascus in the late 6th/12th century, described several such fountains, including one that remained until recently in the Madrasa al-Nuriyya (I.4). Water entered the *madrasa* from beneath a *muqarnas* canopy in the western *iwan*, ran through a channel and emptied into the central pool. Found also in the Ayyubid palace in Aleppo Citadel (VII.1.h), this is a fountain type known as *salsabil*.

Nowhere in Syria is water used more effectively and picturesquely than in Hama, a city that straddles a bend in the River Orontes. Its world-famous *nawa'ir* (sing. *noria*) or waterwheels probably date to Roman times, although Arab technologists were constantly rebuilding and enlarging the concept and, in fact, spread their use to North Africa and Spain. Still extant until recently was a *noria* that carried water to the Mosque and Bimaristan of Nur al-Din, and another across the river that served the Kilani Palace. It also seems likely that the Mosque of Abu al-Fida' had its own *noria*.

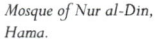
Mosque of Nur al-Din, Hama.

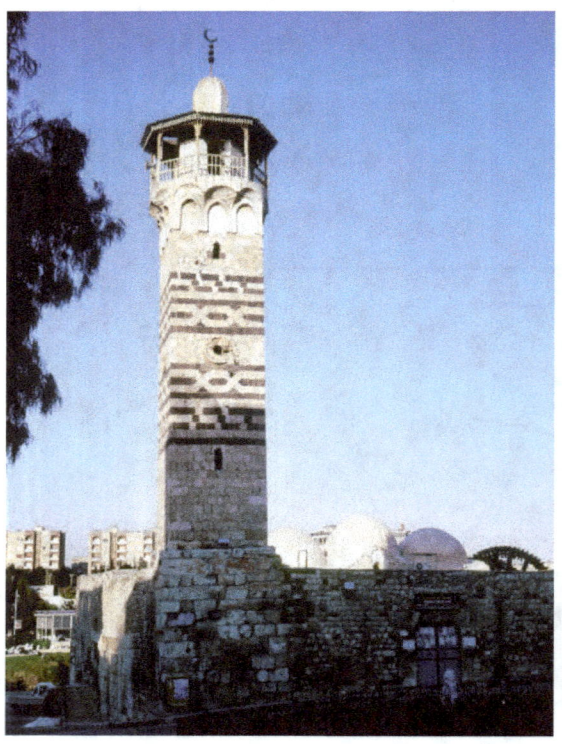

ITINERARY IV   *Water and Hydraulic Works*
Introduction

In fact, Hama underwent major reconstruction and urban development under Nur al-Din's patronage, including the construction of a new Friday Mosque, the Mosque of Nur al-Din and the restoration of the old Umayyad Mosque. He also sponsored *madrasa*s, *hammam*s and *bimaristan*s, all of which were well supplied with water, thanks to his efforts to maintain the *nawa'ir*. Though not much survives of Nur al-Din's original constructions, the status of Hama remained important as one of the more secure cities along the trade routes. Arab rural citadels, such as Shmemis Citadel (supplied by water from deep wells) to the east near the village of Salamiyya Plateau, and Shayzar Citadel (supplied by the river) to the west near the coastal mountains, remained continuously in Muslim hands under the Atabegs and Ayyubids. Even when the Mamluks took over the Ayyubid's leadership and most of Syria, Hama remained a quietly prosperous Ayyubid city in the hands of the last of the Ayyubid rulers, Abu al-Fida' (d. 733/1334). He was a poet-prince who composed significant manuscripts regarding the history and geography of the known world. The Mosque of Abu al-Fida', which still stands today, and within which is his mausoleum, exhibits fine stone-interlacing on its courtyard windows. He also built a palace and a garden nearby, known as the Garden of Wonder, nourished by its own *noria* named "al-Dahsha" or "al-*Duhaysha*", a diminutive of "Wonder" after his garden.

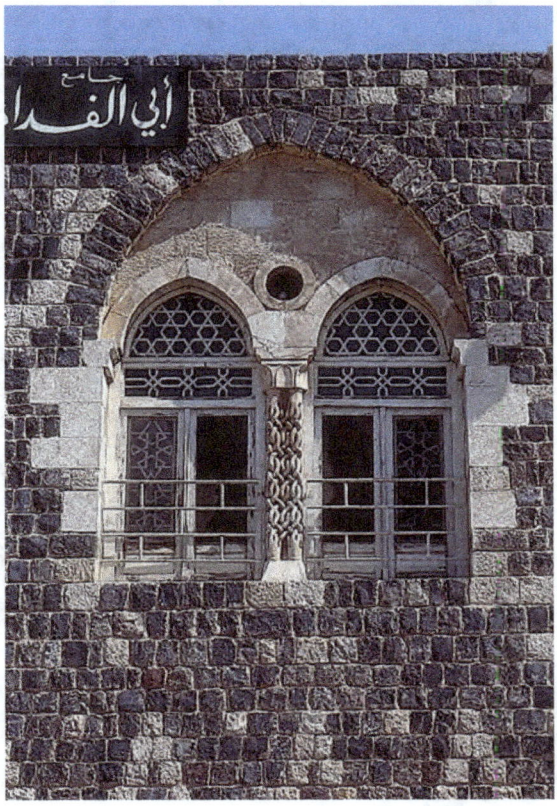

Mosque of Abu al-Fida', detail of a window with the central pillar carved in the shape of intertwined serpents, Hama.

HAMA

The itinerary comprises three sections: An optional citadel requiring a detour south-east of Hama towards the town of Salamiyya, the city and monuments of Hama itself, and a famous Arab citadel to the north-west of the city. In Hama, the itinerary follows a meandering route through the city to allow the visitor to enjoy various views of the noria and the Orontes River.

ITINERARY IV *Water and Hydraulic Works*
Shmemis Citadel

IV.1 SHMEMIS CITADEL
(OPTION)

Located 40 km east of Hama is the Shmemis Citadel. Instead of going straight to Hama city from Homs, take the exit towards the town of Salamiyya. Alternatively, arrive to Hama city and take public transport from there to Salamiyya. The citadel is visible from the road, on a high hill overlooking the surrounding fields. Upon arriving at Salamiyya, negotiate with the driver for the best arrangement back to the citadel, including the necessary waiting time and the drive back. Alternatively, have the driver drop you off on the track leading from the highway to the citadel, and hike the 4 km up to it and then back to the highway.

Caution is highly recommended on site, as the citadel is in poor condition and is not on the usual track of tourists, so beware of the slippery limestone hill. This adventure is strictly for those seeking a taste of medieval conquest.

Shmemis Citadel is advantageously located on the caravan route between the urban settlements of western Syria and the Syrian Steppes in the east. It was refortified during the Ayyubid period when Shirkuh II rebuilt its walls and dug a moat to surround it in 628/1230. It remains picturesquely on a volcanic hill amidst fertile plains, with 11 salient towers along its exterior, a northern gate and traces of a square fortress (35 m x 35 m). It is supplied by an 80 m-deep well in its interior.

IV.2 HAMA

A walk around Hama by this itinerary includes various urban institutions built by the Atabegs and the Ayyubids between the 6th/12th and 7th/13th centuries and a stroll along the River Orontes to feel the sights and sounds of Hama's famous waterwheels. These monuments are all located around a central tell that was once towered by the Citadel of Hama and now serves as a beautiful park.

IV.2.a Noria Jisriyya and Ma'muriyya

Arriving to down town Hama, head to the city's central square, called Orontes Square, which straddles the river. The Noria Jisriyya is the waterwheel to the left of the square, on the eastern bank of the river, while the Ma'muriyya is the large waterwheel with a cluster of smaller ones on the right western bank.

These *norias* have been carefully restored in recent years. The Jisriyya is known to have irrigated a wide expanse of orchards called Bustan al-Shahiqa and a long part of its aquaduct arcade is still standing.

The Ma'muriyya is the largest *noria* on the Orontes, second only to the Muham-

Shmemis Citadel, general view, Hama.

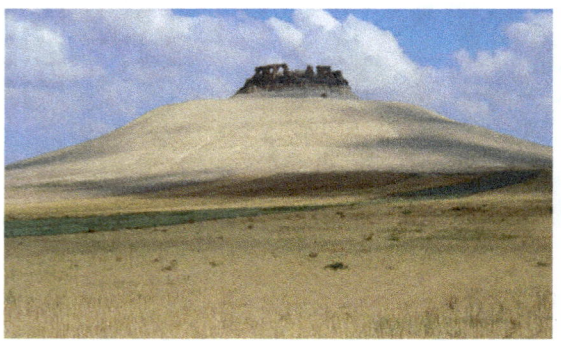

madiyya located to the north of the city. It measures a diameter of 21 meters with a total of 120 buckets. All these *noria*s are known to have been used since early Roman times, as indicated by archaeological findings at the tower bases below the water, and they were certainly strengthened and restored during Nur al-Din's reign, and continued to be restored regularly to this day. But unlike most of the *noria*, this one carries an inscription commemorating the *noria*'s renovation by an Ottoman governor in 857/1453.

Next to the Ma'muriyya are two smaller *noria*s called al-Uthmaniyya and al-Mu'ayadiyya. These smaller wheels are some of the smallest on the Orontes, the former has a diameter of 11 m while the latter a mere 7. They were originally meant to function as mills and, in more recent times, serve as workshops for the water-wheel carpenters.

IV.2.b Noria Ja'bariyya, Sahuniyya, and Kilaniyya

With the Ma'muriyya noria to your right, walk further northwards through the recently restored neighbourhood called Hayy al-Tawafra, passing by a Mamluk period hammam and the Ottoman period Azm palace. The next set of norias appear where there is a dam in the river facing the Nur al-Din Mosque on the left bank.

The Noria Ja'bariyya is one of a group of three which rest on a dam crossing the river with the Nur al-Din Mosque on the left side. The Ja'bariyya was originally composed of two wheels and there are remains of an aqueduct that reveal these

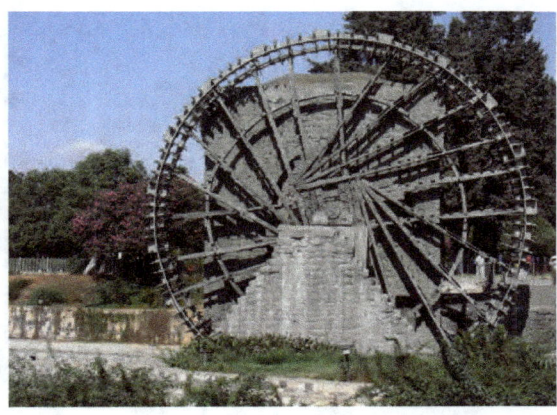

Noria Jisriyya, Hama (photo courtesy of Zena Takieddine).

two wheels were of varying sizes. Only the larger wheel survives. The gardens which these two wheels would have irrigated no longer survive, but the Hammam al-Sultan further north is known to have been supplied by the Ja'bariyya.

Next to the Ja'bariyya is small *noria* with a single wheel, called the Sahuniyya, and on the opposite bank of the river is the Noria Kilaniyya, named after the Kilani family which grew prominent in the late-Ottoman period and owned many lands, gardens, and a palace.

IV.2.c Mosque of Nur al-Din

The Mosque of Nur al-Din is the large building on your left, with the noria Ja'bariyya in front of it. It can be visited respecting appropriate dress codes and conduct, but it is likely to be closed apart from prayer times (approx 11.00–13.00). A small donation is advisable.

ITINERARY IV   *Water and Hydraulic Works*
Hama

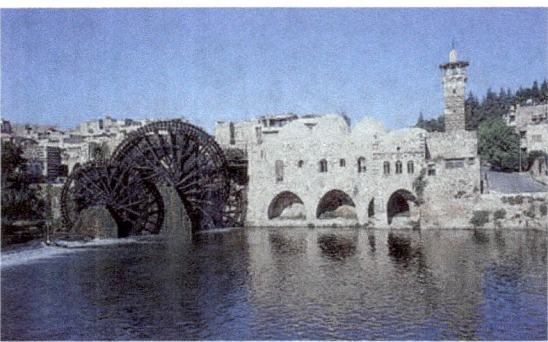

Mosque of Nur al-Din, general view with Noria Ja'bariyya and Noria Sahuniyya, Hama.

Mosque of Nur al-Din, epigraphic inscription, Hama.

The mosque, built by Nur al-Din in 558/1164 in the city of Hama as a second Friday mosque, is located on the River Orontes' left bank, next to the Sheikh Bridge connecting the two parts of the city. It comprised the main part of a monumental complex that was sponsored by Nur al-Din, which also included a *madrasa* and a *bimaristan* and probably also a *noria*, as still exists today. The sociopolitical background for Nur al-Din's sponsorship of urban infrastructure was part of his ideology of nourishing Islamic awareness and unity in order to propagate holy war or *jihad* against the Crusaders. Incorporated into the architecture of the mosque are Crusader *spolia*.

The Nur al-Din Mosque consists of a courtyard surrounded by three cross-vaulted porticos along the west, south and north walls. On the east wall is a long chamber topped by three domes. The middle chamber is fluted into 24 alcoves and rises over dodecagonal drum with windows, a style similar to the domes of the Great Mosques of Damascus and Aleppo, dating to the Ayyubid period.

On the northern façade of the mosque is a dedicatory inscription that runs over 7 m in length, executed in monumental and clearly legible cursive *thuluth* script. Unlike most other dedicatory inscriptions, it begins with the name of God and the *shahada*, or confession of faith, which immediately highlights the religiosity of Nur al-Din's position and possibly meant to address the contemporaneous Christian population. The use of *mujahid*, "the fighter for the faith", and other

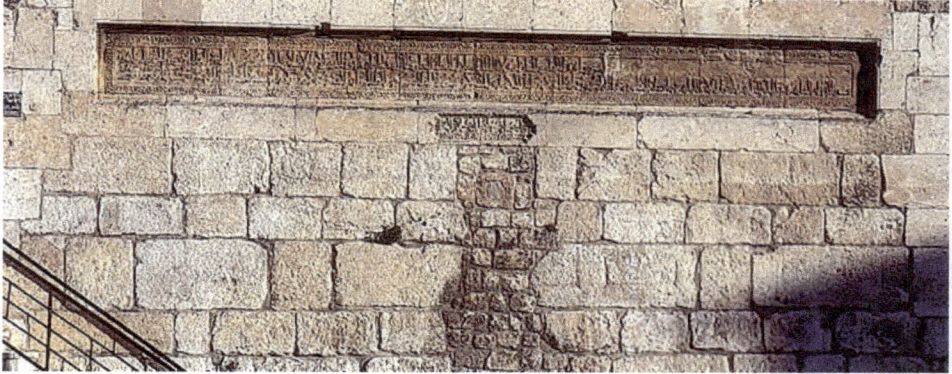

ITINERARY IV   *Water and Hydraulic Works*
Hama

jihad-related epithets such as "keeper of the outposts", "saviour of the public", "vanquisher of the rebels" and "killer of the infidels and polytheists", are meant to go hand-in-hand with the inscriptions on the monumental wooden *minbar*, currently in Hama Archaeological Museum. Thus, both the Mosque of Nur al-Din and its symbolic furnishings are very much historically oriented towards the propagation of knowledge and a strengthened Islamic identity in defiance of the Crusader threat.

Meanwhile, the lower part of the mosque's façade reveals the continuity of the classical Syrian architectural style, elegantly coupled with the Islamic characteristics of the building.

The minaret, located in the north-west corner, is very similar to that at the Great mosque of Hama, but the one at Hama is older. Nur al-Din's is square in plan and built in alternating courses of black basalt and yellowish limestone (*ablaq*) after a manner peculiar to Hama in the Ayyubid period, distinctive for its diamond-shaped designs.

There are many restorations and reparations from later periods, especially during the reign of the Ayyubid Muzaffar II Mahmud (624–6/1227–9) – who added some pillars to support the north wall and ordered the roof over the prayer-hall – and during the rule of Abu al-Fida' Ismai'l (710–33/1310–33) during Mamluk hegemony – who rebuilt the *mihrab*. The most recent changes occurred under the Ottomans with restoration of the west-wing.

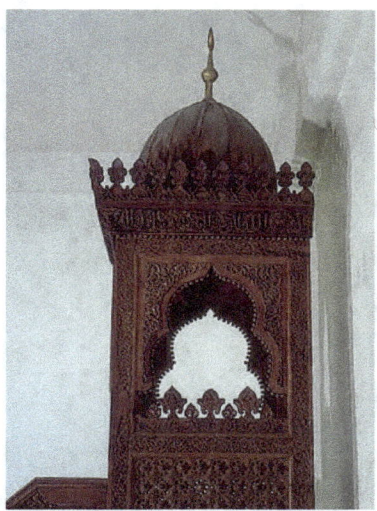

Detail of the wooden minbar from the Mosque of Nur al-Din, Hama Archaeological Museum (Inv. Num. 3256).

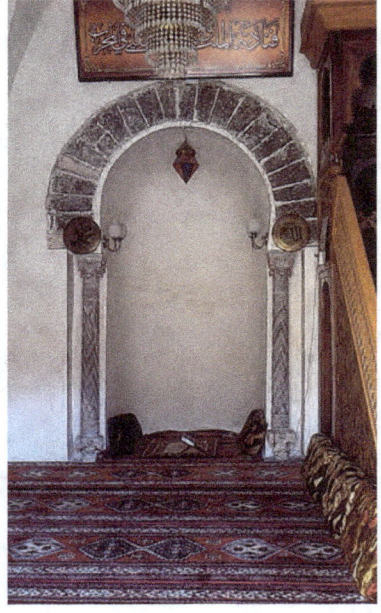

Mosque of Nur al-Din, view of the mihrab, Hama.

ITINERARY IV   *Water and Hydraulic Works*
Hama

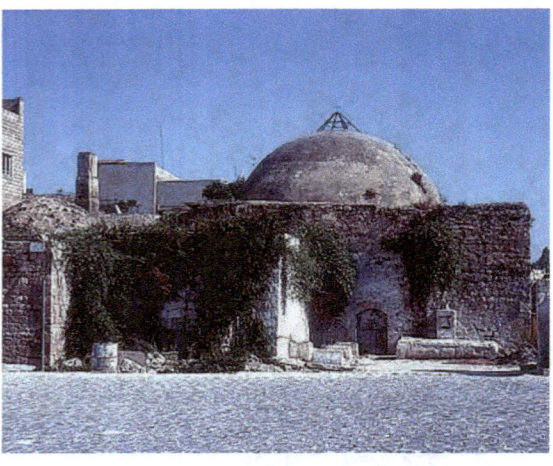

Hammam al-Sultan, Hama.

IV.2.d **Hammam al-Sultan**

Leaving the Mosque of Nur al-Din from its north entrance, the Hammam al-Sultan is easily recognisable by its domes, and is a mere 20 m north of the entrance to the mosque. The building is closed for restoration, but access to the hammam *might be possible with the permission of the proprietor of the carpenter's shop nearby.*

The *hammam* is located on the River Orontes left bank, to the north of the Mosque of Nur al-Din. An open space left by the now-destroyed Madrasa al-Nuriyya al-Kubra, separates the two buildings.

The *hammam* dates to the reign of the Ayyubid ruler al-Mansur I (d. 617/ 1220–1). It is rectangular in shape, its northern side accessible through a narrow passageway that leads to the *barrani*, or exterior chambers, which are the cold rooms. The *barrani*, surmounted by a large, brick dome that ascends some 11 m above ground level, has a water-basin made of limestone and is surrounded on all four sides of the room by *mastabas* – stone ledges to seat bathers. From the *barrani* a corridor leads to the *wustani*, or middle chambers, which are the warm rooms. Similar to the Hammam Nur al-Din of Damascus (I.5), this room is the focal point of the construct, surmounted by one large, main dome surrounded by several smaller domes that cover the symmetrically laid-out annexations, known as *maqsuras*, which have marble panelling. The smaller domes, decorated with small geometric-shaped openings sealed by coloured glass known as *qamariyyat*, illuminate the *hammam* interior, with the addition of creating an aesthetically pleasing and atmospherically therapeutic touch for the benefit of the bathers. The *juwwani*, interior chambers, are the hot rooms, located on the west side of the *hammam*, next to the furnace. Hot water runs in pipes beneath the marble surface of this chamber to keep the steam from condensing, resulting in a sauna effect.

The bathers begin by gradually moving from the cold room area through to the warm rooms and up to the interior-most hot rooms. This gradual transition to chambers of different temperatures is a necessary part of a healthy *hammam* experience, which the bather repeats in reverse on exiting, moving from hot to cold.

Noria Ja'bariyya, located to the east of the Nuri Mosque, supplied the *hammam* with water.

ITINERARY IV *Water and Hydraulic Works*
Hama

IV.2.e **Hama Archaeological Museum**

This new museum is located 2 km north of the city centre on Ziqar Street. Opening times are Wed–Mon 9.00–18.00 during the summer, 9.00–16.00 during the winter. Closed on Tuesdays and during Friday prayers (approx 11.00–13.00). There is an entrance fee.

Noria mosaic
This is the first visual record of the magnificent hydraulic waterwheel-structure known as *noria*. The Byzantine mosaic panel, originally located in Apamea, has a date AD 469. It measures 148 cm x 170 cm and is irregular in shape due to loss of material. Despite its fragmentary state, the different elements that make up the *noria* are evident, such as the wooden beams and circular frame of the wheel, the streams of water that pour from the buckets as it rotates, and the triangular structure made of stone blocks that supports the *noria*'s axle. Various colours feature in the *tesserae* of the mosaic: grey, brown, beige, yellowish beige and pinkish beige – to distinguish the different media of the *noria*.

Shaduf jar
Like the *noria*, the *shaduf*, is another method of water-collecting technology, which is similarly ancient. The *shaduf* is a more provincial construct, and the wheel is generally smaller in size The *shaduf*, unlike the *noria*, is not propelled by the momentum of the river, but is instead driven by animal power; a mule, for example, would walk in circles to rotate

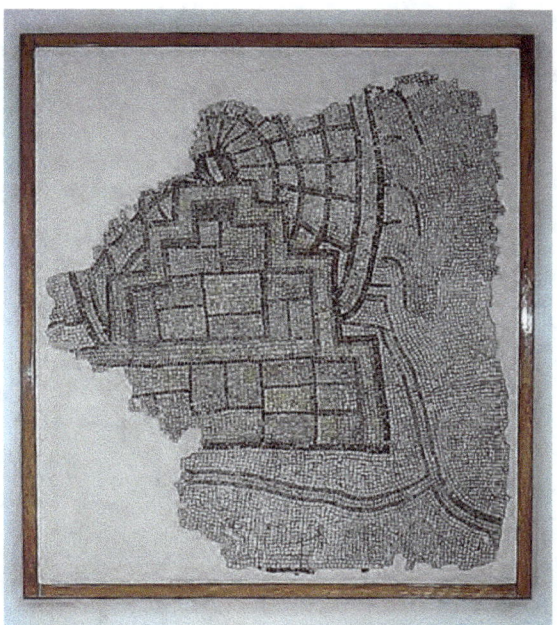

Noria mosaic, Hama Archaeological Museum.

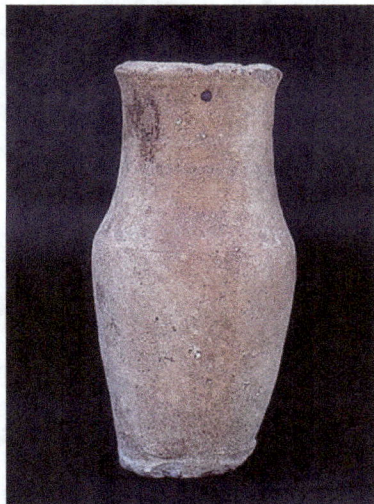

Shaduf jar, Hama Archaeological Museum.

167

ITINERARY IV   *Water and Hydraulic Works*
Hama

the wheel. Attached to the mechanism by way of a rope around the neck or through a pierced hole, these distinctively shaped jars held the water collected by the *shaduf*. The exact date and place of production of *shaduf* jars is unknown, but they are indigenous to the Hama region, and probably date back to some time between the 6th/12th and 8th/14th centuries. Indeed, to this day there is a village called "Tel Shaduf", located to the north of the Salamiyya and Shmemis citadels. On average, the dimensions of these *shaduf* jars are 28.5 cm high, 7.5 cm wide at the base, and 11.5 cm wide at the rim.

Minbar of Nur al-Din

This *minbar* was originally part of the new Mosque of Nur al-Din in Hama, its beauty matched only by its strong political message relating to Islamic piety and Holy War. Standing tall and copiously carved, it is made of wood, 84 cm wide, 318 cm long and 425 cm at its utmost height; the crescent-shaped finial above the domed seat. Geometric designs and calligraphic inscriptions executed in *naskhi* script indicate the name and titlature of the patron, Nur al-Din, and the date of its execution, 559/1263–4. The top of the seat back is decorated with an arched frame with carved-interlacing hexagonal patterns, amidst which is the testimony of faith "*La Ilaha Illa Alla*" ("There is no god but God"), and "*Muhammad Rasul Allah*" ("Muhammad is God's Prophet"), carved in two cartouches and executed in broad calligraphy set on a delicate background of spiralling tendrils. The lower part of the seat back is composed of a hexagonal and triangular grid with pierced brackets that highlight the pattern and make the structure itself less heavy. A magnificent cornice, with floral carving and sculptural floral crenellations along the rim, gives the *minbar* a throne-like quality accentuated by the dome and its far-reaching crescent finial.

The banisters currently on the *minbar* are modern restorations, but one of the original banisters hangs on the wall to the right of the *minbar* and presents the original features of Nur al-Din's inscription, executed in *naskhi* script, all along the frame. The body of the banister, carved with a matrix of criss-crossing lines with diamond-shaped piercing at the intersections, has a zigzag design along the periphery.

IV.2.f **Mosque of Abu al-Fida'**

Sometimes known locally as the Jami' al-Hayyat (Mosque of the Serpents), it is located on the north bank of the Orontes, near the Palestinian Refugee Camp. On leaving the museum, turn to the left and carefully cross the street to return towards the river. The Mosque is discernable by its black-and-white façade and the diamond-shaped stonework on its south elevation. It can be visited respecting appropriate dress codes and conduct, but it is likely to be closed apart from prayer times (approx 11.00–13.00). A small donation is advisable.

It is known that Ayyubid rule lasted longer in Hama than it did in Damascus and elsewhere in Syria. In 727/1321, the ruler al-Mu'ayyid Isma'il, known as Abu al-Fida', built a mosque incorporating

Water and Hydraulic Works
Hama

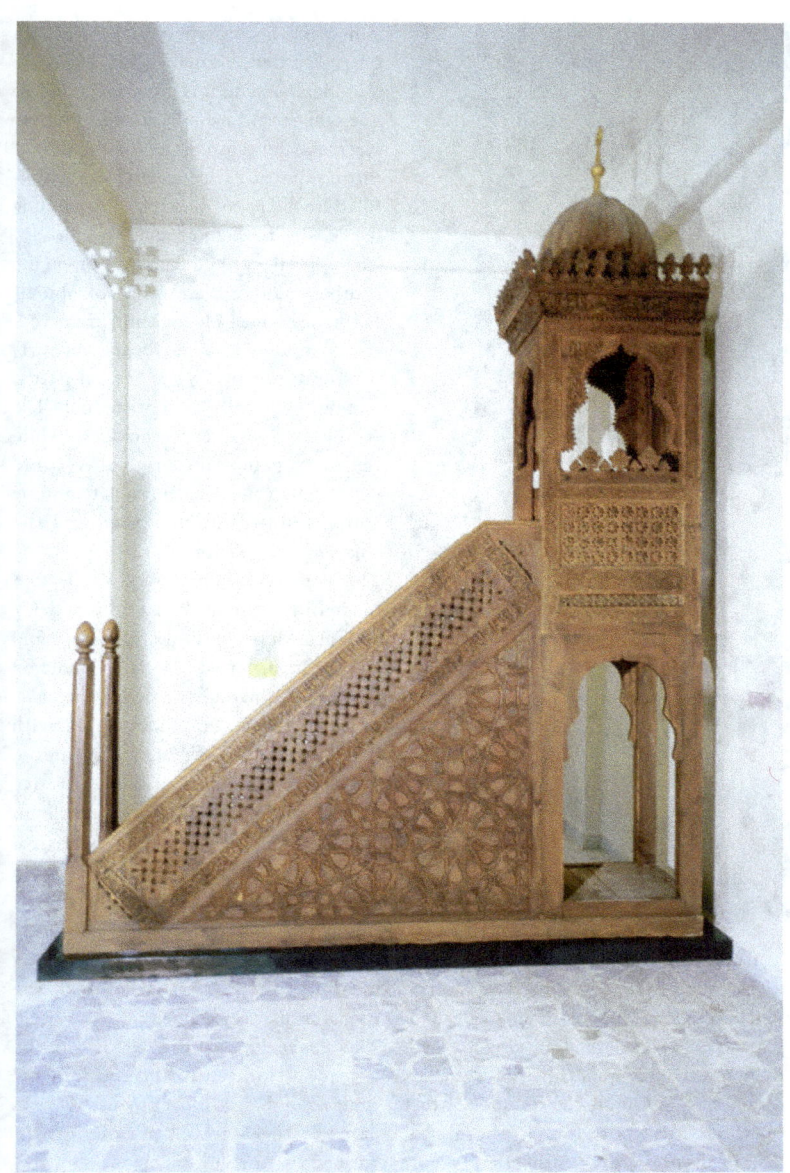

Minbar *of Nur al-Din*, *Hama Archaeological Museum (Inv. Num. 3266).*

ITINERARY IV   Water and Hydraulic Works
Hama

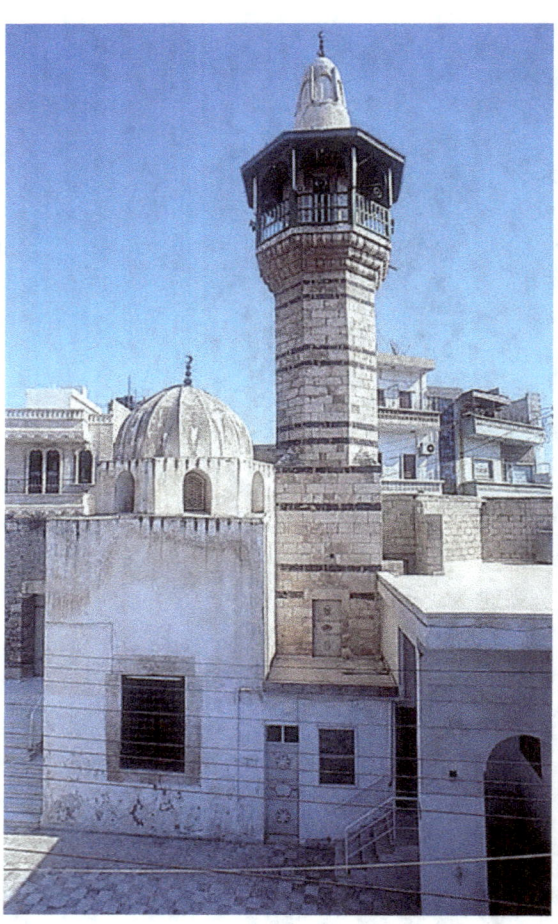

Mosque of Abu al-Fida', view of the minaret and mausoleum, Hama.

a mausoleum for himself on the right-hand bank of the River Orontes. The site lay north of Hama Citadel, in an area called Bab al-Jisr (The Gate of the Bridge), in a region where his grandfather, al-Muzaffar I Taqi al-Din Omar, the founder of the Ayyubid Dynasty of Hama, was laid to rest in 587/1191 in a mausoleum.

Abu al-Fida' constructed a palace with a large garden, known as the Garden of Wonder, next to this great mosque. To keep the royal garden lush and to supply water for the ablutions of worshippers at the mosque was a requirement easily fulfilled by the *noria*, which is still standing to the west of the mosque.

The original Ayyubid construction on the southern side of the Mosque of Abu al-Fida' and his mausoleum is still preserved. It is composed of a small central courtyard entered by two identical gates, although originally there were four. The west gate is small and renovated, while the north gate is the original Ayyubid construction and leads through to a stone staircase into the courtyard and the adjacent Mausoleum of al-Mu'ayyid.

The mausoleum, an average-sized room made of limestone with a domed brick roof of 24 lobes, follows in the Ayyubid style. On the west side is an attached limestone minaret executed in the *ablaq* motif of contrasting black-basalt with limestone, here distributed in an uneven manner that is typical of the decorative architecture in Hama. The Mausoleum and the minaret remain in their original states; it appears that the location chosen for the minaret was in order that it supported the mosque, for the location of the mausoleum, separate from the mosque, was a habitual style of the Ayyubid rulers of Hama.

The *haram*, or sacred space, of the mosque is located to the south of the central courtyard. Most of what survives dates to the Mamluk period, distinguished by its south-facing façade over-

ITINERARY IV   Water and Hydraulic Works
Hama

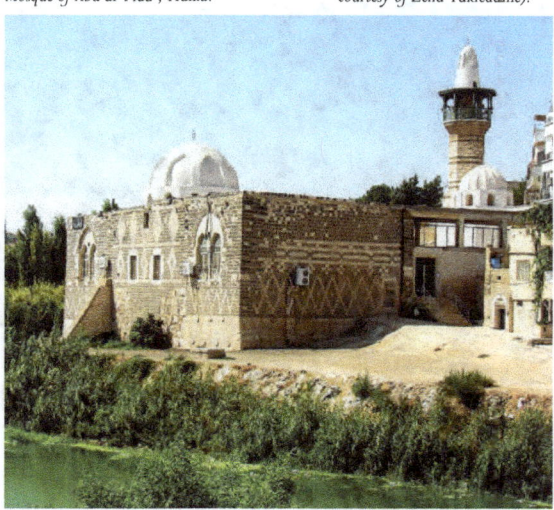

Mosque of Abu al-Fida', Hama.

Noria al-Khudra and Noria al-Dawalik, Hama (photo courtesy of Zena Takieddine).

looking the River Orontes. It is easy to discern the two different styles at work: the first made of large limestone blocks dates to the Ayyubid period and may even be part of the al-Muzaffar's mausoleum, while the latter is of a more recent reconstruction. The mosque's two windows are both decorated with a central pillar carved in the shape of intertwined snakes or serpents; for this reason the mosque is known colloquially as Jami' al-Hayyat, "Mosque of the Serpents".

IV.2.g Noria al-Khudra, al-Dawalik and al-Dahsha

Walk down al-Asad Bridge and continue up the street with the river to your right and tell to your left. More norias are to be seen, on either side of the river.

Another set of three water wheels around a dam are found north of the tell upon which the citadel of Hama once towered. These are the Noria al-Khudra and the Noria al-Dawalik, on the left side of the bank, and the aforementioned Noriat al-Dahsha on the opposite side, irrigating the green fields on the lower slopes by the Mosque of Abu al-Fida'. The largest of the three, al-Khudra, measures about 17.50 meters with the smaller Noria Dawalik just next by. The Dahsha is smallish in size, but it features some interesting structural peculiarities. For example, the triangle upon which the axle of the wheel rests is actually rectangular in shape and the buckets around its perimeter alternate in size.

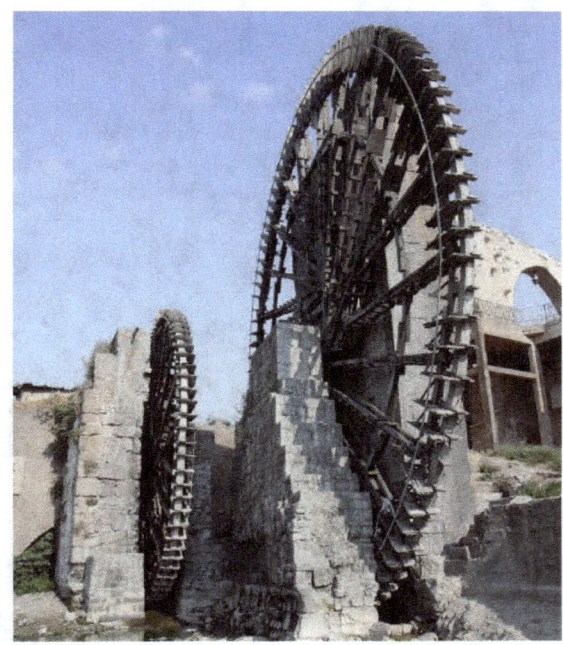

ITINERARY IV Water and Hydraulic Works
Hama

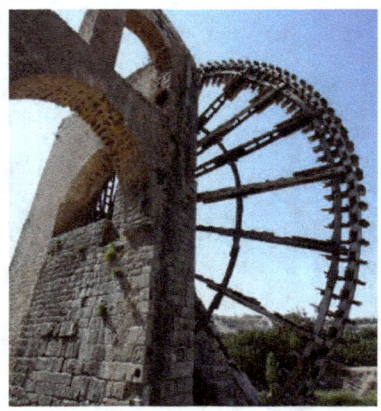

Noria al-Muhammadiyya, detail, Hama (photo courtesy of Zena Takieddine).

a good length of its aquaduct is still standing, a total of some 14 arcades. This *noria* is also one of the rare waterwheels to feature an inscription commemorating the construction of the *noria* in 763–1361 for the purpose of channelling water to the Great Mosque of Hama by a Mamluk governor of the city. Originally, mills functioned next to this important *noria*, supplying wheat for the city and, more importantly, the citadel. Traces of such mills can still be found around the bases of the *noria*s and all along the river banks.

IV.2.h Noria al-Muhammadiyya

Continuing further west is the Noria al-Muhammadiyya which is located in an area known as Bab al-Nahr, or The Gate of the River.

This is the most famous *noria* in all of Hama and, alongside the Noria Ma'muriyya on Orontes Square, it is one of the largest. Its diameter measures 21 meters and

IV.2.i Great Mosque of Hama

Turn back towards the tell and cross the traffic circle and take Thawra street eastward for some 200 m to reach the southern entrance of the Great Mosque. It is discernable by its minaret with a particular design of alternating black and white stone. Respecting appropriate dress codes and conduct, it is open any time during the day. A small donation is advisable.

This Great Mosque was the first and biggest Friday Mosque to be built in Hama, located in the oldest quarter of the city, south-west of where the Hama Citadel once stood. In ancient times, the site was a Roman temple dedicated to the God Jupiter and, during the Christian era, it reverted to a church. The Arab conquerer, Abu 'Ubayda al-Jarrah, converted part of the church into a Friday Mosque to accommodate the newly settled Arab community and Muslim converts. Under the Umayyad Dynasty, it became a monumental mosque, but after

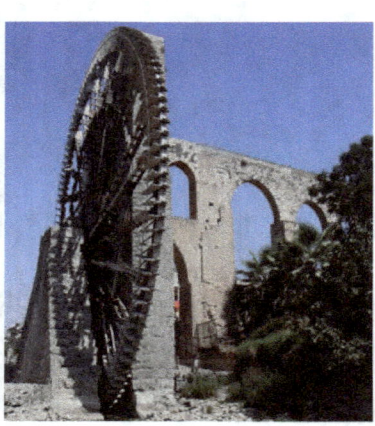

Noria al-Muhammadiyya, Hama (photo courtesy of Zena Takieddine).

ITINERARY IV *Water and Hydraulic Works*
Hama

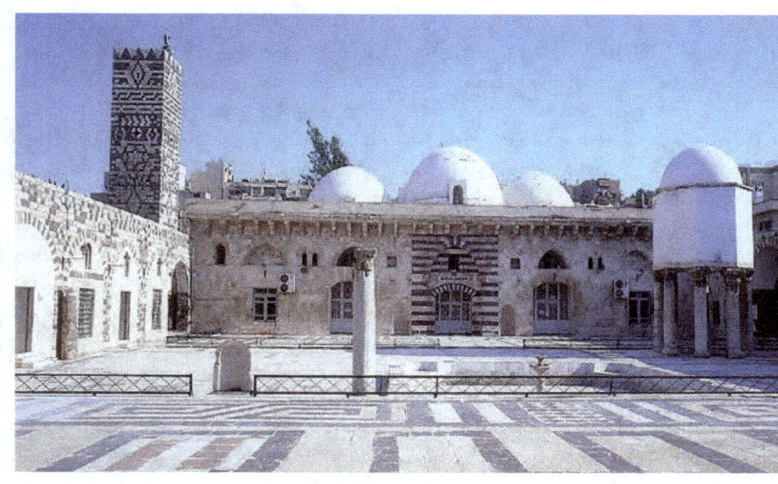

Great Mosque of Hama.

Great Mosque of Hama, the minaret in the south-east corner, with geometric decoration.

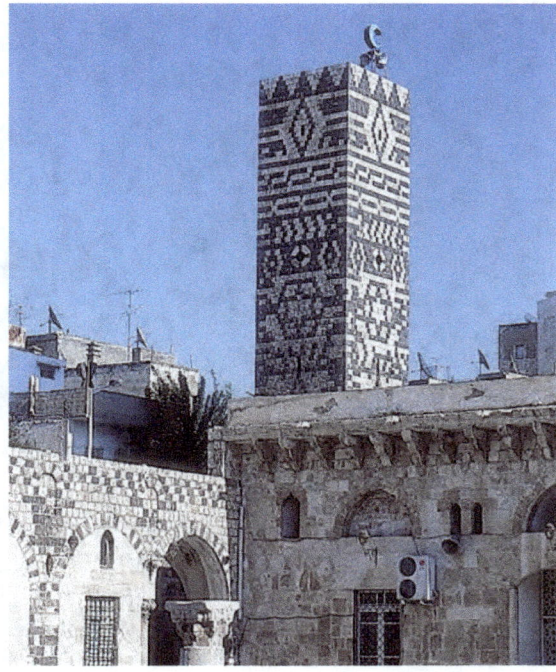

the Byzantine re-occupation of Syria in 357/968, it went back to being a church. The Atabeg and Ayyubid rulers of Hama, therefore, restored its position to the great mosque it had once been. Very similar to the Great Mosque of Aleppo (VI.1.g), it features three cross-vaulted porticoes with the fourth, on the south side, roofed by three domes honouring the prayer-hall. The dome on the south-west corner belongs to the mausoleum of al-Mansur II and his son al-Muzaffar III, the two Ayyubids who ruled during the first half of the $6^{th}/12^{th}$ century. Like the Great Umayyad Mosque of Damascus, there is also a treasury dome located in the courtyard next to the ablutions pool, made of reused columns and capitals from the classical period.

The mosque has two minarets. That in the south-eastern corner is square in plan and built in alternating courses of contrasting black basalt and yellowish limestone after

ITINERARY IV *Water and Hydraulic Works*
Hama

a manner peculiar to Ayyubid Hama, with recognised geometric decorations known as *ablaq*. The other minaret stands next to the north gate and dominates the exterior façade of the mosque. Built in 790/1388 in the Mamluk style, it has decorative windows and perfectly designed *muqarnas* niches.

IV.2.j Mosque of al-Hasanayn

Exiting the Great Mosque from its northern entrance on Hasanayn Street, continue walking eastward towards the foot of the tell. The mosque is found on 7 Nisan Square, a low-lying building with a stout minaret. It can be visited respecting appropriate dress codes and conduct, but it is likely to be closed apart from prayer times (approx 11.00–13.00). A small donation is advisable.

This small mosque is located to the south of where the Hama Citadel once stood, facing its main gate. It is one of Nur al-Din's constructions, built in 554/1161, as is clearly indicated in the inscribed stone panel located above the door. Its stone patterning is distinctive of Hama.

The dimensions of the mosque are approximately 17 m x 11 m with a newly renovated entrance on its south side in which the original foundation-panel is preserved. Renovations have also taken place in the north and east porticos. Four rows of large-sized limestone blocks on the southern façade, similar to the stones found in the Mosque of Nur al-Din in Hama, along with two small domes are all that survive from the Zangid-period construction. The two domes vary in size and height and serve to indicate the

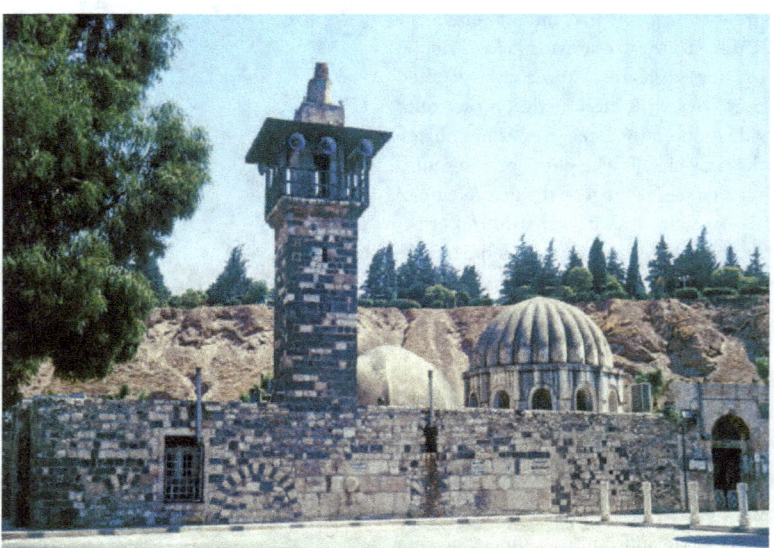

Mosque of al-Hasanayn, general view, Hama.

holiness of the prayer-hall, known as the *haram* or the *musalla*. A small and simple *mihrab* in the south-facing wall is located centrally between the two domes overhead. The larger one peaks at 4 m above ground level, its surface is smooth and it rests on four meticulously designed fan-shaped squinches. The smaller dome peaks at 3 m and its surface is lobed into 24 sections, a style that was common in Hama, Damascus and Aleppo during the Atabeg period, pointing to architectural influences from the East. After the pair of domes and a vaulted chamber, the mosque's small, square-based minaret rises to approximately 8 m in height, made of the black-basalt stone traditionally imported from Hauran and Bosra. There is a wooden-balcony construction at the top of the minaret.

IV.3 QAL'AT SHAYZAR

Located 30 km north-west of Hama, on the road to Jisr el-Shughur, take public transport from Hama to the town of Mharde, discernable by its large industrial complex. From there, take public transport to the village of Shayzar lying at the foot of the citadel. Negotiate with the driver to drop you off at the citadel gate. Alternatively, secure a ride to Shayzar directly from Hama. It might be a good idea to rent a car, useful for the subsequent itineraries as well. Opening times are Wed–Mon 9.00–18.00 during the summer, 9.00–16.00 during the winter. Closed on Tuesdays and during Friday prayers (approx 11.00–13.00). There is an entrance fee. In the unlikely event that the citadel

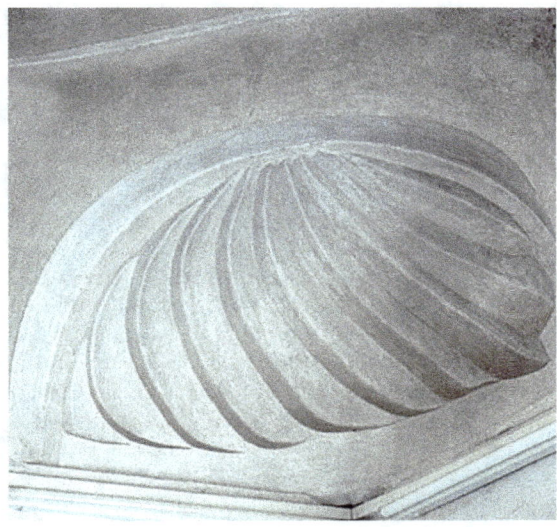

is locked residents of the houses opposite may be able to help you in locating the caretaker.

Mosque of al-Hasanayn, detail, Hama.

Based on the layout of the mountainous escarpment on which it stands, this Arab citadel is located 25 km north-west of Hama. Approximately 50 m wide and 450 m long, the citadel dominates the narrow passageway between the River Orontes and the Ghab Plains, on the road between Damascus and Antakiyya, through Middle Syria. The area witnessed long and violent struggles as well as two devastating earthquakes during the medieval period.

The first mention of a fortress at Shayzar dates to the Hellenistic period when the site was known as Larissa. During the Byzantine reoccupation of northern Syria and the costal mountains, at the end of the 4th/10th century, the fort was developed.

ITINERARY IV *Water and Hydraulic Works*
Qal'at Shayzar

It was the princely family of the Banu Munqidh, a local Arab tribe, who took control over the citadel and the surrounding area in the 474/1081. Usama bin Munqidh, the medieval warrior whose memoirs have survived as a precious record of these turbulent times grew up in this citadel, where he probably penned his diary. The citadel suffered massive damage in an earthquake of 552/1157 and many of the Munqidh family perished, at which point Nur al-Din supervised its restoration, which he renewed after another earthquake in 565/1170. After Nur al-Din's death in 560/1174, integration of Shayzar Citadel into the Ayyubid leadership saw that the surviving members of the Banu Munqidh continued to play a chivalrous role in the fight against the Crusaders and the defence of the Ayyubid Dynasty. It remained a strong defensive fort and, following the devastation of the Mongol attacks, the Mamluk Sultan al-Zahir Baybars reinforced it along with many other fortresses in Syria.

The most important remnant of the citadel is its impressive entrance supported by a well-constructed stone glacis on its north side and a deep ditch to the south. Large, strong towers once stood along its 1 km surrounding wall. Evidence of storage areas and a two-storey residential building at the far south of the citadel are in evidence. This, the south tower, is the main construction dating to Nur al-Din's era and exemplifies the massive fortified-building type of the period with its two still-standing storeys and decorated façade built with well-hewn, large limestone. A monumental inscription made on the original stone was added under the reign of the Ayyubid ruler of Aleppo, and patron of the great Citadel of Aleppo, al-Zahir Ghazi, dated 631 (1233).

Perfectly formed and decorated arrow slits and machicolations defend this tower along with the other towers in the citadel, revealing the architectural mastery of the Arabs in military construction. Thus, **Qal'at Shayzar** is a fine example of medieval Islamic fortifications, especially in that it was a site never conquered by the Crusaders.

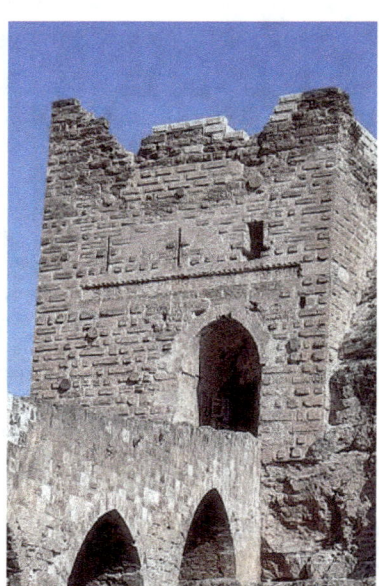

Qal'at Shayzar, detail of the entrance gate, Hama.

ITINERARY IV *Water and Hydraulic Works*
Qal'at Shayzar

Qal'at Shayzar, general view, Hama.

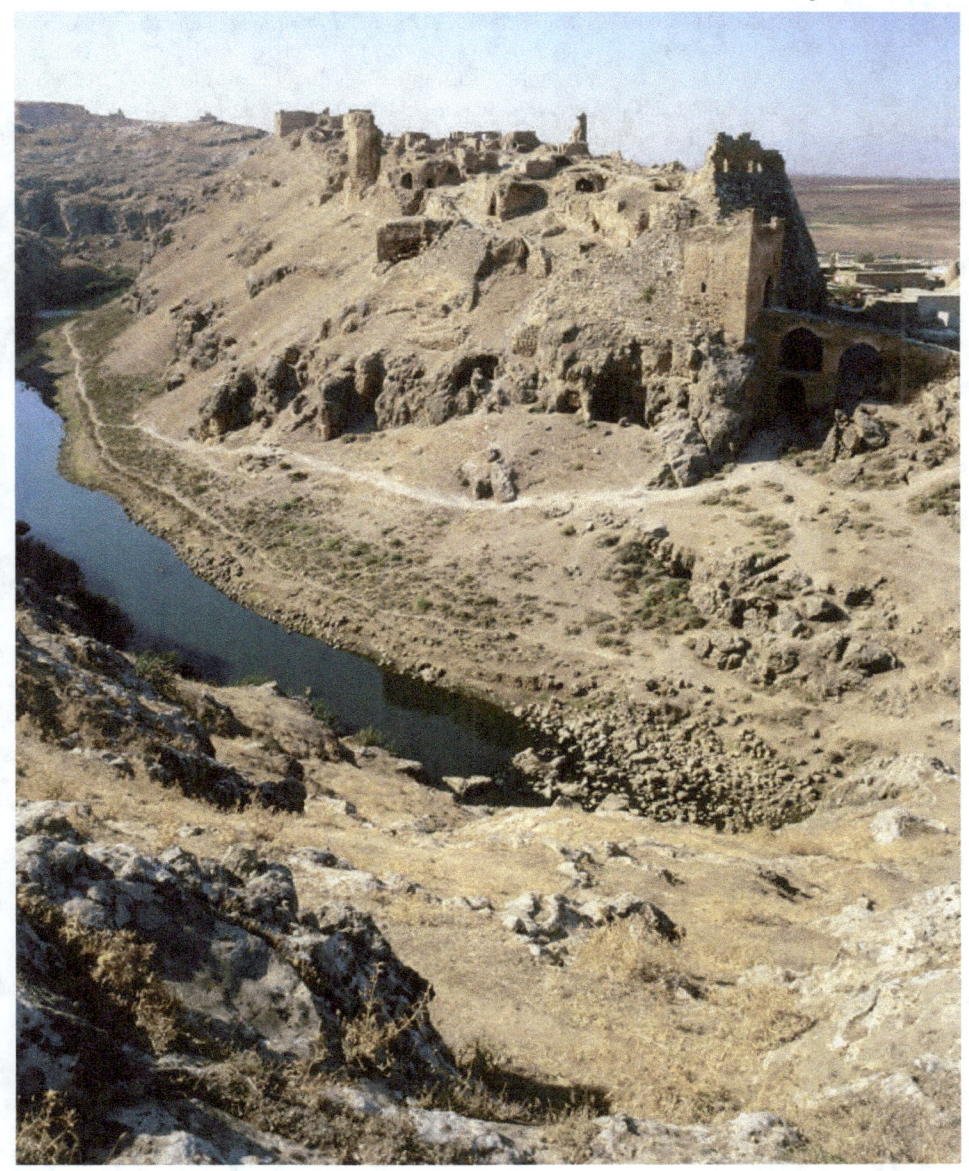

MEMOIRS OF AN ARAB KNIGHT

Yasser Tabbaa

Usama bin Munqidh's long life (488–584/1095–1188) almost exactly overlaps with the early Crusades. Born to a family of feudal lords in Shayzar near Hama, Usama trained from his youth in the arts of horsemanship, hunting, falconry and poetry. He also grew to become a physician, statesman and a noteworthy man of letters.

Disenchanted by his prospects in Shayzar, Usama left the city in 533/1138 for the Burid court of Damascus, and not long after that King Fulk of Jerusalem employed him as his emissary. He was never to return to Shayzar, which in 550/1156, suffered a massive earthquake that killed all the inhabitants and destroyed the city. Usama's life was one of constant movement among the many Muslim courts of the 6th/12th century, including Cairo, Mosul and especially Damascus, where he resided for a total of 33 years and where he died at the age of 94.

Usama, best known today for his memoirs *Kitab al-I'tibar* (*Book of Instruction by Example*), which describes in candid and vivid detail his numerous encounters with the Crusaders: great kings, brave knights, pious monks, foolish doctors and cuckolded husbands. Written from the perspective of a curious but conservative Muslim mind, the book provides a window into the world of the Crusaders, who condoned the familiar or beneficial, while disparaging the foreign or crude.

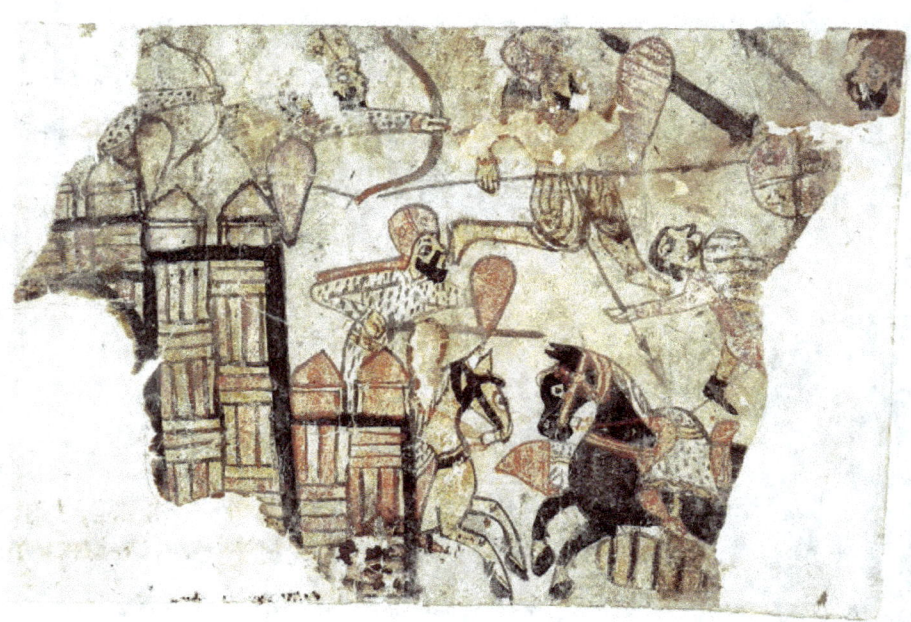

Fragment of a painting depicting a battle scene, 12th century, Ayyubid Dynasty, British Museum, London (Inv. Num. 1938,0312,0.1; © Trustees of the British Museum, London). Although made in Egypt, probably after the death of Usama bin Munqidh, he may have witnessed sieges similar to the scene depicted here.

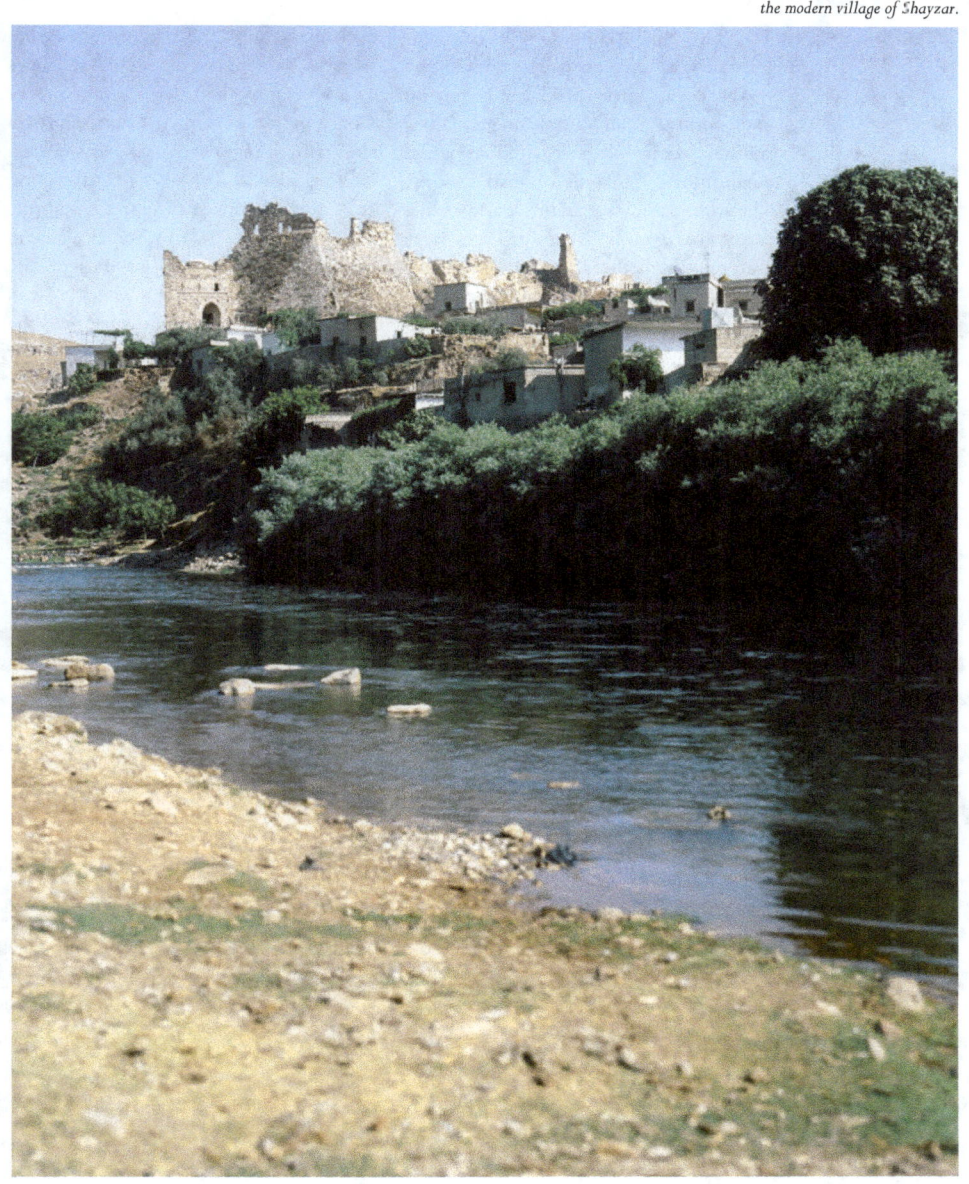

Qal'at Shayzar overlooking the modern village of Shayzar.

NORIA CONSTRUCTION

Wa'al Hafian

The craft of *noria* construction and maintenance is an ancient, deeply rooted one in the community of Hama based on engineering, architectural and geometric skilfulness, carefully calculated ratios and harmoniously designed constructions. The stone skeletal structure consists of a narrow passageway, which draws the river water towards the wheel and regulates the level of water. A rectangular tower on one side, and a triangular one on the other, flanks the passageway of water. The triangular tower carries the weight of the wheel's axle while the rectangular tower acts as a water receptacle, receiving the water in buckets at the top-most level. The water distribution to the surrounding areas is according to a calculated time-cycle that ensures sufficient water supplies to parks, gardens and other public facilities as overseen by the town's legal council. Construction of the wheel is usually on site, with the supportive tower set up on its vertical axis. The wheel construction is generally out of poplar or walnut, although other types of wood available in the River Orontes Valley are used. The diameter and width of the wheel, as well as the level of the river, determined the amount of water the wheel could lift per rotation.

Taking into account the length of the Orontes River, the city of Hama includes the greatest density of *nawa'ir* within close vicinity of each other. At one time, the *nawa'ir* totalled 20, but there are now

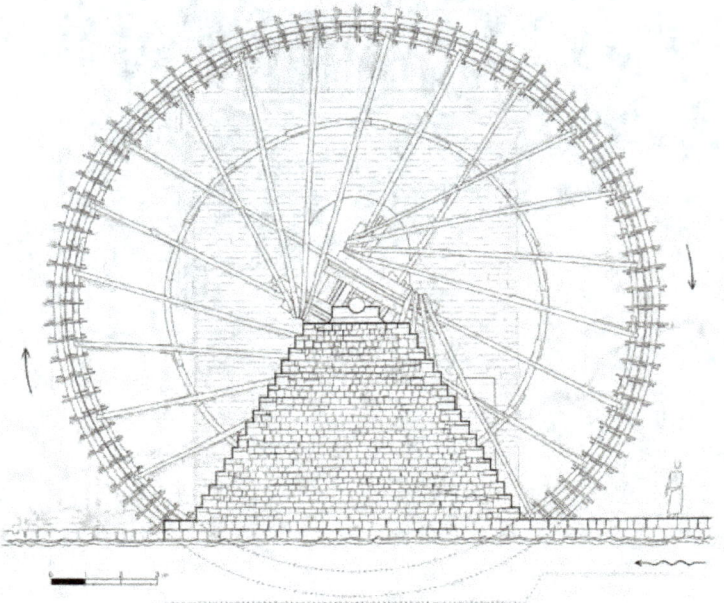

Sketch of a noria (Delpech, Girard, Robin, Roumi, 1997, fig. 79).

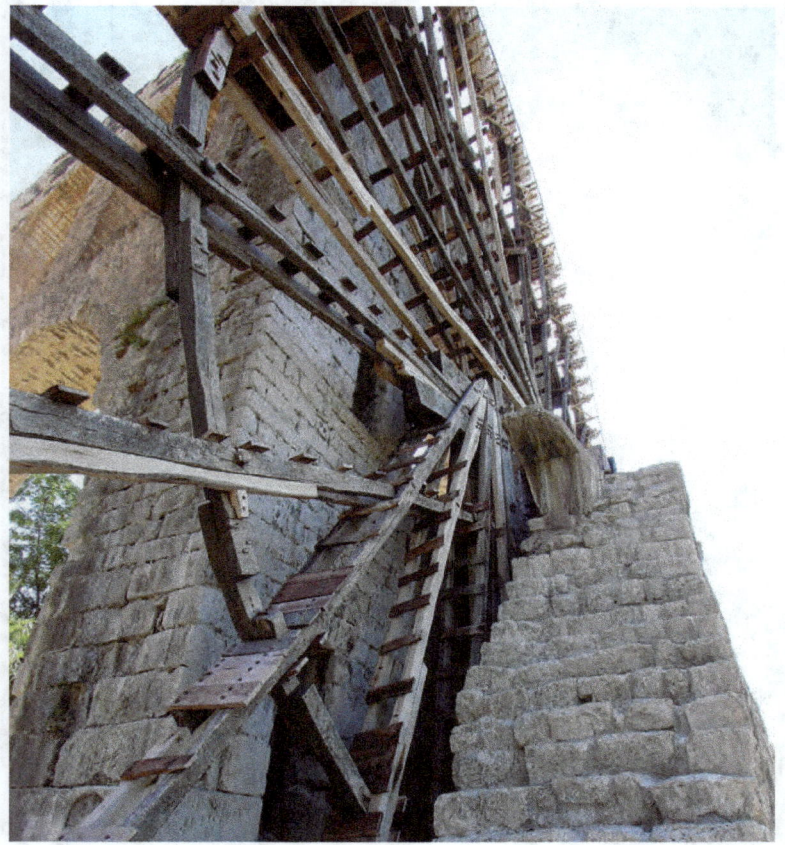

Noria al-Muhammadiyya, detail of the structure: the wooden wheel, the triangular tower and the rectangular tower, Hama (photo courtesy of Zena Takieddine).

only 17. They vary in size the largest (21 m in diameter) is the al-Muhammadiyya, located to the west of the city and featuring a Mamluk-period inscription. The Ma'muriyya, also with a dated inscription, is located to the east and forms part of a group of *nawa'ir* constructed during the Ottoman period. All the *noria*s have undergone restoration over the centuries, as the wooden beams of the *noria* require changing regularly, about every 15 years. Nevertheless, the act that the Mosque of Nur al-Din, the Madrasa al-Nuriyya al-Kubra, the Hammam al-Sultan, the Bimaristan al-Nuri, and the Citadel of Hama were all functioning institutions during the Zangid period, there is no doubt that these *nawa'ir* were equally well-maintained at that time.

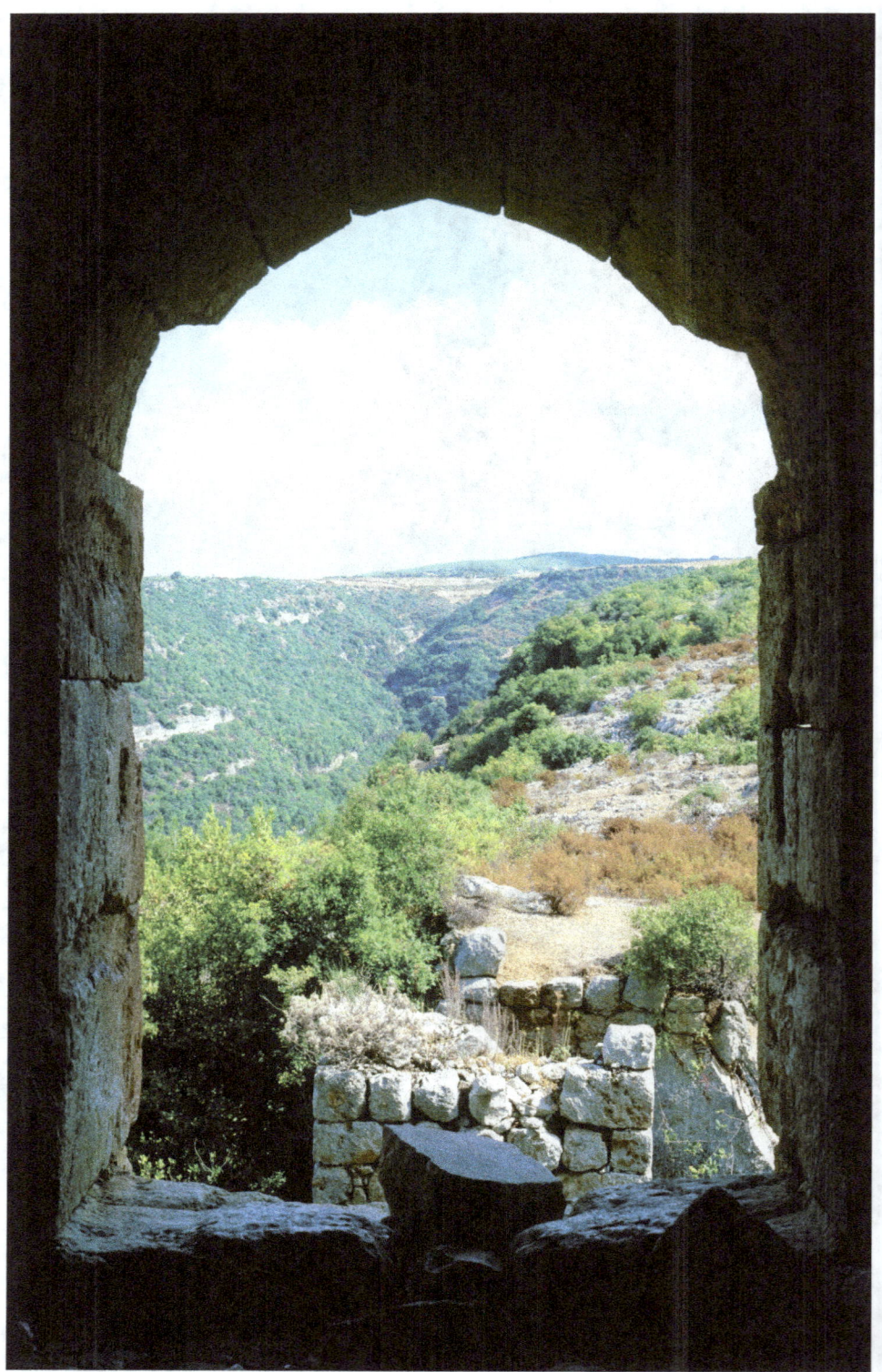

ITINERARY V
First day

Confrontation and Coexistence: Fortifications in western Syria

Introduction: Benjamin Michaudel;
Monuments: Benjamin Michaudel, Balázs Major, Haytham Hasan

HAMA

V.1 QAL'AT ABU QUBAYS (OPTION)
V.2 QAL'AT MISYAF
V.3 CRAC DES CHEVALIERS
V.4 SAFITA
    V.4.a Burj Safita

TARTUS

V.5 TARTUS
    V.5.a Old City Walls and Citadel

The Isma'iliyya Emirate of Syria   Haytham Hasan

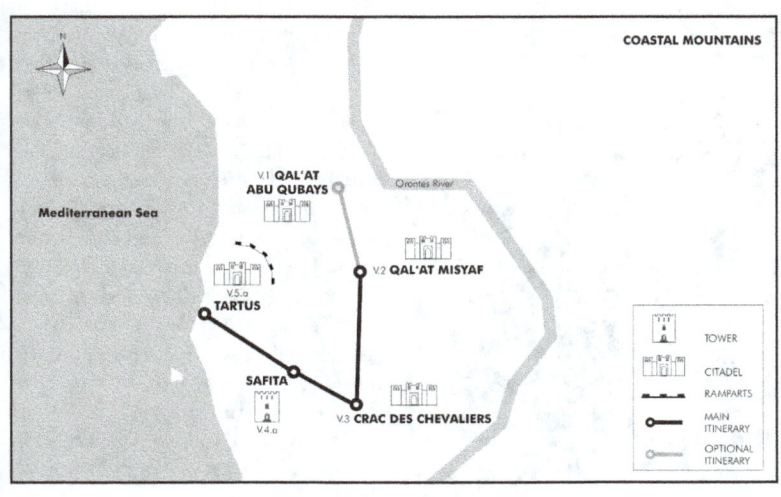

Qal'at Salah al-Din, window overlooking the surrounding mountains.

ITINERARY V *Confrontation and Coexistence: Fortifications in western Syria*
Introduction

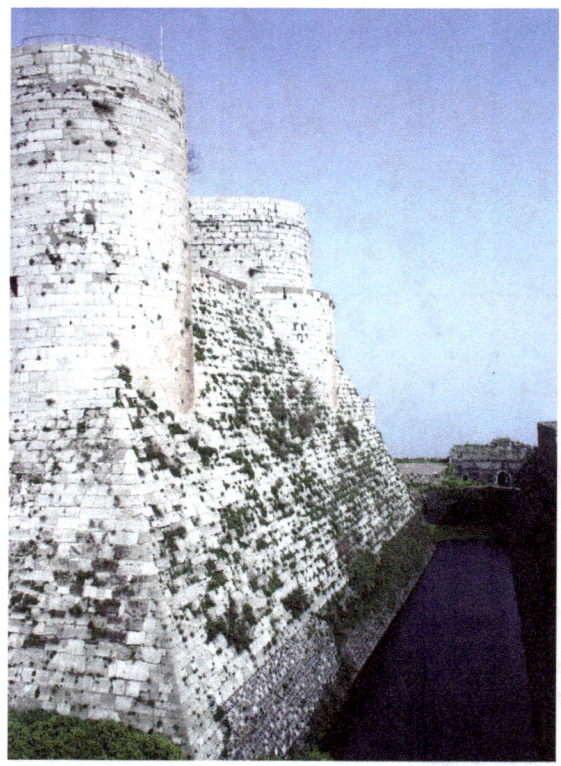

Crac des Chevaliers, view towards the southern side of the qilla: the donjon, the glacis and the ditch (photo courtesy of Yasser Tabbaa).

During the period of the Crusades, the encounters of Frankish and Muslim armies in the Bilad al-Sham were continuous, lasting for over two centuries. It generated among the opponents a concern for the affirmation of their political, religious and military identities in visual media, particularly through intense architectural activity on both sides. Some were fortresses serving to guarantee the stability of the borders and the defence of the fiefs, or *iqta'*, some were lookout towers along communications routes to ensure the safe passage of troops, while some were vital storehouses for food and weapons. There were also the palatial residences of rulers, the army dormitories and shelters for the locals. Castles represented the pillars of the establishment for both Crusader and Muslim powers and, built in abundance, they dotted the landscape of western Syria. This vast territory included the Syrian coastline, which stretches across some 160 km, through the steep and rocky mountains along the coast of Syria known as Jibal al-'Alawiyyin, and the northeastern Ghab Plains.

From the end of the 5th/11th century, the Crusaders coveted the area. When they conquered it at the beginning of the 6th/12th century, the region, divided into two parts, became the principality of Antioch in the north and the County of Tripoli in the south. Due to a serious shortage of troops, the Franks, as the Arabs called them, realised that their survival in the region was only maintainable through a dense defensive network. They initiated a large fortification policy, supervised at first by the feudal lords and fiefdoms in the 6th/12th century, and then progressively given over to the control of the Templars and Hospitallers. Erected in western Syria during this period were some Jewels of Crusader fortification, including Crac des Chevaliers, Marqab, Burj Safita, the Citadel of Salah al-Din, as well as the town of Tartus and Arwad Island.

At the same time, several mountain citadels were sold and/or bequeathed by their local Arab rulers to the Nizariyya

ITINERARY V Confrontation and Coexistence: Fortifications in western Syria
Introduction

Isma'iliyya or "Fellowship of the Guided Calling", as they called themselves, but who were known to the Franks as the "Assassins". This powerful and esoteric Shi'ite sect settled in the heart of the coastal mountains, known as the Mountain of the Alawites, during the latter half of the 6th/12th century. They showed a careful concern for the defence of their territory and were adept at protecting their strongholds, even though they took over an enclave coveted for its strategic importance by both the Crusaders and by the Sunni Muslims. The Isma'ilis recovered dozens of citadels from the hands of Crusaders and local tribes. They prodigiously improved their impregnability and defences, as can be seen in Misyaf, their headquarters, as well as al-Kahf and Abu Qubays.

Both the Crusader coastal defences and the Isma'ili mountain citadels played an important role in limiting the expansion and unification endeavours of the mid-6th/12th-century Seljuq-Zangid Atabeg Nur al-Din. While Nur al-Din was able to fortify Qal'at al-Mudiq near Hama, and the Citadel of Ma'arrat al-Nu'man further north, the Crusader and Isma'ili citadels of western Syria prevented the progress of the Seljuq armies further west.

The Ayyubid Sultan Salah al-Din faced the responsibility of reshaping the region at the end of the 6th/12th century. He launched a military campaign in the northern part of western Syria, which led to the conquests of the main feudal citadels held by the Crusaders, including the Chateau de Saone, which became

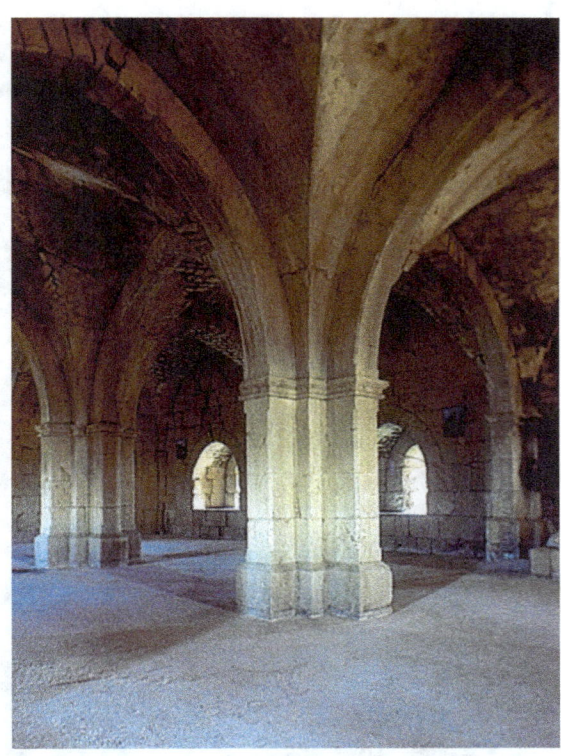

Burj Safita, interior, detail of the pillars and vaults of the hall that was probably the Templars' dormitory.

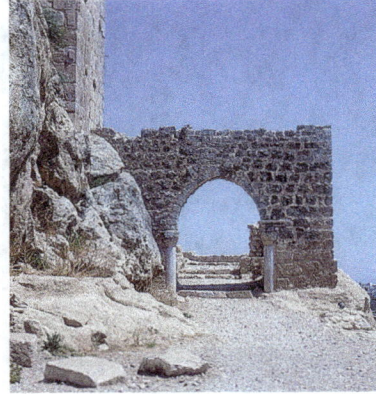

Qal'at Misyaf, remains of a gate.

ITINERARY V *Confrontation and Coexistence: Fortifications in western Syria*
Introduction

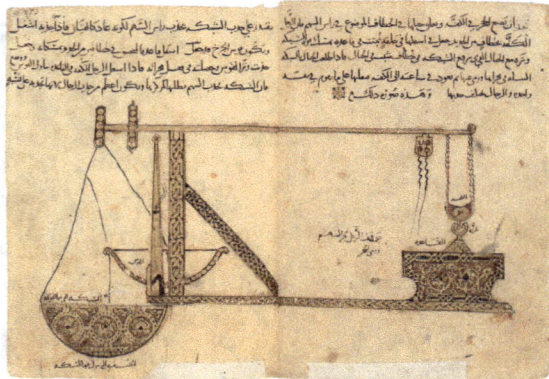

An illustration from Murda ibn 'Ali al-Tarsusi's treatise Tabsirat Arbab al-Albab fi Kayfiyyat al-Najat fi-l-Hurub min al-Aswa', *dedicated to Salah al-Din, Bodleian Library, Oxford (Inv. Num. MS. Huntington 264, fols. 134b–135a;* © *Bodleian Library, University of Oxford).*

Qal'at Marqab, general view.

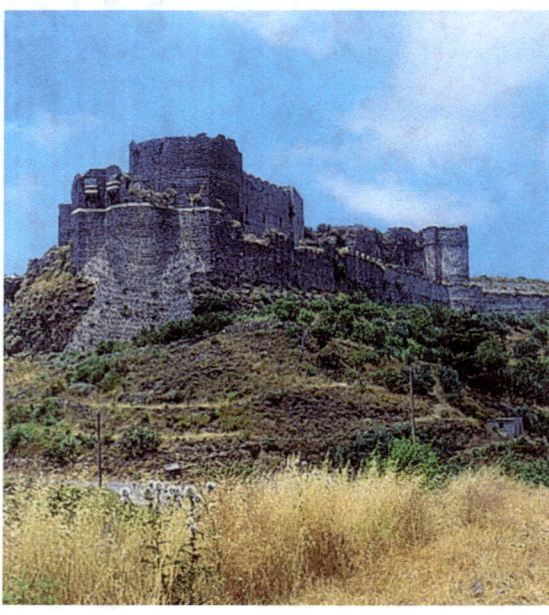

known as the Citadel of Salah al-Din. The main sites conquered by the Seljuq Zangids and the Ayyubids were refortified to be used as a form of military prowess against the Crusaders. The art of fortification witnessed a major evolution, partly due to the increasing popularity of the counterweight trebuchet or great mangonel, known in Arabic as the *Manjaniq*, and used for laying siege to fortified castles or citadels. The incorporation of civil and religious concerns into military architecture is also evident in many of the constructions of this period, the citadels of Salah al-Din and Ma'arrat al-Nu'man being just two examples.

The Mamluks of Egypt finally defeated the Crusaders and the Isma'ilis in western Syria, led by the sultans Baybars and Qalawun, in the second half of the 7th/13th century. The last of the Frankish citadels conquered during Mamluk military campaigns, Crac des Chevaliers and Marqab, for example, also became subject to refortification and renovation programmes. Transformed into symbols of Mamluk political and military supremacy, they signified the twilight of the Crusader period.

Although it is possible to cover this itinerary without a private vehicle, having your own rented car will make things significantly more pleasant and less complicated. Start early in the morning, at around six or seven, and pack a picnic as there are multiple scenic spots en route. Arrange beforehand for an overnight stay in Tartus, 145 km away from Hama, the city you will be arriving at during nightfall.

V.1 QAL'AT ABU QUBAYS (OPTION)

This citadel is located 75 km north-west of Hama. If available, take public transport to the town of Tal Salhab, and from there find someone to drive you to the village of Abu Qubays and drive 1 km further to the more remote village of 'Ayn al-Jard. At the picnic spot near the river, there is a steep dirt track up the mountain path to the left of the road leading to the citadel, with a spectacular view. The building is always open to the public.

The Citadel of Abu Qubays reaches a peak of 950 m, strategically located overlooking the Ghab Plains. Intermittently taken over by the Franks, the citadel came under Isma'iliyya Nizariyya leadership in 526/1132. The Franks Latinised its name to "Bochebeis". Its main exterior gate, located on its north-eastern side, is protected by two circular towers with interior grooves that once held a sliding iron gate, or portcullis, a distinctive defensive feature of the 6th/12th century. The gate, protected further by one immense tower, several smaller towers and an indirect passageway, also has a steeply built stone glacis on the east side. A large, square-based tower, rising at the east end of the mountain, watches over the communication routes and, facing the Isma'iliyya command centre, the Citadel of Misyaf.

V.2 QAL'AT MISYAF

If you are driving from Abu Qubays, the town and citadel of Misyaf is located 30 km south. Driving from Hama, it is 45 km to the west, on the Hama/Banyas Highway. The citadel appears eerily on the horizon and is easily discernable from the highway. Opening times are Wed–Mon 9.00–18.00 during the summer, 9.00–16.00 during the winter. Closed on Tuesdays and during Friday prayers (approx 11.00–13.00). There is an entrance fee.

The city and Citadel of Misyaf is located on the eastern slopes of the coastal mountains of Syria some 45 km west of Hama, on top of a rocky cliff surface. For military movement especially, the citadel (approx 70 m x 170 m) is very well positioned strategically on the fork of the communications routes between coastal Syria and the interior, and along the north–south route. The location had been

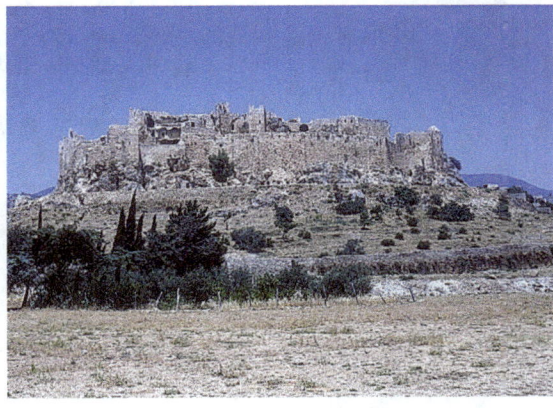

Qal'at Misyaf, general view.

ITINERARY V *Confrontation and Coexistence: Fortifications in western Syria*
Qal'at Misyaf

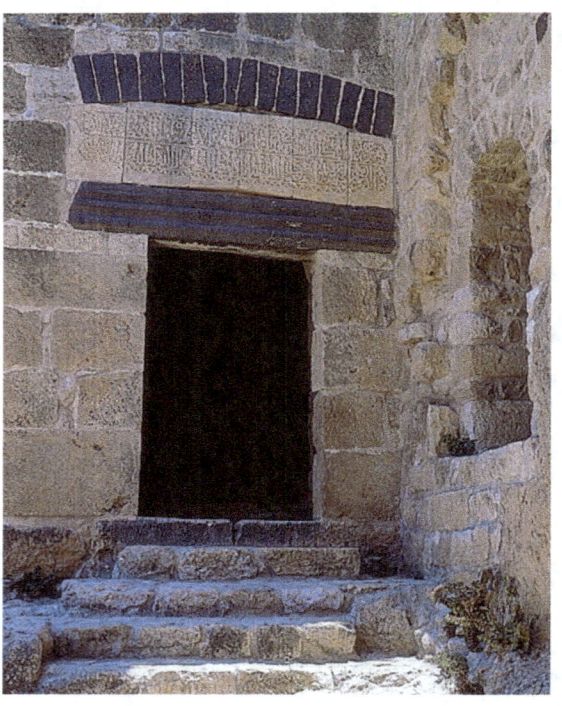

Qal'at Misyaf, detail of an epigraphic inscription.

a coveted for its strategic position since Roman times, and Septimius Severus who was Roman Emperor from AD 191 until AD 217 used it as the military headquarters.

During the medieval period in 389/999, Misyath Fortress, as it was known then, was destroyed by the Byzantine Emperor Basil II. Two subsequent Muslim Dynasties, the Hamdanid and Mirdasid then repossessed it. With the arrival of the Seljuqs, who bestowed the castle on the Banu Munqidh of Shayzar, it was used as a seigneurial residence and summertime location. In 535/1141 the Isma'iliyya al-Nizariyya, a clandestine missionary group who called themselves *Ashab al-Da'wa al-Hadiya*, or "Fellowship of the Guided Calling" took over the citadel. Under the leadership of Sinan Rashid al-Din (r. 558–88/1163–93; known as the greatest Isma'iliyya leader of Syria more famously known as "The Third Sheikh of the Mountain"), Misyaf became the official capital of the Isma'iliyya al-Nizariyya Emirate of Mount Bahra. Well defended, the citadel even succeeded in defying a siege by Salah al-Din in 572/1176. Cordial relations between the Isma'iliyya leadership and the Ayyubid rulers, particularly al-Zahir Ghazi of Aleppo, followed.

The castle continued to be governed by several Isma'ili leaders sent from Almut in Iran during the first half of the $7^{th}/13^{th}$ century. In 655/1258, the Mongols captured the castle, but the Mamluks freed it subsequently in 658/1260.

The citadel's nucleus is the interior fortress, or *qilla*, standing on the southern section of the cliff top. It is square with four towers, one on each corner, and a central ground-level courtyard or *castrum*. The *qilla*, enclosed by a wall with five square towers, once surrounded the entire surface of the cliff. A second, lower, wall surrounds the exterior and is similarly fortified by a number of square-based towers provided with arrow loops. Added during the $6^{th}/12^{th}$ century, the new exterior entrance-block was of huge dimensions and had formidable defences. A non-direct or elbow-shaped passageway that turns at a right angle northward for about 65 m and which is carved into the rock-face, connects the two great gates.

More towers were added, made of larger stones and taller arrow loops, some 170 cm long.

At the end of the 6th/12th century, when Sinan Rashid al-Din took over, the citadel witnessed a comprehensive renovation programme that included the construction of pentagonal-based towers on all sides. Each tower had five large arrow loops, thus highlighting the important military role played by the citadel during this period. The spaces between the interior and exterior walls were reworked to include reception halls and multi-purpose buildings. A palace, built on the upper level of the citadel's interior and distinguished by an ornamented gateway whose inscriptions attribute it to Hasan bin Mas'ud in 622/1226, is now more or less in ruins.

The main gate of the citadel was also rebuilt, with the addition of a *postrum* and the construction of a *barbacane*, which included a *hammam*. During the Mamluk period, the castle witnessed major renovation works, such as the merlons along the southern and eastern rooftops, new halls on the second level of the exterior and redecoration of the palace.

V.3 CRAC DES CHEVALIERS

Known locally as Qal'at al-Hosn, the castle is located 80 km south of Misyaf and there are many signs on the road to guide the visitor, as Crac des Chevaliers is a very popular destination. From Misyaf take the road to Tell-Kalakh near the Syrian-Lebanese border. Opening times are everyday 9.00–18.00 during the summer, 9.00–16.00 during the winter. There is an entrance fee.

Considered one of the most emblematic castles of the Crusades, Crac des Chevaliers, known in Arabic as Qal'at al-Hisn, represents a remarkable example of the evolution of Crusader and Islamic military architecture in the Near East during the 6th/12th and 7th/13th centuries. The citadel, situated half-way between

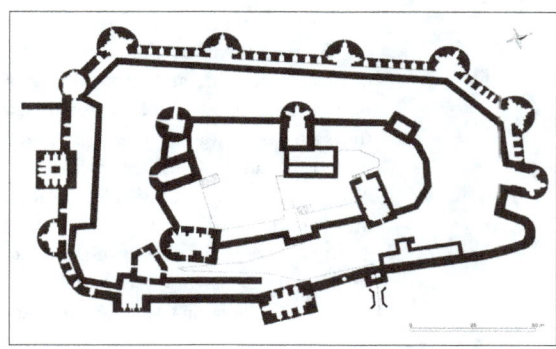

Floor-plan of Crac des Chevaliers.

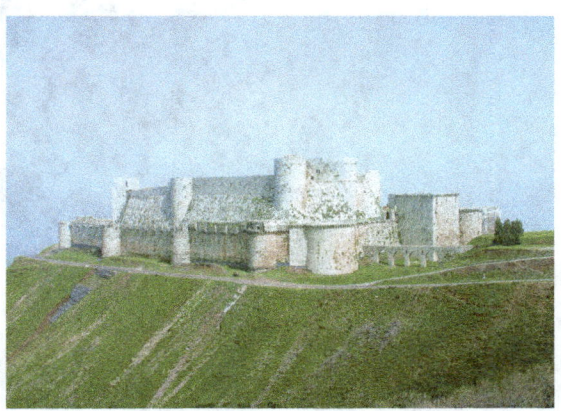

Crac des Chevaliers, general view (photo courtesy of Yasser Tabbaa).

ITINERARY V *Confrontation and Coexistence: Fortifications in western Syria*
Crac des Chevaliers

the Port of Tartus and the city of Homs on the southern buttresses of Syria's coastal mountains, stands at an altitude of 650 m, watching over the Gap of Homs, the main passageway between the Muslim hinterland and the Crusader coastline.

The site underwent its main fortification after the Crusader conquest of 504/1110, and especially after its donation to the military Order of the Hospitallers in 537/1142. It held on to by the Crusaders and protected by the Hospitallers for more than 120 years, withstanding two major Muslim forces; Nur al-Din's in 558/1163 and Salah al-Din's in 584/1188. The latter, though he kept the castle standing, destroyed the rest of the Count of Tripoli's territory. Crac des Chevaliers finally fell to the Mamluk Sultan Baybars in 669/1271. Restored and refortified it became the symbol of Mamluk sovereignty in the region and the residence of the Mamluk governors. It remained militarily occupied until the end of the Ottoman period and remained inhabited until the period of the French Mandate in the 1930s.

Lying on a basaltic trapezoidal-shaped spur, and separated from the mountain on the south side by an artificial ditch, the citadel divides into two defensive areas. The high citadel, known in Arabic as the *qilla*, built on a rocky promontory in the middle of the site, is organised around a central courtyard and a double trapezoidal-shaped surrounding wall. It constituted the private area of the Hospitallers, and held the most impressive buildings of the Frankish occupation. The religious complex included a chapel, a capitular room and a cloister gallery. The donjon, made up of three huge towers on the south front, was utilised as the headquarters and main residence for the Hospitaller elite. Architectural remains of the Crusader settlement in the low courtyard around the high citadel include the western and northern ramparts, the stable, the reservoir on the south front and the "barbacane" on the north-eastern front.

Mamluk architectural contribution to Crac des Chevaliers is substantial. The most significant works, achieved during the last third of the 7th/13th century, comprise restoration works and major improvements of the Hospitallers' original fortifications. These included new ramparts and several flanking towers built on the south and east fronts of the low courtyard, overhung by continuous galleries of machicolations and box-machicolations. The Mamluk's use of the site as a regional administrative centre led

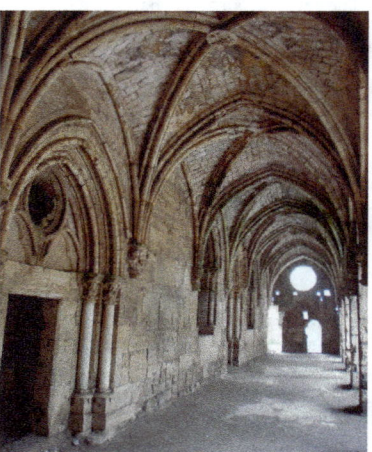

Crac des Chevaliers, the cloister gallery.

to the construction of residential and palatial buildings, like the governor's house on top of the donjon, decorated rooms overhanging the high castle and a *hammam* in the low courtyard.

V.4 SAFITA

The town of Safita is located 25 km west of Crac des Chevaliers, follow the street signs.

V.4.a Burj Safita

Beautifully located on the top of a hill covered with olive groves, the Safita Donjon can be reached from any of the multiple snaking alleyways ascending from the town. The donjon is now serving as one of the town's churches. In the unlikely event that the donjon is locked, the caretaker of the restaurant facing can help locate the responsible priest.

Safita, boasting the largest Crusader tower or *burj* of the Levant, is located at one of the best observation points in Syria's mountain ranges. It is also a unique example of an église-donjon, a keep incorporating a chapel. The first verifiable mention of Safita comes from the year 505/1112 as being in the hands of the Crusader County of Tripoli. Located very near to Muslim territories, the fortifications, carried out by the Order of the Temple, were complete by 506/1152. However, even they were unable to hold it against the armies of Nur al-Din who briefly took the area in 562/1166–7 and again 566/1171.

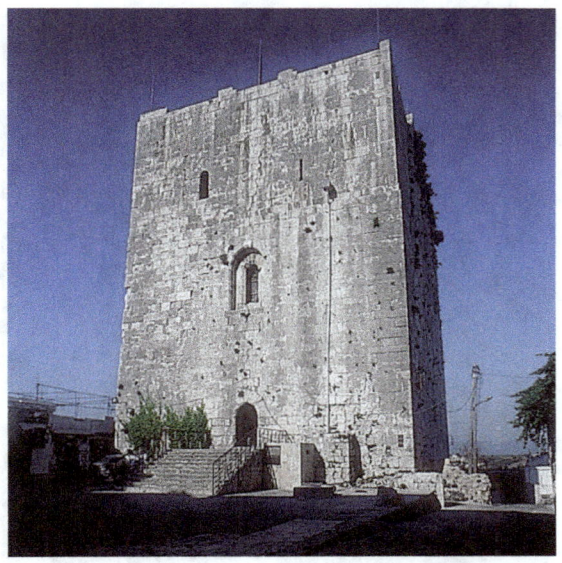

Burj Safita, general view.

During the reign of the Count of Tripoli, Raymond III, the Crusaders repossessed Safita; building of the donjon probably commenced after these events and following the ravages of the earthquake that struck in 565/1170. The campaign of Salah al-Din in 584/1188 passed Safita by, but another earthquake in 598/1202 did much damage.

The Franks assiduously attended to the damage wrought by the earthquake of 598/1202, together with the siege conducted by the Ayyubid prince al-Malik al-Ashraf in 615/1218. Some sources mention the French King, Louis VII's participation in improving Safita's fortifications. Safita went mostly unmolested until 569/1271, when the Templar garrison surrendered the castle to the Mamluks.

ITINERARY V *Confrontation and Coexistence: Fortifications in western Syria*
Safita

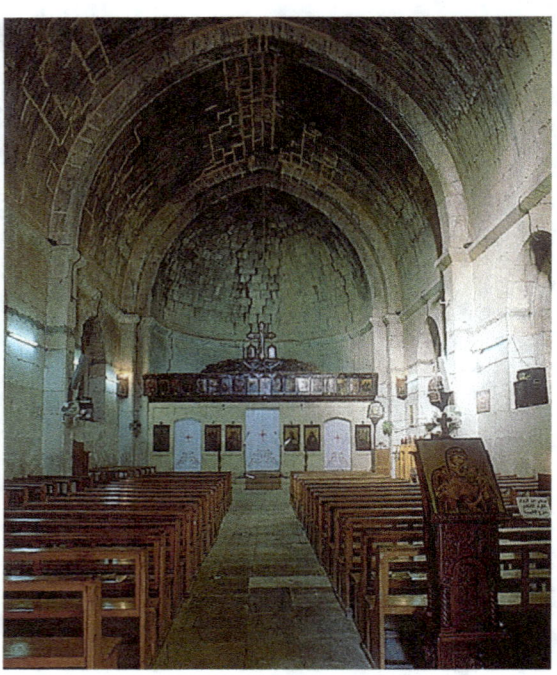

Burj Safita, interior, general view of the chapel.

A 27 m-high donjon, or central tower within a castle, dominates the remains of the Citadel of Safita. The donjon, which was practically unknown in Syria before the arrival of the Crusaders, became a regular feature in contemporary European military architecture. Regardless of its European origins the intention of the design for the tower of Safita was to accommodate Levantine requirements. Unlike many of its western contemporaries, its roof is flat and its interior spared from wooden elements. These developments are probably in response to the fear of combustibles used in war, a highly developed weapon in the Near East.

The tower, this time similar to its Latin counterparts, consisted of two vaulted levels. On the ground floor, there was a 13.5 m-high grandiose chapel covered by a pointed barrel-vault. This chapel follows the style used by the military orders residing in castles. The Greek Orthodox community of Safita continues to use it as a liturgical area, dedicated to Saint Michael.

From the left of the entrance, defended by slot machicolations, a stairway leads up from within the thickness of the walls to the first floor hall, which probably served as the dormitory of the Templar Knights' elite. This elegant hall is divided by three pillars, which support a cross-groined vault of eight bays. The flat roof above the hall preserves remnants of the original crenellations and offers a sweeping view over the surrounding countryside. The Donjon of Safita stood as the strategic centre of the region from where almost all the citadels and towers of the surrounding area were visible, including the Crac des Chevaliers. Large cracks currently seen on the façades of the tower are very possibly evidence of earthquake damage and restoration from the early 7th/13th century.

Of the two enceintes surrounding the tower, only the outer one, approximately 165 m x 100 m, still visible, remains. Its eastern stretch incorporates the western façade of a large rectangular building of two storeys. The springing of the ribbed-vault in the first-floor room bears close resemblance to a similar hall in the Citadel of Tartus.

V.5 TARTUS

From the town of Safita drive westwards towards the coast following the road signs to Tartus.

V.5.a Old City Walls and Citadel

The walls lie along the modern seafront of the city, across from the large placard advertising the new urban and touristic development of the city. Remains of the citadel lie directly behind the walls.

Tartus was the town held the longest by the Crusaders in the Levant. The buildings erected during their long stay, especially the superbly preserved cathedral, give a good impression of the general shape of a medieval coastal city in the Near East during the 6th/12th century.

Tartus sprang up as a satellite settlement off Arwad Island, which was the centre of the settlement pattern in ancient times. Tartus rose to prominence in the Romano-Byzantine period, its fame enhanced by two early Christian relics: the altar, according to legend, consecrated by the Apostle Peter during his short stay; the miraculous icon, allegedly one of four painted by Saint Luke. Disregarding a short period of Byzantine reconquest in the second half of the 4th/10th century, Tartus was in Muslim hands from the Arab conquests in the first half of the 1st/7th century up until the advent of the Crusades. While the army of the First Crusade briefly occupied the town in 492/1099, the firm establishment of Crusader control was not realised until 495/1102, when one of the Crusader leaders, Raymond of Saint Gilles, made it his base for the conquest of the future County of Tripoli. The campaign of Nur al-Din in 546/1152 succeeded in occupying and devastating the town, which led the bishop to transfer the lordship of the settlement to the Order of the Temple in return for protection. The town of Tartus then became the northern headquarters of the Templars. Even though Salah al-Din's army destroyed the town and part of the citadel in 594/1188, the Templars resisted them in the donjon. Tartus, rebuilt after Saladin's departure,

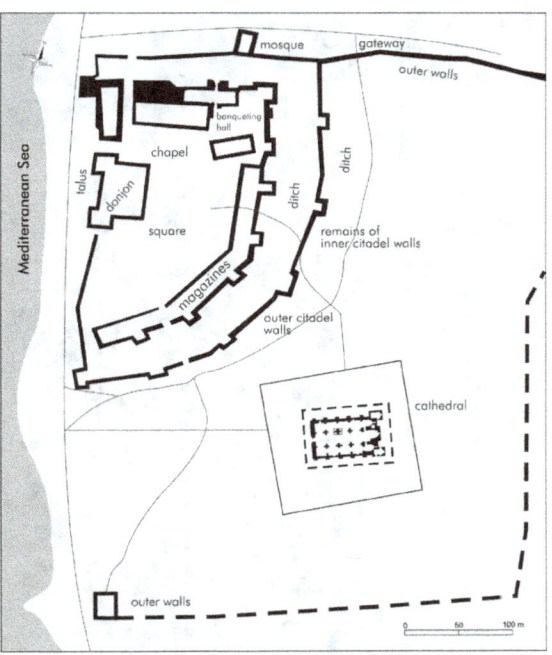

Map of Tartus City.

ITINERARY V *Confrontation and Coexistence: Fortifications in western Syria*
Tartus

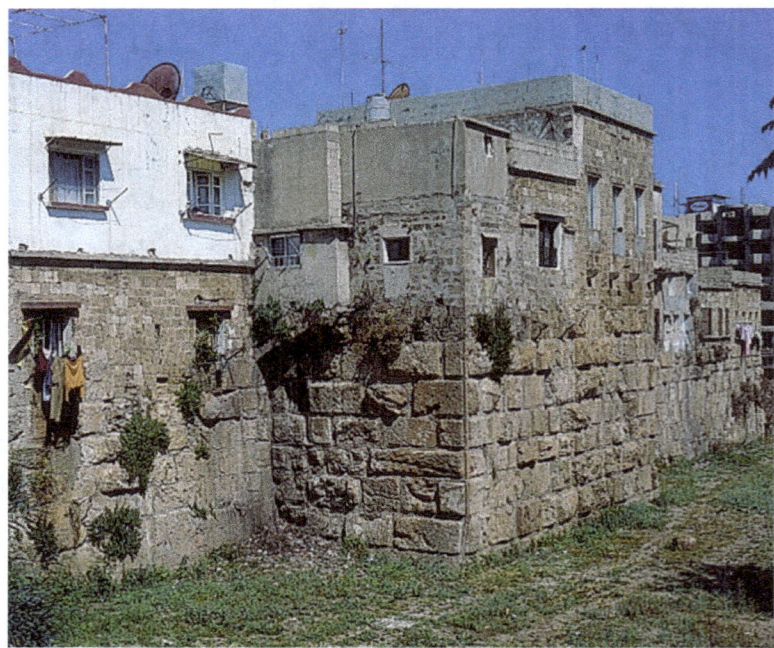

Remains of the old city walls, Tartus.

remained in Crusader hands until in 590/1291.

A surrounding ditch and town wall with rectangular projecting towers defended the medieval town of Tartus. The part of the gateway most intact is in the western part of town, and it is the best-preserved Crusader town gate in the region. The gate stood at the point where the town wall joined the fortifications of the citadel. The Templars built the citadel in the north-western corner of the walled rectangle, with direct access to the town, the sea and the fields to the north.

The castle plan is oval-shaped and concentric, with a double circuit of walls on its landward side, surrounded by rock-cut moats. The enclosures were built of large bossed ashlars, a favourite construction material of the Templars, and flanked by large oblong towers, which is also characteristic of 7th-/13th-century Templar defensive architecture. At one point, the inner wall survived to its full height (25.5 m), with good examples of different kinds of loopholes on several of the preserved levels. The high inner wall was supported in the interior by huge vaulted ranges, which were also used as storage areas.

The main entrance to the citadel was through an enormous gatehouse, which

ITINERARY V *Confrontation and Coexistence: Fortifications in western Syria*
Tartus

now functions as a mosque. Though much overbuilt later by houses, the interior of the castle still preserves the most important elements characteristic of the fortifications of the military orders. One was the large rectangular building on two levels, the upper storey most probably containing the Great Hall of the knights. Another was the chapel, a typically austere building covered with gothic ribbed-vaults. The third, main element of the castle was the donjon, which stood by the seaside. Its shooting galleries (which opened from a glacis at ground level) were constructed around an older donjon, possibly that which held out against Salah al-Din. Separated from the rest of the castle by a large ditch, the donjon, with its long seaward façade, had two flanking towers to provide additional defences.

Leaving the bases on the south-west corner tower of the inner castle, one reaches the sloping glacis of the south-west tower of the town wall, opposite the entrance to the harbour, from which Arwad Island is reached. Being the only habitable island on the Syrian coast and offering the best natural harbour of the region, Arwad was an important military base for the Templars, where they held out until 701/1302. Their castle was in the middle of the island, but was largely demolished and remodelled in later periods.

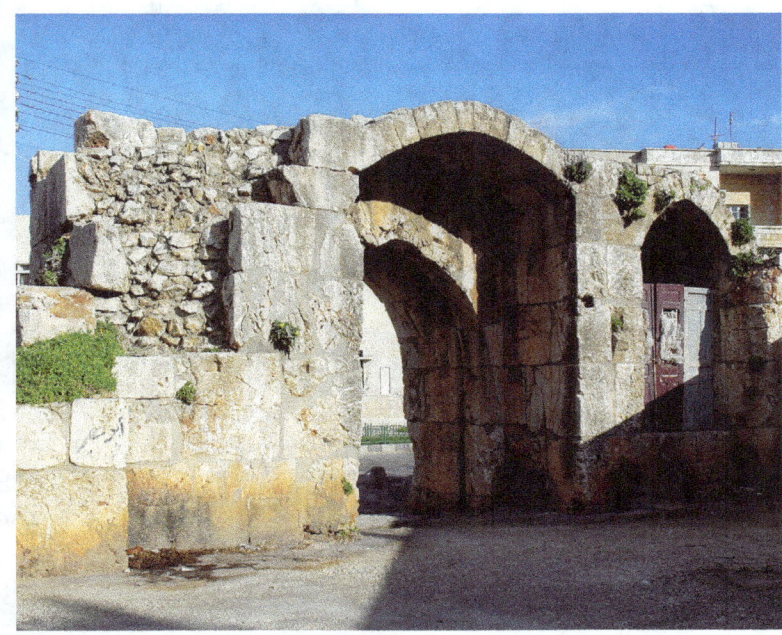

Tartus city, St. Helen, Crusader gate (photo courtesy of Balázs Major).

THE ISMA'ILIYYA EMIRATE OF SYRIA

Haytham Hasan

The Isma'iliyya is one of the major branches of Shi'ite Islam, itself having numerous sub-divisions. Its name derives from the seventh Imam, known as Isma'il bin Ja'far al-Sadiq (d. 148/765). As a minority group with secretive tendencies, the orthodox Muslim histories have generally not been even-handed in their portrayal of the sect. The Isma'ilis have been known as Qaramatians (after al-Qarmati), Fatimids (after Fatima the Prophet's daughter), al-Batina (the Esoterics), but also al-Rafida (the Refusers), al-Hashashashin (the Drug-users) and al-Malahid (the Atheists). Nonetheless, the Isma'ilis were also philosophers, and one of their most important manuscripts, *Rasa'il Ikhwan al-Safa* (*Epistles of the Brethren of Purity*), survives as a fine example of manuscript art and also as an encyclopaedia of Isma'ili epistemology. Authors of this work were indeed an esoteric group, thought to reside in the Salamiyya region of Syria, lying east of Hama. Members of the Isma'iliyya Nizariyya sect emerged with the death of the Fatimid caliph al-Mustansir in 487/1094 due to a controversial succession. Followers of his younger son al-Musta'li took the throne in Cairo while followers of his elder son, Nizar, refused the former's legitimacy. Quarrels ensued, and the Nizari Isma'ilis left Egypt for Syria, forging strong links to the Nizaris of Iran. Their existence relied mostly on the thick chain of castles and fortresses that were in the process of development along difficult-to-reach mountain ranges, amounting to over 100 bastions. The Persian Isma'ilis, led by Hasan al-Sabah, occupied the formidable Castle of Alamut in 483/1090 and sent missionaries to Syria who took advantage of its western mountains and possessed many strategic castles in the area.

During the Crusader period, the Ismai'li sect became a major player on the military and political scene of Syria. They called themselves *Ashab al-Da'wa al-Hadiya* (Fellowship of the Guided Calling) or the *Sinaniyya* after their ruler Sinan Rashid al-Din (d. 558–88/1163–93), who came to Misyaf from Alamut and was famously known as the "Old Sheikh of the Mountain". Among the Franks, they were known as the "Assassins".

Sinan's policy of political assassination against his enemies afforded him an infamous reputation throughout the eastern Mediterranean region, causing kings and sultans to pay tribute to him. As Sinan's power grew, he severed his relations with the mother centre of Almut Iran, bestowing on the rising Emirate of Misyaf a great degree of independence. Sinan negotiated with the great powers of the region, making alliances with the Franks, such as King Amalric of Jerusalem. Between them were gifts exchanges and embassies, as well as occasional turbulence, which Sinan managed to his credit. Sinan went into conflict with the Nur al-Din bin Zangi and against Salah al-Din, who finally destroyed the Fatimid caliphate in Egypt, and then tried to defeat Sinan in Aleppo. When Salah al-Din's siege of Misyaf failed, he gave up trying to subdue the Isma'ili power and, instead, the two formed a long-term peace treaty. Greater stability in the region was achieved by cordial relationships between the ruling Ayyubid family and the Isma'iliyya in Misyaf.

The Isma'iliyya Emirate in Syria retained its power until the first half of the 7th/13th century. The Mongol invasion destroyed the mother centre in Almut in 653/1256, and overpowered several of the Isma'ili castles in Syria. The Isma'iliyya's final defeat arrived at the hands of the new Mamluk Sultanate, led by al-Zahir Baybars, who decisively took over Misyaf in the year 668/1270.

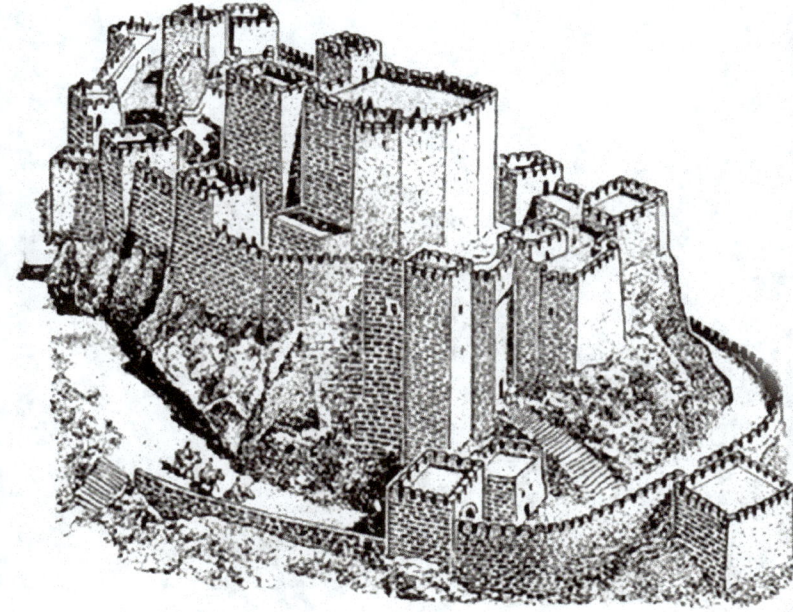

Sketch of Qal'at Misyaf (Hiller.brand, 1999, fig. 7.67; Leacroft, 1976).

Cathedral of Our Lady of Tortosa / Museum of Tartus.

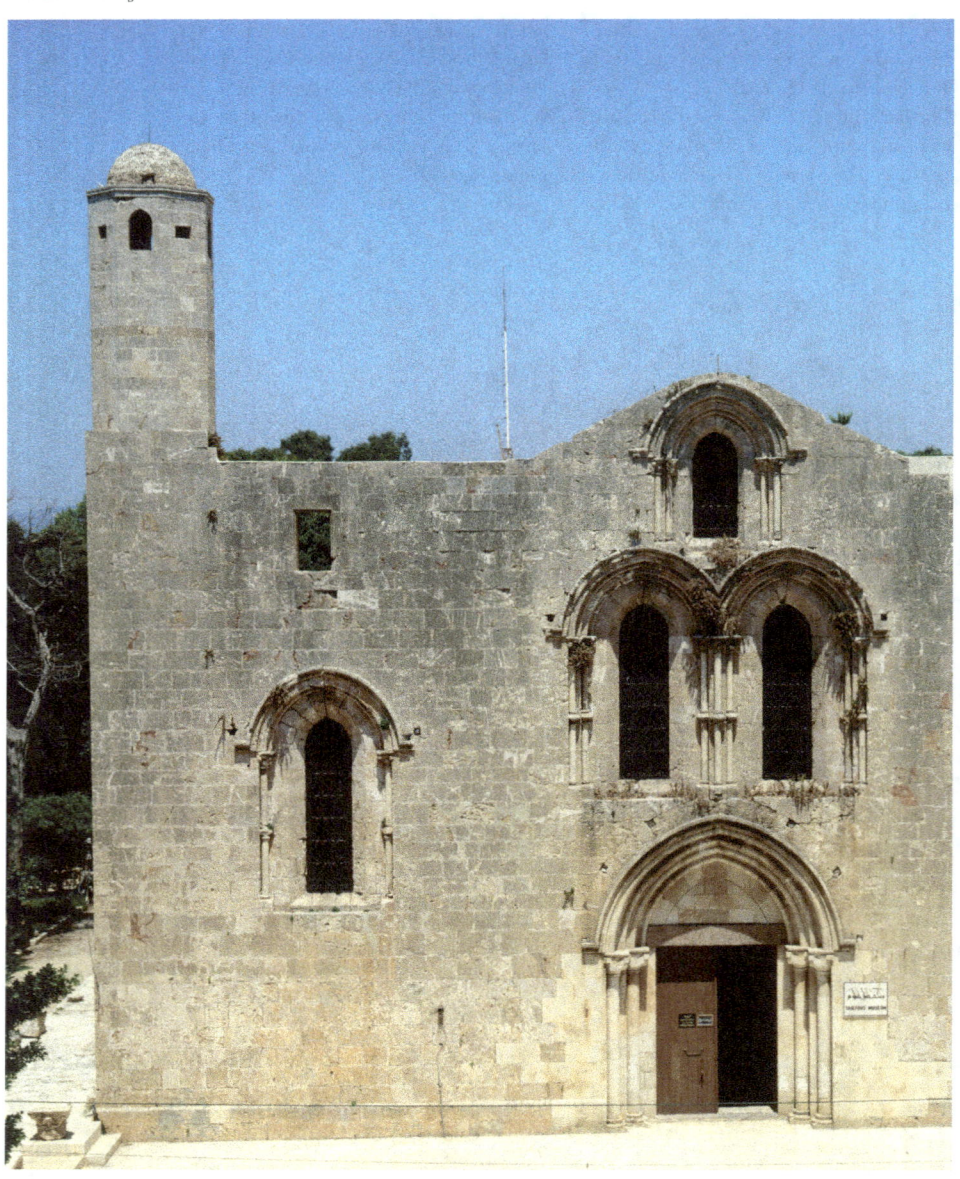

ITINERARY V
Second day

Confrontation and Coexistence: Fortifications in western Syria

Introduction: Benjamin Michaudel;
Monuments: Benjamin Michaudel, Balázs Major, Haytham Hasan

TARTUS

V.5 TARTUS
   V.5.b Cathedral of Our Lady of Tortosa/Museum of Tartus

V.6 QAL'AT MARQAB

V.7 QAL'AT SALAH AL-DIN

V.8 MA'ARRAT AL-NU'MAN
   V.8.a Town of Ma'arrat al-Nu'man: Great Mosque, Madrasa, Citadel

Memoirs of Salah al-Din   Yasser Tabbaa

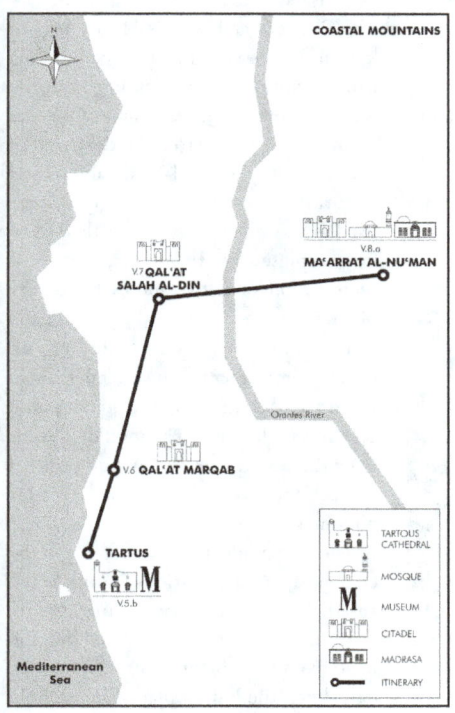

V.5 TARTUS

Although it is possible to cover this itinerary without a private vehicle, having a car will make things significantly more pleasant and uncomplicated. Start early with a quick walk around Tartus, then prepare for a long day on the road. Pack a picnic, as there are multiple scenic spots en route. Arrange beforehand for an overnight stay in Aleppo, the city you are likely to arrive at after nightfall.

V.5.b Cathedral of Our Lady of Tortosa / Museum of Tartus

The cathedral / museum is in the middle of a small public park off Minshiye Street. Walk south from the citadel and the building appears amongst the trees.

The Cathedral of Our Lady of Tortosa was erected on the site of the Altar of Saint Peter. Construction of the cathedral started in 517/1123, interrupted by two Muslim conquests, and completed by 542/1130. The cathedral is a rare and important survivor of Latin architecture in the region, based on a Byzantine eastern church destroyed in an earthquake of 387 AD. An icon of the Virgin Mary painted by Saint Luke survived the destruction and its preservation thought of as miraculous. The church itself is one of the earliest religious locations to be associated with the Virgin Mary, and thus, it has long attracted pilgrims and visitors. The Museum of Tartus was established in the Cathedral in 1956.

The Crusader cathedral is 41 m x 34.5 m x 15 m. The eastern end of the building is of a typical basilica plan begun in the Romanesque style, but when work was resumed, perhaps after the destruction carried out by Salah al-Din, capitals and decorative motifs of a later style were used. The western façade was the last to be completed. At this point, the architects no longer felt bound by the legacy of their predecessors and followed the European Gothic style of the $7^{th}/13^{th}$ century, implementing five slender lancet windows set in recessed arches and columns in the jams. The moulded bands over the pointed arched windows are a typical decorative feature in Crusader buildings.

Besides the gradual change of style in the cathedral, another curious feature is the small, arched passageway built underneath the westernmost pier dividing the nave from the northern aisle. This may have been the hiding place for the holy

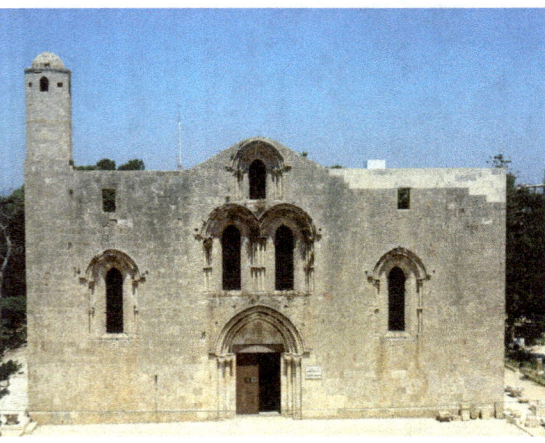

Cathedral of Our Lady of Tortosa, general view.

icon, observable through a slit-window opening in the west wall of the passage. With the growing danger posed by the establishment of the Mamluk state in Egypt in the second half of the 7th/13th century, the cathedral itself was fortified by two arrow-slitted towers to its east end. Plans for similar implementations for its west side never came to anything.

Fresco

The fresco wall painting depicts the Virgin Mary putting Christ the Child in the arms of Saint Simeon, while a woman stands in the background overlooking them. All four figures have golden halos around their heads, shaped like a disk within a thin white, then black, frame. Painted below the outstretched hands of the Virgin Mary, the infant Christ and Saint Simeon, is what appears to be a gem-incrusted bound copy of the Holy Scriptures. Between the Virgin Mary and Saint Simeon is a small unidentifiable male figure who probably symbolised a kneeling worshipper. The date of the fresco is some time between 566–669/1171–1271, and it was originally located on the exterior wall of Crac des Chevaliers. Its peculiar location has spurred several interpretations: a pious donation, a protective icon to secure the citadel, or perhaps a painting that was part of the decoration of a cemetery east of the citadel.

Amphora

The shape of this amphora with its wide base allows it to be considered a suitable vessel for storage of foodstuffs traded overseas, particularly olive oil and wine.

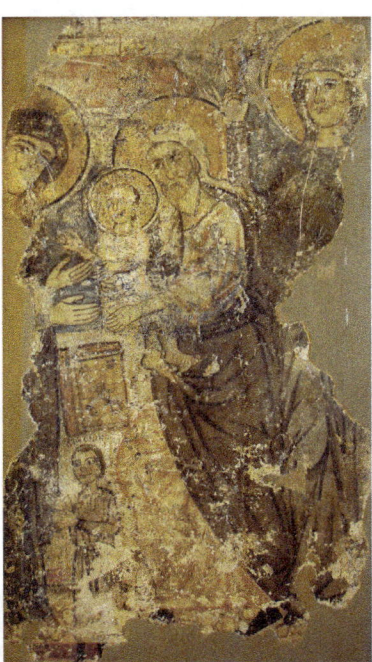

Crusader fresco depicting the Virgin Mary, Christ Child and St. Simeon. Museum of Tartus.

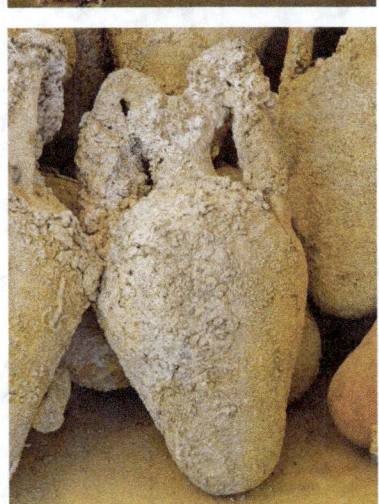

Amphora (probably Crusader), Museum of Tartus.

Tartus

Excavated underwater and dated using carbon dating, it has been attributed to the 6th/12th century. It was probably onboard a ship belonging to a Crusader fleet.

Reliquary
This lidded, marble box was to keep sacred relics in, in the Crusader holy places. Dated to between 555–700/1150–1300, the carving comprises two small crosses and three Latin letters that symbolise the name of Christ. Believers maintain that the remains of saint's bones were stored within it. The pierced lid allowed oil to be poured over the bones of the saints. A small hole in the bottom of the box allowed the sanctified oil to run out and a previously prepared dish collected the oil for believers to use for blessings. Excavated from an abandoned monastery north-east of Tartus, it is a rare find, with only one other known example extant, made of basalt stone, and found in the National Museum of Aleppo.

Sword
This straight Crusader sword with a small handle survives without a sheath and with a slight break. It is decorated with a pair of parallel lines carved into the length that curve and intersect near the tip. The dimensions of the blade are 46.8 cm long and 3.8 cm wide, while the length of the handle is 9.0 cm. It survives in relatively good condition but requires further study for date and attribution.

Column capital
A square-based capital carved with figurative motifs showing Central Asian

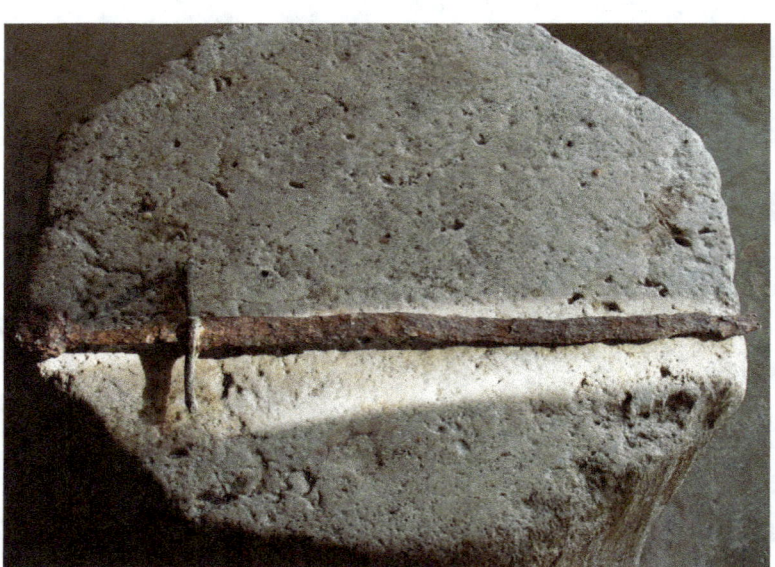

Crusader sword, Museum of Tartus (photo courtesy of Balázs Major).

ITINERARY V Confrontation and Coexistence: Fortifications in western Syria
Qal'at Marqab

facial features and probably indicating the period of Mongol acquisition of the citadels of Isma'iliyya during the first half of the 8th/14th century. The heart-shaped design has links to the Isma'ili sect known as the Isma'iliyya Nizariyya.

V.6 QAL'AT MARQAB

This citadel lies 30 km north of Tartus. Drive north from Tartus on the Tartus/Lattakia Highway. Take the exit to the town of Baniyas, just before a basalt watchtower. Follow the road that winds up past the olive groves as it ascends to the citadel, a basalt structure that is very clearly visible from the highway below. Opening times are Wed–Mon 9.00–18.00 during the summer, 9.00–16.00 during the winter. Closed on Tuesdays and during Friday prayers (approx 11.00–13.00). There is an entrance fee.

The citadel is a very good example of a coastal Crusader and Hospitaller fortification, such that it is often presented as the basalt counterpart to Crac des Chevaliers. It controlled the coastal route and protected the Port of Banyas, which the Crusaders used to export musk, wine, sumac, almonds and figs and, on an artistic level, pottery.

The earliest mention of the Qal'at Marqab was in the year 453/1062–3 as a site fortified by a local tribe. The citadel was temporarily in the possession of the Byzantines at the beginning of the 6th/12th century, and definitively conquered by the Crusaders under the

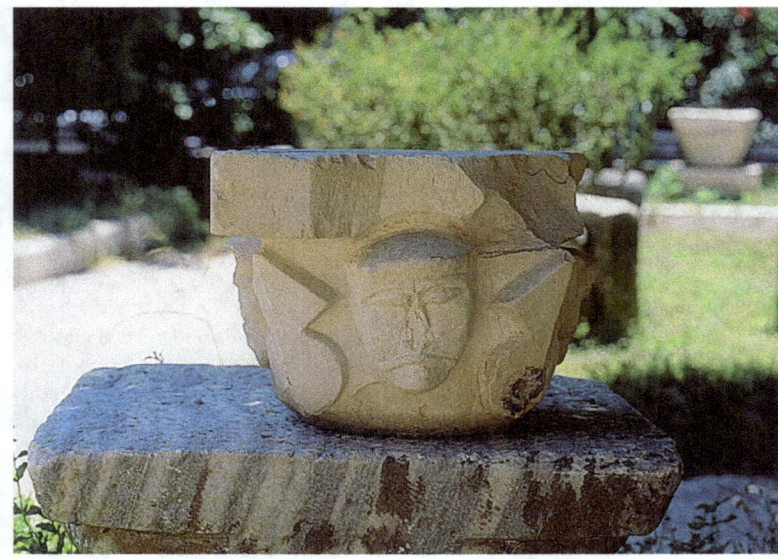

Column capital (probably 14th century), Museum of Tartus.

203

ITINERARY V *Confrontation and Coexistence: Fortifications in western Syria*
Qal'at Marqab

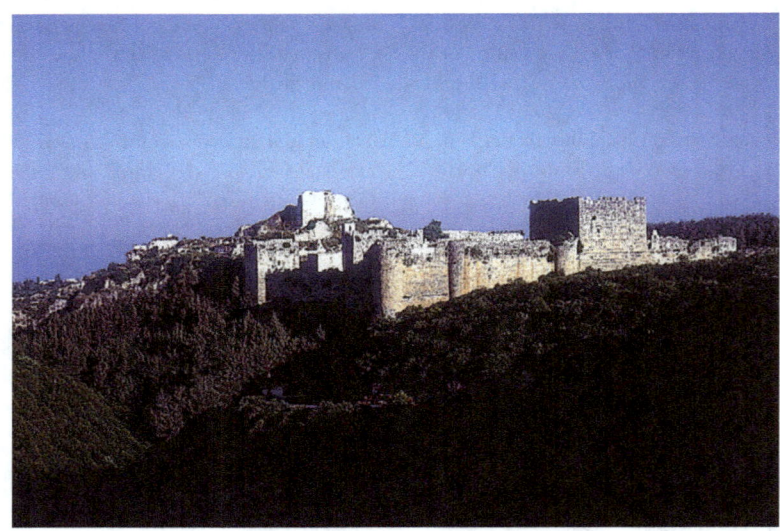

Qal'at Salah al-Din, general view.

leadership of knight Renaud I Masoiers in 511/1117–18. The site became an important headquarters for one of the most powerful fiefs of the Principality of Antioch.

Marqab was handed to the Hospitallers, alongside Banyas, in 581/1185–6. It remained in their hands for a century, during which time it witnessed two main fortification programmes. The citadel was able to ward off Saladin's attack of 584/1188, but fell finally to the Mamluk Sultan Qalawun in 682/1285.

Situated about half way between the Syrian ports of Jabla and Latakia, Marqab Citadel occupies a triangular shaped cliff rising 350 m above the Syrian littoral, 2 km south-west of Banyas. The citadel divides into two complementary areas. The south point of the cliff holds the stronghold devoted to the Hospitallers'

elite, while the northern area of the cliff was a village and *faubourg*, or suburb. The stronghold is organised around a central courtyard of trapezoidal plan. During the first construction programme of the late 6th/12th early 7th/13th centuries, several oblong rooms on two or three levels surrounded the courtyard. These were utilised as residences, a refectory, a storage area and ramparts and defended by numerous arrow loops. South of the courtyard, a chapel was built, its interior plan consisting of two bays with a barrel-vaulted apse, and four lancet windows for illumination. Fresco wall paintings depicting the *Pentecost* are located in the north sacristy, suggesting they belong to the first fortification programme. Surrounding these buildings was an external defensive wall. Sometime after 601/1204–5, saw the erection of Burj al-Sabi, a square

ITINERARY V   *Confrontation and Coexistence: Fortifications in western Syria*
Qal'at Marqab

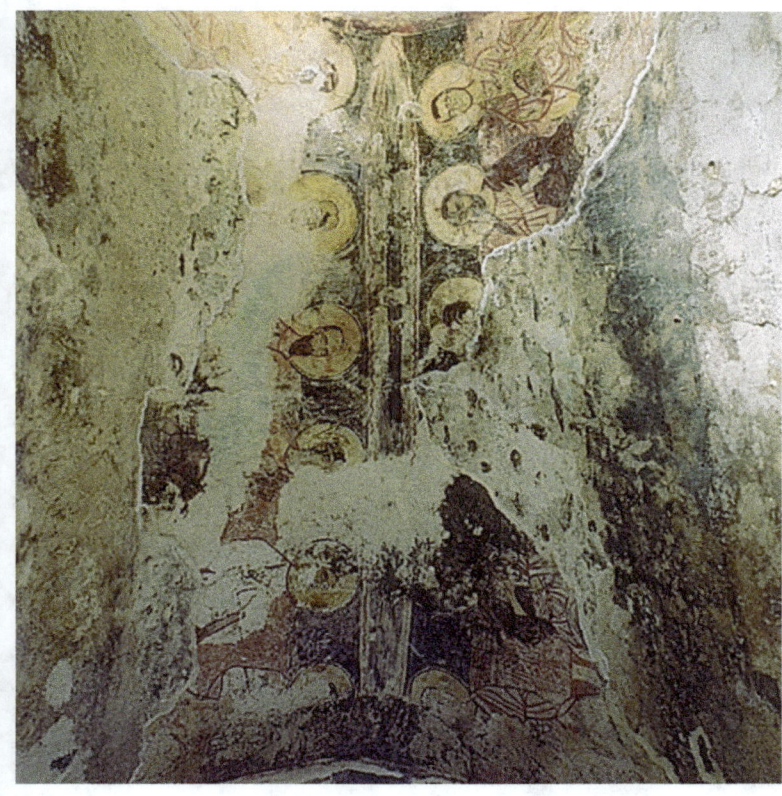

Qal'at Marqab, interior, fresco.

watchtower that overhung the coastal road 1.5 km to the west. The Port of Banyas retains evidence of a ruined mill, possibly dating from this period. During the second Hospitaller fortification programme in the 7th/13th century, the addition of a donjon made up of a residential tower and a circular keep to the south of the central courtyard was made at the same time as a long wall fortified by semi-circular towers was erected around the *faubourg*.

The takeover of the castle by the Mamluks in 683/1285 did not cause major damage but led to restorations and defensive improvements, notably the building of a massive tower overhung by box-machicolations on the south point of the stronghold undermined during the Frankish siege. It also led to the citadel's transformation into the administrative centre of the province as a district of Tripoli.

V.7 QAL'AT SALAH AL-DIN

There are two main roads from Marqab to the Qal'at Salah al-Din, either along the coast road or through the mountains. One can return to the coastal highway and drive northwards to Latakia. Five kilometres before arriving at Latakia, take the Aleppo Highway and drive eastwards to the town of Heffe, from which one can follow the signs to the castle. Alternatively, it is possible to take the scenic route through the mountains, through the villages and the pines, following the signs to Heffe, from which it is straightforward to find the dramatically positioned castle. Opening times are Wed–Mon 9.00–18.00 during the summer, 9.00–16.00 during the winter. Closed on Tuesdays and during Friday prayers (approx 11.00–13.00). There is an entrance fee.

The Castle of Salah al-Din, considered one of the most elaborate of the Eastern Mediterranean, is an example of Byzantine, Frankish, Ayyubid and Mamluk military architecture. Located in the northern part of western Syria, about 30 km north-east of the Port of Latakia along the northern buttress of the Alawite coastal mountains, it controlled the road between Latakia and the northern Ghab Plains. This castle was mostly a county residence rather than a garrison citadel.

Appearing in the historical sources during the 4th/10th century, the Byzantines occupied the site until the end of the 5th/11th century and launched ambitious fortification campaigns. Kept for a short time by the Seljuqs, the castle was then conquered by the Crusaders between 507/1114 and 513/1119 and granted as a fief to the knight, Robert, son of Foulques and his successors. Significant improvements were made to the castle fortifications possibly with the help of the military orders. It was finally conquered by Salah al-Din in 584/1188 and subsequently granted as an *iqta'* to the Mengüverish *emir*s. Following the Mongol menace of the mid 7th/13th century, the Mamluk Sultan Baybars recovered the

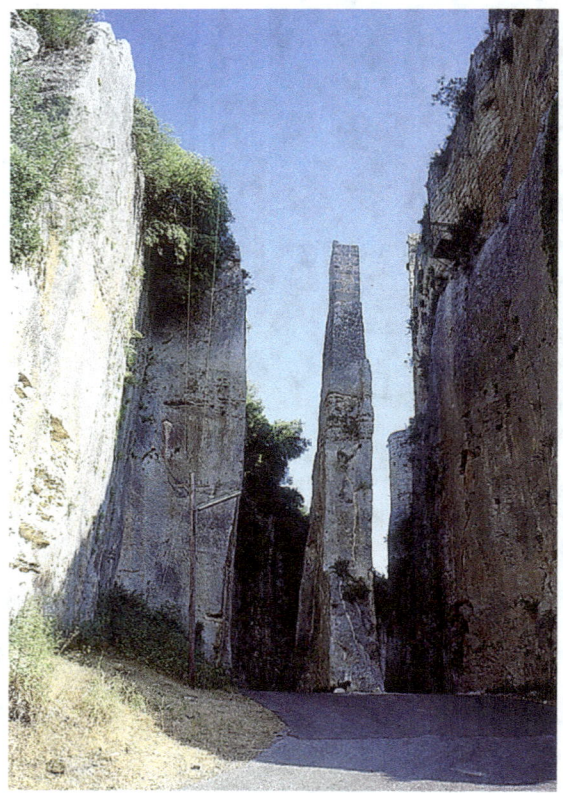

Qal'at Salah al-Din, view of the eastern ditch.

castle peacefully in 671/1272, and granted it to the governor in his charge. After the advent of Sultan Qalawun in 679/1280, the anti-sultan, Sunqur al-Ashqar transformed the castle into his headquarters and kept it until its final conquest by Qalawun in 686/1287. Qal'at Salah al-Din was then transformed into a provincial administrative centre within the Mamluk Empire.

The triangular shaped castle, built on a rocky spur, is isolated from the mountain by a wide, artificial ditch about 30 m deep. The spur measures about 700 m east to west and has 120 m of maximal width along the eastern ditch, where there towers a pinnacle for the drawbridge. It has two topographical areas divided by a central ditch, deepened by the Byzantines so that the castle was on the high, eastern side and the defensive towers on the low, western side.

The high courtyard to the east was initially the heart of the Byzantine citadel, with a small polygonal castle built at the top of a hillock and defended by four successive surrounding walls on the east side, lined by polygonal and semi-circular salient towers. Transformed into a manorial area by the Crusaders during the 6th/12th century, it included a huge square keep, two large cisterns, numerous surrounding towers and partial digging of the eastern ditch. Later, the Ayyubids improved the defences and built a large palatial complex combining a *hammam* and reception rooms on two levels, following the same model as that of the Citadel of Aleppo (VII.1.h). Two additional *hammams* and a mosque were built around this complex during the Mamluk period with a reception tower astride the west wall of the high courtyard. The low courtyard to the west was also improved defensively during the Crusader and Islamic occupations with the construction of two gate-towers and the completion of the surrounding wall.

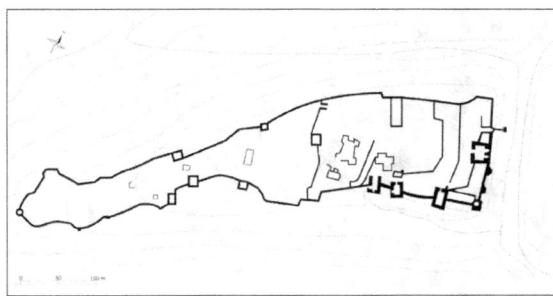

Floor-plan of Qal'at Salah al-Din.

V.8 MA'ARRAT AL-NU'MAN

The town lies 75 km south of Aleppo, and it will take a good three hours to reach from the Castle of Salah al-Din. After visiting the city's monuments, return to the Damascus–Aleppo Highway and continue north to your pre-arranged accommodation in Aleppo.

V.8.a Town of Ma'arrat al-Nu'man: Great Mosque, Madrasa, Citadel

The minaret of the town's great mosque, echoing the famous minaret in Aleppo (VI.1.g) is the town's most important landmark, found in the centre of the old city.

ITINERARY V *Confrontation and Coexistence: Fortifications in western Syria*
Ma'arrat al-Nu'man

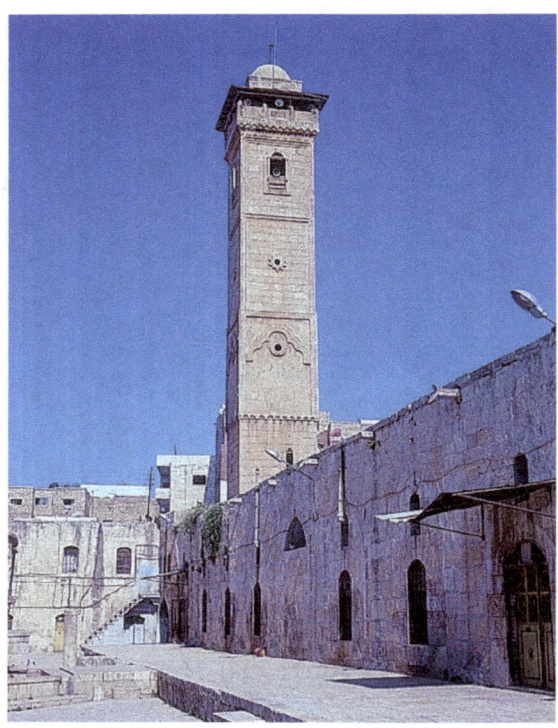

*Great Mosque,
Ma'arrat al-Nu'man.*

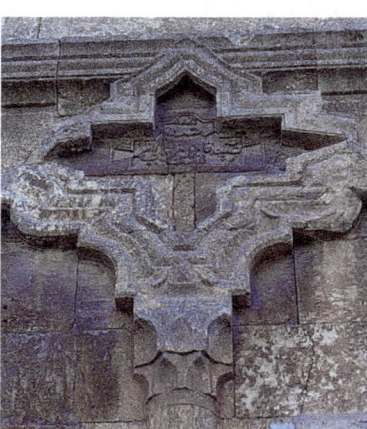

*Great Mosque,
epigraphic inscription,
Ma'arrat al-Nu'man.*

Ma'arrat al-Nu'man is a good example of a frontier town, lying on the crossroads between Aleppo, Antioch, Hama and Homs and witness to much medieval warfare. Having been recovered by the Seljuqs, and then governed by the Ayyubids, the town experienced a period of reprieve. Its main monuments reflect the Islamic artistic and architectural styles of this period.

The town is a minor one, named after Nu'man bin Bashir al-Ansari, the companion of the Prophet and governor of the region under the Umayyads. Because of its coveted strategic position in northern Syria, the town was conquered repeatedly during the medieval period. Throughout the 4th/10th and 5th/11th centuries, the town was subjugated by the Hamdanids, Byzantines, Fatimids, Seljuqs and Mirdasids successively and became the preferred target of the Franks during the First Crusade. It suffered a very difficult period of war and famine, particularly during the Crusader siege of 492/1098. The fall of Ma'arrat al-Nu'man to the Crusaders, and the dreadful massacre of the city's population, shocked everyone; the episode recounted in detail in Muslim historical literature. In 529/1135 the Seljuq Atabeg, 'Imad al-Din Zangi, reconquered Ma'arrat al-Nu'man and it reverted back to the Muslims. After Salah al-Din's successful expeditions throughout western Syria in 584/1188, the town lost some of its strategic significance and was relieved of its wartime pressure, allowing for its architectural and infrastructural development. During the first half of the 7th/13th

ITINERARY V   *Confrontation and Coexistence: Fortifications in western Syria*
Ma'arrat al-Nu'man

century, rivalling Ayyubid principalities of Damascus and Hama contested the town's possession. It was finally granted by the Mamluks as an *iqta'* to the Prince of Hama.

Two main monuments from the constructive Ayyubid period are the renovated Great Mosque and the new Madrasat Abu al-Fawaris, both easily discernable in the town's main square. The Umayyads constructed the Great Mosque in the $2^{nd}/8^{th}$ century, the Byzantines destroyed it in 358/969 and the Seljuqs then restored it in the first half of the $6^{th}/12^{th}$ century. The mosque was damaged and repaired by Nur al-Din after the earthquakes of 552/1157 and 565/1170; the mosque and the minaret were given a last major restoration in 595/1199 and epigraphically signed by the architect Qahir al-Sarmani. The elegant, square minaret is clearly inspired by the monumental minaret of the Umayyad Mosque in Aleppo.

The Ma'arrat al-Nu'man Madrasa, now known locally as Jami' Nur al-Din, was built by the same architect as the mosque and in the same year, 595/1199. It belonged to the *Shafi'i* rite and first named Madrasat Abu al-Fawaris. It offers a typical *madrasa* plan ubiquitously adapted in Syria, a *muqarnas* entrance that leads to a central courtyard surrounded by an *iwan* to the west, a prayer-hall with a *mihrab* to the south and the founder's tomb-chamber on the north-east corner. As for the castle, it lies today in a bad condition on a hill to the north-west of the town. Built on a circular plan and initially defended by a ditch, the castle

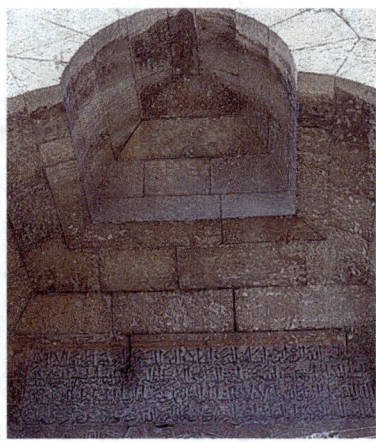

Madrasat Abu al-Fawaris, detail of the upper part of the entrance portal with inscription, Ma'arrat al-Nu'man.

suffered from a recent occupation that led to the dismantling and re-use of its construction stones, except for the outer wall, which is partly preserved and is constructed from mixed courses of small blocks and of large smooth ashlars.

Remains of the citadel, Ma'arrat al-Nu'man (photo courtesy of Balász Major)

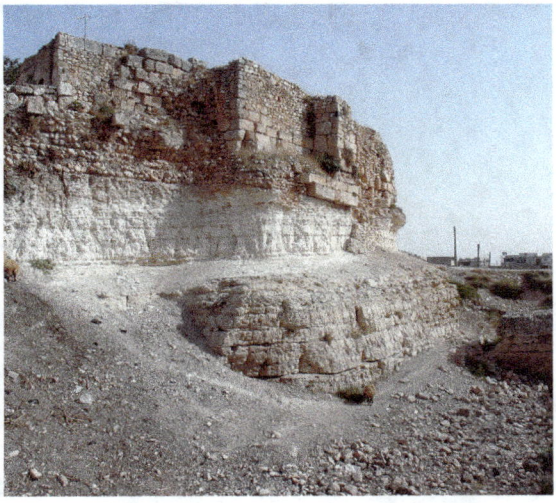

209

MEMOIRS OF SALAH AL-DIN

Yasser Tabbaa

Vanquisher of the Fatimids, founder of the Ayyubid Dynasty and liberator of Jerusalem, Salah al-Din's life story is a mixture of fact and legend, truth and hyperbole. Born in Tikrit and brought up in Damascus, Salah al-Din enters history in 559/1164 as a lieutenant in Nur al-Din's expedition to Egypt. Within a few years, he became the de facto ruler of Egypt and, in 569/1171, he declared the end of the Isma'ili Fatimids. Driven by enormous political ambition and military prowess, Salah al-Din took advantage of Nur al-Din's death in 569/1174, to declare his rule over Egypt and to begin his methodical conquest of Syria, which he achieved in 583/1183.

Salah al-Din, however, would only become immortalised after his astonishing success at the Battle of Hittin of 583/1187 and his subsequent conquest of Jerusalem after 90 years of Frankish rule.

In a period otherwise noted for its political fragmentation and internecine fighting, Salah al-Din became the hero of Islam, equated with the Caliph 'Umar (d. 23/644), the second Rightly Guided Caliph, companion of the Prophet and a leader renowned for his passion. Although he was certainly feared and hated by the Franks, Salah al-Din was also admired, both for his dedication to his faith and for his magnanimity towards the helpless inhabitants of Jerusalem.

The biography of Salah al-Din was written soon after his death by Baha' al-Din ibn Shaddad (d. 632/1235), Salah al-Din's head lieutenant in Palestine, who was also a prominent figure in the courts of 'Abbasid Baghdad, Atabeg Mosul and Ayyubid Aleppo. Ibn Shaddad dedicated a work on *jihad* to Salah al-Din, but his most important composition is Salah al-Din's biography, *Al-Nawadir al-Sultaniyya wa al-Mahasin al-Yusufiyya* (*Sovereign Rarities and Yusufi Merits*), which offers rare insight into Salah al-Din's personality and eye-witness accounts of various battles between the Islamic and Crusader armies. Unlike the lore of later histories, this biography is an accurate and balanced account, tying in the events of Salah al-Din's time with analyses of military administration and political interaction.

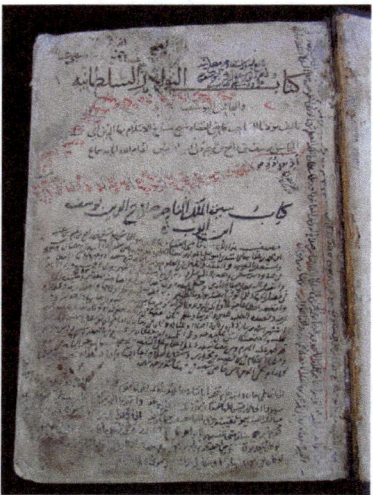

Page from Ibn Shaddad's biography of Salah al-Din Al-Nawadir al-Sultaniyya wa al-Mahasin al-Yusufiyya, *Islamic Museum, al-Aqsa Mosque (Inv. Num. 203), Jerusalem.*

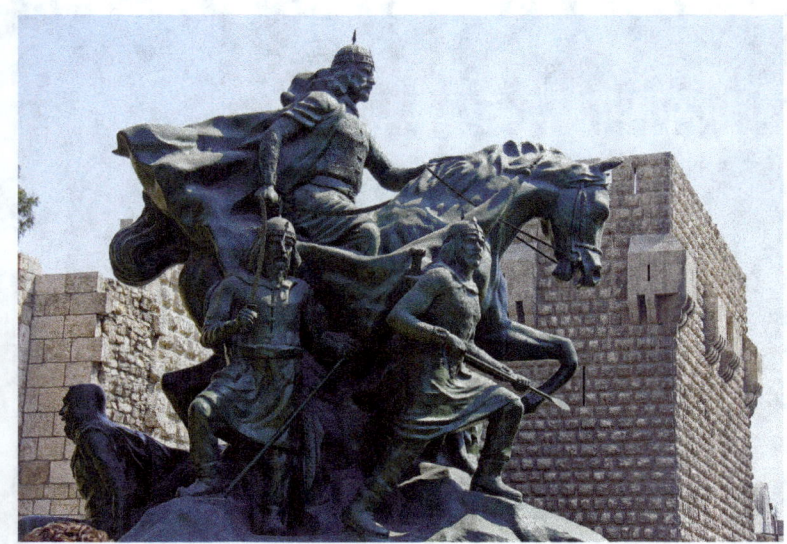

The modern statue of Salah al-Din, Damascus (photo courtesy of Zena Takieddine).

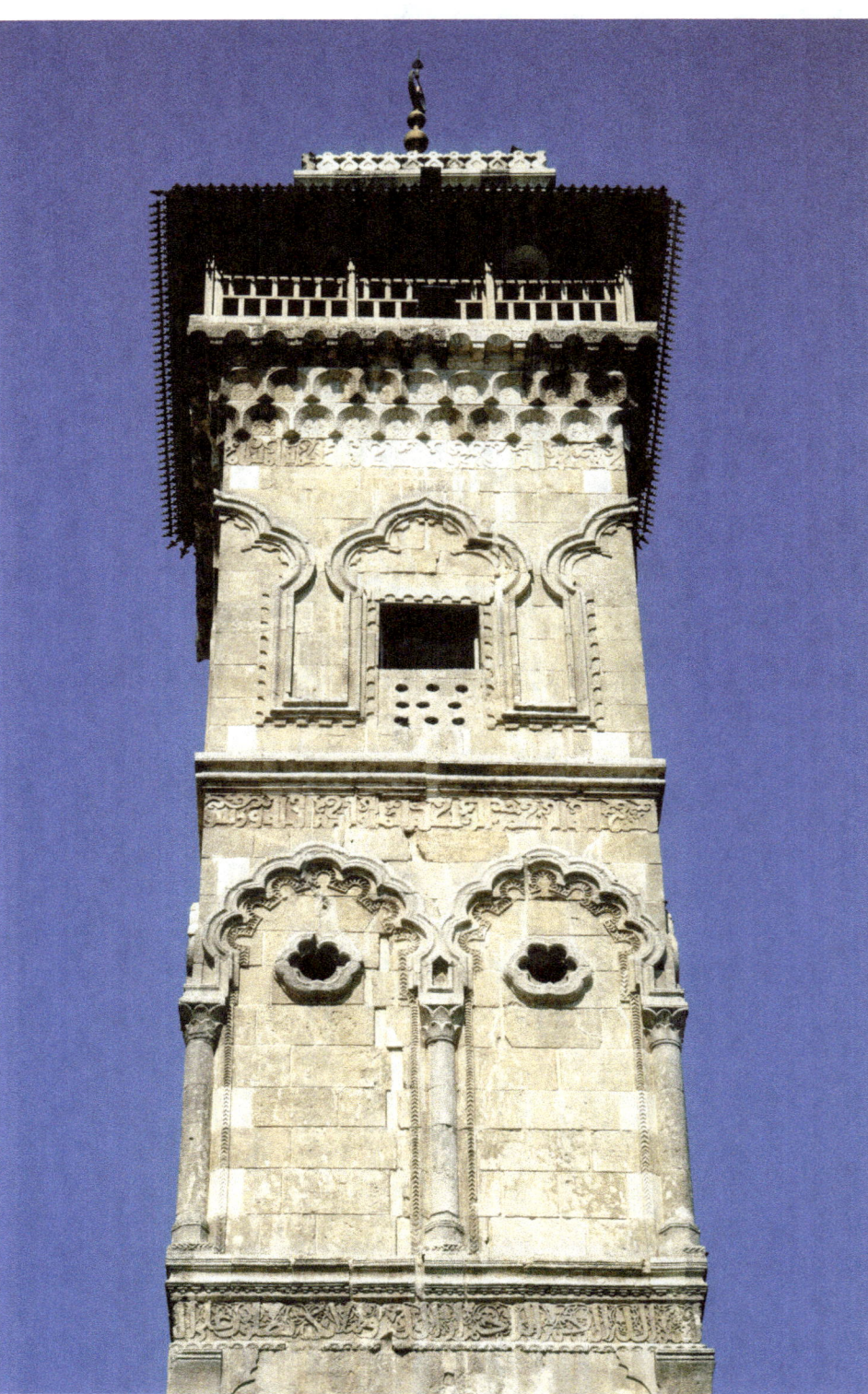

ITINERARY VI

Commerce and Daily Life

Yasser Tabbaa

VI.1 ALEPPO
- VI.1.a National Museum of Aleppo
- VI.1.b Bab Antakiyya
- VI.1.c Madrasa al-Shu'aybiyya
- VI.1.d Madrasa al-Muqaddamiyya
- VI.1.e Bimaristan Nur al-Din (Bimaristan al-Nuri)
- VI.1.f Madrasa al-Hallawiyya
- VI.1.g Great Mosque of Aleppo
- VI.1.h Hammam al-Nahassin
- VI.1.i Madrasa al-Shadhbakhtiyya
- VI.1.j Madrasa al-Sultaniyya

Suq of Aleppo — Yasser Tabbaa

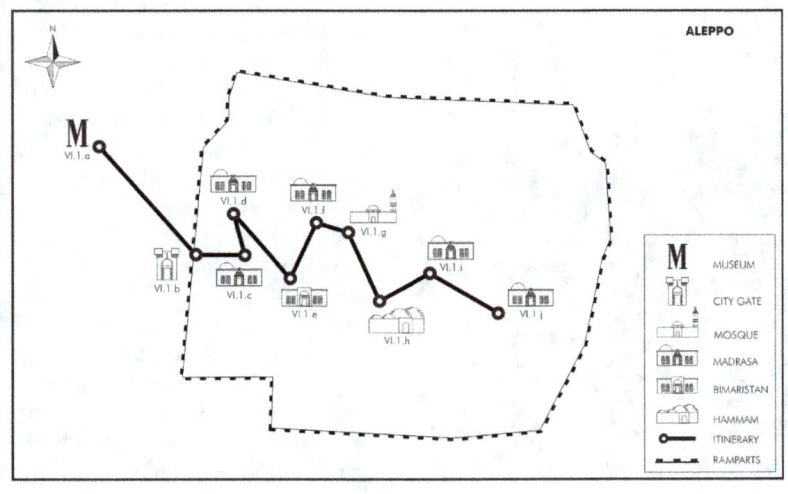

Great Mosque, minaret, Aleppo.

ITINERARY VI   *Commerce and Daily Life*
Introduction

Atabeg and Ayyubid Aleppo was a typical medieval Middle Eastern city, comparable to her neighbouring cities such as Damascus, Mosul and Jerusalem. Although all these cities assumed an increasingly Islamic character during the Umayyad and 'Abbasid periods – seem mostly in their congregational mosques and *suqs* – in the 6th/12th and 7th/13th centuries, pervasive architectural and socio-political transformations altered their form and function for many centuries to come. These included a citadel and fortified enclosure, a compact urban form, ethnically and religiously divided quarters, and numerous religious, charitable and educational institutions.

Whether in terms of the size and plurality, their populations, or the development of their infrastructure, Middle Eastern cities outranked contemporary European cities. Aleppo, with a 7th-/13th-century population estimated at 70,000, was larger than most European cities, although it lacked their corporate and municipal structure. Furthermore, the varied inhabitants of Aleppo and other Middle Eastern cities were not citizens with specific rights and obligations but rather urban dwellers, who often had sectarian, tribal and ethnic attachments that could override their allegiance to their respective cities.

Without being well-defined municipal entities, the intention of Islamic cities nevertheless was to provide their inhabitants with three main assets: security, religious life and economic opportunity. Security in this period was most clearly manifest in a citadel and a well-defended enclosure. Religious life was ultimately guaranteed by *shari'a* (religious law), which was during the period implemented by the newly developed institutions of the *muhtasib* (market supervisor), the *dar al-'adl* (tribunal), and by other legal institutions specific to a particular sect or religion. Religious culture, on the other hand, increasingly resided within the institutional structure provided by *madrasa*s, *khanqa*s and shrines.

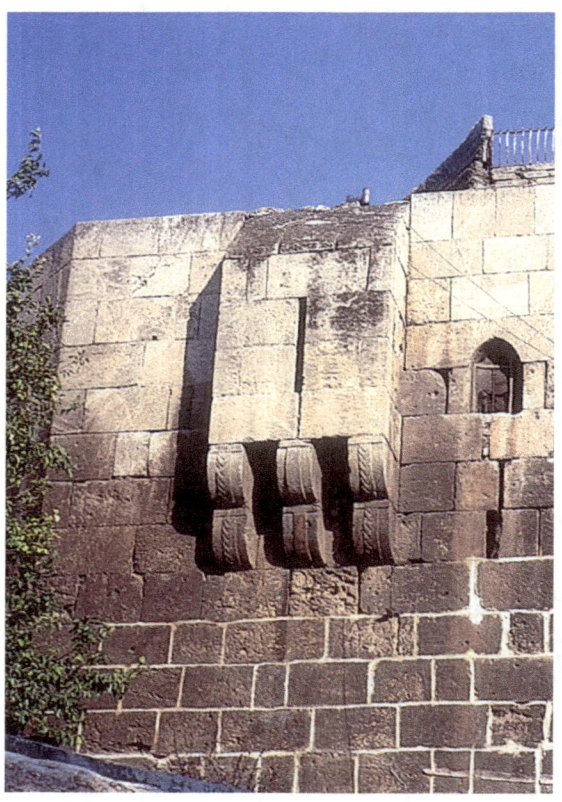

Bab Antakiyya, detail of a defensive arrow slit, Aleppo.

ITINERARY VI *Commerce and Daily Life*
Aleppo

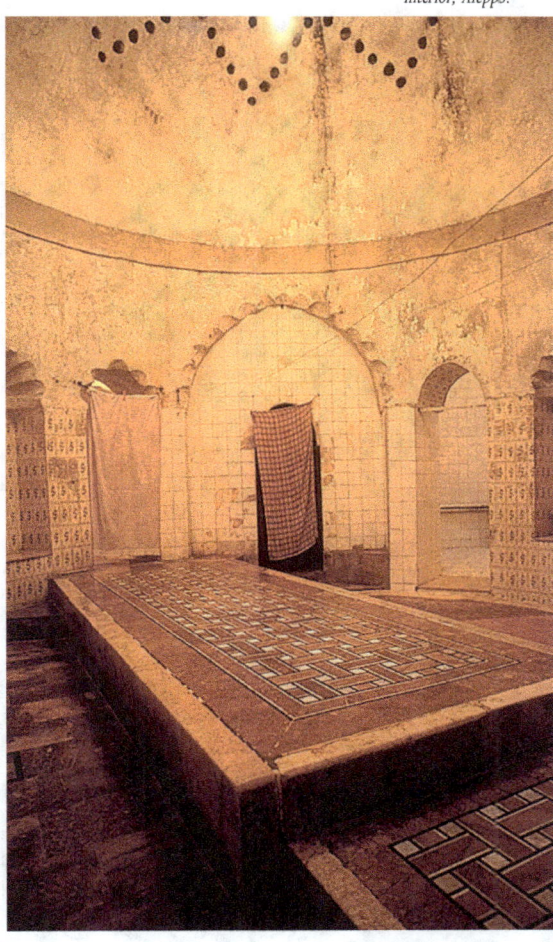

Hammam al-Nahassin, interior, Aleppo.

Economic opportunity resided, as it had since early Islam, in the *suq*: an exclusive centrally located zone dedicated to trade, retail and wholesale. The Suq of Aleppo, one of the largest in the Islamic world, dates back to the early Islamic period. Although much of the existing *suq*, including most of its existing *khans* (wholesale markets), date to the Ottoman period, it should be noted that these later developments rested on the resilient foundations created under the Ayyubids. It was also precisely in the first decades of the 7th/13th century that a series of commercial contracts were struck between the Ayyubid sultans and Venice that resulted in the building of a *fondaco*, an inn and place of commerce for travelling Venetian merchants. As a commercial centre for local inhabitants, travelling caravans and European merchants, medieval Aleppo was a thriving market, which, with its mosques, *madrasas*, *bimaristans* and *hammams*, carried all the emblems of Islamic urbanism.

VI.1 **ALEPPO**

VI.1.a National Museum of Aleppo

The museum is located in the heart of Aleppo, on the corner of Baron Street and al-Ma'arri Street. Opening times are Wed–Mon 9.00–18.00 during the summer, 9.00–16.00 during the winter. Closed on Tuesdays and during Friday prayers (approx 11.00–13.00). There is an entrance fee.

The National Museum of Aleppo, best known for its Ancient Near Eastern and Mesopotamian collections, also contains some of Syria's most important Islamic artefacts particularly from the medieval period.

ITINERARY VI   *Commerce and Daily Life*
Aleppo

Ceramic stand, National Museum of Aleppo.

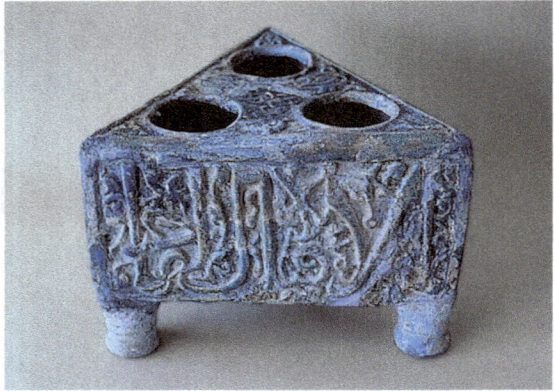

Ceramic stand

This blue-glazed ceramic object is a type of Raqqa ware considered used as a stand. Such stands are an Ayyubid innovation, becoming a regular product of Syrian ceramics in the first half of the 7th/13th century. Most common was a rectangular form, but triangular and octagonal forms also occur. They are typically made of monochrome-glazed, moulded fritware and copy the designs of carved wooden furniture. This particular stand presumably served to hold vessels steady and upright, either drinks or, most probably, writing materials like quills, ink and sand.

Stone relief of a lion

This carved stone block featuring the emblem of a prowling lion is one of a pair found in the north-western area of old Aleppo, near Bab al-Faraj, which was rebuilt by the Ayyubid ruler, al-Zahir Ghazi (d. 613/1216), as part of his expansion of the city. Such lions are extremely common during this period, not only in Syria but also in the architectural decoration of Anatolia to the north and Mesopotamia to the east, often appearing on city walls, gates and other places of fortification.

Stone cenotaph

This large, rectangular, profusely decorated stone cenotaph belongs to a type that was widely distributed in Syria and Mesopotamia during the 6th/12th century. The decoration shows a magnificent Qur'anic inscription in floriated *kufic* script containing *Ayat al-Kursi*, (2:255) the "Throne Verse". Four small, vertical cartouches in the middle of each side of the cenotaph mention the deceased, Husayn bin Hasan al-Shukri, but no date. The form and decoration of this cenotaph belongs to the theme of classical continuity in stone carving, typical of northern Syria during the early Zangid period. The intricate inscription has a close counterpart in the epigraphy of the Madrasa al-Shu'aybiyya, dated 545/1150, which is

Stone relief of a lion, National Museum of Aleppo (Inv. Num. 559).

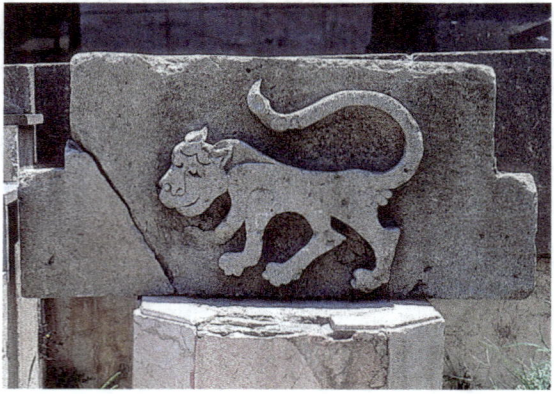

ITINERARY VI *Commerce and Daily Life*
Aleppo

one of the last examples in Syria of the use of *kufic* script in monumental architecture before it was generally replaced by the cursive *naskhi* and *thuluth* scripts.

Lustre dish
Excavated at Qal'at Ja'bar (VIII.3.), this large dish features a reddish-brown hue of lustre ornamentation beneath a transparent green glaze. It follows a distinctive type of luxurious fritware produced in the region of Raqqa. The extensive decoration on this piece, along with the central design of a radiating sun with a figurative face that has slanted eyes, reveals the dominance of Eastern – specifically Persian – artistic repertories, on northern Syria. Planetary symbols and zodiacal signs were popular features on contemporary metalwork, here translated on to pottery.

VI.1.b Bab Antakiyya

Exiting the museum, walk east down Ma'arri Street, then turn right and walk south for 500 m down Bab Antakiyya Street, keeping the city walls to your left. The gate will duly appear on your left.

Defending Aleppo from its most vulnerable side, Bab Antakiyya was the most important gate of the city, the reason for its constant rebuilding between the 4th/10th and 9th/15th centuries. It is also the best-preserved Ayyubid gate in Aleppo. Beyond the ramshackle shops built against it, there are two massive towers (each 24 m x 12.50 m) with chamfered fronts, firmly constructed from large stones. The northern tower, built with three vaulted compartments and an array of arrow slits, was for the sole purpose of defending the entrance to the city, while the southern tower, entered by turning right into a spacious chamber, also contains deep niches with arrow slits built into the thickness of the wall.

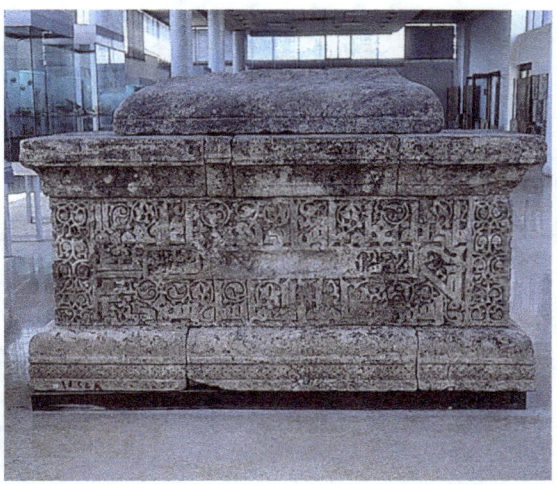

Stone cenotaph,
National Museum
of Aleppo
(Inv. Num. 330).

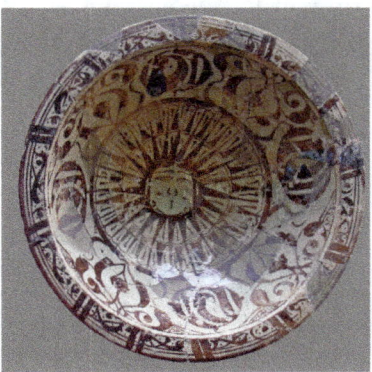

Lustre dish,
National Museum
of Aleppo
(Inv. Num. 56').

ITINERARY VI Commerce and Daily Life
Aleppo

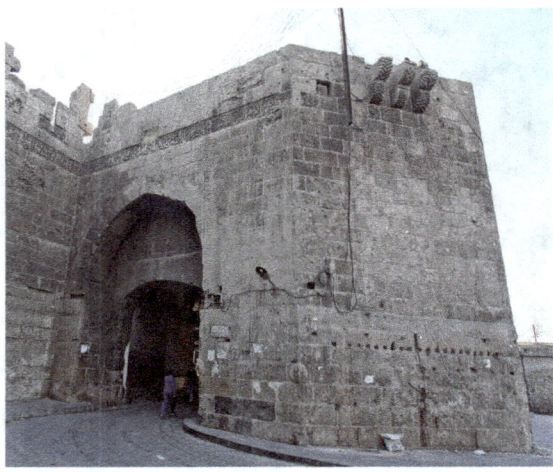

Bab Antakiyya, Aleppo.

Madrasa al-Shu'aybiyya, detail of the kufic inscriptions, Aleppo. On the left: a sketch of the inscriptions (Herzfeld, 1955, plate LXXXVIII).

VI.1.c Madrasa al-Shu'aybiyya

Enter the old city through Antioch Gate and walk west for 50 m. The madrasa *stands facing you directly on a v-shaped intersection. Access to the building might prove to be difficult as the* madrasa *is currently undergoing restoration.*

Built by Nur al-Din in 545/1150, possibly as a monument to celebrate his recent victorious campaigns against the Crusaders, the Madrasa al-Shu'aybiyya consists of a projecting porch supported on three pointed arches and crowned by a heavy classicised entablature. A wealth of floriated *kufic* inscriptions and arabesque ornamentation cover all parts of the projecting entablature, contributing to its curious appearance. Attached to the porch is a small mosque, but the building otherwise completely lacks the necessary components of a functional *madrasa*, particularly in not providing rooms for students. Attached to the space of the *madrasa* is the Qastal al-Shu'aybiyya, a water distribution system constructed by Nur al-Din n the 6th/12th century as part of his water-development projects for the city.

VI.1.d Madrasa al-Muqaddamiyya

Walk west into Suq al-Sakatiye for 300 m, then turn right into a small lane (third after Madrasa al-Shu'aybiyya) and walk down here for 70 m. Madrasa al-Muqaddamiyya appears on your left, discernable by its muqarnas portal, and is located just before the cross vault covering the alley. It now functions as a mosque and can be visited respecting appropriate dress codes and conduct, but it is likely to be closed apart from prayer times (approx 11.00–13.00). A small donation is advisable.

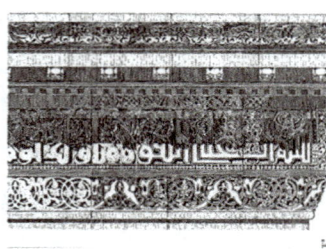
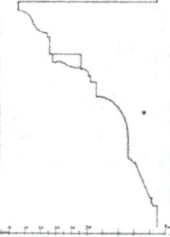
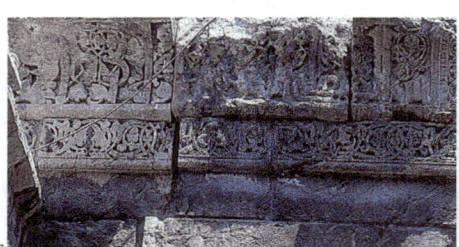

Muhammad Ibn al-Muqaddam, a Kurdish military commander in the service of Nur al-Din, patronised the construction of Madrasa al-Muqaddamiyya in 563/1168. Only the portal and parts of the mosque, particularly the *mihrab*, remain of the original construction, making it difficult to determine the original plan. The portal, an outstanding example of northern Syrian stonework and capped by a cross vault, is framed by a tri-lobed arch. The *mihrab*, which is located in the middle of a typical tripartite sanctuary, is in fact the earliest of a long tradition of marble-reveted *mihrabs* in Syria. Two freestanding columns with simplified Corinthian capitals support a slightly pointed arch, flanked by a simple knot design made of overlapping stone-courses in different colours. A wide continuous moulding frames the columns and separates the niche of the *mihrab* from its hemispherical conch.

VI.1.e Bimaristan Nur al-Din (Bimaristan al-Nuri)

Return to the main suq axis, and walk for 20 m. Turn into another small lane (fifth after Madrasa al-Shu'aybiyya) *and walk for 100 m. As the building is still undergoing restoration, access is irregular, although one can peek into the building through the window grilles that overlook the lane.*

The Bimaristan al-Nuri, first built by Nur al-Din in around 545/1150, is the earliest surviving hospital in the Islamic world. Entered from the east through a vaulted portal which is framed by a chevron moulding, the recently restored hospital is disposed around two courtyards, the larger of which dates to the original foundation, while the smaller was added in 655/1257. The larger courtyard is surrounded by iwans to the south and west, while a third, northern, *iwan* may have once existed before the 7th-/13th-century expansion. Inserted on one level between these *iwans* were the patients' chambers. Surrounding the once vaulted, smaller courtyard on three sides are individual cells, entered through a single door with a window above it, an arrangement also seen in the Bimaristan al-Kamili in Aleppo, built in the late 7th/13th century.

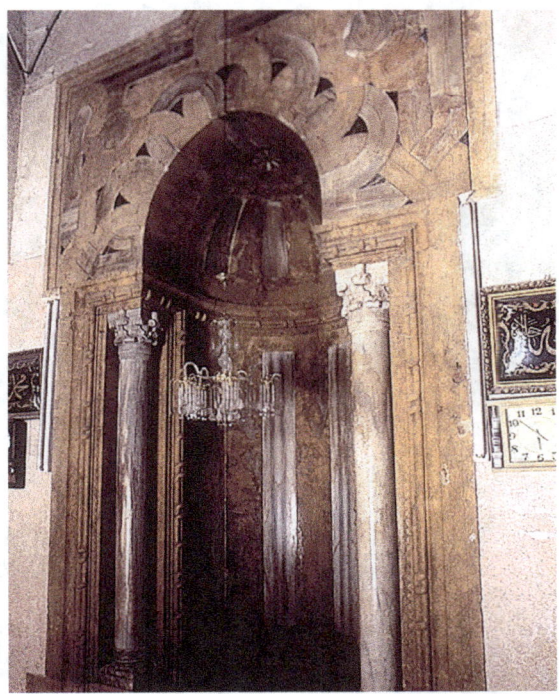

Madrasa al-Muqaddamiyya, mihrab, Aleppo.

ITINERARY VI   *Commerce and Daily Life*
Aleppo

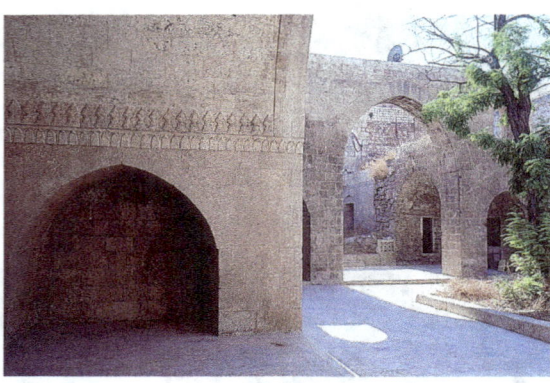

Bimaristan Nur al-Din, the courtyard, Aleppo.

VI.1.f **Madrasa al-Hallawiyya**

Return to the main suq axis and walk west, turning north at Khan al-Jumruk. Continue to walk north, towards the Great Mosque and the modern plaza facing the mosque on its northern edge. The Madrasa al-Hallawiyya *faces the west gate of the mosque. The* madrasa, *now a mosque, is open respecting appropriate dress codes and conduct, at any time during the day. A small donation is advisable.*

Across a narrow road from the north-west corner of the Great Mosque is the Madrasa al-Hallawiyya, rebuilt in the 6th/12th century over the remains of the Byzantine Church of St Helena. An inscription by Nur al-Din dates it to 543/1149, although the courtyard and the large dome above the Byzantine apse appear to be Ottoman. A separate chamber next to the dome contains the magnificent wooden *mihrab* offered to the *madrasa* by Ibn al-'Adim, an important figure in legal and political circles who served as *qadi* (judge) vizier (minister) and historian of Aleppo during the Ayyubid reign. Inscribed by the historian himself, this *mihrab* is one of the masterpieces of Arabic woodwork and calligraphy.

VI.1.g **Great Mosque of Aleppo**

Exiting Madrasa al-Hallawiyya *enter the Great Mosque from the western gate directly facing you. Respecting appropriate dress codes and conduct, it is open any time during the day. A small donation is advisable, and a small fee may be due for foreigners.*

The Great Mosque, built by the Umayyads on the grounds of a Byzantine cathedral,

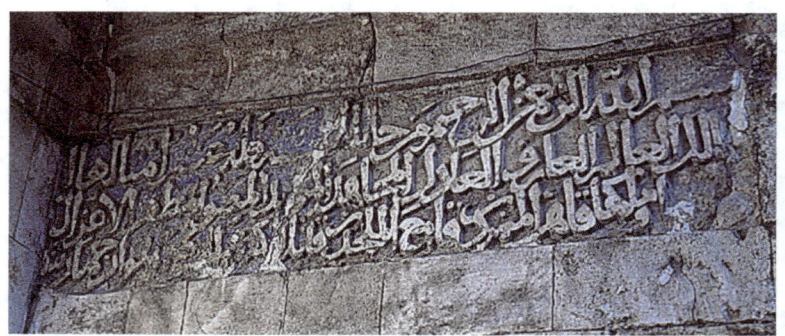

Madrasa al-Hallawiyya, detail of Nur al-Din's inscription in the courtyard, Aleppo.

220

ITINERARY VI *Commerce and Daily Life*
Aleppo

stands at the heart of Aleppo. Restored and rebuilt over the centuries, the only Atabeg vestiges extant are a few arches in its eastern courtyard and the splendid minaret, founded by the *qadi* Ibn al-Khashshab during the rule of the Atabeg, Aq Sunqur in 483/1090. Frequently compared to classical architecture, the minaret of the Great Mosque is actually more stylistically linked to the 5th- and 6th-century AD churches west of Aleppo, such as Qalb Lozeh or Qal'at Sim'an. In this respect, it may represent a continuity of Syrian Late-Antique architecture.

This minaret is one of the great masterpieces of medieval Aleppo. Towering to a height of more than 45 m the square shaft, broken up with cornices and inscriptions into six zones, has four decorated with pilasters, foliate arches and continuous mouldings. The stone-carved inscriptions found along the minaret's friezes offer a variety of angular and cursive designs, including some of Syria's best examples of Atabeg *kufic* calligraphy. On the highest level the *basmala* "in the name of God ...", and the dedication to the Seljuq Sultan Mahmud bin Malik Shah. On the next level down there is a dedication to the Seljuq Atabeg of Aleppo, Aq Sunqur. The third level has a dedication to the *qadi* Ibn al-Khashshab, while the fourth holds a Qur'anic blessing to mosque builders in general. The ground level is undecorated, with only a cartouche naming the architect and date of construction: "Made by Hasan bin Mufarraj al-Samani in the year three and eighty and four hundred", which corresponds to AD 1091.

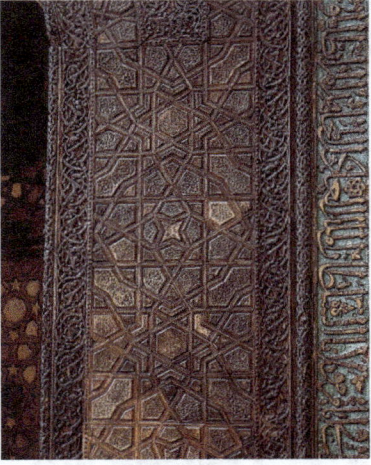

Madrasa al-Hallawiyya, wooden mihrab, *detail of the decoration and inscription, Aleppo.*

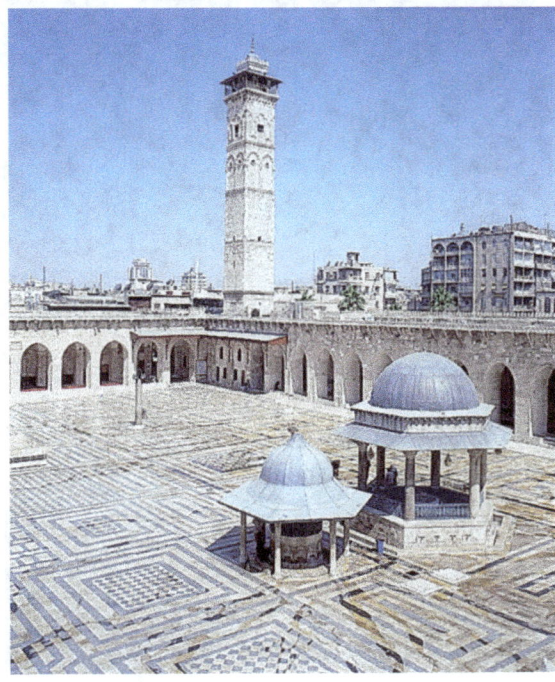

Great Mosque, *courtyard and minaret, Aleppo.*

ITINERARY VI Commerce and Daily Life
Aleppo

Great Mosque, minaret, southern side, examples of kufic *inscriptions on the lower section, Aleppo.*

Hammam al-Nahassin, interior of a dome with qamariyyat, *Aleppo.*

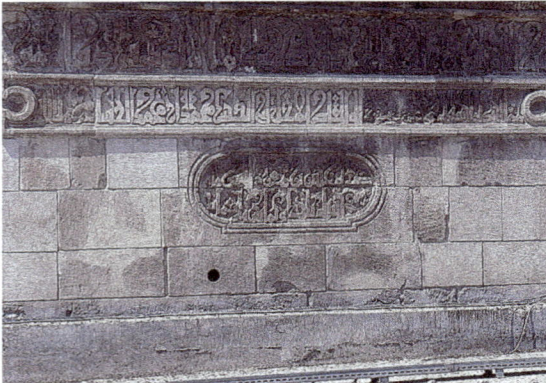

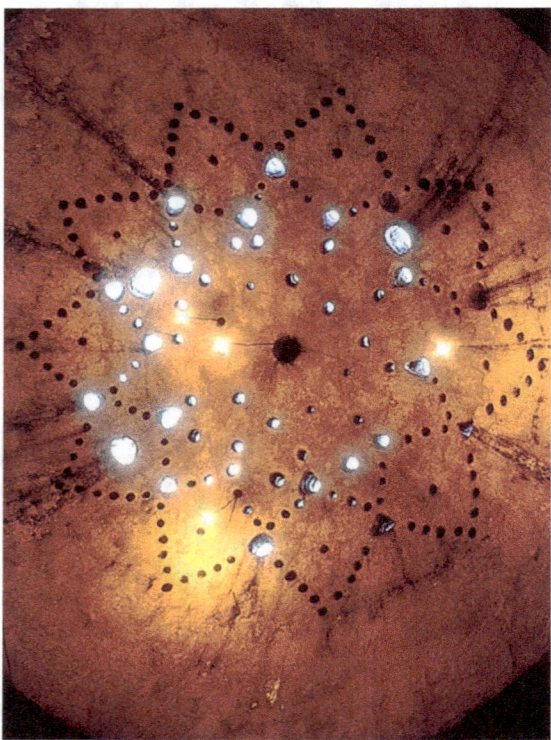

VI.1.h Hammam al-Nahassin

Return to the main suq axis and enter Suq al-'Attarin, from here turn south into Suq Mahmas and Khan al-Nahassin. The hammam, which directly faces the entrance to the khan, should appear on your left.

The Hammam al-Nahassin, like most *hammams*, consists of three bathing and grooming chambers – the *barrani* (exterior areas), *wastani* (middle areas), and *juwwani* (interior areas) – which are often preceded by the *mashlah*, a large domed chamber serving as a changing-room and a place for relaxation after bathing. With the exception of the dome over the *mashlah* that has a windowed drum and a lantern, the other domes in the *hammam* lack a drum and windows, receiving light through thick glass roundels known as *qamariyyat* inserted into the dome itself. Clay pipes distributed hot water around the *hammam* from the wood-burning furnace, called *bayt al-nar*.

VI.1.i Madrasa al-Shadhbakhtiyya

Return to Suq al-'Attarin, and continue to walk west into its extension known as Suq al-Zarb that leads to the citadel. The Madrasa al-Shadhbakhtiyya today, known as Jami' Sheikh Ma'ruf, is located 50 m into Suq al-Zarb on your right. Access to the building might prove to be difficult as the madrasa *is currently undergoing restoration.*

The Madrasa al-Shadhbakhtiyya, known today as Jami' Sheikh Ma'ruf, was founded in 583/1187 by Jamal al-Din

ITINERARY VI *Commerce and Daily Life*
Aleppo

Shadhbakht, a court official of Nur al-Din and his son al-Salih Isma'il. Although originally freestanding, during the 19th century an extension to the *suq* surrounded it with shops on three sides and encroached on its plan. A *muqarnas* portal leads through a domed vestibule into a rectangular courtyard enclosed by a tripartite prayer-hall to the south, a large *iwan* to the north and a series of cells on one floor to the east. The northeastern corner of the building is occupied by another tripartite hall that contains the shrine of Sheikh Ma'ruf, a local holy man whose name, Ma'ruf, is common among mystics. The prayer-hall, consisting of a dome flanked by two rectangular sail vaults, stands on an axis with the northern *iwan*. Its *mihrab*, lined with marble slabs and topped by polychrome-marble interlacing, is the first of a series of such *mihrabs* in Aleppo, which includes those in the Madrasa al-Sultaniyya and Madrasat al-Firdaws.

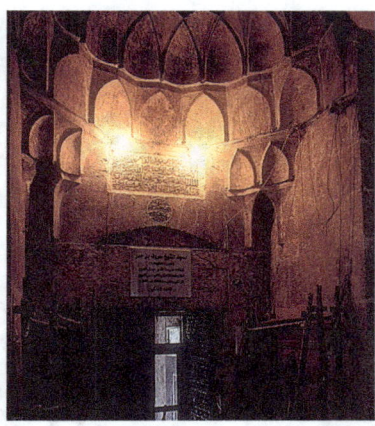

Madrasa al-Shadhbakhtiyya, muqarnas portal, Aleppo.

Madrasa al-Shadhbakhtiyya, general view, Aleppo.

VI.1.j Madrasa al-Sultaniyya

Exit Suq al-Zarb and walk south, clockwise, around the citadel mount. Walk 20 m past the cafes facing the castle entrance, and Madrasa al-Sultaniyya sits behind the small garden. The madrasa, now a mosque, is open respecting appropriate dress codes and conduct, at any time during the day. A small donation is advisable.

Construction of Madrasa al-Sultaniyya probably began under the auspices of al-Zahir Ghazi at around the same time

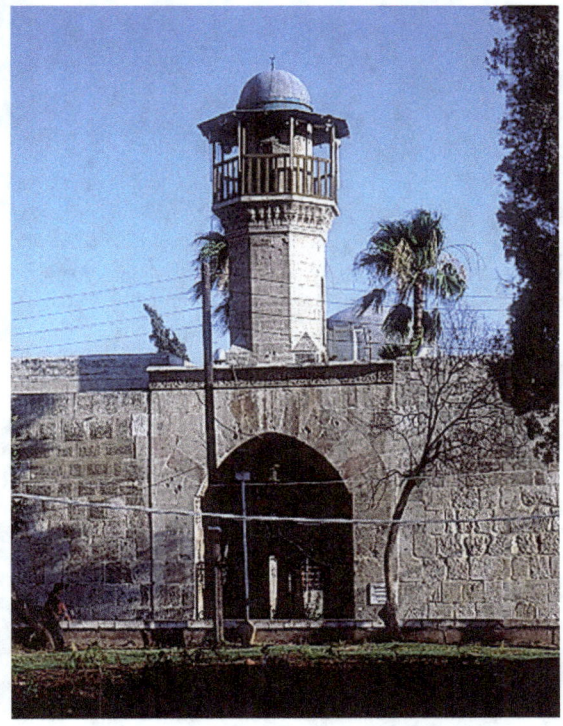

ITINERARY VI *Commerce and Daily Life*
Aleppo

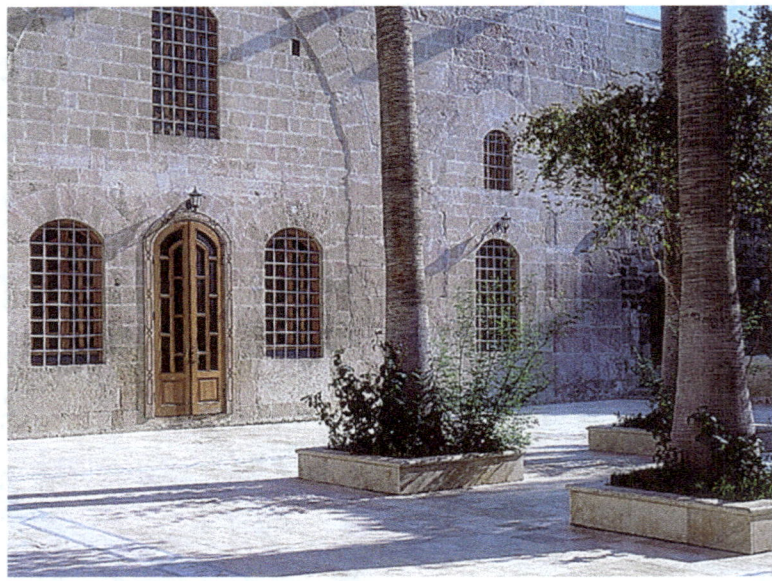

Madrasa al-Sultaniyya, courtyard and walled up tripartite arcade, Aleppo.

that he rebuilt the Citadel of Aleppo (c. 610/1214), but his minister Toghril did not complete it until 620/1223. The entrance is on the north side through a simple portal surmounted by a minaret, which leads to a spacious courtyard surrounded on the east and west sides by double rows of rooms for students, and from the south by the mosque. A tripartite arcade, now walled up, leads to a spacious prayer-hall with a single dome and a beautiful *mihrab*, a simpler version of the one at Madrasat al-Firdaws. At the east end of the mosque is a door that leads to al-Zahir Ghazi's mausoleum, a plain, domed chamber with three grilled windows that project slightly into the street. These windows, which bear three identical inscriptions on the outside, would have attracted the prayers of pedestrians. It is a good example of refined Ayyubid architectural simplicity.

SUQ OF ALEPPO

Yasser Tabbaa

As it stands today, Aleppo Suq covers a huge rectangle (around 600 m x 400 m), largely made up of many narrow but orthogonal streets lined with numerous small shops and interspersed with several *khans*. As with other *suqs*, Aleppo Suq is organised according to two main principles: specialisation and value, such that the sale of all like-merchandise was in specific areas within the *suq*, while the *suq* itself would be organised in a radial from the Great Mosque outwards. The most valuable goods were located in or near the centre of the *suq*. This merchandise included the gold and silk bazaars, the garment's zone, women's wear, and dry goods. The more modest products, such as light industrial and agricultural goods and services (i.e. wool, rope, tents and farm tools) were located at the periphery of the *suq*.

It is nearly impossible today to distinguish the Atabeg-Ayyubid portions of the *suq* from its later additions and accretions. Nevertheless, we know that in 564/1169 Nur al-Din restored Aleppo Suq just south of the Great Mosque after a major fire. He also built a *qaysariyya* (a covered market) for textiles south-east of the mosque. Finally, in 576/1172, two new markets — Suq al-Bazz al-Kabir and Suq al-Khali' — were added by Nur al-Din, and a third was built subsequently by Majd al-Din Ibn al-Daya, a local jurist and patrician, and named after him.

In 576/1180, the *suq* suffered a major fire. In 591/1195, al-Zahir Ghazi rebuilt it dedicating some of its revenue as a *waqf* for his extramural *madrasa*. Finally, in 650/1252 al-Nasir Yusuf, the last Ayyu-bid sultan, built several *suqs* including Suq al-Bariyya and Suq al-Dhira'. Interestingly, the names of most of these newly built *suqs* have to do with textiles and garments, an industry for which Aleppo had always been famous.

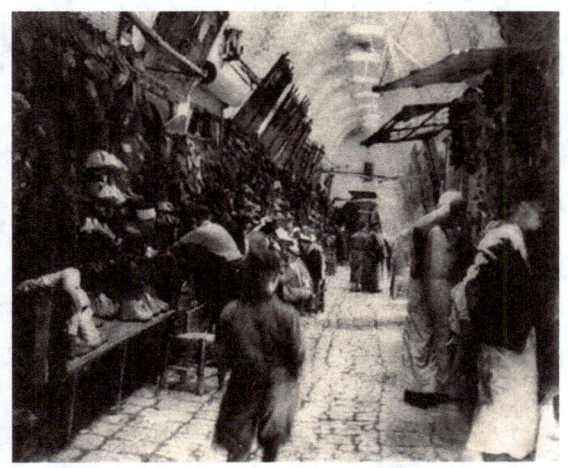

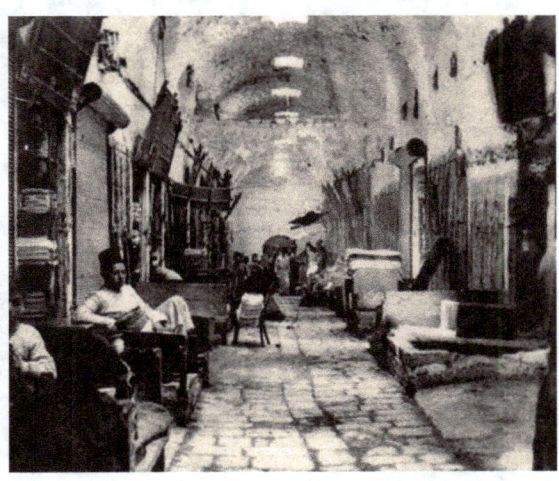

Old photos of Aleppo Suq by. J. Sauvaget (Sauvaget, 1941, plate XIX).

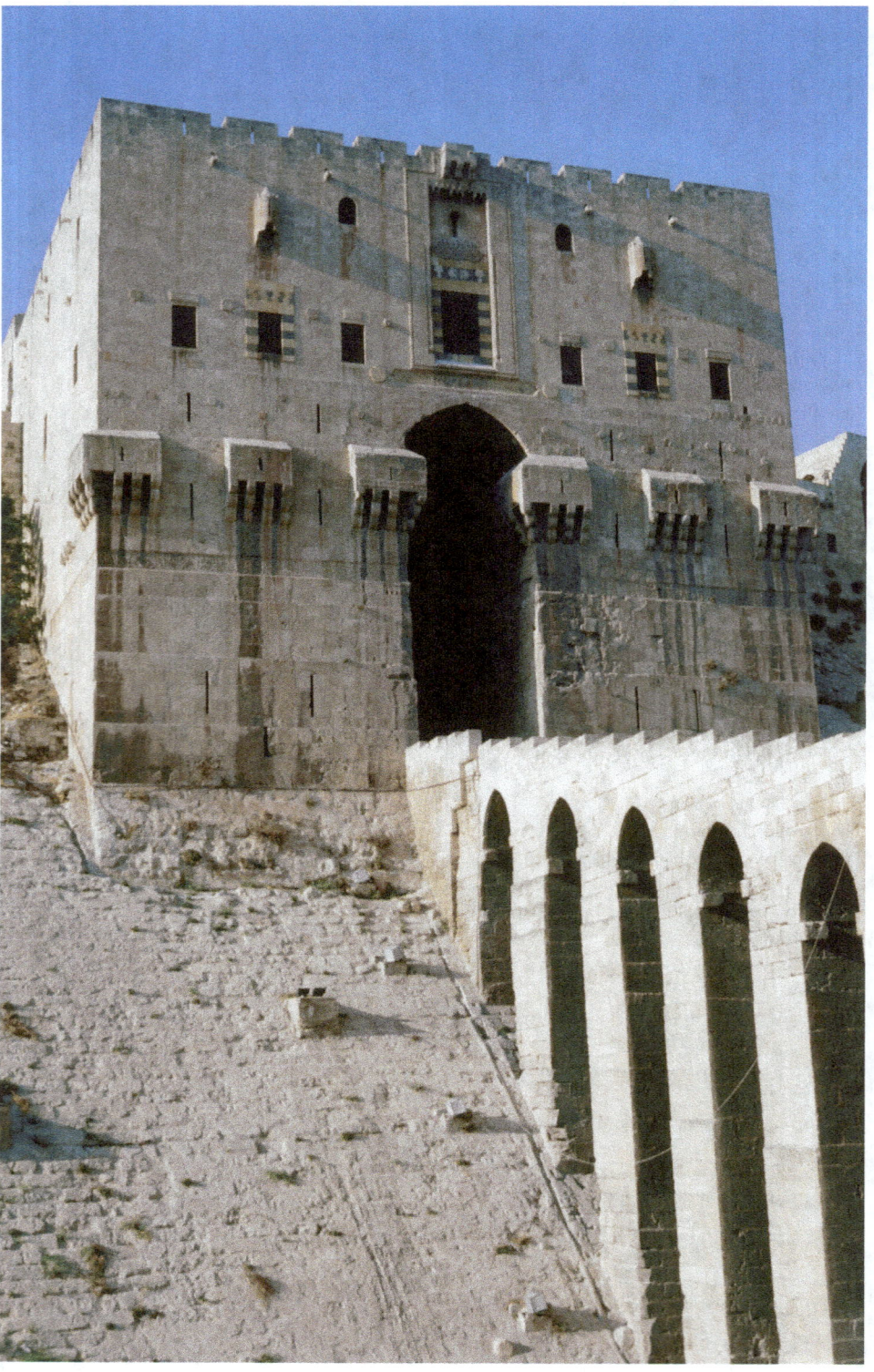

ITINERARY VII

Patronage and Court Life under the Atabegs and Ayyubids in Syria

Yasser Tabbaa

VII.1 ALEPPO
    VII.1.a Mashhad al-Hussein
    VII.1.b Mashhad al-Dikka
    VII.1.c Bab Qinnisrin
    VII.1.d Bab al-Maqam
    VII.1.e Madrasa al-Zahiriyya
    VII.1.f Madrasat al-Firdaws
    VII.1.g Madrasa al-Toruntayya al-'Adimiyya
    VII.1.h Aleppo Citadel (in three parts: Entrance Block, Palace and Mosque)
    VII.1.i Matbakh al-'Ajami
    VII.1.j Khanqa al-Farafra (Option)
    VII.1.k Bab al-Nasr

Inscriptions and Public Texts	Yasser Tabbaa
Female Patronage in Urban Development and Education	Abd al-Razzaq Moaz

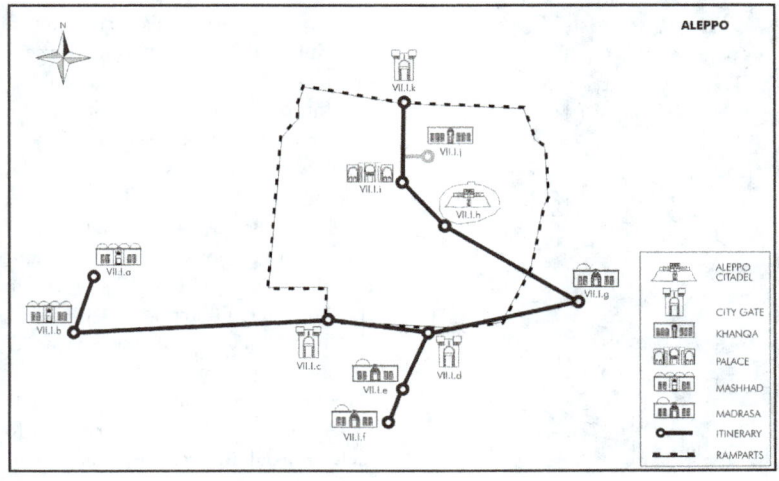

Aleppo Citadel, entrance.

ITINERARY VII *Patronage and Court Life under the Atabegs and Ayyubids in Syria*
Introduction

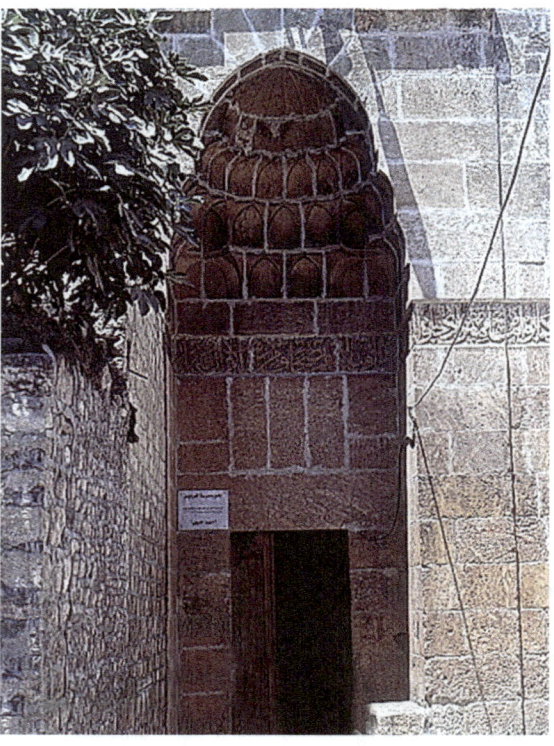

Madrasat al-Firdaws, Aleppo.

Syrian cities witnessed a pronounced rise in architectural patronage in the 6th/12th and 7th/13th centuries, likely to be attributable to the development in economic and dynastic factors. Economically, the systematisation of the *waqf* as an instrument of architectural patronage made it possible for a larger sector of the aristocracy, court officials and urban notables to build various religious, charitable and educational institutions. Dynastically, Atabeg and Ayyubid sultans, as with the rulers before them, used architectural patronage as a means of projecting an image of Islamic piety and royal power. While early Islamic monuments reflected the power of the great dynasties that ruled in the name of the *umma*, the "entire Muslim community", those built in the medieval period link more directly with particular patrons who personally provided the funds for construction. This personal identification is often reflected in the naming of these institutions – for example, that of al-Zahir Ghazi – Madrasa al-Zahiriyya – and by the fact that the patron and members of his or her household were often buried within their own foundations.

Beyond their symbolic image, the *madrasa*s, mausoleums, *khanqa*s and *bimaristan*s built by Atabeg and Ayyubid sultans also fulfilled important urban and social functions. Some of these institutions, for example the Ayyubid *madrasa*s south of Aleppo, or in the Salihiyya district north of Damascus, became nodes for subsequent urban development. Socially, *madrasa*s and *khanqa*s in particular provided employment and sustenance for generations of jurists and mystics, whether students or teachers, in accordance with the provisions of their *waqf*s. While conforming to the precepts of Islamic charity, this linkage between royal patrons and scholars of theology also served to influence their religious outlook and manner of teaching. The three *madrasa*s in the Maqamat Quarter – al-Firdaws, al-Zahiriyya and al-Kamiliyya – exemplify Ayyubid religious architecture in Aleppo. This period also witnessed a remarkable expansion in the basis of patronage, to include, in addition to the sultans them-

ITINERARY VII *Patronage and Court Life under the Atabegs and Ayyubids in Syria*
Introduction

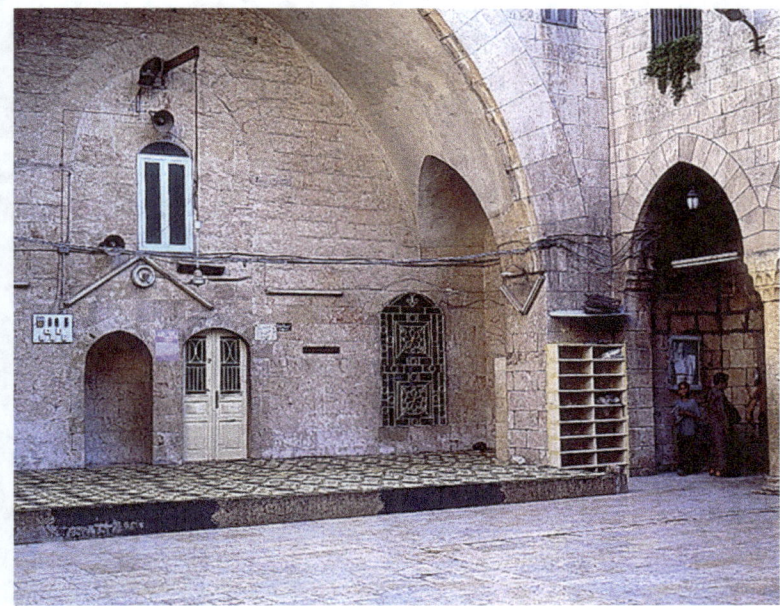

Madrasa al-Toruntayya al-'Adimiyya, courtyard, Aleppo.

selves, state officials, urban patricians and women of the court. Court officials, such as Shadhbakht, Toghril and Ibn al-Muqaddam (VI.1.d) often completed their master's buildings, in addition to founding their own institutions. Patrician families, such as Banu al-'Ajami and Banu al-'Adim in Aleppo, built numerous mosques and *madrasa*s, some vying in size with those built by the sultans themselves. The case of Kamal al-Din ibn al-'Adim (d. 662/1262), the greatest historian of Aleppo, is quite telling in this regard. Historian, jurist, poet and calligrapher, he founded an important *madrasa* outside Bab al-Nayrab, known as Madrasa al-Toruntayya and, as seen in the previous itinerary, also donated a magnificent wooden *mihrab* to the Madrasa al-Hallawiyya, in which he was a teacher.

*Madrasa*s, even more than mosques, formed the core of Atabeg and Ayyubid patronage, as seen in Damascus, since they were dedicated to the theological and legal analysis of the four rites, or *madhahib*, of Sunni Islam, which dictated the precept of public and private life. Political patrons also renovated shrines dedicated to martyrs, known as *mashhad*s, in order to tap into their religious resonance and popular appeal. The pious act of building *khanqa*s, centres of learning dedicated to spiritual and Sufi knowledge, was another form of Atabeg and Ayyubid patronage. The elegant Madrasat al-Firdaws was dedicated to the more mystical

ITINERARY VII *Patronage and Court Life under the Atabegs and Ayyubids in Syria*
Introduction

aspects of Islamic experience and was sponsored by the female regent of Aleppo, Dayfa Khatun, who ruled for nearly 20 years. Unlike Iranian or Anatolian *madrasa*s, which closely follow the four-*iwan*s-in-axial-symmetry plan, Syrian madrasas adopt a more flexible canon that calls for a tripartite prayer-hall, a single *iwan* and rooms for study and residences on two floors, all disposed around a courtyard with a central pool. Perhaps the most striking feature of Ayyubid *madrasa*s in Aleppo are their exteriors, which appear like massive stone blocks whose severity is only partly softened by one or more domes, *muqarnas* portals and inscription bands.

The ruling dynasty provided the provision of security and protection, implemented most directly by the building of fortifications. By the 6th/12th century, walls and citadels had become an absolute necessity, to the extent that urban life was inconceivable without them. The rebuilding of Aleppo's enclosure and gates, not to mention the magnificent citadel, began under al-Zahir Ghazi (581–613/1186–1216) and continued under his successors until the middle of the century.

VII.1 ALEPPO

VII.1.a **Mashhad al-Hussein**

This building is on the western outskirts of Aleppo nestled within the slopes of Jabal al-Huss, behind the Shahba Park. Those unfamiliar with Aleppo should probably consider taking a taxi to the site of the Mashhad. The Mashhad building is behind the contemporary theological institute that has a large car park. It can be visited respecting appropriate dress codes and conduct, at any time during the day. A small donation is advisable.

Aleppo is a city of shrines, of which two important Shi'ite examples have survived about 2 km west of Bab Antakiyya, at the foot of Jabal Jawshan. Mashhad al-Hussein is the larger and more important of the two; in fact, it is the most important medieval Shi'ite structure in the whole of Syria and continues to function as a pilgrimage shrine attracting thousands of visitors. Nevertheless, it is a thoroughly Ayyubid building that was constructed over several interrelated phases between the late 6th/12th and early 7th/13th centuries. In 1920, a massive explosion damaged the shrine badly. It remained in ruins

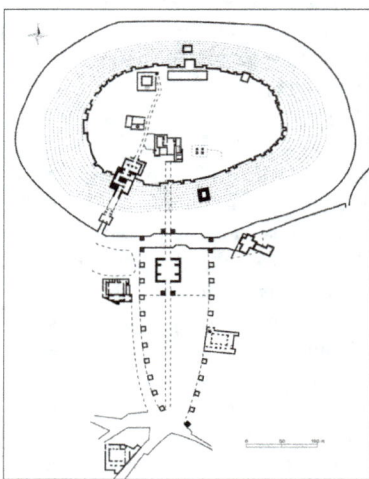

Floor-plan of Aleppo Citadel.

ITINERARY VII *Patronage and Court Life under the Atabegs and Ayyubids in Syria*
Aleppo

for about 50 years, until methodically and scientifically restored to its original appearance by 1983. Briefly used as a local mosque, there was a sudden transformation a few years later, that saw it change from an exquisite Ayyubid-style building into a modern Shi'ite shrine with a covered courtyard and a glittering cenotaph inserted into its main *iwan*.

The original shrine, measuring 70 m by 40 m, consists of two parts: an unfinished enclosure surrounded by small rooms and, a few steps higher, the main courtyard. The main entrance to the shrine is from the east, through an elaborate *muqarnas* portal framed by a wide arch with radiating stonework. The foundation text above the door, framed within a splendid braided design, has above it a frieze of tiny lamps suspended within a continuous arcade. It is likely that the light imagery alludes to the radiance that is often associated with Imam Hussein.

The central part of the shrine is disposed around an almost-square courtyard, which is focused on an elevated western *iwan* and flanked by two smaller arches surmounted by an interlace motif. A large panel with

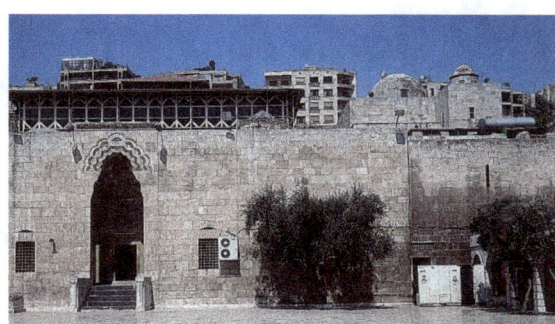

Mashhad al-Hussein, general view, Aleppo.

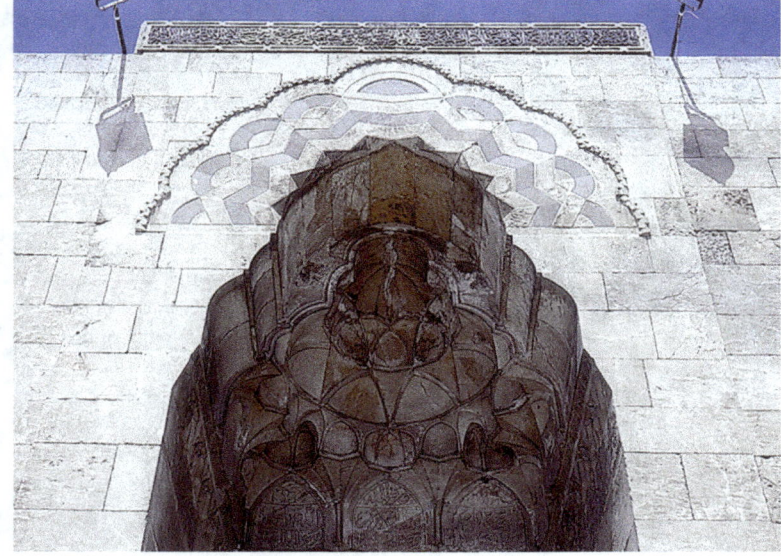

Mashhad al-Hussein, main entrance, Aleppo.

ITINERARY VII   *Patronage and Court Life under the Atabegs and Ayyubids in Syria*
Aleppo

a Shi'ite inscription that gives the names of the 12 Imams crowns the *iwan*. The south side has a five-domed prayer-hall, balanced on the north side by four domed bays. Also contributing to the balance and unity of the courtyard is a cornice raised on brackets that surrounds the courtyard on three sides.

North of this courtyard are two independent units, added in the early 7th/13th century, each consisting of two vaulted chambers. The western unit consists of two adjoining chambers covered by exquisite domes, one resting on eight squinches, and the other on a halo of *muqarnas* cells. It seems likely that the first of these chambers was for study and meditation, while the second served as a residence for the sheikh of the shrine, since it includes a small latrine hidden discretely in a corner. The eastern unit, which has its own entrance, was entirely utilitarian, including a kitchen and a set of seven latrines. These functions are entirely in keeping with the character of a pilgrimage shrine.

VII.1.b **Mashhad al-Dikka**

Exiting Mashhad al-Hussein, walk through the car park and exit from the small gate at the south-west corner. Walk out onto the dirt track towards the cypress trees in the distance. At the point where the dirt track meets an asphalted road, turn right and walk up the steps. This shrine is also known as Mashhad Sheikh Muhsin and it can be visited respecting appropriate dress codes and conduct, at any time during the day. A small donation is advisable.

The Mashhad al-Dikka or Imam Muhsin was first erected in 351/962 by Sayf al-Dawla, the Hamdanid ruler of Aleppo. It was subsequently restored and expanded by several leaders, 'Imad Zangi in 437/1143; Nur al-Din Mahmud bin Zangi in 541/1146; al-Zahir Ghazi in 585/1189 and al-'Aziz Muhammad in 631/1234. Proceeding chronologically, it seems that the double-domed mausoleum in the south-eastern corner dates to 'Imad Zangi, while the projecting cubical mass at the north-eastern corner represents the water facilities installed by Nur al-Din. The *muqarnas* portal in between these structures bears an inscription from the time of al-Zahir Ghazi who probably rebuilt the mosque. Under Ghazi's reconstruction, Mashhad al-Dikka features the earliest extant stone *muqarnas* portal in Aleppo. The mosque and the rest of the building are entirely plain and have been painted in modern times.

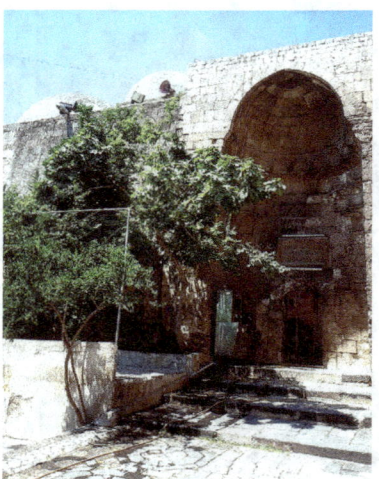

Mashhad al-Dikka, muqarnas *portal, Aleppo.*

ITINERARY VII Patronage and Court Life under the Atabegs and Ayyubids in Syria
Aleppo

VII.1.c **Bab Qinnisrin**

Take a taxi back towards the old city to Bab Qinnisrin, southwestern part of the old city walls.

Bab Qinnisrin stands today as a masterpiece of medieval Syrian military architecture, second only to the entrance gate of the Citadel of Aleppo. Although similarly repeatedly rebuilt and restored between the 4th/10th and 9th/15th centuries, much of its late Ayyubid form, dated to 654/1256, is retained. Before losing its east tower, Bab Qinnisrin consisted of two massive and unequal towers with chamfered fronts, of which the west tower was defensive, while that on the east contained the actual portal. This portal, which is equipped with a defensive sliding gate called a portcullis, leads to two rectangular halls separated by another portcullised gateway. A third defensive gate opens up to a final square chamber providing access to the city. More than just a gate, Bab Qinnisrin was a fortress in its own regard, with two wells and a water cistern, flourmills, facilities for the production of olive oil, a bakery and an arsenal.

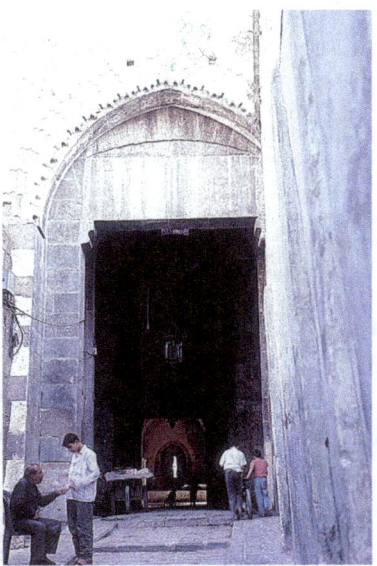

Bab Qinnisrin, Aleppo.

VII.1.d **Bab al-Maqam**

Enter the old city through Bab Qinnisrin and walk eastward for about 450 m, keeping parallel to the walls. Today the gate is free standing, separated from the city walls, and situated on the corner of two streets: Bab Maqam and Said 'Ass.

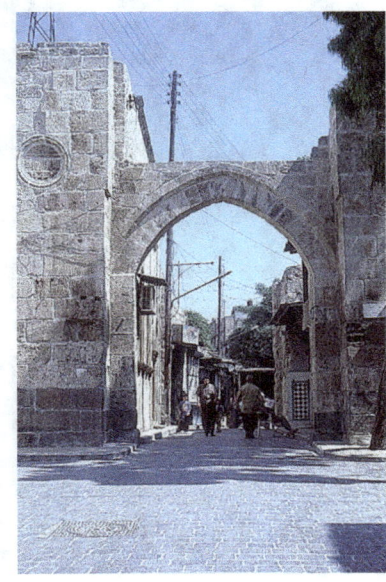

Bab al-Maqam, Aleppo.

The initial construction of Bab al-Maqam was under the auspices of al-Zahir Ghazi, but completed by his son, Muhammad, in around 627/1230; extensive alterations took place during the Mamluk period. Far less impressive than other Ayyubid gates, it differs from them by its lack of towers and by the fact that its original design was one of a triple gate with a large central opening flanked by two smaller ones, the traces of which are still visible in the masonry. Such tripartite gates were practically unknown in medieval Syria as they only had minimal defensive capabilities. Bab al-Maqam was most likely a ceremonial gate that stood on the road linking the Ayyubid monuments in the Maqamat with the citadel.

VII.1.e Madrasa al-Zahiriyya

Walk south for 400 m until you reach a v-shaped intersection. Fifty meters to the left of this intersection is a large building with a monumental muqarnas *entrance. Access to the interior might prove to be difficult as the* madrasa *is undergoing restoration.*

The Madrasa al-Zahiriyya, which lacks a foundation inscription, was undoubtedly built by al-Zahir Ghazi as a *madrasa* and as a mausoleum intended for members of his household. The *madrasa* is accessible axially through a *muqarnas* portal that leads to an oblong courtyard framed on the north and south ends by triple porticos, on the east by a deep *iwan* and on the west by small rooms on two levels. The south portico leads to a mosque with three domes and a *mihrab*, which has lost its marble revetment, but retains flanking panels with exquisite geometric ornamentation. The north-western part of the *madrasa*, with about 20 identical rooms on two levels, is entirely residential. One of the most interesting features of this *madrasa* is the incorporation of Romanesque Crusader capitals. The incorporation of capitals, columns and other *spolia* from Crusader monuments was common practice in Ayyubid constructions. Many examples can be

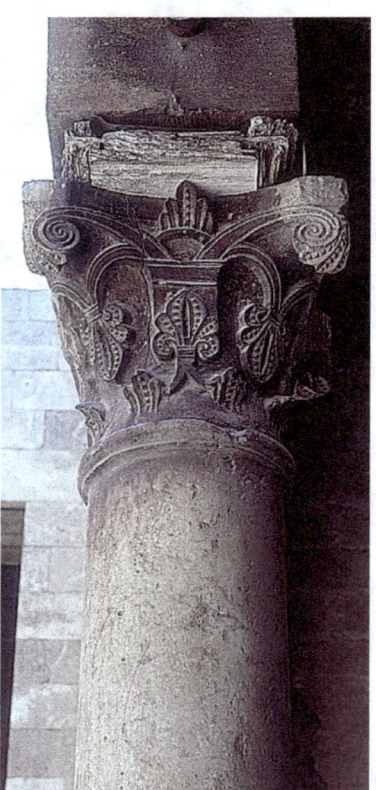

Madrasa al-Zahiriyya, Crusader capital, Aleppo.

ITINERARY VII   Patronage and Court Life under the Atabegs and Ayyubids in Syria
Aleppo

found in Jerusalem but also in Hama, as can be seen in the Mosque of Nur al-Din built in 558/1164 (IV.2.c) and in the Hanabila Mosque in the Salihiyya district of Damascus built in 604/1206 (I.16). The use of *spolia* in this way is generally interpreted as the acquisition of victory trophies.

VII.1.f **Madrasat al-Firdaws**

Walk south for a further 250 m, keeping the cemetery to your right, even at the point where the road becomes much narrower. Walk a further 80 m and take the lane to your right, the madrasa *will appear before you. The* madrasa, *now a mosque and the site of several graves of distinction, is open to the public respecting appropriate dress codes and conduct, at any time of the day. A small donation is advisable.*

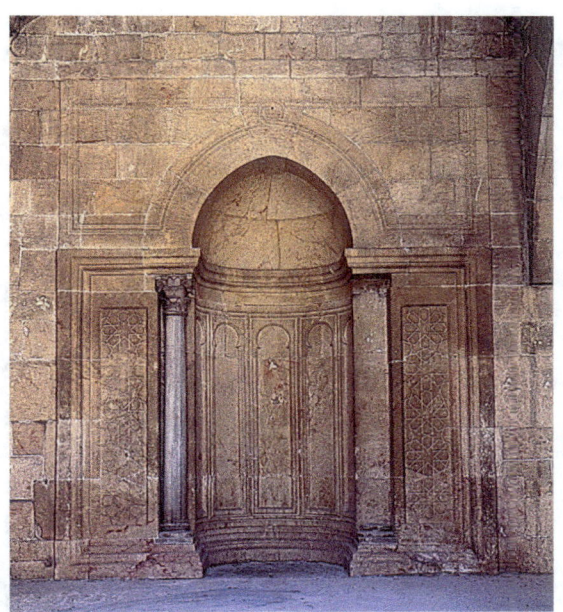

Madrasat al-Firdaws, built by the regent queen Dayfa Khatun in 633/1235, is without doubt Syria's most important Ayyubid religious building. Its size (43.5 m x 55 m), with 11 undulating domes and an exterior *iwan*, which once faced a garden, further contribute to its uniqueness. The entrance is on its eastern side through a *muqarnas* portal, shot through by a long inscriptional frieze that starts with Qur'anic descriptions of Paradise and continues with honorific titles to Dayfa Khatun. Unfortunately, later encroachments have marred this entrance along with the other façades of this important building.

The glory of this building is its pristine rectangular courtyard, which is sur-

Madrasa al-Zafiriyya, mihrab, Aleppo.

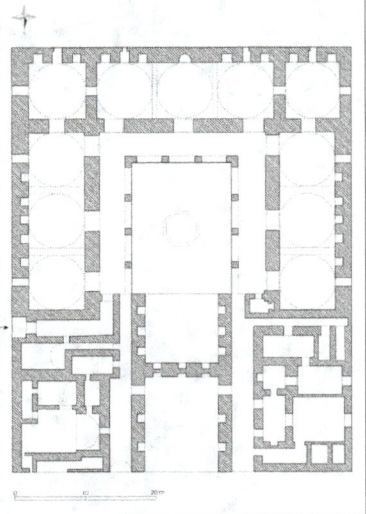

Floor-plan of Madrasat al-Firdaws.

235

ITINERARY VII *Patronage and Court Life under the Atabegs and Ayyubids in Syria*
Aleppo

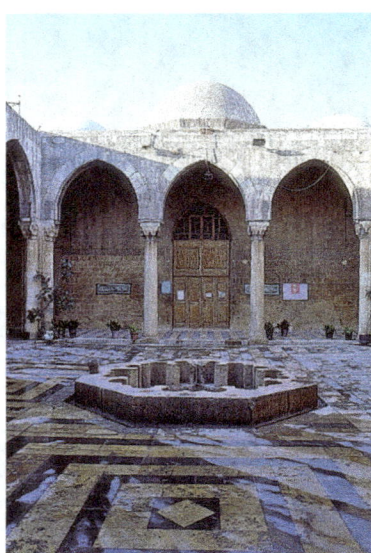

Madrasat al-Firdaws, courtyard, view towards the southern side with the prayer hall, Aleppo.

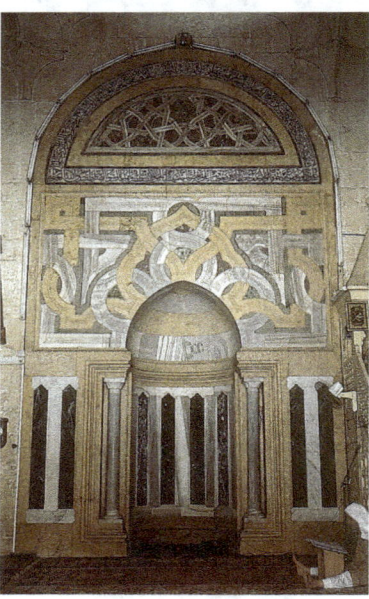

Madrasat al-Firdaws, mihrab, Aleppo.

rounded by arched porticos on the east, south and west sides, and by a large *iwan* to the north. The porticos lead to three long chambers, each with three domes, the southern one of which serves as a mosque. This mosque contains a splendid marble *mihrab*, surmounted by a polychrome interlaced spandrel, which is the largest and finest of several examples from Aleppo. It should be noted that these interlaces were not superficial inlay work but rather deeply engaged stonework, whose visible surfaces have been manipulated into various geometric swirls. Perhaps because of its ingenuity and spectacular effect, this decorative feature was subsequently exported from Aleppo to Anatolia, Palestine and Egypt.

The Madrasat al-Firdaws is a heavily inscribed Ayyubid building, with exterior and interior inscriptions that total more than 150 m in length. The religious inscriptions are some of the most outstanding in all Islamic architecture. Using prose, poetry and Qur'anic references, it vividly and passionately describes the actions and aspirations of the Sufis who worshipped at al-Firdaws. Their night vigil and ecstatic worship would be rewarded by entry to Paradise and by a vision of God we are told. Although called a *madrasa*, al-Firdaws was most likely a *khanqa* that, in its time, housed deep forms of Sufi practice, and hence the use of the word, *madrasat* to indicate that it was both a shrine and religious school.

VII.1.g Madrasa al-Toruntayya al-'Adimiyya

Retrace your steps back to Bab al-Maqam and take a taxi heading east towards Bab al-Nayrab Square. The madrasa *is on a small hill 500 m from the square and is recognisable by its* muqarnas *portal and the concrete steps ascending the hills. The still-functioning* madrasa *is open, respecting appropriate dress codes and conduct, at any time of the day. A small donation is advisable.*

The Madrasa al-Kamaliyya al-'Adimiyya, known today as Jami' Toruntay, is located on a small hill about half a kilometre east of Bab al-Nayrab. Most scholars attribute it to the famous historian of Aleppo, Kamal al-Din ibn al-'Adim, and is dated to between 639/1241 and 649/1251. Architecturally, the 'Adimiyya differs from all other Ayyubid *madrasas* in having two, rather than one, *muqarnas* portals: one leading to the *madrasa* proper and the other to a residential unit for the head of the *madrasa*. The main portal leads to a spacious courtyard (10.80 m x 14.50 m) flanked on the east and west by exquisite arcades resting on four granite columns. This *madrasa* is a living spiritual space still steeped in devout religious practice with hundreds of young children learning the Qur'an and sheikhs teaching the faith of Islam.

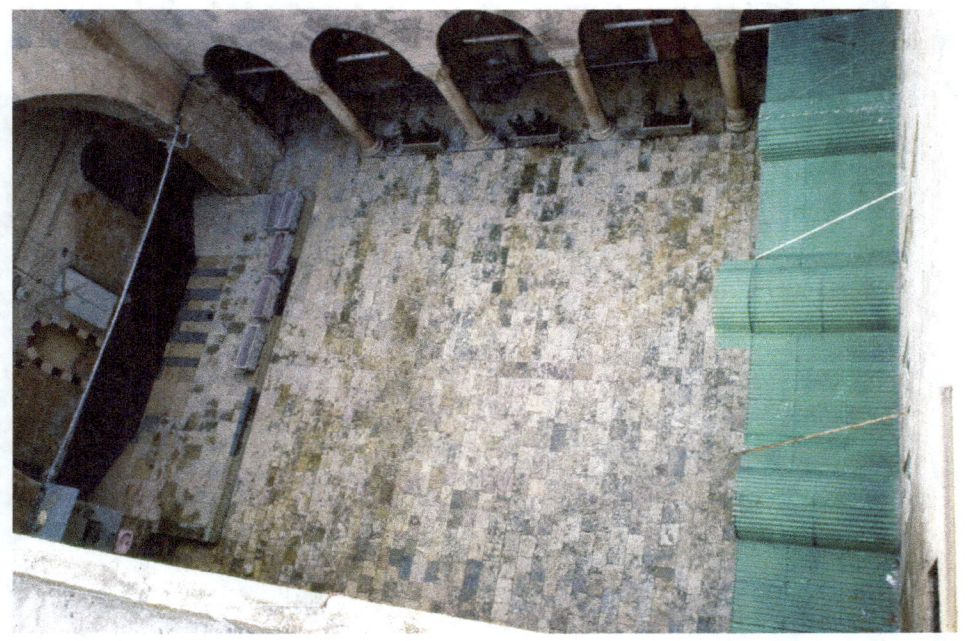

Madrasa al-Toruntayya al-'Adimiyya, courtyard, Aleppo (photo courtesy of Yasser Tabbaa and AKDC. © Yasser Tabbaa Archive, Aga Khan Documentation Center at MIT).

ITINERARY VII Patronage and Court Life under the Atabegs and Ayyubids in Syria
Aleppo

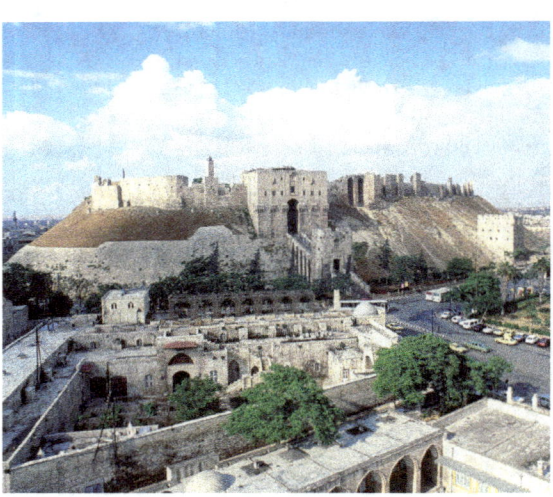

Aleppo Citadel

VII.1.h **Aleppo Citadel**
(in three parts: **Entrance Block, Palace and Mosque**)

In the heart of Aleppo, the citadel will be very easy to find. Opening times are Wed–Mon 9.00–18.00 during the summer, 9.00–16.00 during the winter. Closed on Tuesdays and during Friday prayers (approx 11.00-13.00). There is an entrance fee.

In terms of both its height and the greatness of its entrance block, Aleppo Citadel ranks far above all the other urban citadels in Syria and her neighbouring countries. Seen from any angle, the entrance block alone is an impressive sight. Linked with the city by means of a ramp supported on seven arches, it rises like a great monolith pierced by numerous arrow slits and machicolated brattices. Its two massive towers hide behind them a U-shaped corridor that would force an attacking army to change direction six times, all the while being exposed to projectiles and hot liquids poured from openings in the vaults above them. Indeed, the strength of the entrance block was reinforced by use of powerful imagery, such as the intertwined dragons at the first gate and the two lion sculptures at the last.

The Ayyubid palace complex is located on high ground near to the south end of the citadel and is reached by stairs to the right of the main ramp. Built initially by al-Zahir Ghazi and rebuilt by his son 'Aziz Muhammad in the early 6th/13th century, the palace complex measures about 50 m x 40 m. It consists of the palace proper, a *hammam* with three chambers, and a warren of guardrooms and arsenals, which are currently under excavation, to the south. The palace entrance is on the west side through a monumental portal, which is quite striking in its richness and complexity, combining, as it does, *muqarnas* vaulting, geometric ornamentation and colour. Although *muqarnas* portals were fairly commonplace in this period, this one is the tallest and most elaborate example in Aleppo.

Moving through a vestibule for guards one passes through a small courtyard (4.5 m sq) before entering a more spacious courtyard, (about 10 m sq), which forms the centre of the palace. With an octagonal pool in the middle and four coaxial *iwans*, the palace resembles other Ayyubid palaces, in particular that seen at Qal'at Najm (VIII.1.). The northern *iwan*, undoubtedly the most privileged, has the remains of a *salsabil* fountain hooded by a *muqarnas* vault. Originally,

238

ITINERARY VII *Patronage and Court Life under the Atabegs and Ayyubids in Syria*
Aleppo

Aleppo Citadel Mosque

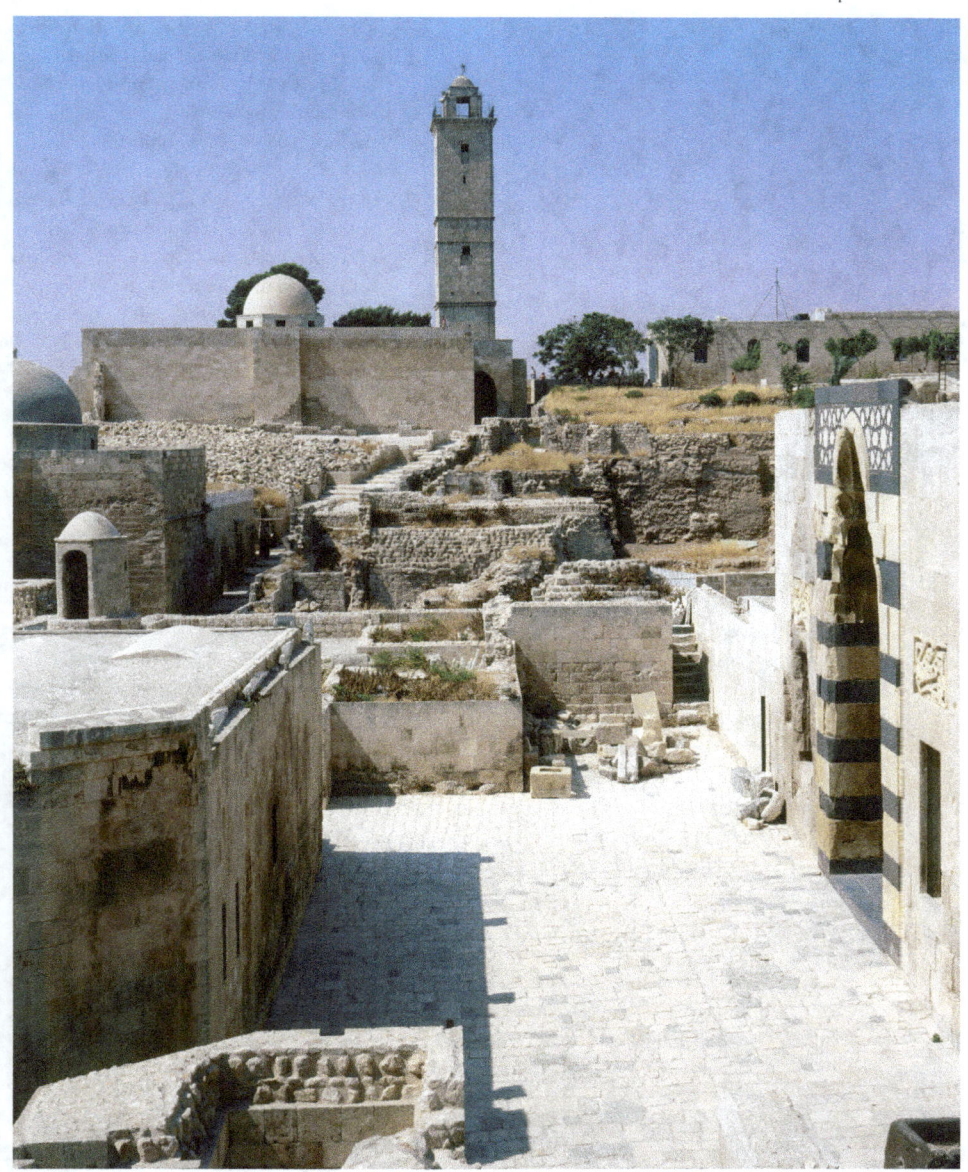

ITINERARY VII Patronage and Court Life under the Atabegs and Ayyubids in Syria
Aleppo

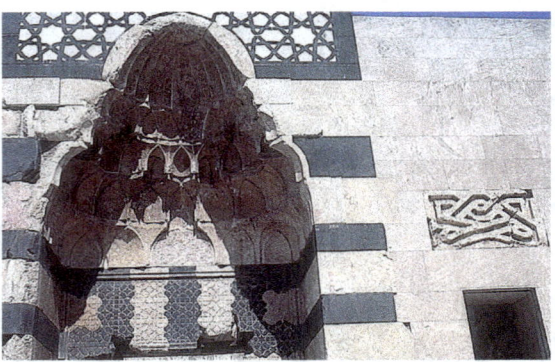

Aleppo Citadel, Palace, detail of the muqarnas portal.

water would have flowed down a carved marble slab, into a partially open and part-covered channel, and emptied into the central pool.

Perched at the highest point in the citadel, the mosque's inscription on the portal dates it to 610/1214. Externally, it has a simple and traditional form, consisting of a large rectangular block with a central dome and a tall, square minaret. Internally, the mosque is equally traditional, with a rectangular courtyard and a tripartite prayer-hall with a dome and a plain, stone *mihrab*. In fact, the mosque is interesting chiefly for its minaret, whose height and square section recall the older minaret of the Great Mosque below.

VII.1.i **Matbakh al-'Ajami**

Return to the large plaza north of the Great Mosque. Walk east for 100 m until you face the entrance of the large Khan al-Wazir and the small plaza before it. Directly facing the khan and the above-mentioned smaller plaza to the north is the matbakh. Access to the building might prove to be difficult.

The so-called Matbakh al-'Ajami was originally an Ayyubid palace that likely belonged to the 'Ajami family. About a third of this palace was demolished when the street to the south of it was widened, and the palace was given a false façade in the Mamluk style. An inconsequential entrance leads to the north-east corner of a spacious courtyard surrounded by four *iwans* and covered by a dome on *muqarnas* pendentives, possibly the largest preserved Ayyubid dome in Syria. All four *iwans* are flanked by narrow, arched openings, forming a tripartite-façade composition typical of Ayyubid palaces. The northern *iwan*, framed by an elaborate arch with pendant voussoirs, has an exquisite *muqarnas* vault that resembles a starry sky.

VII.1.j **Khanqa al-Farafra** *(Option)*

Return to the citadel and walk around clockwise around it. Take the alleyway that leads into the Farafra district, north of the citadel. The Khanqa al-Farafra will appear to your right, discernable by its muqarnas entrance, but it will probably be off access.

It was also founded by Dayfa Khatun in 634/1237 and intended for Sufi women. As such it is the only survivor of about a dozen medieval *khanqas* in Aleppo. A *muqarnas* portal in the middle of a plain wall leads through a bent-axis vestibule to a squarish courtyard (10 x 11 meters) centered around an octagonal pool with a polylobed interior. A three-bay mosque with a central dome occupies the southern side, a spacious *iwan* faces it on the north, while the eastern and western sides are taken up by residential rooms arranged on two levels. The mosque is relatively plain except for a deeply recessed mihrab which is completely reveted in veined white marble and green diorite.

Dayfa Khatun's architectural patronage reveals her inclination to learning and Sufism, while many contemporary chroniclers have recorded her justice and charity: "She was just to her subjects, very charitable and loving towards them. She removed various taxes in all the regions of Aleppo. She favoured jurists, ascetics, scholars and people of religion, and extended to them many charities", records the Syrian historian Ibn al-Wasil (604–97/1208–98).

VII.1.k Bab al-Nasr

From Khanqa al-Farafra, continue north towards Sijn / Mutanabbi Streets. Cross the street then turn left and walk for 75 m. A few steps further to your right you will arrive in a neighbourhood full of shops selling stationary. The gate is discernable amongst the shops.

Rebuilt by al-Zahir Ghazi in 609/1212, Bab al-Nasr, or the Gate of Victory, is the most important gate in the northern enclosure. It has a typical Ayyubid form, with two projecting towers, but with a double, instead of the usual single, bent-axis entrance. This was made by adding a vaulted chamber built into the thickness of the wall between the first bend and the final entrance into the city.

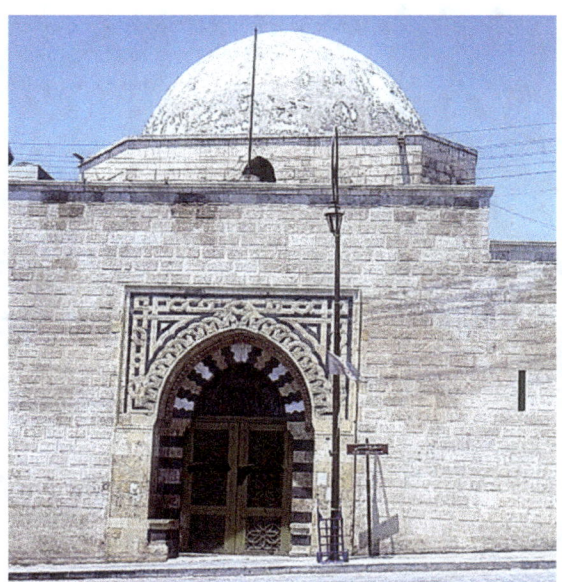

Matbakh al-'Ajami, Aleppo.

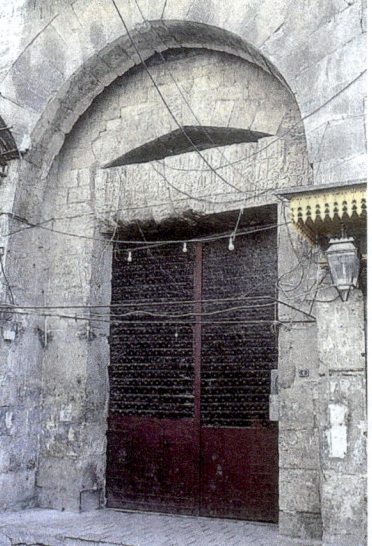

Bab al-Nasr, Aleppo.

INSCRIPTIONS AND PUBLIC TEXTS

Yasser Tabbaa

Monumental inscriptions on the exterior of buildings begin in full force under the Fatimids in Cairo, where inscription bands in floriated *kufic* script become commonplace from the late 4th/10th century onwards. The practice spread to Syria in the 5th/11th century, where it is known as Atabeg *kufic*. The style is magnificently displayed in the minaret of the Great Mosque of Aleppo, dated 483/1090, whose four inscription bands in floriated *kufic* script mark a peak in this exacting calligraphic style.

In Syria the switch from *kufic*, an angular script, to a cursive one is quite abrupt and can be directly attributed to Nur al-Din. Beginning with his inscription in the Madrasa al-Hallawiyya in Aleppo, dated 543/1149, thenceforth all monumental inscriptions in Syria are in the cursive *thuluth* style. In effect, this new epigraphic style marks a clean break with Fatimid practice, supplanting their floriated *kufic* script with the perfect legibility of the *thuluth* style. Introduced in the middle of the 6th/12th century, this calligraphic style continues with minor refinements up until the end of the Ayyubid period.

Another good example are the inscriptions of Nur al-Din and his son Isma'il in the Maqam of Ibrahim in Aleppo Citadel dated 563/1168 and 575/1179 respectively. They display a squat but tapered script that uses all the marks of vocalisation and orthography necessary for perfect legibility. Thus, changes in the style of calligraphic scripts relate

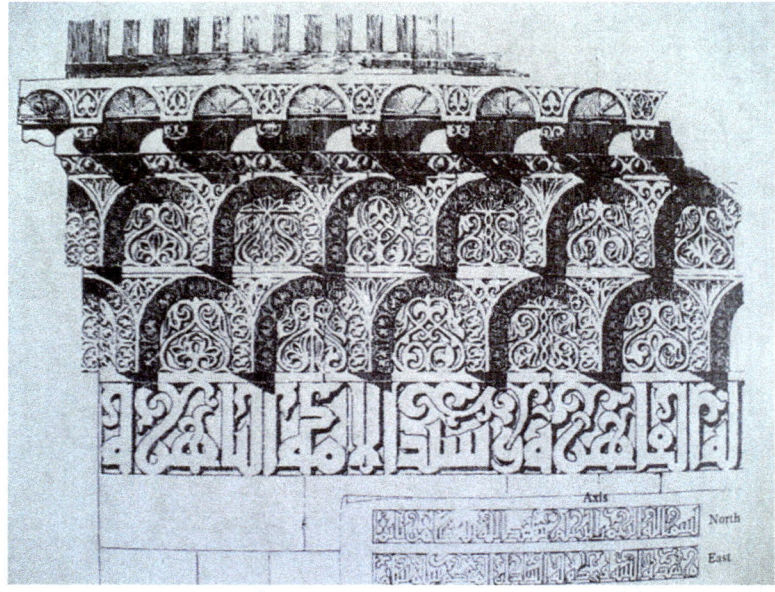

Minaret of Aleppo, transcribed Atabeg kufic inscription, drawing (Herzfeld, 1955, plate LXII).

to the need for functional clarity with regard to recording patronage, details of endowment (*waqf*) and renovations of a given monument. Later inscriptions from the time of al-Zahir Ghazi, or those of Dayfa Khatun in Aleppo, or al-Ashraf Musa in Damascus, are somewhat more sinuous and more attenuated giving them greater elegance, but they are still just as legible. Some monuments feature cursive and *kufic* inscription panels, the latter used decoratively while the former is actually informative.

The content of Atabeg and Ayyubid inscriptions tends to be largely dynastic and historical with the inclusion of occasional Qur'anic verses and, more rarely, information about the *waqf*. As such, these inscriptions are especially useful for the purposes of dating, attribution, titulature, function and even iconography. In exceptional cases, such as at Madrasat al-Firdaws in Aleppo, the inscriptions help to elucidate the function of the building and flesh out the iconography of the monument.

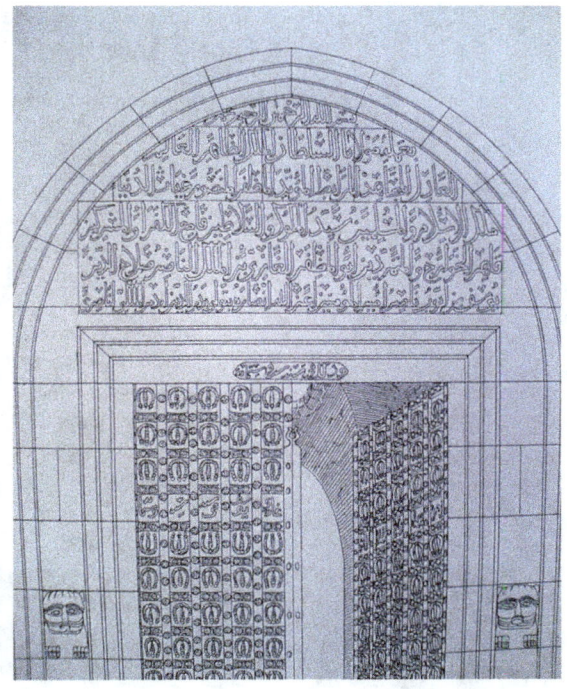

Aleppo Citadel, Lion Gate, transcribed inscription, drawing (Herzfeld, 1955, plate XXXVIII).

FEMALE PATRONAGE IN URBAN DEVELOPMENT AND EDUCATION

Abd al-Razzaq Moaz

The active role of women in medieval Islamic society is seen by the abundant number of urban, educational and religious institutions sponsored by female members of the Seljuq, Zangid and Ayyubid courts. These women were themselves scholars unlike, for example, the Mamluk women of the 7th/13th and 8th/15th centuries, many of whom were Turkish speakers and illiterate in Arabic, though they too sponsored beautiful architecture. Safwat al-Mulk (d. 512/1119) was one of the most prominent personalities of her time, and perhaps a trendsetter for women patrons. She built a *khanqa* and a mausoleum in Damascus as part of the Seljuq-period reconstruction of the city. Sitt al-Sham, Rabi'a Khatun and Dayfa Khatun, all sisters of Salah al-Din, were some of the most prominent figures of Syrian Ayyubid urbanism, famous for their *madrasa*s, and active not only in architectural patronage, but also in education, leadership and commerce.

In Aleppo, probably the definitive example of Ayyubid architecture sponsored by a woman is the Madrasat al-Firdaws, built by Dayfa Khatun, who ruled the city for nearly 20 years and was famous for the prosperity of her reign and for her mystical tendencies. She sponsored several institutions, particularly *khanqa*s, such as Khanqa al-Farafra, and always disposed of healthy *waqf*s for the perpetual maintenance of her charitable institutions.

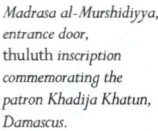

Madrasa al-Murshidiyya, entrance door, thuluth inscription commemorating the patron Khadija Khatun, Damascus.

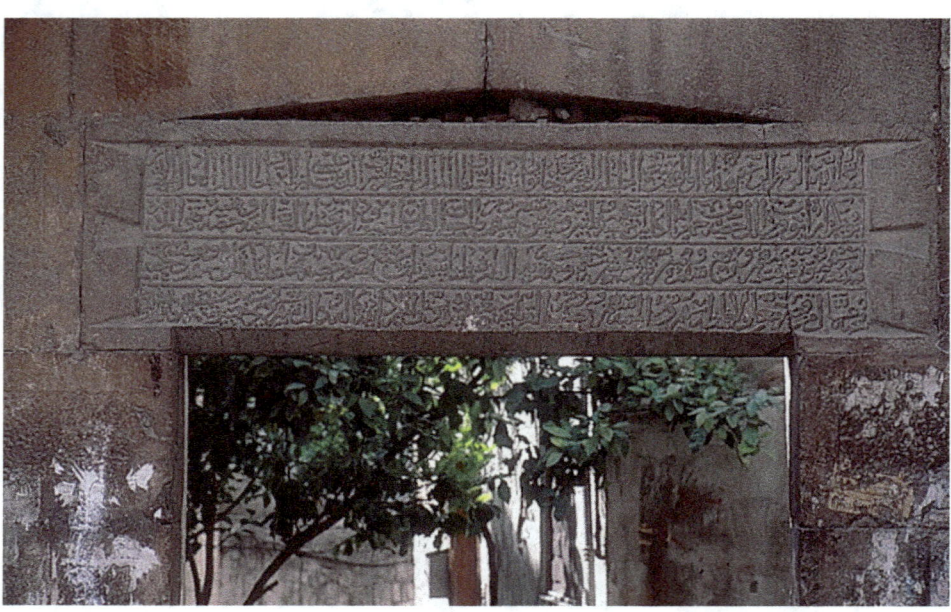

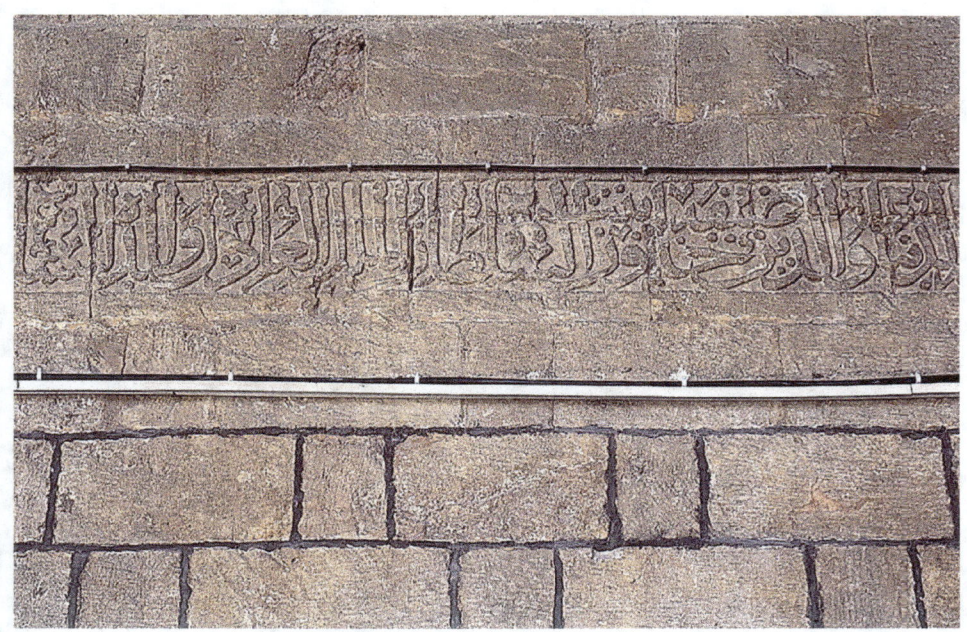

Madrasat al-Firdaws, exterior, thuluth inscription on the eastern façade presenting the honorific titles of the patron Dayfa Khatun. Aleppo.

In Damascus and the Salihiyya district, scores of women devoted their attention to urban development and the foundation of didactic institutions. The Murshidiyya of Khadija Khatun, the Sahiba founded by Rabi'a Khatun, the Shamiyya patronised by Sitt al-Sham are all madrasas constructed by daughters of the Ayyubid dynasty; while the Farukhshahiyya and the Atabakiyya were founded by the wives of Ayyubids, and the Hafiziyya by a freed-women of an Ayyubid prince, and this is to name but a few. These patrons would also participate in scholarly lectures and religious discussions, with many afforded diplomas or *ijaza* subsequently, allowing them to become teachers on their own merit. The contemporary historian Ibn 'Asakir gives thanks to over 80 female teachers for their wisdom, intellectual discussion and generous patronage. Rabi'a Khatun composed many religious studies, and is known to have attended the opening lecture at the Madrasa al-Sahiba, which she founded. 'Ismat al-Din Khatun, the princess-wife of Nur al-Din and subsequently Salah al-Din, built a *madrasa*, *turba*, *khanqa* and a *funduq*. Amat al-Latif was a prominent female figure of the Ayyubid court and an expert in the Hanbali rite. Often called *al-'Alima*, or "the Knower", she commissioned both a *madrasa* and a *Dar al-Hadith* in the al-Salihiyya district.

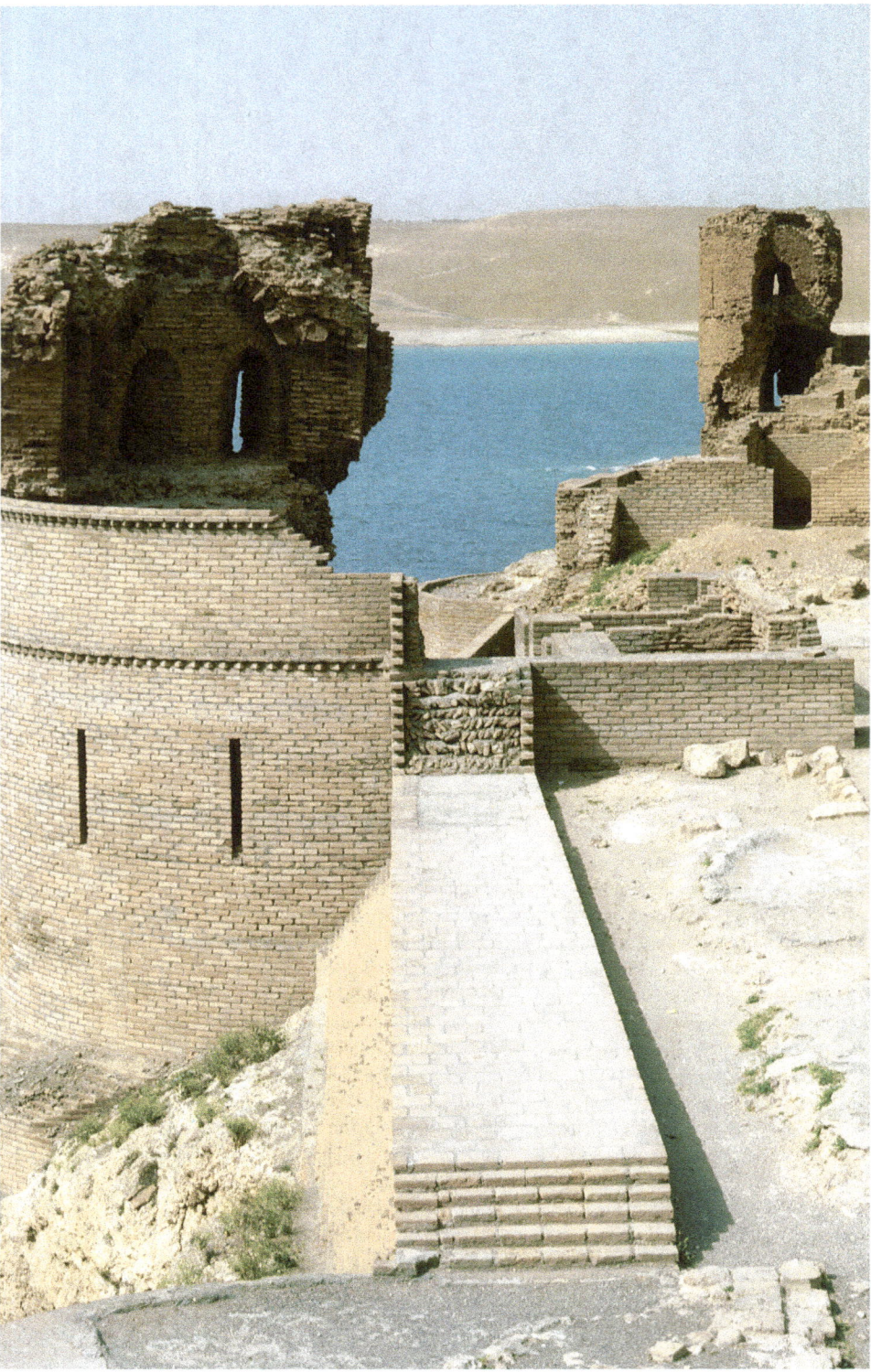

ITINERARY VIII

The Euphrates Region: Window onto Mesopotamia

Verena Daiber

VIII.1 QAL'AT NAJM
VIII.2 MASKANEH, MEDIEVAL BALIS
VIII.3 QAL'AT JA'BAR
VIII.4 RAQQA
    VIII.4.a Raqqa Museum
    VIII.4.b Great Mosque of al-Rafiqa
    VIII.4.c Qasr al-Banat
    VIII.4.d Bab Baghdad

SCENIC OPTION
VIII.5 TADMUR
    VIII.5.a Qal'at Tadmur

The Eastern Influence in Syria   Verena Daiber

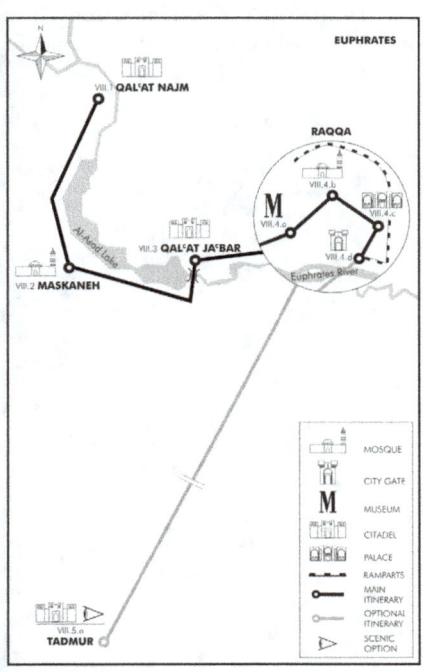

Qal'at Ja'bar.

ITINERARY VIII   The Euphrates Region: Window onto Mesopotamia
Introduction

The area to the east of the Euphrates belongs geographically to the northern half of Mesopotamia. This area, called *al-Jazira*, "the Island", due to its geographical position, lies engulfed between the Tigris and the Euphrates. Historically, the Jazira was divided into three parts, each named after the early Islamic tribes that controlled the area, and it is the western part, named Diyar Mudar, which now largely constitutes the north-eastern part of modern Syria. The area of the Jazira owned the communications routes between Iraq, Anatolia and the Armenian-Iranian regions that bordered on Syria. Thereby it was a fertile and cultivated area supplied with water from several rivers such as the Balikh and the Khabur, tributaries of Euphrates. The abundant water nourished livestock including sheep and horses, as well as agricultural produce such as cereals, rice, olives, other fruits and cotton. The production of charcoal also supported light-industry. Shipping trade and local crafts flourished on the Tigris and the Euphrates, with Balis being one of the main Syrian ports out of which left exported goods.

From the beginning of the 4th/10th century, the area witnessed a period of destabilisation. The central power of the 'Abbasids declined, while regional dynasties such as the Tulunids, Ikhshidids and Hamdanids came to power. Successful Byzantine campaigns in northern Syria and the Jazira further weakened 'Abbasid authority in the area, while the Fatimids from Egypt attempted to take hold of Syria from the

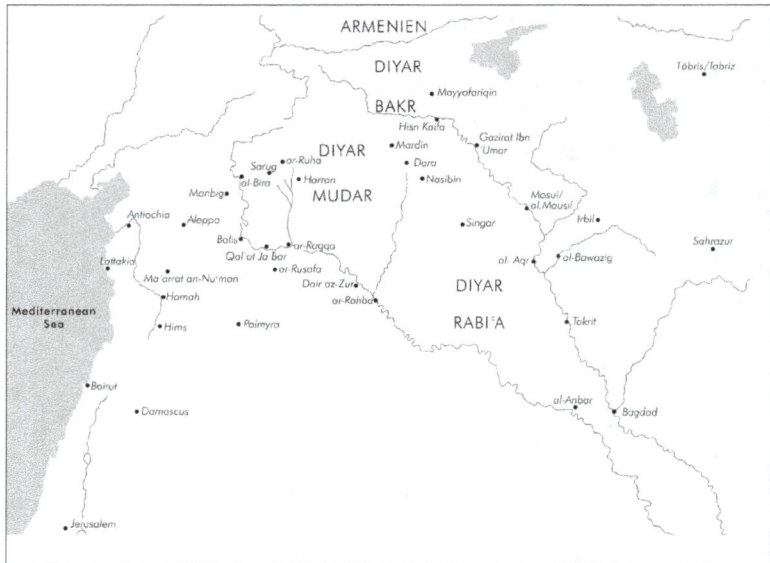

Regional map of al-Jazira.

ITINERARY VIII   The Euphrates Region: Window onto Mesopotamia
Introduction

Qal'at Najm.   *Qal'at Ja'bar.*

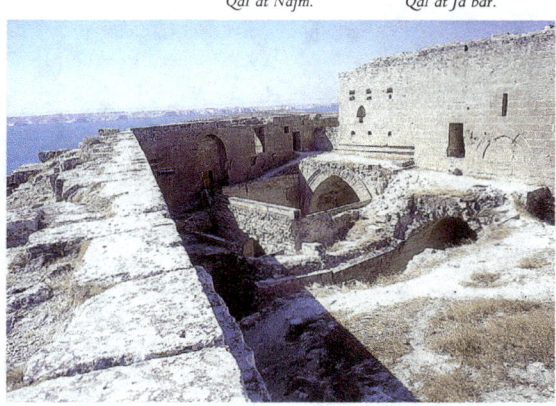

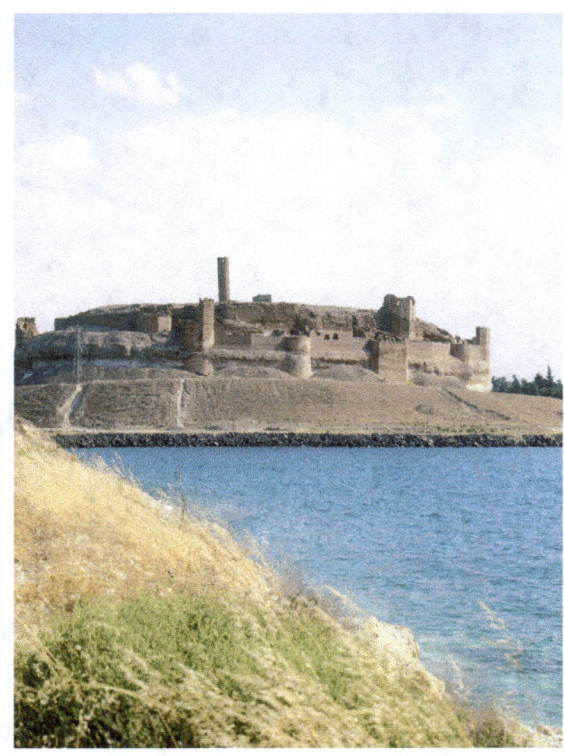

south, conquering Damascus in 358/969 and reaching as far north as Aleppo in 404/1015. Perpetual raids of local Bedouin tribes were an additional destabilising factor. In this atmosphere of chronic warfare and insecurity, local rulers, among them numerous Bedouin chiefs, fortified significant positions to establish strongholds for protecting their own entourage. As a consequence, strongholds were not only established at major towns and commercial centres but also in rural areas, serving as protective outposts for the people settled in the neighbourhood and guarding commercial roads and strategic points such as river crossings.

Qal'at Najm was one such rural fortification established in the 4th/10th century, and known as Jisr Manbij in historical sources. Here, either a bridge or a shallow part of the river provided a crossing over the Euphrates to reach Qal'at Ja'bar and Harran, major centres of the Diyar Mudar. Positioned on the main road to Harran, Ja'bar also gained considerable strategic importance during these insecure times.

The Seljuq Atabeg 'Imad al-Din Zangi (r. 521–40/1127–46) was the first to unite and stabilise Syria. In 522/1128, he began his conquest of the Jazira and took Raqqa, the main city of the Diyar Mudar, in 529/1135. His son Nur al-Din (r. 540–68/1146–74), continued the expansions begun by his father and succeeded in 549/1154 to unite all of Syria under Muslim rule, with the exception of the coastal strip held by the Crusaders. Nur al-Din was patron of a vast range of building and restoration activities all over his territory, especially after the destructive

249

ITINERARY VIII   The Euphrates Region: Window onto Mesopotamia

Introduction

earthquakes of 552/1157 and 565/1170. Ja'bar is an interesting example of the politics of alliances during the time of the Crusader states established after 492/1099. In around 497/1104, Ja'bar Citadel was taken by the Crusaders and incorporated into the County of Edessa. From then on, the fortress mainly came under the rule of the local dynasty of the 'Uqailids who in turn became important allies of the Franks. Their close relationship was probably due to the fact that one of the 'Uqailid lords married a Frankish woman. In 540/1146, during an attempt to conquer Ja'bar, 'Imad al-Din Zangi was killed in front of the walls of the fortress by a Frankish eunuch. Finally, his son Nur al-Din ibn Zangi succeeded in taking the castle from the 'Uqailids in 564/1168. He gave it as an *iqta'* to his milk-brother but, after his death in 569/1174, his son who was lord of Aleppo, violently regained control of the place. The struggle for power over Ja'bar reflects more or less the changes in supremacy in Aleppo and shows its strategic importance, since it controlled the major communications routes in the region. It was not only the principal crossing point on the Euphrates but also an important trade route between Aleppo and Mosul, thereby commanding control over virtually all movement in the region.

The history of the medieval city of Balis, also known by its modern name of Maskaneh, shows that it was closely related to Ja'bar and that it can be described as the economic centre of the area. Throughout medieval history Balis was continuously conquered together with Ja'bar. Nur al-Din gave both cities away to his son as a fief and although Balis was the main shipping port in the Middle Euphrates, its importance was not only based on economic-strategic considerations, but also on agricultural strength, as it was situated in the middle of rich and fertile land and, therefore, an utmost profitable fief.

As for the city of Raqqa, once the capital of the 'Abbasid Empire under the famous caliph Harun al-Rashid (r. 179–93/ 795–809), it too benefited from the restored safety and refortifications brought about by the Zangid father and

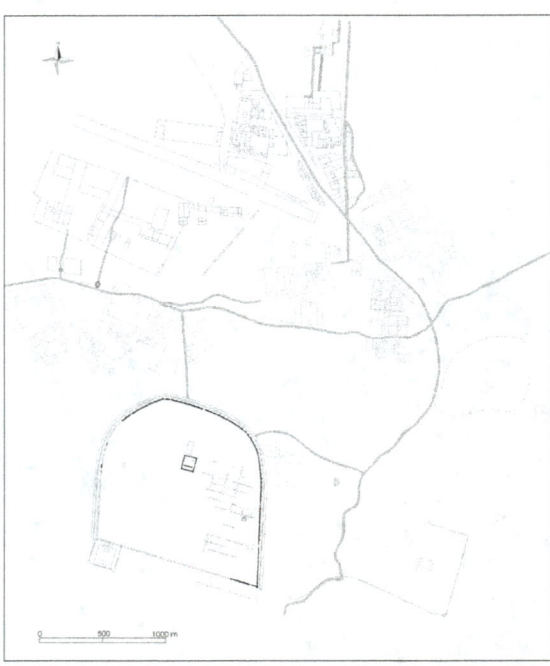

Plan of al-Raqqa.

ITINERARY VIII   The Euphrates Region: Window onto Mesopotamia
Introduction

son. Their patronage improved the communications routes and revived long-distance trade for their Ayyubid successors. Raqqa became the main town of the Diyar Mudar. Historical sources have recorded the establishment of *madrasa*s, a *bimaristan* and *khanqa*. It is also probable that one of the Zangids built a palace called Qasr al-Banat. Nur al-Din in particular continued the architectural development of the city and extensively restored the Friday Mosque in al-Rafiqa in 544/1149. Glass and ceramic industries started to flourish and Raqqa became the main production centre for a typical ceramic style using innovative techniques in decoration.

Although isolated as a frontier province the north-western area of the Jazira remained critical to the Ayyubid state in the face of the hostile Zangids of Mosul. Under Zangid rule, the Ayyubid state was a confederation of local principalities, each led by a more or less autonomous ruling member of the Ayyubid family, thereby keeping the fortresses on the Euphrates in Arab hands. The founder of the dynasty, Salah al-Din established his son al-Zahir Ghazi as ruler in Aleppo bestowing on him both Balis and Ja'bar, and demonstrating once again the close ties with Aleppo. Also, in Qal'at Najm, several inscriptions attributable to al-Zahir Ghazi document his sovereignty over the place.

Following the Ayyubid conquest in 578/1182, Raqqa remained under the rule of the Zangids of Sinjar, but under the supremacy of the new Ayyubid authority. Salah al-Din's successor in Raqqa, al-Ashraf Musa (r. 626–34/1229–37) laid out several gardens within the city as well as palaces and a hammam. There are also reports of the construction of a citadel but, unfortunately, none of these Ayyubid buildings has survived. Only the abundance of the delicately produced and extensively traded Raqqa-ware ceramics found in excavations all over the Bilad al-Sham testify to the continuation of the second flourishing of Raqqa during the Zangid and Ayyubid periods.

Attempts at centralisation of government and increasing warfare between the principalities weakened the Ayyubids power and made them easy prey for the Mongol raids of 657/1259. Cities throughout the Euphrates region were subject to decisive destruction and abandonment. There are records of only smaller restoration works in the following periods. The re-appointment of Raqqa as the main city of the province did not happen until 994/1586.

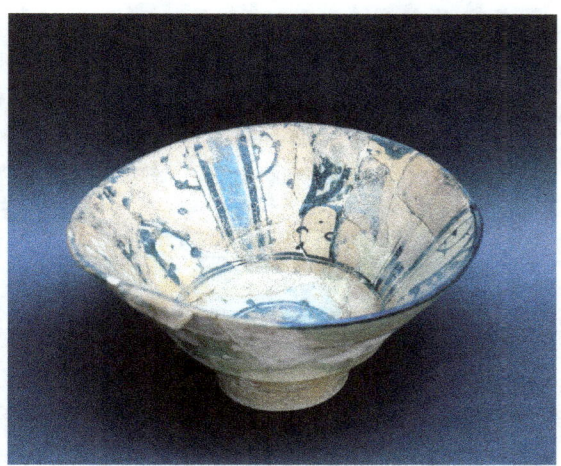

Conical bowl, Raqqa Museum.

ITINERARY VIII   The Euphrates Region: Window onto Mesopotamia
Qal'at Najm

Start early in the morning having prepared yourself for a long trip in an arid landscape. Leave Aleppo via the Aleppo–Jezira Highway. It is possible to schedule an overnight stay in Raqqa (200 km), Deir Ezzor (a further 150 km) or even Palmyra (330 km) from Aleppo.

VIII.1 QAL'AT NAJM

Gloriously situated on the right bank of the River Euphrates, this castle is situated 100 km north-east of Aleppo. Follow the highway to al-Bab (35 km away), Menbij (a further 35 km), then take the south-east exit at Jubb al-Qader. Drive through the village towards the river, arriving in the surreal setting of the castle with the river in the background and the village graveyard in the foreground. Opening times are Wed–Mon 9.00–18.00 during the summer, 9.00–16.00 during the winter. Closed on Tuesdays and during Friday prayers (approx 11.00–13.00). There is an entrance fee.

Arriving via the Aleppo Road, a field of gravestones stretching about 1 km in front of the castle itself provides a surreal setting for the two religious monuments in the middle of this open landscape. One of them is a *maqam*, or small sanctuary, in good condition. The other one is a ruin but still showing the clear outline of proper Ayyubid architecture. It was probably a *madrasa* or *ribat*; arranged around a square courtyard of 7 m sq, with an arch flanked by two smaller entrances on the north and east walls. There is a huge single arch leading to a cross-vaulted *iwan* on the east wall, while the area to the south probably accommodated what was presumably a barrel-vaulted prayer-hall, indicated by the *mihrab*, with a central dome. The sober style of the thoroughly dressed stones along with the execution of the vault attachments, imply a date shortly after the early 7th-/13th-century extension to the castle.

Approaching the castle, dramatically situated high above the banks of the River Euphrates, it rises to a natural elevation of 380 m. This ascending terrain not only provides a natural defensive position but also allows a towering view over the river plain. The castle is completely surrounded by a glacis of dressed stones. The south side also shows remains of a large moat. The defensive wall itself is divided but by slight projections rather than by proper towers.

An inscription above the entrance gateway records the patronage of the Ayyubid prince of Aleppo, al-Zahir Ghazi (d. 613/1216) between 605/1208 and 612/1215. This gateway with two towers to protect it, gives access to a great vaulted passageway with chambers on either side, leading to the upper level. The

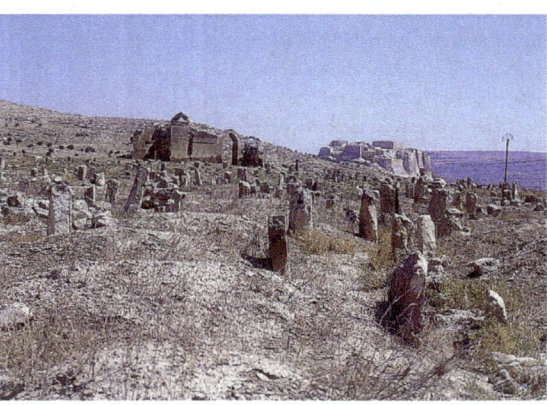

The landscape surrounding Qal'at Najm, with the old graveyard and the citadel in the background.

252

ground-floor arrangement of the palace is around a perfectly square central courtyard 7.05 m sq with an octagonal basin. The *iwans* on the west and east sides have three doorways, while the other two, larger, *iwans* emphasise the principal north–south axis. The layout and the octagonal basin show a remarkable resemblance to that in the Ayyubid palace of Aleppo Citadel, which further supports attribution to the same patron, al-Zahir Ghazi. Attached to the palace is a *hammam* and, at the eastern end of this level, the remains of what was probably a residential structure, forming a terrace offering a magnificent view over the Euphrates valley. At the centre of the first floor is an arsenal divided into several barrel-vaulted halls, which overlooks the fortification. On the same floor, directly above the main gate there is a mosque, indicated by the *mihrab* and featured above the entrance another building inscription attributed to al-Zahir, dated 612/1215.

Thoroughly dressed, stone architecture constructed in the tradition of Aleppine Ayyubid architecture betrays close ties to western Syria. This is in contrast to sites further south-east in the Euphrates Valley where the Mesopotamian/Iranian influence on the Syrian Ayyubid territories is more clearly visible.

VIII.2 MASKANEH, MEDIEVAL BALIS

Return to Menbij. From there, take the highway south following the road signs to Maskaneh, 100 km away. Upon arriving at the modern town, drive east towards the village of Hosn, separated from Maskaneh by an irrigation canal. The minaret, which was moved 5 km into the village, overlooks Lake Asad. The site is always open to the public.

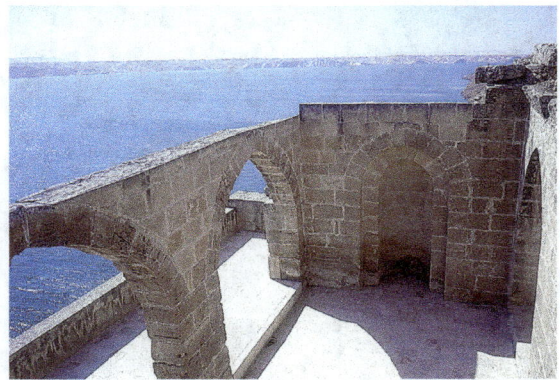

Najm Castle.

Originally, the city sat on a terrace by the river meadows. Still visible are the Byzantine city walls, measuring 400 m x 450 m, and used as defences even in Islamic times. In the 1970s, construction of a dam further south of the river caused the eastern half of the city to drown. Thus, currently, much of Balis sunk beneath the waters of Lake Asad. From afar, an octagonal minaret marks the location of this ancient site. This is the westernmost example of Mesopotamian-influenced mud-brick architecture. The minaret, erected on a square base, has four ornamented bands with inscriptions to indicate the different levels. These inscriptions are either formed from inlaid-brickwork cartouches, or shaped in relief by projecting bricks. The first and third inscriptions mention the ruler

ITINERARY VIII   *The Euphrates Region: Window onto Mesopotamia*
Qal'at Ja'bar

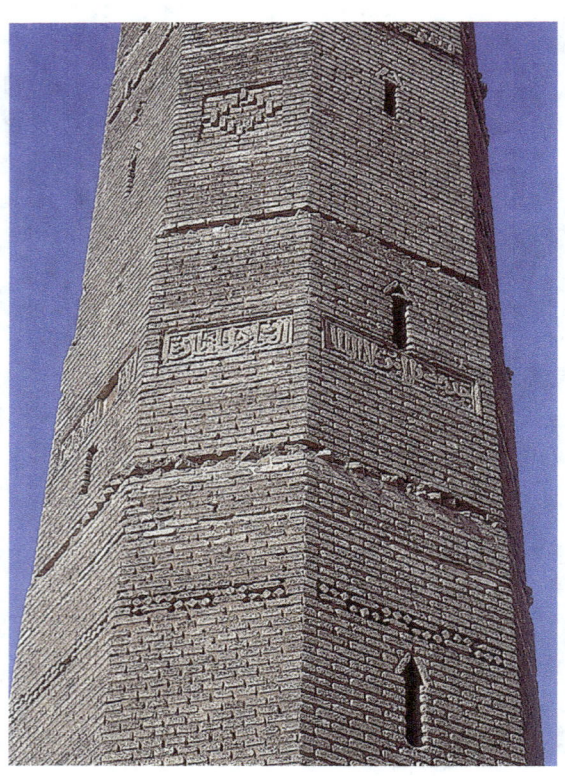

The octagonal brick minaret, Maskaneh, medieval Balis.

to the south of the city wall at a height of about 2 km. It was re-erected in the centre of a square structure built of large limestone blocks, which by that time was still unexcavated and formed a roughly square elevation. Its layout with the projecting bastions on the outer walls, and stucco decoration and wall paintings revealed in the latest excavations, suggest that this structure dates to the Umayyad period (15–132/636–750).

Four km north of the city wall, a mosque with a tripartite prayer-hall once stood. Its *mihrabs*, lavishly decorated with stucco panels, are now in the National Museum of Damascus (I.11). The stucco framing of floral motifs, vine tendrils and inscriptions in floriated *kufic* script, mention the master-builder and the dates 464/1071–2 and 469/1076–7.

VIII.3   QAL'AT JA'BAR

From Maskeneh, drive east towards the modern town of al-Thawra. Cross the Euphrates dam to the north bank of the river and follow the road that curves back towards the lake from which the castle will appear. In order to cross the dam, foreigners must present to the guard-on-duty their passports. Photography is not allowed.

of Aleppo al-'Adil Abu Bakr, uncle of al-Zahir Ghazi, and the name of the master builder. The second inscription details the construction date of 607/1211, while the top one is given over to devotional quotations. Further embellishment comes in the form of ornamental arrow-slit-shaped windows and a row of brickwork lozenges midway up the minaret.

Originally, the Great Mosque to which the minaret belonged was in the part destroyed area of the city but, before flooding the area, the minaret was moved

Qal'at Ja'bar uses a natural elevation as a strategic setting, surrounded by defensive walls and a ditch. The strategic importance of the site is still obvious, overlooking as it does the Euphrates. Now situated on the shore of Lake Asad, its visual impact has increased and it currently forms a peninsula surrounded

ITINERARY VIII   The Euphrates Region: Window onto Mesopotamia
Raqqa

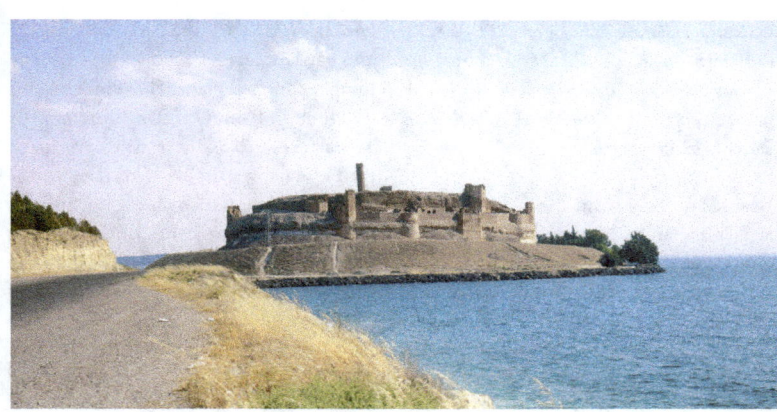

Qal'at Ja'bar, general view.

by the intensely blue waters of the artificial lake.
The fortification stretches 320 m from north to south and 70 m from east to west, surrounded by two curtain walls both provided with more than 35 salient towers. In the lower part, the towers are of limestone. The upper parts – largely restored after 1972 – are made of baked bricks of semi-circular, semi-octagonal or rectangular shapes. The walls between the towers are provided with niches containing arrow slits.
The entrance at the south-west corner of the walls, topped by a small arch, has two towers that guard it. Integrated into the south-western curtain wall, a large building with a particularly well-preserved brick decoration rises immediately above the entrance. The huge inner-vault construction is partly preserved.
A cylindrical minaret on a 5 m-high square base rises from the middle of the fortress. Constructions attached to its east side were probably from a mosque that was later during the Mamluk period converted into workshops. An inscription dating to 569/1173, and naming Nur al-Din who was the patron of vast restoration works at the site, marks the upper part of the minaret. The inscription, flanked by two bands of continuous saltire crosses, is topped by a row of dogtooth moulding. Four arched windows, connected by pearl borders alternating with inlaid lozenges of patterned brick, appear on the upper part of the minaret.

VIII.4 RAQQA

Return to the highway and drive eastwards for the remaining 25 km to the city of Raqqa.

VIII.4.a Raqqa Museum

Raqqa Museum is located on Rashid Street just north of its crossing with al-Jalaa street.

ITINERARY VIII   *The Euphrates Region: Window onto Mesopotamia*
Raqqa

Opening times are Wed–Mon 9.00–18.00 during the summer, 9.00–16.00 during the winter. Closed on Tuesdays and during Friday prayers (approx 11.00–13.00). There is an entrance fee.

Besides objects from the 'Abbasid palaces in the area, a vast collection of Zangid-Ayyubid glazed pottery is on show in the main room and the two first-floor side rooms to the left. Raqqa was famous for its sophisticated industry of fine glazed wares in the Middle Ages for which broad evidence exists at the industrial sites of Tell Zujaj and Tell Aswad, west of the ancient city walls. The showcases in the central and upper left-hand rooms contain wasters, caked together shards and raw material such as kiln bars and lumps of melted glass. These indicate the existence of once-active kilns nearby as wasters such as these were produced in the glazing process. Sketches of the kilns elucidate the advanced techniques used for the production of ceramics in medieval Raqqa. In other rooms, one can admire the finished pieces that are of different qualities and decorated with various patterns: incised wares of the $5^{th}/11^{th}$ and $6^{th}/12^{th}$ centuries, and the technically more advanced underglaze painted wares with turquoise or transparent glazes from the $6^{th}/12^{th}$ and early $7^{th}/13^{th}$ centuries. The most precious pieces among them are the lustre-decorated wares. The decoration, which shines golden in different tinges, was applied to the glaze in a complicated procedure that required two thoroughly directed firing processes. Most remarkable are the lustre-decorated tiles showing human figures. Glazed tiles would have decorated the walls of prestigious buildings such as palaces.

The turquoise-glazed tiles (in the main, central, room in the showcase on the left wall) were floor tiles. Stucco was very popular as interior decoration for prestigious buildings, and had various decorative uses such as for inscription panels and floral motifs. The fragments from stucco windows with coloured glass from the Qasr al-Banat offer a glimpse of the interior furnishings for an early medieval palace at Raqqa.

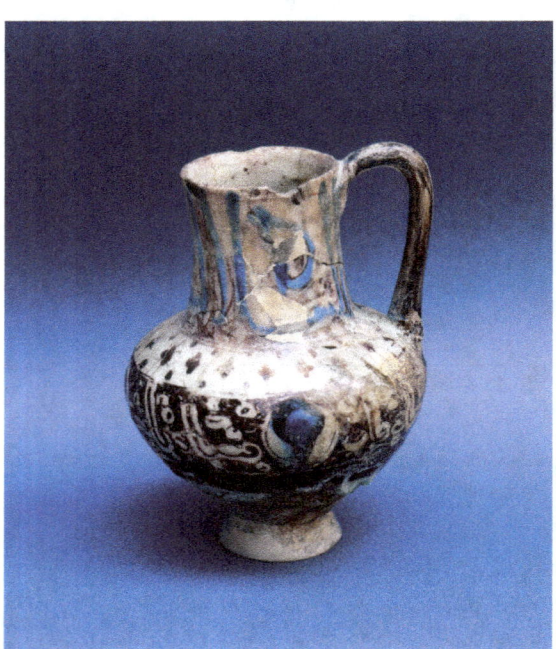
Ewer, Raqqa Museum.

ITINERARY VIII   The Euphrates Region: Window onto Mesopotamia
Raqqa

Turquoise blue fragment,
Raqqa Museum.

Painted stucco,
Raqqa Museum.

Painted tiles,
Raqqa Museum.

Turquoise blue fragment

The pale colour of the clay seen on this fragment of ceramic indicates that both the brilliant turquoise and the blue underglaze are both features of Syrian 6th/12th century pottery made in Raqqa, which lasted until the middle of the 7th/13th century. Measuring 5.5 cm in length and 5 cm in width, the fragmentary decoration reveals a band of beautiful *thuluth* calligraphy in relief. This period also witnessed the transition from angular *kufic* script to the more cursive scripts, although it was popular to use *kufic* for decorative purposes.

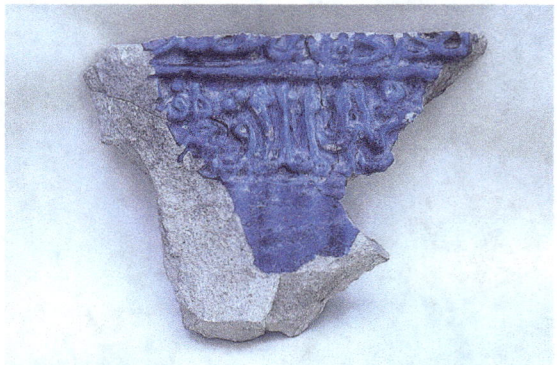

Ewer

This ewer dates to the first half of the 7th/13th century, typical as it is of the type of luxurious Raqqa ware produced before the Mongol invasion of 658/1260. It has a bulbous body, cylindrical neck with a slightly flaring rim and a handle that juts out at rim-level descending to the edge of the body at a right angle. More usually, decorations on such vessels are arranged in bands featuring glittering lustre patterns with underglazed dots and stripes of cobalt blue.

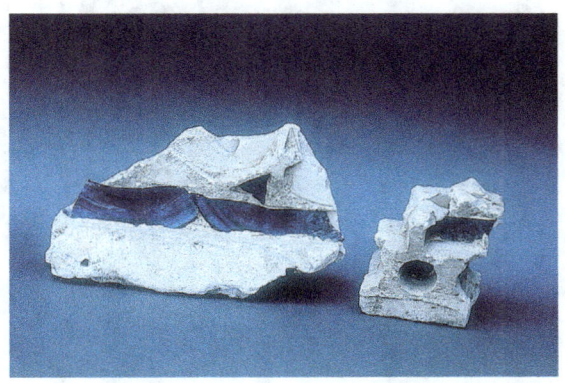

Painted stucco

The fragments featured here come from the pierced windows of Qasr al-Banat and date to the middle of the 6th/12th century during which time the palace was under Zangid rule. The fashion of decorating buildings with carved and painted stucco was most prominent in the region of Raqqa. The style came from the East under the patronage of the Atabeg and

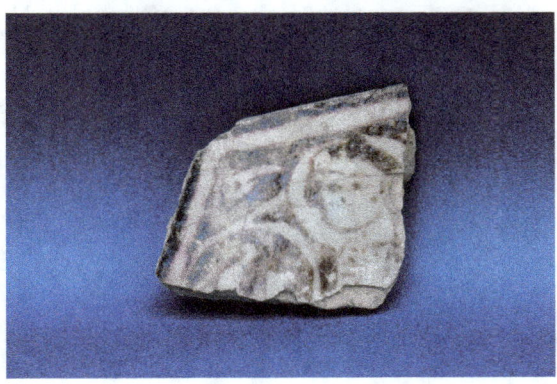

ITINERARY VIII   *The Euphrates Region: Window onto Mesopotamia*
Raqqa

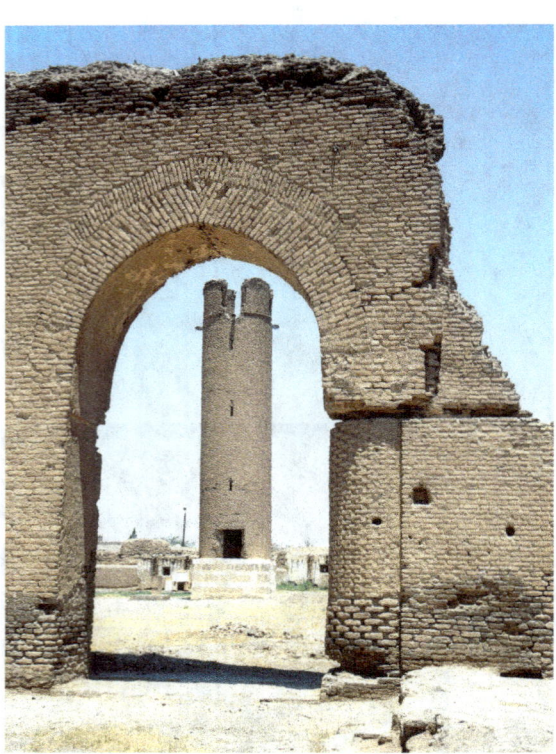

Great Mosque of al-Rafiqa.

by the aesthetic appeal of the beauty mark often seen on the cheek; all such images had swirling arabesque fillers. These particular examples, although fragmentary, still offer glimpses of their fine, lustre decoration. They also came from Qasr al-Banat.

VIII.4.b Great Mosque of al-Rafiqa

From the museum, turn east to reach Seyf al-Dawla street. From there walk north towards the centre of the old city for some 400 m, crossing the main east-west axis called 23 Shbat Street. All that remains of the original mosque is the minaret and part of the courtyard's hypostyle hall. The site is always open to public.

The original structure, with monumental dimensions of 112.6 m x 97.3 m, dates to the 'Abbasid caliph al-Mansur in 155/773. Access to the mosque is through one of several doors: there are two doorways in the west wall, two in the east wall and three in the north wall. Double arcades on three sides surround the almost-square courtyard, while the prayer-hall to the south is divided into three aisles by two rows of columns. According to the inscription on the façade of the prayer-hall, or *qibla riwaq*, the reconstruction works were supported by Nur al-Din bin Zangi in 561/1166.

A square, stone base supports the cylindrical minaret, which appears to have been set, randomly, in the courtyard. The sole decoration is a vertical row of arrow-slit-shaped windows with a row of four, arched windows above.

Ayyubid rulers, with examples found in Bosra and Damascus.

Painted tiles

These tiles were luxurious items destined for palatial settings. They would have hexagonal-, octagonal-, or star-shaped formations and be placed next to each other as wall-to-wall tessellations. Often, the tiles feature floral and vegetal designs, animal motifs, hunting scenes, and figurative portraits of courtly life, like musicians and entertainers distinguished

Stylistically, the minaret strongly resembles that of Qalʿat Jaʿbar, erected by Nur al-Din, and is therefore attributable to the reconstruction activity documented in the inscription of the *qibla riwaq* by the same ruler.

VIII.4.c Qasr al-Banat

From the Rafiqa mosque, walk east towards the old city walls and keeping the walls to your left turn south crossing again 23 Shbat street. Just past the point where there is a break in the wall are the remains of Qasr al-Banat located in a small public garden. If you find the gate to the site is closed, residents from the house opposite may help you secure access.

Going inside the city wall, about 400 m north of the Gate of Baghdad and 150 m from the eastern wall, we find the Qasr al-Banat, "The Maidens' Palace". There is no reference to a palace inside the city walls in the historical sources, and the name is supposed to have come from a local tradition that bears no relation to the original structure. The lack of historical information also makes the dating and the attribution to a certain ruler impossible. According to the ceramic material and the coinage found in sondages in the palace, the foundation of the building was conducted in ʿAbbasid times, probably during the reign of Abu Jaʿfar al-Mansur or Harun al-Rashid, followed by several later phases of renovations. References to a Zangid palace in the historical sources, along with stylistic criteria relating to the stucco decoration and the four-*iwans*-in-axial-symmetry layout that later became

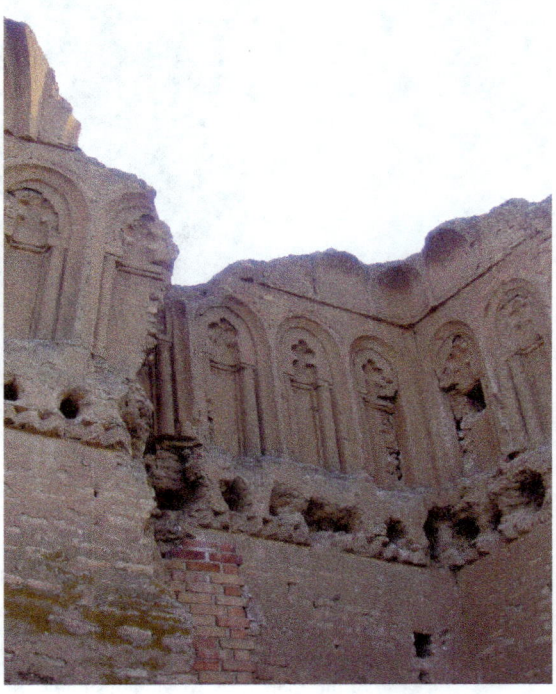

Qasr al-Banat, Raqqa.

a distinctive feature of Ayyubid palatial architecture, point to a date some time in the Zangid period.

The roughly square structure measuring 42 m x 44 m contains 40 so far excavated rooms. The entrance is on the north wall; after crossing two rooms, one turns left and reaches the core of the monument: a square courtyard provided with an *iwan* on each side. A brick-built well that probably had a marble basin furnishes the centre of the courtyard, itself paved with stone slabs. The west, south and east sides

Raqqa

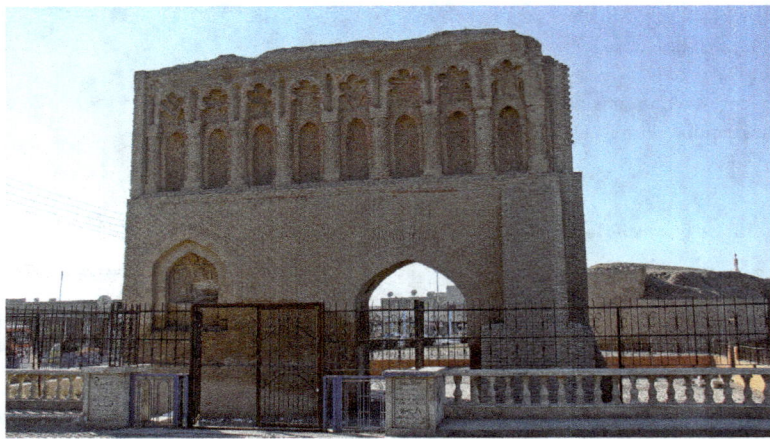

Bab Baghdad (Baghdad Gate), Raqqa.

comprise a single *iwan*, while a tripartite *iwan* accentuates the north side of the courtyard.

Most remarkably in the western part of the palace, there is a square room with a row of decorative stucco niches on the upper part of the 8.7 m-high walls, still extant. A similar room exists in the eastern part of the monument where most of the rooms are paved with stone slabs. Exceptional also is the additional room to the north-west of the entrance that was paved with octagonal and round, glazed tiles. Remains of stucco-decorated windows and wall decorations, as well as wall paintings found during excavation works, give some idea of the once lavish decoration of the palace.

VIII.4.d Bab Baghdad

From Qasr al-Banat walk 600 m southward parallel to the cornice street which runs along the old city walls. Located on the south-west corner of the horseshoe-shaped medieval city of Raqqa, and on the corner of the modern Corniche and Hisham bin 'Abd Malek Streets, Bab Baghdad is a freestanding structure that today stands separated from the city walls to its north and east.

Probably the earliest monument going back to the revival of the medieval city after its heyday as the 'Abbasid capital in the $2^{nd}/8^{th}$ century is the so-called Gate of Baghdad. It is located on the southeast corner of the thoroughly restored inner city wall. Originally, the gate was integrated into the outer city wall, but this exterior structure has not survived. The noticeable lack of any fortifications on this gate indicates that it may have served for ceremonial purposes.

The brick-built monument must have been 14.5 m deep in its original state. The gate was not a solid block but included chambers and it must have been about 18 m wide. Designed with a symmetrical façade and a main, central gate flanked by blind windows, it is surmounted by a row of decorated niches. These carved niches follow a style closely related to the late 3rd-/9th-century Qasr al-'Ashiq in Baghdad.

Since decorated niches were in use up until the Zangid period in the mid-6th/-12th century, the sophisticated construction of four-centred arches is a later development. It is likely that the Gate of Baghdad, constructed in the 4th/10th or even 5th/11th centuries, belongs to the first phase of rehabilitation works. The works are attributable either to the local dynasties of the Numairids (r. 401–64/1010–1071/2), or to the 'Uqailids (r. 464–529/1071/2–1135), who held the area under Seljuq suzerainty after their conquest of the Jazira in 479/1086.

SCENIC OPTION

VIII.5 **TADMUR**

The wonderful oasis of Palmyra lies 280 km south-east of Raqqa when driving through the desert. Take public transport or drive across the Bridge of al-Raqqa from Corniche al-Nahr street and turn west for some 30 km. At al-Mansoura take the south-bound route all the way to al-Sukhneh and from there turn west again to reach Tadmur, or Palmyra. Public transportation is available from there back to Damascus.

Tadmur is one of the most enchanting places in Syria. Its ancient wealth grew out of the desert trading routes between Mesopotamia to the east, the Mediterranean to the west, as well as trade from Arabia in the south.

VIII.5.a **Qal'at Tadmur**

A towering medieval fortress rises on an elevation of the Palmyran mountain range overlooking the impressive ruins of Roman Palmyra.

During the Ayyubid period, Palmyra belonged to the principality of Homs. Within the Roman city there are inscriptions that testify to the transformation of the Temple of Bel, located at the southern end of the colonnaded street, into a fortress by the Seljuq ruler Nasir al-Din Muhammad bin Shirkuh in 532/1137 who later, in 576/1180, added a mosque.

The medieval citadel is similar to the many other Arab citadels visited during this exhibition. A deep ditch surrounds this towering medieval fortress, only accessible via a bridge that rests on three pillars. The rooms, arranged around five courtyards, rise in elevation towards the north-west tower on the most prominent part of the hill. So far, the citadel's origins are largely unexplored, but ceramic evidence dates the site back to the Ayyubid period and suggests that it took over the function of the citadel that had once been the Temple of Bel.

THE EASTERN INFLUENCE IN SYRIA

Verena Daiber

Most striking is the abundant and almost exclusive use of mud bricks – a common building material in Iraq and Iran. This material, naturally available along the banks of the River Euphrates, had already been used for centuries at Raqqa, once the 'Abbasid capital and therefore under influence of the architecture of the 'Abbasid heartland. Taking into consideration the geographical setting of Raqqa as the western extension of Mesopotamia, clearly separated from the densely populated urban centres of western Syria by an expansive desert, it is considered to be the Mesopotamian part of Syria and the westernmost extension of Iraqi and Iranian architectural modes.

The advent of the Seljuqs in 447/1055, who held their capital in Isfahan, gave a new impetus to the fashion for building techniques and decorative modes in the Eastern style, popular throughout the middle-Euphrates area. The earliest example of the revival of the Eastern influence is probably the 5th-/11th-century Baghdad Gate in Raqqa. The row of decorative blind niches follows the façade layout of the last great 'Abbasid palace in Samarran, Qasr al-'Ashiq (built 264–9/878–82), a tradition that continued in a whole series of Iraqi monuments of the 5th/11th and 6th/12th centuries. The four-centred arch of the gate is an Iranian structure that is simply not feasible if built with large stones. Other adaptations of Iranian ornamental forms, arising from the type of material used, are high-relief inscriptions, stalactites, patterned colonnettes and geometrical designs. In Qal'at Ja'bar, Raqqa and Abu Hurayra, round minarets – a predominant shape in Iran – were built in contrast to the square

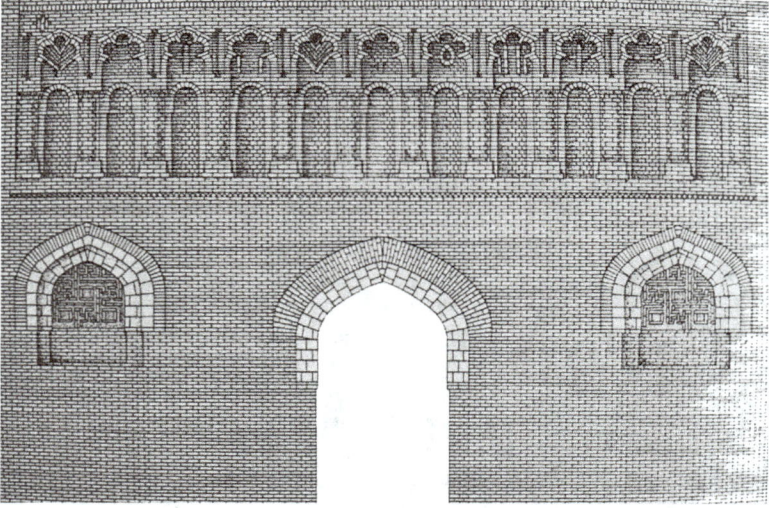

A drawing reproducing Bab Baghdad (Korn, eds Daiber and Becker, 2004, fig.2).

counterparts of western Syria. Another ground plan that has a long tradition in Iran is the four-*iwans*-in-axial-symmetry structure around a courtyard. This layout becomes very common in later Ayyubid architecture and appears for the first time in the early 6th/12th century Qasr al-Banat in Raqqa.

The Iranian influence is also apparent in interior design. Pierced stucco windows and carved stucco wall-panels are clear signals of the use of materials and workmanship from the East. In Qasr al-Banat, stucco windows with coloured inlaid glass and a frieze of arched stucco niches supported by columns, recall the brickwork niches of the Gate of Baghdad. Lavish stuccos from a mosque and houses in Balis, dated to the late 5th/11th century, feature floral decorations that echo the Samarran and Sassanian forms of the East, rather than influences from the classical tradition.

Eastern influences are also visible in everyday objects. In the early 6th/12th century, Raqqa became the main centre for the production of ceramics. The introduction to the world of ceramics of a new material called Fritware – a fine white material with a high mineral content – helped the development of the technique of underglaze painting. Bright, white and delicate, it imitated the texture of Chinese porcelain. Usage of black or polychrome black, blue and red painting, applied under the glaze also show close ties in colouring and style to the contemporaneous Iranian *mina'i* wares, distinguished from the Syrian wares by their use of the overglaze-painting technique. Some

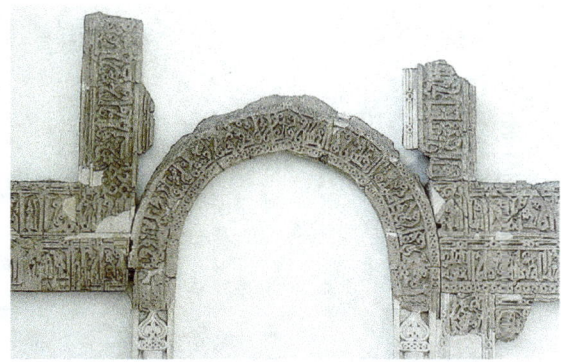

figurative portrayals show strong Asian features; almond eyes and the "moon face" that were a typical Seljuq ideal of beauty. A striking example is the so-called Horseman of Raqqa. The ceramic figurine is 46.5 cm high, depicting a cavalryman in warrior pose with conspicuous Mongol facial features, hairstyle, military dress and horse accoutrements.

Carved stucco panels and niches from Maskaneh, medieval Balis

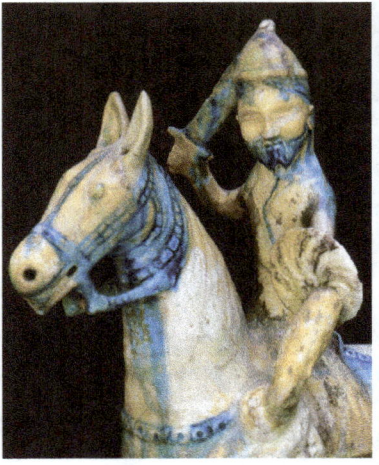

The "Faris al-Raqqa" or the "Horseman of al-Raqqa", National Museum of Damascus (Inv. Num. 5819/٢).

GLOSSARY

Ablaq	From the Turkish *"iplik"*, "rope" or "thread", it is a decorative building technique consisting of alternating courses of contrasting masonry, usually basalt and limestone.
Amir	Military commander, prince or senior official.
Amir al-Mu'minin	Prince of Believers.
Al-Andalus	The name of the Iberian Peninsula (Spain and Portugal) under Muslim rule, which lasted from 92/711 to 896/1491.
Arabesque	Arabic design of intertwined leaves and geometric shapes developed during the Islamic era.
'Ashura	Tenth day of Muharram, the first month of the Muslim calendar, commemorated as a holy day to mourn the martyrdom of the Prophet's grandchildren, al-Hasan and al-Husayn.
Astrolabe	Scientific tool used in astronomy to measure the altitude of the sun or the stars and to establish directions in navigation.
Atabeg	Commander-in-Chief of armies and tutor of young princes in matters of leadership.
'Atiq	Freed-slave.
Ayat al-Kursi	Literally, "The Verse of the Chair", which is an excerpt from the Qur'an (2: 255), popularly memorised and regularly inscribed on amulets and monuments. It is a favourite verse among Muslims because it mentions the many names of God.
Bab	Gate, door.
Banu/Bani	Literally "Sons of", members of a clan.
Barbicane	A tower that is part of a defensive structure.
Barrani	Literally the "outer area". In the *hammam*, it designates the cold room because it is located farthest from the furnace.
Basmala	Islamic blessing by calling the name of God.
Bilad al-Sham	Geographical area that includes contemporary Jordan, Palestine and Syria.
Birka	Man-made lake.
Burg/Burj	Fort, bastion or tower, sometimes surrounded by an outer wall.
Calidarium	(From Latin) hot room.
Caliph	From Arabic *Khalifa*, literally "successor", the supreme head of the Muslim community and the lineage of whom descends directly to that of the Prophet.
Caliphate	Charge or territory under the power of the caliph.
Caravanserai	Hostel along main communication routes to accommodate travellers and safeguard their goods.
Cavea	Seats in the auditorium of a theatre.
Darb al-Hajj	The pilgrimage route.
Dervish	Member of a Muslim religious order noted for devotional exercises.
Dinar	Islamic gold coin.
Dirham	Islamic silver coin.
Diwan	Literary compilation.
Donjon	Inner tower, keep or stronghold of a castle.

Glossary

Faranj/Ifranj	The term used by the medieval Arabs for the Franks and used to designate the Crusaders.
Faris	Equestrian, knight.
Faubourg	An ancient French term approximating "suburb"; a town or city.
Fils	Islamic bronze coin.
Fritware	Type of delicate ceramic with high quartz content, which imitates porcelain.
Funduq	Hostel for merchants and their pack animals; store for merchandise and a commercial centre, equivalent to a *caravanserai* or a *khan*.
Hadith	Body of traditions related to the sayings and actions of the Prophet Muhammad and his companions.
Hajj	The "fifth pillar of Islam", the great pilgrimage to Mecca and holy places, which every believer must accomplish at least once during his lifetime if he has the means to do so.
Hammam	Bathhouse.
Hanafi	One of the four Sunni legal schools (Orthodox Islam).
Hanbali	One of the four Sunni legal schools (Orthodox Islam).
Haram	Sacred space that also indicates the prayer-hall of a mosque.
Hashashin	Followers of a Syrian Isma'ili sect known as the Isma'iliyya Nizariyya, known also as the Assassins.
Hijaz	The western district in the Arabian Peninsula.
Hijra	Denotes a departure from one's country and marks Muhammad's flight from Mecca to Madina in the year 622 of the Christian era. The term commemorates the beginning of the Muslim calendar (Arabic *hijra*).
Hisn	Arabic term for a fortified area, such as a tower or citadel.
Hypostyle	Method of building that relies on multiple columns to support a ceiling over a large space.
Ibn/bin	Son of (Arabic).
Imam	One who presides over Islamic prayers, a guide, chief, spiritual model or cleric; sometimes also a politician in Muslim society.
Iqta'	Land granted as payment for administrative and military services.
Isma'ili	Shi'ite sect that accepts Isma'il as the seventh and last imam.
Iwan	Vaulted hall, walled on three sides with a large opening arch.
Jabal	Mountain or mountainous terrain.
Jahiliyya	Pagan period before the advent of Islam.
Jami'	Main mosque used for daily prayers, but one that is large enough for the Friday communal prayers and sermons.
Jihad	Striving towards moral and religious perfection. It can lead to fighting "on the path to God" against dissidents or pagans; holy war undertaken to protect and defend Islamic territories.
Jizya	Personal Tax on non-Muslims within a Muslim State.
Ka'ba	Meaning literally "cube". Temple in Mecca, centre of the Islamic religion.
Khalwa	Small room or cell with few or no windows to which Sufis retreat for solitary meditation.

Khan	An inn offering lodgings for travellers and merchants on the main caravan routes, it also provided a store and was seen in large urban, commercial centres; it designates a stopover along communication routes (see also *funduq* and *caravanserai*).
Khanqa	Monastery or hostel for Sufi travellers and dervishes.
Khatun	Arabised term of the Turkish *"hatun"*, a title of respect for upper-class women.
Khutba	Sermon of the Friday payer.
Kitab	Book.
Kufic	Type of Arabic calligraphy with angular and stylised characters, often highly decorated, used both in early Qur'ans and in foundation inscriptions. Its name is probably due to its attribution to the city of Kufa in Iraq.
Lala	Turkish title for "educator" or "upbringer".
Laqabi	Type of ceramic, the grooves and protrusions of which are highlighted with the application of different coloured glazes.
Lustre	Type of metallic glaze applied to pottery through a sophisticated firing technique.
Machicolation	Defensive architectural structure with protrusions above the gates, towers and walls, through which soldiers would pour hot oil over their enemies below. See also *saqqata*.
Madhhab	Islamic judicial school, the four great Orthodox or Sunnite Islamic submissions of which are: Shafi'i, Malikite, Hanafi and Hanbali.
Madrasa	Islamic school of science (theology, law, Qur'an, etc.) with lodgings for students.
Maliki	One of the four Sunni legal schools (Orthodox Islam).
Manjaniq	Catapult used for siege warfare and introduced into medieval military strategies some time during the 6th/12th century.
Maqam	Structure of one or more architectural units, it usually has a dome that contains the tomb of an important religious figure; a place of worship frequented by pilgrims.
Maqsura	Area of sanctuary in congregational mosques reserved for the *caliph* or the *imam* during public prayer times, usually separated by a latticed screen.
Mar	Saint.
Mashhad	Mausoleum for a martyr, literally "place of witness".
Masjid	Mosque, literally "place of prostration".
Mastaba	Long stone bench against the walls on either side of the entrance to a building.
Mazwala	Sundial.
Mihrab	Arched niche in the wall that indicates the direction of Mecca towards which worshippers face when praying.
Mina'i	Type of over-glazed polychrome ceramic that was popular in 5th-/11th-century Iran and which had a strong impact on regional productions.
Minbar	Pulpit in a mosque from which the *imam* preaches his sermon *(khutba)* to the faithful every Friday at noon prayers.

Glossary

Muhtasib	(Literally, "he who keeps count"). A person in charge of supervising the *suq* to make sure all dealings are fair and legal.
Muqarnas	Architectural decoration made up of concave spherical prisms carved in a stalactite or honeycomb pattern.
Musalla	Prayer hall.
Naskhi	(Literally "copied") one of the most widespread styles of Arabic calligraphic script.
Niello	A black pigmentation used decoratively to accentuate the contrast of in-laid metals.
Noria	Waterwheel (pl. *nawa'ir*).
Order of the Hospital/Hospitallers	Religious and military order, which originated in Europe around the time of the first Crusade (1096–99).
Portcullis	Sliding gate typical of 6th-/12th-century military constructions.
Qadi	Muslim judge.
Qal'a/Qal'at	Citadel, castle.
Qamariyyat	Glass knobs inserted into domes in a rhythmic pattern used both decoratively and as a means of illuminating the space.
Qanat	Subterranean conduit of water; part of a water-distribution network.
Qashani	Ottoman tiles from the 10th/16th century, predominantly blue and green in colour, used to renovate important religious buildings.
Qasr	Palace or castle, from Latin *castrum*.
Qaysariyya	Covered market.
Qibla	Direction of the Ka'ba towards which believers orient themselves for prayer.
Qilla	Keep of a castle.
Qimmim	Colloquial term referring to the furnace of a *hammam*.
Qubba	Dome. By extension, a domed monument or chamber usually built over the grave of a holy person.
Qur'an	(From the root qr', "to recite, to read"). Sacred text of the Islamic revelation, transmitted by the Archangel Gabriel to the Prophet Muhammad.
Riwaq	Arcaded space.
Sabil	Charitable building designed to provide drinking water. A public fountain.
Sahn	Flat, open space. Courtyard preceding the prayer room of a mosque.
Samarra Style	Style of stucco carving popularised in the Abbasid capital of Samarra and categorised into "Samarra A", "Samarra B", and "Samarra C" in which the carving techniques range between floral compartments and flowing abstract lines.
Saqqata	(From the root "s-q-t", "to drop"); the Arabic term for machicolations, a defensive architectural feature usually found protruding from towers and walls and from which hot oil was poured on top of enemies.

Scaena	Stage in a theatre (Roman).
Shafi'i	One of the four legal schools of Orthodox Islam.
Shahada	Profession of Muslim faith: *"La ilaha illa Allah"* ("There is no god but Allah").
Shari'a	(Literally "route", "road"). Islamic precept that the believer must follow in order to stay on the right road to God. Shari'a rules the behaviour of the faithful in the spiritual, legal, social and political spheres and in the concrete aspects of daily life.
al-Sham	Territories including Syria, the Lebanon, Palestine and Trans-Jordan, nowadays Syria.
Sha'riyya	Arabic term to designate a separate quarter for women's prayers.
Shaykh/Sheikh	Elderly man respected for his age and wisdom. Tribal chief or leader of the brotherhood.
Shi'a	Properly Shi'at 'Ali, meaning "the party of 'Ali" whereby 'Ali was the Prophet Muhammad's first cousin, his son-in-law and one of the first believers in Islam. His followers believe him to be the true successor of the Prophet and. therefore, suppressed by the "Sunni" majority.
Shi'i	(Literally "Scission", "section", "party") meaning partisans of 'Ali and of his descendants. Shi'ites reject the legitimacy of the caliphs who succeeded after the Prophet's death.
Spandrel	Triangular area between two arches, or between the outside curve of an arch and the horizontal line from its apex, and the vertical line from the pillar supporting it.
Spolia	(Latin *spolium*). Architectural elements taken from earlier monuments.
Squinch	Arch placed diagonally at each corner of a square and filled decoratively with a variety of methods, providing the transition from the cubical walls to the sphere of the dome.
Stucco	Plaster applied to cover architectural surfaces often decorated by carving, piercing and painting.
Sufi	Mystical or ascetic order in Islam. Mystic or devotee.
Sufism	Derived from "suf" meaning wool, the fabric in which ascetics (*Sufis*) clothed themselves. Since the $2^{nd}/8^{th}$ century, the term denotes Islamic mysticism.
Sultan	Title used for a supreme sovereign such as a political leader without ousting or imposing on a caliphate.
Sunna	For Orthodox Islam, traditions of the Prophet in which legal advisers and theologians find support and the foundations on which to establish the content of Islamic law arising from the Qur'an.
Sunni	Follower of Sunna. "Sunnism", a political and religious system constituting the majority of the Muslim community and opposed to "Shi'ism". Sunnites are divided into four theological schools: Maliki, Hanbali, Hanafi, Shafi'i.
Suq	Market.
Sur	Wall, ramparts.
Sura	Chapter of the Qur'an.
Tabula ansata	Rectangular tablet generally used for inscriptions having triangular "handles".

Glossary

Templars	Members of a religious military order founded by the Crusaders in Jerusalem 1118–1312.
Tepidarium	Warm areas of a public bath.
Tessera	(Latin term, pl. tesserae). Small pieces of ceramic that make up a mosaic.
Thuluth	Cursive calligraphic script commonly used in monumental inscriptions in Muslim religious buildings.
Turba	Private burial place, mausoleum, tomb.
'Ulama	Experts of Islamic theological and legal sciences.
Waqf	Endowment in perpetuity, usually land or property, the revenues from which pay for the upkeep of religious foundations.
Warraqat	Paper-mill.
Zarif	Beautiful.
Zawiya	Edifice for religious teaching, dedicated to prepare men to become sheikhs. It includes the shrine of a saint and constructed in the place of his birth.
Zellij	Small enamelled-ceramic tiles used to decorate the exterior or interior of buildings.

SELECTED HISTORICAL PERSONALITIES

This list offers further but not exhaustive information on the personalities, dynasties and places mentioned in this book. The information is organised into categories, each ordered chronologically where appropriate.

Personalities from the Early Islamic period

Khidr
A popular legendary figure mentioned in the Qur'an (18: 60–82) who bears some resemblance to the Christian figure of St George. His name relates him with lush greenery and, by extension, water sources. His role is to guide and encourage travellers to have patience during their hardships.

Bahira
A Syriac Christian monk residing in the city of Bosra, southern Syria, in the late 6th century AD. According to Islamic historiography, he met the child (or adolescent) Muhammad when the latter was travelling with his uncle on a Meccan caravan and predicted Muhammad's future.

Khadija (d. 619/three years before Hijra)
The first wife of the Prophet Muhammad and the first convert to Islam, she was a successful merchant and a main supporter of her husband.

Fatima (d. 11/632)
The daughter of the Prophet Muhammad and Khadija, she became the wife of 'Ali bin Abi Talib, the Prophet's cousin. She is the only child of Muhammad to have a continuous line of descendents.

'Umar bin al-Khattab (r. 13–23/634–44)
The second caliph of Islam and a major force behind the creation and expansion of the Islamic Empire, conquering lands beyond the Arab peninsula and establishing new Islamic cities. He was famous for being strong-willed, austere and valiant.

Hussein bin 'Ali (Imam Hussein)
Grandson of the Prophet Muhammad, the second son of Fatima and 'Ali. His death, at Karbala on 10 Muharram 61/10 October 680, is a focal point in Islamic history and a tragedy that is mourned by all Muslims.

Imam Muhsin
Alleged great-grandson of the Prophet Muhammad, an aborted child of Hussein.

Al-Walid bin 'Abd al-Malik (r. 86–96/705–15)
The sixth caliph of the Umayyad Dynasty and founder of the Great Umayyad Mosque in Damascus.

'Umar II bin 'Abd al-'Aziz (r. 99–101/717–20)
The eighth caliph of the Umayyad Dynasty, known for his pious modesty and his aversion to worldly materialism.

Isma'il bin Ja'far al-Sadiq (d. 148/765)
The son of the seventh Shi'i Imam. His followers grew into a considerable movement by the 4th/10th century and were generally persecuted as a subversive political movement, except during the Fatimid Dynasty when they prospered.

Main Islamic Leaderships

Rightly Guided Caliphs (11–40/632–61)
The first four successors of the Prophet Muhammad. Their leadership focused on the consolidation of the Muslim community after the Prophet's death, massive territorial expansion and the establishment of civil welfare, particularly in securing water and nourishment for all the new settlements, and the careful division of booty from their conquests.

Umayyad Caliphate (41–132/661–750)
The first Islamic Dynasty, founded by the Banu Umayya, a wealthy family of merchants from the Quraysh tribe in Mecca. They made Damascus their capital and constructed the first consciously Islamic monuments such as the Dome of the Rock in Jerusalem and the Great Umayyad Mosque of Damascus, as well as Arabising the systems of administration and coinage. The Umayyads were defeated by the 'Abbasids. One member of this dynasty, 'Abd al-Rahman al-Dakhil, escaped massacre and fled to al-Andalus (Muslim Spain and Portugal) where a large Muslim community from Arabia and Syria had already settled. The Arabs remained in Spain until 897/1492.

'Abbasid Caliphate (132–656/750–1261)
The second Islamic Dynasty, founded by Banu 'Abbas and tracing their ancestry to the family of the Prophet. Due to several political and economic factors, they revolted against the Umayyads, defeated them in 132/750, and moved the capital of the Islamic Empire to Mesopotamia where they founded the city of Baghdad. This is considered one of the Golden Ages of Islam, which witnessed a great scientific and literary renaissance, transmission of knowledge, wealth and culture. The 'Abbasids ruled for a long time and autonomous dynasties emerged within their realm, especially in the later years. They were defeated by the Mongols in 656/1261. A makeshift 'Abbasid caliphate was set up by the last caliph's uncles who had fled to Cairo, where he gave legitimacy to the Mamluks and helped fill the political vacuum. This puppet caliphate lasted until 750/1517, when the Mamluks were defeated by the Ottomans.

Fatimid Caliphate (297–567/909–1171)
An Arab Islamic Dynasty that became the first Shi'ite caliphate, reigning for 300 years and causing a schism in the history of the Islamic community, since they denied the legitimacy of the 'Abbasids. The Fatimids traced their ancestry to Fatima, the daughter of the Prophet and they established their stronghold in Tunis. From there, they conquered Egypt and founded the victorious capital city of Cairo in 358/969, launching a period marked for its creative and artistic production and wealth. The Fatimids dominated the Mediterranean taking rule of Tunis, Sicily, Sardinia, Egypt, Palestine and the Hijaz, including the holy cities of Mecca, Medina and Jerusalem. They were contained by the Seljuqs, Turkish warriors, and finally defeated by Salah al-Din, founder of the Ayyubid Dynasty, in 567/1171.

The Seljuq Sultanate (431–590/1040–1193)
Turkish warrior nomads who achieved great military and political power in Iran and Iraq establishing a powerful dynasty within the heart of the 'Abbasid court in Baghdad. Toghril Beg

(d. 455/1063) was the first Seljuq Sultan to take control of Baghdad, the 'Abbasid capital, seeking to empower 'Abbasid authority against both the Fatimid Caliphate and the Byzantine Empire. The influential Nizam al-Mulk (d. 485/1092) was Grand Vizier of the first and second Seljuq Sultans in Baghdad where he became a patron of some of the earliest *madrasa*s. He was also the first to be given the title of Atabeg. Some Seljuq Turkish warrior tribes settled in Asia Minor, where they were known as the Seljuq al-Rum, while ruling over Syria and Jerusalem, making Damascus their capital.

The Ayyubids (564–658/1169–1260)
This relatively short-lived but influential dynasty followed in the Seljuq spirit of militarisation and active re-education. It was founded by Salah al-Din bin Ayyub (Saladin) who first established power in Egypt and then took Damascus as his capital in 570/1174. He conquered Aleppo in 579/1183, liberated Jerusalem in 583/1187, and left a long line of succession that ruled over Egypt, Syria, Palestine and Yemen as a dominant military power with strong mercantile ties. The Ayyubids were defeated by the Mongols and succeeded by the Mamluks.

The Mamluks (648–922/1250–1517)
Military slaves who founded an enduring and powerful sultanate in Egypt and Syria in succession to the Ayyubids. The early Mamluks, mostly of Turkish Circassian origin, followed in the footsteps of the Ayyubids, playing a decisive role in saving Islam from both Crusader invasions and Mongol raids.

The Ottomans (698–1342/1299–1922)
A dynasty of Turkish warriors, which rose to power in western Anatolia after the Seljuq al-Rum. In 856/1453, the Ottomans took over the Byzantine capital Constantinople, becoming a world power. Their supremacy peaked during the reign of Suleyman the Magnificent (926–73/1520–66) when they came to dominate the largest territory including parts of Eastern Europe, the Near East and North Africa.

Some Medieval Dynasties

Buyids or Buwayhids (321–410/933–1019)
A Persian tribe that took over Iran, Iraq and the Jazira. They were defeated by the Seljuqs.

Hamdanids (333–406/944–1015)
An Arab tribe that ruled in Aleppo and Mosul. They were defeated by the Buyids in Mosul and by the Fatimids in Aleppo.

'Uqailids (370–489/989–1069)
An Arab tribe in Mosul, the Jazira and Aleppo. They were defeated by the Seljuqs.

Mirdasids (402–72/1011–79)
An Arab tribe belonging to the Banu Kilab in Aleppo and its environs. They were defeated by the 'Uqailids.

The Seljuqs in Syria (471–97/1094–1104)
A short-lived but influential Turkish dynasty that was founded by Taj al-Dawla Tutush (d. 487/1094) and his wife Safwat al-Mulk (d. 512/1119) who made themselves autonomous

Selected Historical Personalities

from the Seljuq leadership in Baghdad. Their two sons, Ridwan (d. 508/1113) and Duqaq (497/1104), rivalled each other and ruled over Aleppo and Damascus respectively. Defeated by the Atabegs, who founded the Burid Dynasty.

The Burids (471–549/1078–1154)
A dynasty founded by the Atabeg of the Seljuq princes in Syria to rule over Damascus and Aleppo. Defeated by Nur al-Din bin Zangi.

The Atabegs (478–577/1085–1181)
Military warriors, usually Turkish, appointed as teachers to young Seljuq princes. They often became powerful governors of cities under the Seljuq domain.

The Artuqids (483–778/1090–1376)
Turkish dynasty in Mardin and Diyar Bakr (northern Syria and Asia Minor) who were defeated by the Ottomans.

The Zangids in Syria (541–69/1146–73)
A short-lived but influential dynasty that was begun by the Atabeg 'Imad al-Din Zangi (521–41/1127–46) of Mosul and Aleppo and continued by his son Nur al-Din Mahmud bin Zangi (541–69/1146–73) who took over Damascus and unified the Syrian cities under his rule. Defeated by the Ayyubids, but Zangid branches continued to exist in the Jazira and Mesopotamia up until the 7th/13th century.

Sequence of the Ayyubid Dynasty in Syria (570–658/1174–1260)

564–89/1169–93: Al-Nasir I Salah al-Din (Saladin)

DAMASCUS	592/1197: Al-Afdal Nur al-Din 'Ali
	615/1218: Al-'Adil I Sayf al-Din Abu Bakr
	624/1227: Al-Mu'azzam Sharaf al-Din 'Isa
	635/1237: Al-Ashraf Muzaffar al-Din Musa
	635/1237: Al-Salih 'Imad al-Din Isma'il (first reign)
	637/1240: Al-'Adil II Sayf al-Din Abu Bakr
	637/1240: Al-Salih Najm al-Din Ayyub (first reign)
	643/1245: Al-Salih 'Imad al-Din Isma'il (second reign)
	647/1249: Al-Salih Najm al-Din Ayyub (second reign)
	648/1260: Al-Mu'azzam Turanshah
	658/1260: Al-Nasir Salah al-Din Yusuf
HOMS	574–81/1178–85: Muhammad
	637/1139: Al-Mujahid Shirkuh
	644/1245: Al-Mansur Ibrahim
	661/1262: Al-Ashraf Muzaffar al-Din
HAMA	574–87/1178–91: Al-Muzaffar I Taqi al-Din 'Umar
	617/1220: Al-Mansur I Muhammad
	626/1229: Al-Nasir Qilij Arslan
	642/1240: Al-Muzaffar II Taqi al-Din Mahmud

	683/1284: Al-Mansur II Muhammad
	698/1298: Al-Muzaffar III
	The dynasty continued in Hama under the Mamluk reign as follows:
	710–33/1310–31: Al-Mu'ayyid 'Imad al-Din Isma'il Abu al-Fida'
	742/1341: Al-Afdal Nasir al-Din Muhammad
ALEPPO	579–613/1193–1216: Al-Zahir Ghiyath al-Din Ghazi
	(Succeeded by wife Dayfa Khatun who died in 636/1238)
	634/1236: Al-'Aziz Ghiyath al-Din Muhammad
	658/1260: Al-Nasir Salah al-Din Yusuf

Scientists, Poets, Scholars and Artisans

Al-Akhtarini (5th/11th century)
An artisan from Aleppo, famous for his carpentry and inlaid work, the most famous of which is the *mihrab* of Madrasa Hallawiyya in Aleppo.

Abu al-'Ala' al-Ma'arri (449/1057)
A Syrian philosopher, linguist and poet. His most famous work is *Risalat al-Ghufran* (Epistle on Forgiveness).

Ibn al-'Arabi, Muhyi al-Din (d. 638/1240)
One of Islam's greatest mystic philosophers (Sufis), a teacher and a writer. He was born in Murcia (Muslim Spain), travelled widely, and settled in Damascus where his tomb continues to be an important site of pilgrimage. His most famous works are *Futuhat Makkiyya* (Meccan Illuminations) and *Fusus al-Hikam* (Bezels of Wisdom).

Abu Shama, Shihab al-Din (665/1267)
A professor and historian of Damascus during the Zangid and Ayyubid periods. He taught in the Madrasa al-Rukniyya. He is author of *Kitab al-Rawdatayn fi Akhbar al-Dawlatayn* (The Book of the Two Gardens in the News of the Two States).

Muhammad al-Ghazali (d. 505/1111)
An influential scholar and theologian who was patronised by the Seljuq court in Baghdad and later resided in Damascus. Author of *Ihya' 'Ulum al-Din* (Revival of the Religious Sciences).

Al-Jazari, Abu al-'Izz Badi' al-Zaman
A genius scientist and inventor. He was chief engineer at the Artuqid court for which he composed his illustrated guide to the construction of automata entitled *Al-Jami' bayn al-'Ilm wa-l-'Amal al-Nafi' fi Sina'at al-Hiyal* (A Compendium on the Theory and Practice of the Mechanical Arts).

Ibn Jubayr (d. 614/1217)
A pilgrim traveller from al-Andalus and a chronicler. He visited the Holy Lands and Syria during the Ayyubid period.

'Abd al-Karim al-Harith al-Muhandis (5th/11th century)
A geometrician from Damascus, famous for his wood carving on the gates of Bimaristan Nur

al-Din.

Al-Mutanabbi (4th/10th century)
A famous Syrian court poet and panegyrist during the Hamdanid period.

Abu Qasim 'Ali ibn 'Asakir (d. 571/1176)
A great historian of the city of Damascus and member of the prominent Banu 'Asakir family, which was active between 470–660/1077–1261. His work is entitled *Tarikh Madinat Dimashq* (History of the City of Damascus).

Ibn Khaldun (d. 732–84/1332–82)
A prominent thinker, politician and educator of the Arab Muslim world. He is considered the founder of modern sociology.

Usama bin Munqidh (d. 584/1188)
A high-ranking knight and poet from a prominent Arab tribe in Syria, Banu Munqidh, who resided in Shayzar Castle, west of Hama.

Ibn Mutran (d. 587/1191)
A medical scientist and prominent physician at the court of Salah al-Din (Saladin).

Ridwan ibn al-Sa'ati
A Damascene clockmaker and author of the scientific treatise *Fi Sina'at al-Sa'at wa Faw'iduha* (On the Construction of Clocks and Their Uses).

Ibn Shaddad, 'Izz al-Din al Halabi (b. 613/1217; d. 684/1285)
Syrian author of topographical and historical works. His most famous work is entitled *Al-A'laq al-Khatira fi Dhikr Umara' al-Sham wa al-Jazira* (The Crucial Essence in the Mention of the Princes of Syria and the Jazira).

Ibn Shaddad, Baha' al-Din (d. 632/1234)
A military judge (*qadi 'askar*) during Salah al-Din's reign, he also wrote a biography of Salah al-Din entitled *Al-Nawadir al-Sultaniyya wa al Mahasin al-Yusufiyya* (The Rare and Excellent History of Saladin).

Sibt ibn al-Jawzi (d. 655/1257)
A charismatic preacher and historian who settled in Damascus under the Ayyubids. He was the author of *Mir'at al-Zaman* (Mirror of Time).

Ibn al-'Adim (d. 660/1262)
A judge (*qadi*) of Aleppo who travelled widely in the Seljuq and Ayyubid realms of Damascus, Jerusalem, Baghdad, the Hijaz and Cairo. His family, the Banu 'Adim, held office as *qadi*s for generations, and he himself became an important historian of Aleppo and the author of *Bughyat al-Talab fi Tarikh Halab* (The Wanted Request in the History of Aleppo).

Ibrahim al-Kurdi (d. 604/1208)
An artisan who designed the Hanabila Mosque's wooden *minbar* in the al-Salihiyya district of Damascus.

Ibn Battuta (703–67/1304–68?)
A North African traveller and chronicler whose voyages covered the full expanse of the known Muslim world of his time.

Nasir-i Khusro (d. 480/1088)
A Persian traveller and chronicler during the Fatimid period.

Murda al-Tarsusi (c. 6th/12th century)
A scholar of military technology during the reign of Salah al-Din for whom he composed *Tabsirat Arbab al-Albab fi Kayfiyyat al-Najat fi-l-Hurub min al-Aswa' wa nashr a'lam al-i'lam fi-l-'Udad* (A Treatise on How to Survive War). His illustrated composition presents different types of military equipment, especially those used in siege warfare.

Ibn al-Wasil (604–97/1208–98)
A judge, scientist, teacher and prominent historian during the Zangid, Ayyubid and early Mamluk periods. Originating from Hama, he travelled widely between Baghdad, Aleppo, Hama, Damascus and Cairo.

FURTHER READING

AALUND, F. ET AL., *Islamic Bosra: A brief guide.* Damascus: German Archaeological Institute, 1990.
AALUND, F. AND M. MEINECKE, *Bosra – Islamische Architektur und Archäologie*, with contributions by S. Heidemann et al., ed. L. Korn. Rahden, Westfalia: Verlag Marie Leidorf GmbH, 2005.
ABU AL-FARAJ AL-'USH, M., *A Concise Guide to the National Museum of Damascus.* Damascus: General Directorate of Antiquities and Museums, 1969.
ABU AL-FIDA', ISMA'IL, "Taqwim al-Buldan", *The Memoirs of a Syrian Prince. Abu'l-Fida', sultan of Hamah (672–732/1273–1331)*, trans. with Introduction by P. M. Holt. Wiesbaden: Franz Steiner Verlag GmbH, 1983, pp. 58, 59.
ABU SHAMA, SHIHAB AL-DIN AL-MAQDISI, *Kitab al-Rawdatayn fi Akhbar al-Dawlatayn al-Nuriyya wa al-Salahiyya*, vol. I, ed. M. H. Ahmad. Cairo: Wizarat al-Thaqafa, 1956–1962.
AL-JAZARI, ISMA'IL, BADI' AL-ZAMAN, *The Book of Knowledge of Ingenious Mechanical Devices: Kitab fi ma'rifat al-hiyal al-handasiyya*, trans. P. Hill. Dordrecht: Springer Science & Business Media B. V., 1973.
AL-MAQRIZI, TAJ AL-DIN AHMAD, *Kitab al-Mawa'iz wa al-I'tibar bi-Dhikr al-Khitat wa al-Athar.* Cairo: Dar al-Tiba'a al-Misriyya, 1270/1853–54.

BURNS, R., *Monuments of Syria. An Historical Guide.* London/New York: I.B. Tauris, 1999.

CAHEN, CL., *Orient et Occident au temps des Croisades.* Paris: Aubier, 1983.
CAHEN, CL., "Ayyubids", in: H. A. R. Gibb, et al. (eds), *Encyclopaedia of Islam*, 2nd edition, vol. I (A–B). Leiden: E. J. Brill, 1986, pp. 796–807.
CANARD, M., "Fatimids", in: B. Lewis et al. (eds), *Encyclopaedia of Islam*, 2nd edition, vol. II (C–G). Leiden: E. J. Brill, 1991, pp. 850–62.
CHAMBERLAIN, M., *Knowledge and Social Practice in Medieval Damascus, 1190–1350.* Cambridge: Cambridge University Press, 1994.
CRUICKSHANK-DODD, E., "The Monastery of Mar Musa al-Habashi near Nebek, Syria", *Arte Medievale: periodico internazionale di critica dell'arte medievale*, 2nd series, vol. 6, no. 1 (1992): pp. 61–132.

DAIBER, V. AND A. BECKER (eds), *Raqqa III. Baudenkmäler und Paläste I.* Mainz am Rhein: Verlag Philipp von Zabern, 2004.
DELPECH, A. ET AL., *Les Norias de l'Oronte: Analyse Technologique d'un Élément du Patrimoine Syrien.* Damascus: IFEAD, 1997.
DELPONT, E., *L'Orient de Saladin, l'art des Ayyoubides.* Paris: Gallimard, 2001.

ECOCHARD, M. AND C. LE COEUR, *Les Bains de Damas*, 2 vols. Beirut: Institut français de Damas, 1942–43.
EDDE, A. M., *La Principauté Ayyoubide d'Alep (579/1183 658/1260).* Stuttgart: Franz Steiner Verlag, 1999.
ELISSEEFF, N., *La Description de Damas d'Ibn 'Asakir.* Damascus: Institut français de Damas, 1959.
ETTINGHAUSEN, R. ET AL., *Arte y Arquitectura del Islam, 650–1250*, vol. 1. Madrid: Cátedra, 1997.
ETTINGHAUSEN, R. ET AL., *Islamic Art and Architecture 650–1250.* New Haven: Yale University Press, 2001.

HASSAN, A. Y. AND D. R. HILL, *Islamic Technology: An Illustrated History.* Cambridge: Cambridge University Press, 1986.
HERZFELD, E., "Damascus: Studies in Architecture – I", *Ars Islamica*, vol. 9 (1942): pp. 2–11.
HERZFELD, E., "Damascus: Studies in Architecture – III", *Ars Islamica*, vols 11–12 (1946): pp. 1–71.
HERZFELD, E., *Materiaux pour un Corpus Inscriptionum Arabicum*, part 2: *Syria du Nord. Inscriptions et Monuments d'Alep*, tome. 1, vol. 1. Cairo: Institut français d'Archaeologie Orientale, 1955.
HILLENBRAND, R., "Eastern Islamic Influences in Syria: Raqqa and Qal'at Ja'bar in the later 12th Century", in: J. Raby (ed.), *The Art of Syria and the Jazira 1100–1250.* Oxford: Oxford University Press, 1985, pp. 21–48.
HILLENBRAND, R., *Islamic Architecture: Form, Function and Meaning.* New York: Columbia University Press, 1994.
HILLENBRAND, C., *The Crusades: Islamic Perspectives.* Edinburgh: Edinburgh University Press, 1999.

HITTI, PH., *An Arab-Syrian Gentleman & Warrior in the Period of the Crusades. Memoirs of Usamah Ibn-Munqidh*. London: I. B. Tauris, 1987.

HUMPHREYS, R. S., *From Saladin to the Mongols: The Ayyubids of Damascus, 1193–1260*. Albany, NY: State University of New York Press, 1977.

HUOT, J. L. AND A. S. KARDOUS (eds), *Photographies du Levant*. Beirut: Institut français d'archéologie du Proche Orient, 2001.

IBN ABI USAYBI'A (d. 1270), *Uyunul-Anba Fi-Tabaqat Al-Atibaa*, ed. N. Rida. Beirut: Dar Maktaba al-Hayat (1965), pp. 519–21.

IBN ABI USAYBI'A (d. 1270), *'Uyun al-Anba' fi Tabaqat al-Atibba'*. Beirut: Dar al-Thaqafa, 1987.

IBN AL-ATHIR, 'ALI 'IZZ AL-DIN, *Tarikh al-Dawla al-Atabakiyya*, in: C. J. Tornberg (ed.), *Al-Kamil fi-l-Tarikh*, 13 vols. Leiden, 1851–76 (reprint Beirut: Dar Sadir, 1385–7/1965–7), pp. 12–386.

IBN AL-QALANISI, ABU YA'LA HAMZA IBN ASAD, *Dhayl Tarikh Dimashq*; trans. H. A. R. Gibb, *The Damascus Chronicle of the Crusades. Extracted and Translated from the Chronicle of Ibn Al-Qalanisi*. London: Luzac & Co., 1932.

IBN BATTUTA (d. 770s/1370s), *Travels of Ibn Battuta*, trans. T. Mackintosh-Smith. Basingstoke and Oxford: Picador, 2002.

SIBT IBN AL-JAWZI (d. 655/1257), *Mir'at al-Zaman*, ed. J. R. Jewett. Chicago: University of Chicago Press, 1907.

IBN JUBAYR (d. 614/1217), *The Travels of Ibn Jubayr*, trans. R. J. C. Broadhurst. London: Jonathan Cape, 1952.

IBN JUBAYR (d. 614/1217), *Rihlat Ibn Jubayr*. Beirut: Dar Sadir li-l-Tiba'a wa-al-Nashr, 1964.

IBN KHALLIKAN (d. 681/1282), *Wafayat al-A'yan*, ed. Ihsan 'Abbas, 7 vols. Beirut: Dar al-Thaqafa, 1969.

IBN SHADDAD, BAHA' AL-DIN, *Al-Nawadir al-Sultaniyya wa al-Mahasin al-Yusufiyya*. Cairo, 1317/1899.

IBN SHADDAD AL-HALABI, 'IZZ AL-DIN (d. 684/1285), *Al-A'laq al-Khatira fi Dhikr Umara' al-Sham wa al-Jazira*, ed. Sami Dahman. Damascus: IFAPO, 1992.

IBN WASIL, JAMAL AL-DIN MUHAMMAD (d. 697/1298), *Mufarrij al-Kurub fi Akhbar Bani Ayyub*. Cairo: Fuad I University Press, 1973.

KENNEDY, H., *Crusader Castles*. Cambridge: Cambridge University Press, 1994.

KHOULI, M., "Antiquités de la céramique ayyoubide au Musée de Damas", *Les annales archéologiques arabes syriennes: Revue d'archéologie et d'histoire*. Damascus: Direction générale des antiquités et des musées, République Arabe Syrienne, vol. 25 (1975): pp. 151–57.

KLAUSNER, C. L., *The Seljuk Vezirate: A Study of Civil Administration (1055–1194)*. Cambridge, MA: Center for Middle Eastern Studies, Harvard University, 1973, pp. 105–10.

KORN, L., AND A. BECKER (eds), *Raqqa II, Die Islamische Stadt*. Mainz: Verlag Philipp von Zabern, 2003.

KORN, L., *Die Ayyubidische Architektur in Ägypten und Syrien*, 2 vols. Heidelberg: Heidelberger Orient Verlag, 2004.

KORN, L., "Das Baghdad-Tor", in: V. Daiber and A. Becker (eds), *Raqqa III, Baudenkmäler und Paläste I*. Damascus and Mainz: German Archaeological Institute, 2004.

KURAN, A., *Mimar Sinan*. Istanbul: Hürriyet Vakif Yayinlari, 1986.

LEWIS, B, "'Abbasids", in: H. A. R. Gibb et al.–B. Lewis et al. (eds), *Encyclopaedia of Islam*, 2nd edition, vol. I (A–B). Leiden: E. J. Brill, 1986, pp. 15–23.

LORTET, L., *La Syrie d'aujourd'hui. Voyages dans la Phénicie, le Liban et la Judée (1875–1880)*. Paris: Librairie Hachette et Cie, 1884.

MEINECKE, M., "The Old Quarter of as-Salihiya/Damascus: Development and Recent Changes", *Les annales archéologiques arabes syriennes: Revue d'archéologie et d'histoire, Numéro spécial Damas*. Damascus: Direction générale des antiquités et des musées, République Arabe Syrienne, vol. 35 (1985): pp. 31–47.

MEINECKE, M., "al-Rakka", in: C. E. Bosworth et al. (eds), *Encyclopaedia of Islam*, 2nd edition, vol. VIII (NED–SAM). Leiden: E. J. Brill, 1995, pp. 410–14.

MEINECKE, M., *Patterns of Stylistic Change in Islamic Architecture: Local Traditions versus Migrating Artists.* New York and London: New York University Press, 1996.

MINISTERO DELLA CULTURA – DIREZIONE GENERALE DELLE ANTICHITÀ E DEI MUSEI, DAMASCO – ISTITUTO CENTRALE PER IL RESTAURO, ROMA, *Il Restauro del Monastero di San Mosè l'Abissino, Nebek, Siria.* Damascus, 1998.

MOAZ, 'A. R., "Isham al-Mar'a fī al-'Amara bi-Dimashq khilal al-'Ahd al-Ayyubi", *Al-Turath al-'Arabi,* vol. 29 (1987): pp. 216–225.

MOAZ, A. R., "Les madrasas de Damas et d'al-Salihiyya depuis la fin du V/XI siècle jusqu'au milieu du VII/XIII siècle", unpublished PhD thesis, Provence: Université de Provence Aix-Marseille I, 1990.

MULLER-WIENER, W., *Castles of the Crusaders.* London: Thames & Hudson, 1966.

NASIR-I KHUSRO (d. 480/1088), *Sefer Nameh,* trans. W. M. Thackson. Albany, NY: Bibliotheca Persica, 1986.

AL-NU'AYMI, 'ABD AL-QADIR (d. 927/1520), *Al-Daris fi Tarikh al-Madaris,* ed. J. al-Hasani, vol. I. Damascus: Matba'at al-Taraqqi, 1948–51.

PORTER, V., *Medieval Syrian Pottery.* Oxford: Ashmolean Museum, 1981.

RAYMOND, A. AND J. L. PAILLET, *Balis II. Histoire de Balis et fouilles des îlots I et II.* Damascus: IFEAD, 1995.

SAADÉ, G., "Histoire du château de Saladin", *Studi Medievali,* vol. 9, no. 3 (1968): pp. 979–1016.

SAUVAGET, J., "Le cénotaphe de Saladin", *Revue des arts Asiatiques,* vol. 6 (1930): pp. 168–175.

SAUVAGET, J., *Les Monuments Historiques de Damas – Livraison II.* Paris: E. de Boccard, 1938.

SAUVAGET, J. ET AL., *Les Monuments Ayyoubides de Damas: Livraison I.* Paris: E. de Boccard, 1938–50.

SAUVAGET, J., "Caravansèrais Syriens du Moyen Âge", *Ars Islamica,* vol. 6 (1939): pp. 49–55.

SAUVAGET, J., Alep, *Essai sur le développement d'une grande ville syrienne des origines au milieu du XIXe siecle.* Paris: Librairie Orientaliste Paul Geuthner, 1941.

TABBAA, Y., "Monuments with a Message: Propagation of Jihad under Nur al-Din 1146–1174", in: V. P. Goss and C. Bornstein (eds), *The Meeting of Two Worlds: Cultural Exchange between East and West during the Period of the Crusades.* Kalamazoo: Medieval Institute Publications, Western Michigan University, 1986, pp. 223–40.

TABBAA, Y., *Constructions of Power and Piety in Medieval Aleppo.* University Park: Pennsylvania State University Press, 1997.

TABBAA, Y., *The Transformation of Islamic Art during the Sunni Revival.* Seattle and London: University of Washington Press, 2001.

TONGHINI, C., *Qal'at Ja'bar Pottery: A Study of a Syrian Fortified Site of the Late 11th–14th Centuries.* Oxford: Oxford University Press, 1998.

TONGHINI, C. AND N. MONTEVECCHI, "The Castle of Shayzar: The results of recent archaeological investigations", in: N. Faucherre et al. (eds), *La Fortification au temps des Croisades.* Rennes: Presses Universitaires de Rennes, 2004, pp. 137–150.

TURNER, H. R., *Science in Medieval Islam: An Illustrated Introduction.* Austin: University of Texas Press, 1997.

VAN BERCHEM, M. AND E. FATIO, *Voyage en Syrie.* Cairo: Imprimerie de L'Institut Français d'archéologie orientale, 1914.

WATSON, O., *Ceramics from Islamic Lands.* London: Thames and Hudson, 2004.

WILSON, SIR, C. W., *Picturesque Palestine, Sinai and Egypt,* vol. 1. New York: D. Appleton & Co. Publishers, 1881–84.

ZAYYAT, H., *Al-Diyarat al-Nasraniyya fi-l-Islam.* Beirut: Dar al-Mashriq, 1999.

PHOTOGRAPHIC AND PLAN REFERENCES

Photographic references
See also pages 5 and 6
Page 22, Aleppo: Ann & Peter Jousiffe, London
Page 25, Alhambra, Granada: Archivos Oronoz Fotógrafos, Madrid
Page 39: J. L. Huot and A. S. Kardous (eds) (Beirut, 2001), p. 95, photo 39
Pages 53, 69, 197: C. Hillenbrand (Edinburgh, 1999), figs 3.19 (Hillenbrand, 1994), 1.6 (Rice, 1953); fig. 7.67 (Leacroft, 1976)
Pages 57, 225: J. Sauvaget (Paris, 1941), plates XLVIII, XIX
Page 78: L. Lortet (Paris, 1884), engraving of al-Salihiyya
Page 94: Sir C. W. Wilson (New York, 1881–84), p. 389
Page 95: J. Sauvaget (1930), pp. 168–75
Pages 121, 180: A. Delpech et al. (Damascus, 1997), illustration of the *noria* on the River Yazid, fig. 79.
Pages 218, 242, 243: E. Herzfeld (Cairo, 1955), plates LXXXVIII, LXII, XXXVIII
Page 262: L. Korn, in: V. Daiber and A. Becker (eds) (Damascus and Mainz, 2004), pp. 11–18, fig. 2
Page 41. Wikipedia commons: Misyaf Castle, online at Wikimedia.
Pages 44/202, 195, 209. Courtesy of Balázs Major: Crusader sword, Tartus Museum; Tartus city, St. Helen, Crusader gate; Remains of the citadel, Ma'arrat al-Nu'man.
Page 49. Courtesy of Sheila Blair & Jonathan Bloom: Madrasa of al-Salih Najm al-Din Ayyub, Cairo. © Sheila Blair & Jonathan Bloom.
Pages 59, 65, 138. Courtesy of Khaled Moaz: Dar al-Hadith Nuriyya, view of the triple archway leading into the southern bay; Badriyya Mausoleum, Damascus, in the 1950s; Mabrak al-Naqa Mosque/Madrasat Gumushtagin, southern and western *iwans*.
Page 69. Museum of Islamic Art at the Pergamon Museum, State Museums, Berlin: Spherical incense burner with inlaid metalwork decoration, Inv. Num. MIK2774; photo by Johannes Kramer. © Museum of Islamic Art – State Museums, Berlin.
Pages 73, 101, 120, 178. British Museum, London: Bottle, Inv. Num. 1906, 0719.1; Illustration from the 6th/12th-century manuscript *De Materia Medica*, Inv. Num. 1934, 1013, 0.1; Astrolabe, Ayyubid Dynasty, Inv. Num. 1855, 0709.1; Painting, Ayyubid Dynasty, Inv. Num. 1938, 0312, 0.1. © Trustees of the British Museum, London.
Pages 153, 237. Courtesy of Yasser Tabbaa and Aga Khan Documentation Center at Massachusetts Institute of Technology (MIT): Great Mosque of Nur al-Din, the Ayyubid *mihrab*, Homs; Madrasa al-Toruntayya al-'Adimiyya, courtyard. © Yasser Tabbaa Archive, Aga Khan Documentation Center at MIT.
Pages 163, 171, 172, 181, 211. Courtesy of Zena Takieddine: Noria Jisriyya, Hama; Noria al-Khudra and Noria al-Dawalik, Hama; Noria al-Muhammadiyya, detail (top), Noria al-Muhammadiyya (bottom); Noria al-Muhammadiyya, detail of the structure; Modern statue of Salah al-Din, Damascus.
Pages 184, 189. Courtesy of Yasser Tabbaa: Crac des Chevaliers, view towards the southern side of the qilla; Crac des Chevaliers, general view.
Page 186. Bodleian Library, Oxford: An illustration from Murda ibn 'Ali al-Tarsusi's treatise *Tabsirat Arbab al-Albab fi Kayfiyyat al-Najat fi-l-Hurub min al-Aswa'*, dedicated to Salah al-Din, Inv. Num. MS. Huntington 264, fols. 134b–135a. © Bodleian Library, University of Oxford.

Other images from *Discover Islamic Art*
Pages 45, 47, 210. Islamic Museum, al-Aqsa Mosque, Jerusalem: PA 016, Pieces from the Nur al-Din Zangi *minbar*, Inv. Num. 142/40;
PA 02, Marble inscription panel; PA 04, Manuscript *Al-Nawadir al-Sultaniyya wa-l-Mahasin al-Yusufiyya* (Sovereign Rarities and Yusufi Merits).

Plan references
Page 28, Mosque of Damascus: R. Ettinghausen and O. Grabar (Madrid, I, 1997).
Page 29, Mosque of Divrigi and Istanbul; page 30, Mosque of Sivas: Z. Sönmez (Ankara, 1995)
Page 30, Minaret styles: Sergio Viguera, Madrid
Page 31, Mosque and Madrasa Sultan Hassan: S. S. Blair and J. M. Bloom (Madrid, II, 1999)
Page 32, Qasr al-Khayr al-Sharqi: R. Ettinghausen and O. Grabar (Madrid, I, 1997)
Page 33, Khan Sultan Aksaray: A. Kuran (Istanbul, 1986)
Page 58: J. Sauvaget et al. (Paris, 1938–50), fig. 42
Pages 60/112, 114: E. Herzfeld (1946), figs 53, 10
Pages 88, 100: E. Herzfeld (1942), pp. 2–11, fig. 1
Page 91: M. Ecochard and C. Le Coeur (Beirut, 1942–43), fig. III
Pages 109, 189, 193, 207, 235: R. Burns (London/New York, 1999), plans 25, 35, 60, 47, 6
Page 126, 250: M. Meinecke (New York and London, 1996), figs 8 (Directorate General of Antiquities and Museums, Damascus; with additions by Jean-Marie Dentzer and Flemming Aalund), 1 (Norbert Hagen, 1989)
Pages 130, 230: Y. Tabbaa (Pennsylvania, 1997), figs 109, 15
Page 146: J. Sauvaget (1939): pp. 49–55, fig. 19
Page 248: S. Heidemann, in: S. Heidemann and A. Becker (eds) (Mainz, 2003), table 1

AUTHORS

The following short author profiles refer to the period of elaboration of this book.

Dina Bakkour
Is an archaeologist with a degree from the Institute of Archaeology and Museums, University of Damascus, Syria, and a BA in History from the same university. She received her MA (DEA) in Islamic Archaeology from the University of the Sorbonne – Paris 1, and is now preparing her PhD thesis. Dina also holds a degree in Museology from the Ecole du Louvre in Paris. She has participated in conservation and restoration expeditions in Rome, Murcia and Amsterdam. Currently, she works at the General Directorate of Antiquities and Museums, Damascus. She has also participated in many national and European excavations and restoration endeavours in Syria and worked as a teacher at the Institute of Archaeology and Museums in Damascus. She was co-author of an article in the publication *The Restorations of Deir Mar Musa al-Habashi. Nabek-Syria*, published by the Syrian Ministry of Culture and the Istituto Centrale del Restauro in Rome in 1998–99.

Verena Daiber
Has been a researcher at the German Archaeological Institute in Damascus since 2002 where she is preparing her PhD thesis titled "Architectural and cultural history of Damascus in the 18th century". She graduated from the Free University of Berlin where she studied Near Eastern Archaeology and Arabic Literature. In 1990, she obtained her MA with a study of medieval pottery from the citadel of Aleppo. She has participated in numerous excavations in Sheikh Hamad and Aleppo, Syria, and Baalbek, Lebanon. She edited the third volume of the "Raqqa" series, a compilation of studies conducted by several scholars on the site. Her latest publication is a study of fine medieval pottery from Baalbek. In addition to her research, she is also a German/Arabic translator.

Wa'al Hafian
Is a civil engineer working for the Directorate General of Antiquities and Museums, department of Hama, as chief of the Building and Archaeological Sites office. He has been involved in the documentation and archaeological analysis of medieval and Ottoman architectural construction in the city of Hama as well as working on excavations from the Iron Age in the Hama region. The results of his fieldwork on medieval fortifications and Ottoman caravanserais are presently in the process of publication.

Haytham Hasan
Is an archaeologist working at the General Directorate of Antiquities and Museums, Damascus; since 1990 specialising in the medieval sites of the coastal region of Syria. He received his MA from the Sorbonne – Paris IV, which was dedicated to the study of the Isma'ili town and citadel of Misyaf, and he is currently in the process of completing his PhD. He is also the Assistant Director of Excavation in Syria.

Balázs Major
Is an archaeologist, Arabist and historian. He specialises in the field of late antique and medieval settlement patterns and military architecture and has been conducting surveys on the Syrian coast since 2000.

Benjamin Michaudel
Is a scholar in Islamic history, art and archaeology. He is also an Arabist and author of a PhD on the Ayyubid and Mamluk fortifications in coastal Syria. He has been conducting surveys in Syria since 1997.

Abd al-Razzaq Moaz

Is Deputy Minister of Culture, in charge of Cultural Heritage, and Head of EU projects in Syria. He received his BA in History at the University of Damascus in 1985, his MA (DEA) in Archaeology from the University of Provence, Aix-en-Provence in 1987, and PhD in Archaeology from the same university in 1991. He was a scholar at the Institut Francais d'Etudes Arabes de Damas (1991–93) and a Visiting Scholar at the Aga Khan Progam for Islamic Architecture, Harvard University and MIT, USA (1993/4), at Granada University, Spain (1994), at Harvard University (Fulbright Scholar, 1995) and at Harvard University Urban Planning Department (1996). He lectured at Damascus University (1997–99) and as Visiting Professor, Harvard University (spring 1999). He was Director General of Antiquities and Museums, Syria (2000–02). He speaks Arabic, French and English.

Yasser Tabbaa

Is a historian of Islamic architecture. He studied Anthropology at Ohio State University, and History of Art and Architecture at the Institute of Fine Arts at New York University, where he obtained his PhD. He has taught at a number of leading universities in the United States, including Harvard University; the Massachusetts Institute of Technology; the University of Michigan, Ann Arbor; the University of Texas, Austin; and Oberlin College. He has also taught at the University of Jordan, where he is currently Dean of the College of Arts and Design. He is the author of numerous publications on the architecture of the Islamic world, including *Constructions of Power and Piety in Medieval Aleppo* (University Park, PA: Pennsylvania State University Press, 1997); and *The Transformation of Islamic Art during the Sunni Revival* (Seattle and London: University of Washington Press, 2001; paperback edition, 2002).

Zena Takieddine

Is a researcher of Arab history and Islamic art with experience as a freelance editor and writer. She holds a BA in Arab History from the American University of Beirut, a MA in Art and Archaeology from the School of Oriental and African Studies, London, and a Diploma in Art and Antique Connoisseurship from Sotheby's, London. Her topics of interest include pre-Islamic Arabia and the development of Arabic script, early Islamic art and architecture, Arab miniature painting, cross-cultural transmission of knowledge, and post-colonial methodology in the study of history and identity.

Museum With No Frontiers Exhibition Trails and related Travel Books
ISLAMIC ART IN THE MEDITERRANEAN

The following titles have been published in the series:

Portugal
IN THE LANDS OF THE ENCHANTED MOORISH MAIDEN
Islamic Art in Portugal 200 pages

Eight centuries after the Christians re-conquered their lands from the Muslims, towns of the ancient "Gharb al-Andalus" (western Andalusia) have preserved the Legend of the beautiful enchanted Moorish maiden whose spell was broken by a Christian prince; the artistic route of Muslim presence in Portugal also expresses, through a subtle interdependence between constructive techniques and decorative programmes, popular regional architecture. The exhibition gives the visitor a clear view of five centuries of Islamic civilisation (the Caliphate, Mozarabic, Almohad and Mudéjar periods). From Coimbra in the confines of the Algarve, palaces, Christianised mosques, fortifications and cities, all affirm the splendour of past glories.

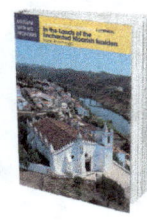

Turkey
EARLY OTTOMAN ART
Legacy of the Emirates 252 pages

Highlighting this exhibition are the works and monuments most representative of the finest period of western Anatolia, the cultural and artistic bridge between European and Asian civilisations. In the 14th and 15th centuries, the transition to a Turkish-Islamic society led artists of the Turkish Emirate to elaborate on a brilliant artistic union culminating in Ottoman art.

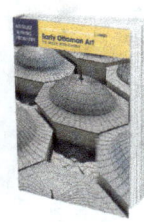

Morocco
ANDALUSIAN MOROCCO
Discovery in Living Art 264 pages

From the beginning of the 8th century, Islamic Moroccans looked beyond the Pillars of Hercules (Gibraltar) and settled in the Iberian Peninsula. From then on, both shores shared the same destiny. From continual cultural, social and commercial exchange animating this extreme of the Maghreb for more than seven centuries, sprang one of the most brilliant facets of Muslim civilisation. Authentic Hispano-Maghreb art left its stamp not only on resplendent, monumental architecture, but also in the characteristics of the cities and traditions of extreme refinement. The exhibition reflects the historic and social wealth of the Andalusi (Andalusian) civilisation in Morocco.

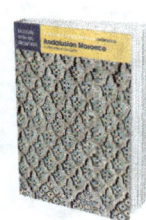

Tunisia
IFRIQIYA
Thirteen Centuries of Art and Architecture in Tunisia 312 pages

Since the 9th century, without breaking with traditions inherited from the Berbers, Carthaginians, Romans and Byzantines, Ifriqiya was able to assimilate and reinterpret influences from Mesopotamia, through Syria and Egypt, and from al-Andalus (Andalusia). This is a unique form of syncretism, of which numerous vestiges prevail even today in Tunisia, from the majestic residences of the Muslim sovereigns in the capital, to the architectonic rigor of the "Ibadism of Jerba". The visitor is invited to look at existing *ribat*s, mosques, *medina*s, *zawiya*s and *gurfa*s (large rooms containing bedroom suites) to witness their imprint on a land abounding with history.

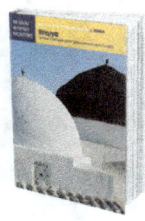

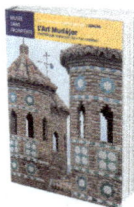

Spain | Andalusia, Aragon, Castilla La Mancha, Castille and Leon, outskirts of Madrid
MUDÉJAR ART
Islamic Aaesthetics in Christian Art 316 pages
The art of the Mudéjars (the Muslim population remaining in Andalusia after the re-conquest) has an unquestionably unique place among all expressions of Islamic art. It deals with the visible manifestation of a splendidly cultured cohabitation with a unique understanding between two civilisations that, in spite of their political and religious antagonism, lived a fructiferous artistic romance. Applying schemes, although rigorously Islamic, the Masters of Works and Mudéjar artisans, famous for their outstanding knowledge in the art of construction, erected for the newly arrived Christians innumerable palaces, convents and churches. The selected works, chosen for their variety and abundance, testify to the exuberant vitality of Mudéjar art.

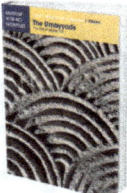

Jordan
THE UMAYYADS
The Rise of Islamic Art 224 pages
Following the Arab-Muslim conquest of the Middle East, the seat of the Umayyad Dynasty (661–750) was moved to Damascus, where the new capital inherited a cultural and artistic tradition dating back to the Aramaean and Hellenistic Periods. Umayyad culture benefited by this move from the frontier between Persia and Mesopotamia and between the countries of the Mediterranean world. The position was favourable for the emergence of an innovative artistic language, in which a subtle mixture of Hellenistic, Roman, Byzantine and Persian influences, produced architectural order and decorative originality. Through the diversity of the works presented, the exhibition also offers the opportunity to reflect on the Iconoclast phenomena.

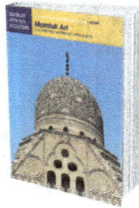

Egypt
MAMLUK ART
The Splendour and Magic of the Sultans 236 pages
Under Mamluk domination (1249–1517), Egypt became a prosperous commercial-route crossing centre. Great riches came to the country. Cairo was one of the most powerful, secure and stable cities of the Mediterranean basin. Scholars from all over the world came to settle there, attracting their followers and students. Mamluk architecture and decorative art displays the vitality of commerce, the intellectual energy and the military and religious force of this period. Characterised by elegant and vigorous simplicity, the purity of line is similar to modern models. The works selected between Cairo, Rosetta, Alexandria and Fuwa represent the height of Mamluk art.

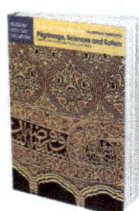

Palestine
PILGRIMAGE, SCIENCE AND SUFISM
Islamic Art in the West Bank and Gaza 254 pages
During the reigns of the Ayyubid, Mamluk and Ottoman Dynasties, numerous pilgrims, from all over the Muslim world came to Palestine. This dynamic tide of religious fervour gave a decisive impulse to the development of *Sufi* thought, through the *zawiyas* and *ribat*s, which multiplied all over the country. Various study centres welcomed the most distinguished scholars. In this way, they obtained considerable prestige and conditions became favourable for the expansion of refined art, which conserves its power to fascinate, even today. The monuments and Islamic architecture proposed for the exhibition clearly reflect these great dimensions of pilgrimages, science and Sufism.

Italy - Sicily
SICULO-NORMAN ART
Islamic Culture in Medieval Sicily   *328 pages*

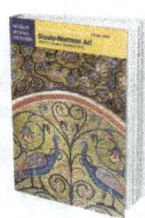

An Island in the middle of the Mediterranean, Sicily is a land of encounter, where various cultures have coincided and adjusted mutually, reaching a new harmony. Unique in the European panorama, Arab-Norman architecture, relatively speaking, is different from that found in the Islamic world. The exhibition presents it from the standpoint of its uniqueness and provides some codes for interpretation permitting better identification. An attentive visitor will better appreciate the admirable fusion of elements, originating from Byzantine, Arab and Norman cultural spheres, employed in this art, which is as original as it is refined.

In preparation

Algeria
ART AND ARCHITECTURE OF THE LIGHT
Legacy of Islam in Algeria
(Provisional title)

See also www.mwnfbooks.net

www.ingramcontent.com/pod-product-compliance
Lightning Source LLC
Chambersburg PA
CBHW071205240526
45470CB00018B/1464